ECUADOR

Alain Legault

ULYSSES
TRAVEL PUBLICATIONS
Travel better... enjoy more

Editorial *Series Director*: Claude Morneau; *Project Director*: Pascale Couture; *Editor:* Daniel Desjardins

Research and Composition *Author* Alain Legault; *Contributors*: Nadia Bini, Tara Haddrell, Jean Roger, Annie-Claude Labbé.

Production *Design*: Patrick Farei (Atoll Direction); *Proofreading*: Jennifer McMorran; *Translation*: Tracy Kendrick, Sarah Kresh, Danielle Gauthier, Christina Poole; *Cartography*: André Duchesne, Steve Rioux (Assistant); *Layout*: Christian Roy, Stephane G. Marceau;

Illustrations: *Cover Photo*: K. Muller (Visa); *Interior Photos*: Élise Berti, Guadelupe Lau, Alain Legault; *Chapter Headings*: Jennifer McMorran; *Drawings*: Lorette Pierson.

Special Thanks to: Oswaldo Muñoz; Daniel Kouperman; Rosario Ayoro; Carmen Mancheno; Patricio Tamariz; Pierre Thomas; Antonio Perone; the Asinc family especially Phil, Andy Grimble, Amando and Inés Ching, Gustavo "Chico" Jimenez Morales, Raymond and Lupe Legault; Olivier, owner of the Luna Runtún Resort; Rodrigo Mora.

Thanks to: SODEC (Québec government) and the Canadian Heritage Minister for their financial support.

Distributors

AUSTRALIA:
Little Hills Press
11/37-43 Alexander St.
Crows Nest NSW 2065
☎ (612) 437-6995
Fax: (612) 438-5762

BELGIUM AND LUXEMBOURG:
Vander
Vrijwilligerlaan 321
B-1150 Brussel
☎ (02) 762 98 04
Fax: (02) 762 06 62

CANADA:
Ulysses Books & Maps
4176 Saint-Denis
Montréal, Québec
H2W 2M5
☎ (514) 843-9882, ext.2232
Fax: 514-843-9448
http://www.ulysse.ca

GERMANY AND AUSTRIA:
Brettschneider
Fernreisebedarf
Feldfirchner Strasse 2
D-85551 Heimstetten
München
☎ 89-99 02 03 30
Fax: 89-99 02 03 31

GREAT BRITAIN AND IRELAND:
World Leisure Marketing
9 Downing Road
West Meadows, Derby
UK DE21 6HA
☎ 1 332 34 33 32
Fax: 1 332 34 04 64

ITALY:
Edizioni del Riccio
Via di Soffiano 164 A
50143 Firenze
☎ (055) 71 33 33
Fax: (055) 71 63 50

NETHERLANDS:
Nilsson & Lamm
Pampuslaan 212-214
1380 AD Weesp (NL)
☎ 0294-465044
Fax: 0294-415054

SCANDINAVIA:
Scanvik
Esplanaden 8B
1263 Copenhagen K
DK
☎ (45) 33.12.77.66
Fax: (45) 33.91.28.82

SPAIN:
Altaïr
Balmes 69
E-08007 Barcelona
☎ 454 29 66
Fax: 451 25 59

SWITZERLAND:
OLF
P.O. Box 1061
CH-1701 Fribourg
☎ (026) 467.51.11
Fax: (026) 467.54.66

U.S.A.:
The Globe Pequot Press
6 Business Park Road
P.O. Box 833
Old Saybrook, CT 06475
☎ 1-800-243-0495
Fax: 1-800-820-2329

Other countries, contact Ulysses Books & Maps (Montréal), Fax: (514) 843-9448

Canadian Cataloguing in Publication Data
Legault, Alain, 1967-
      Ecuador, Galápagos Islands, 2nd edition   (Ulysses travel guides)
      Translation of Équateur
      Includes index.
      ISBN 2-89464-059-5
1. Ecuador - Guidebooks.   2. Galápagos Islands - Guidebooks   I. Titles.   II. Series.
F3709.5.L4313   1997   918.6604'74   C97-940825-3
© July 1997, Ulysses Travel Publications. All rights reserved
ISBN 2-89464-059-5
Printed in Canada

TABLE OF CONTENTS

Help make Ulysses Guides even better!

The information contained in this guide was correct at press time. However, mistakes can slip in, omissions are always possible, places can disappear, etc. The authors and publisher hereby disclaim any liability for loss or damage resulting from omissions or errors.

We value your comments, corrections and suggestions, as they allow us to keep each guide up to date. The best contributions will be rewarded with a free book from Ulysses Travel Publications. All you have to do is write us at the following address and indicate which title you would be interested in receiving (see the list at the end of guide).

Ulysses Travel Publications
4176 Rue Saint-Denis
Montréal, Québec
Canada H2W 2M5
http://www.ulysse.ca
E-mail: guiduly@ulysse.ca

LIST OF MAPS

TABLE OF SYMBOLS

≡	Air conditioning
bkfst	Breakfast
⊗	Ceiling fan
tv	Colour television
☺	Exercise room
⇄	Fax number
hw	Hot water
ℂ	Kitchenette
≈	Pool
pb	Private bathroom
ps	Private shower
ℝ	Refrigerator
ℜ	Restaurant
△	Sauna
#	Screen
sb	Shared bathroom
☎	Telephone number
⊛	Whirlpool

ATTRACTION CLASSIFICATION

★	Interesting
★★	Worth a visit
★★★	Not to be missed

HOTEL CLASSIFICATION

The prices in the guide are for one room, double occupancy, not including taxes.

RESTAURANT CLASSIFICATION

$	$6 or less
$$	$6 to $12 US
$$$	$12 or more

The prices in the guide are for a meal for one person, including taxes, but not drinks and tip.

All prices in dollars in this guide are in American dollars.

Where is Ecuador ?

Ecuador
Capital: Quito
Languages: Spanish and Quechua
Population: 11 500 000
Area: 283 561 km²
Currency: sucre

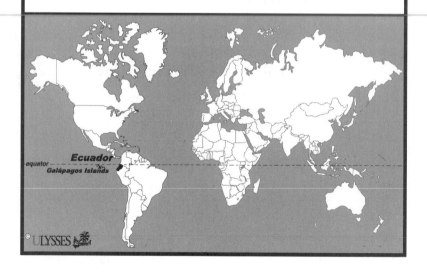

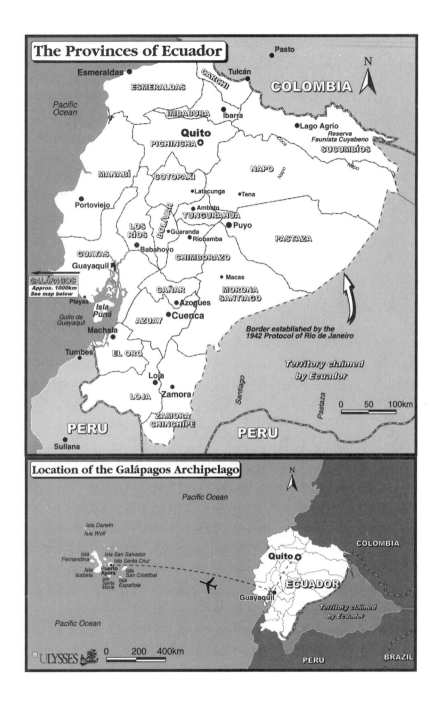

PORTRAIT

The smallest of the Andean republics, Ecuador is nonetheless one of the most interesting countries in the Americas. For over 500 years, this land has been capturing the imagination of men eager to demystify El Dorado, that "mythical land strewn with plains of cinnamon trees, where it is pleasant to live and gold abounds". The list of those bold enough to try their luck is a long one: conquistadors, scientists, monks, travellers and tourists. Today, El Dorado is still a myth, and the gold of the Incas now glitters inside the country's many religious sanctuaries, silent but stirring testimonies to a rich past that was extraordinary in many ways, albeit marked by much bloodshed.

Wedged between Peru and Colombia, this small South American nation lies on the Pacific coast and is bisected by the Andes. It takes its name from the equator, the great circle perpendicular to the earth's axis of rotation and equidistant from its poles, which divides the surface into northern and southern hemispheres and runs through the northern part of the country, right near Quito. An amazingly varied country, Ecuador boasts magnificent scenery, with lofty volcanoes proudly studding the two cordilleras that form the country's backbone, as well as superb religious monuments that bear witness to the era of Spanish colonization; a huge, luxuriant forest that covers the mysterious Amazon region and seems to stretch endlessly into the distance; scores of picturesque little native villages, which, perched in the Andes, seem frozen in the past; and finally, of course, the extraordinary world of the Galápagos Islands.

GEOGRAPHY

Aside from the magnificent Galápagos Islands, Ecuador is divided into three distinct geographical regions: the Costa, the Sierra and the Oriente, which cover a total area of 270,670 square kilometres. In 1941, however, a war suddenly broke out between Ecuador and Peru. The end result was that Ecuador had to surrender part of its territory to the Republic of Peru under the Protocol of Rio de Janeiro (1942). Don't be surprised, therefore, if a map put out in Ecuador doesn't show the same borders as one made elsewhere.

To the west, the low coastal plain commonly known as the Costa runs between the Andes and the Pacific Ocean for the entire length of the country, covering an area of over 70,000 square kilometres of scenery and vegetation that change according to the variations in the climate. This coastal plain ranges in width from 30 to 200 kilometres.

The Sierra is made up of two parallel mountain chains (the Western and Eastern Cordilleras), which run through the country from north to south. It is home to about 60% of the country's population and is studded with over 30 awe-inspiring volcanoes, some of which are still active. The highest is Chimborazo at 6,300 metres, though it is no longer active; the highest active volcano is Cotopaxi at 5,978 metres. These cones are surrounded by many other smaller peaks and form a volcanic massif known as the Avenida de los Volcanes.

The Oriente, located east of the Eastern Cordillera, is part of the Amazon Basin. Although this region accounts for over half of the Ecuadoran territory, less than 10% of the total population lives here. These inhabitants are clustered in small, rustic, semi-autonomous villages linked by a vast river network that is easy for small boats to travel along. However, the discovery of oil in Lago Agrío in 1967 led to the construction of a road across the Sierra to Quito, as well as an oil pipeline.

Made famous by English naturalist Charles Darwin's research, the Galápagos archipelago lies in the Pacific Ocean some 1,000 kilometres west of the Ecuadoran coast, and consists of 15 islands and 40 islets of volcanic origin. These are home to many fascinating plant and animal species, some found nowhere else in the world.

The Principal Geological Characteristics of Ecuador

Ecuador's present geological characteristics are the result of the various movements that affected the earth's crust in this part of the globe in the past, as well as a number of events that have gradually shaped its geography. Of the major events that have helped give the country its present geography, and to a certain degree its widely varied climate, the most important are those that contributed either directly or indirectly to the emergence of the Andes mountain range. The entire history of the formation (orogenesis) of the Andes and its consequences on Ecuador, which straddles this famous cordillera, can be deduced from the country's present relief.

The emergence of the Andes began with the westward drift of the South American continent, which resulted in a collision between the continental shelf, still known as the Guyano-Brazilian Shield, to the east, and the ocean crust or Pacific plate to the west. Gradual as it was, this collision was punctuated by countless earth tremors and volcanic eruptions. This slow drift and the impact of the two tectonic plates ended up fracturing and displacing the continental shelf and the ocean plate, with the latter gradually lodging itself under the former. During the Cretaceous period (a period of geological time 144 to 65 million years ago), the fractures and the subduction of the ocean plate (occurring at a speed of up to 10 centimetres per year) caused magma from the depths of the lithosphere to rise up, creating intense volcanic activity on the surface. The abundant flow of lava eventually formed a solid platform, which now forms the skeleton of the coastal zone and the Western Cordillera. The "pillow lava" found here indicates that these eruptions occurred underwater—that is, before the emergence of the Andes. During this period, the pressure caused by the continental shelf's westward shift transformed the fractured blocks of crystalline rock of which it was composed, and gradually forced them upward.

It was then that the two major geological zones that now characterize Ecuador each took on its own identity: the coastal and northern parts of the Western Cordillera have a substratum of volcanic rock, while the entire Amazon region and the Eastern Cordillera have a substratum of crystalline, metamorphic rock. The widespread upthrust of the Andes occurred during the Eocene epoch, just over 50 million years ago, and continues to this day.

This uplifting has been accompanied by severe erosion throughout the Andes, a phenomenon that has led to a significant accumulation of sediment at the foot of the cordillera, mainly on the Amazon shield east of the mountain chain. This sediment and the organic debris it contains provide a favourable environment for the formation and accumulation of hydrocarbons, a resource Ecuador is beginning to capitalize on.

FAUNA AND FLORA

The diversity of the flora and fauna in this small Andean country is absolutely incredible. Within an area of just 270,670 square kilometres, there are four times as many plant and animal species as in Europe, and twice as many as in Canada and the United States put together. A third of the world's amphibian species, a fifth of its bird species, a sixth of its lepidopterous insects (butterflies) and a seventh of its reptilian species are found in Ecuador.

> Superstitious travellers claim that it is a sign of good luck when a butterfly lands on you. The more scientific explanation is that the butterfly is feeding on the salt in your perspiration.

Fauna

In the coastal region, the province of Guayas alone is home to over 400 species of birds, all as distinctive as they are flamboyant.

Unfortunately, some of these species are endangered. One is the condor, which can occasionally be seen flying over the tops of the Chimborazo, Cayambe and Antisana volcanoes.

The lush Amazon forest is home to all sorts of animals. Some waterways are infested with voracious piranhas. These carnivorous fish, attracted by blood, can devour a man or an animal in the space of a few minutes. Much more appealing than piranhas in many people's opinion, freshwater dolphins are one of the pleasant surprises that travellers might happen upon in the tropical rainforest. Little is known about these friendly mammals. Researchers agree that these dolphins lived in the ocean a long, long time ago, before the emergence of the Andes, and had to adapt to the aquatic environment of Amazon. They have pale, sometimes pinkish skin and are between 2 and 2.6 metres long. They have tiny eyes and are nearly blind. Unfortunately, these dolphins occasionally get trapped in ponds when the water level drops quickly. Unlike saltwater dolphins, who pop up out of nowhere and leap joyfully out of the water when they come up for air, freshwater dolphins only expose a small part of their back.

The giant sea otter is another curious creature that haunts the rivers of the Oriente. Over-hunted for its skin, it is now an endangered species. It weighs between 24 and 34 kilograms, rarely swims alone, and is difficult to observe. Sea lions are usually seen in groups of five to nine. When they are in a state of alert, they all surface at the same time, stick their neck out of the water and make a loud snorting noise. The fauna in the Oriente includes boas, anacondas, pumas, jaguars and caimans, among others.

Llamas, for their part, are scattered about the high, mountainous regions of Ecuador, Peru, Bolivia and some parts of Colombia, Chili and Argentina. Llamas are ruminants belonging to the camel family. There are two wild breeds, the guanaco and the vicuña, and two domestic breeds, the alpaca and the llama, bred for their meat and their wool. The best-known by far is the llama, which can weigh up to 140 kilograms. Used as a pack animal, the llama is very strong and can carry sizeable loads over long distances.

Smaller than the llama, the alpaca can reach up to 80 kilograms. It is bred for its wool, longer and finer than the llama's. Unlike its cousin, however, it is not used as a beast of burden. Alpacas are found near swampy areas, where there are lots of luxuriant pastures suitable for their dietary needs.

The vicuña weighs barely 55 kilograms and is distinguished by its gracefulness, as well as its thin neck and frail-looking legs, which give it a dainty look. Its wool is extremely soft and warm, and is considered the finest animal fibre after silk. For years, the vicuña was aggressively hunted for its high-quality wool, so much so that the species was on the brink of extinction. However, a concerted effort was made to protect vicuñas all over the continent, and their numbers are once again on the rise.

Finally, the guanaco weighs an average of 90 kilograms. A good swimmer, it can also run very fast—up to 55 kilometres per hour. Like the vicuña, it is difficult to domesticate and lives in small herds.

The Galápagos Islands are surely the only place on Earth where species as diverse as penguins, flightless cormorants, giant tortoises, sea lions and iguanas share the same territory. The waters around the islands are inhabited by a fascinating variety of marine animals. Dolphins, whales and numerous species of fish all live in this part of the Pacific Ocean. For more specific information on the animal life of the Galápagos, see p 269.

Flora

Thanks to its topography and varied climate, Ecuador boasts remarkable vegetation. There are over 2,700 species of wild orchids alone!

The Amazon region features giant trees up to 60 metres high, which rise up majestically in the equatorial forest. Their branches are very high, while their broad, flattened tops are made up of thick, dark green leaves, which often end in a narrow point; these drain off the rainwater. The trees are entwined by lianas, which hang from the leafy canopies. Only a little bit of light makes its way through the dense, luxuriant foliage. Contrary to what you might think, the trees in the tropical forest have very shallow roots. This is true even of the tallest ones, which are often felled by the wind and rain, not to mention the countless insects that gnaw upon them mercilessly. The Oriente is covered with thick, seemingly infinite forests, and is home to over 25,000 species of plants—a far greater number than in all of North America.

The landscape of the Costa ranges from semi-arid regions to lush tropical forests and huge grasslands covered with rice paddies, and the vegetation varies accordingly, while the Sierra is dominated by snow-capped mountains where few trees grow. The *páramo* is typical of the Andes. One of the first definitions of this term was provided by the Spanish, for whom it meant a very high and inhospitable stretch of land that was cold, windy and rainy. Today, *páramos* can be found at altitudes ranging from 3,000 to over 4,000 metres. They are home to fascinating plants known as *fralejónes*, which have lots of little thorns, spread out gracefully and can protect themselves from the wind, sun and ice. These are found mainly in the Reserva Ecológica El Ángel.

For a century now, the eucalyptus, a precious plant imported from Australia, has been thriving in Ecuador, quickly adapting to the widely varied climate. It adapts easily to the surrounding climatic conditions and grows very quickly. Unfortunately, the eucalyptus absorbs a lot of water, and the substances it feeds on dry out and impoverish the soil. Furthermore, its dead leaves, which contain toxins, affect the soil when they fall, preventing other plant species from growing.

The Mangrove Swamp

The mangrove swamp is home to several species of mangrove trees, all distinguished by their large roots. These trees can grow as high as 30 metres and are able to withstand submersion and salt. One of the varieties found in the salty waters along the shore of the Costa is the red mangrove. A great many sea birds and all sorts of insects inhabit this strange forest. The growth of the shrimp industry has led to a great deal of development in this swampy part of the shore. Unfortunately, the increase in the

Red mangrove

number of people living here has brought about the destruction of the greater part of the coastal forest. Nevertheless, patches of it can still be found here and there, most notably in the Reserva de Churute, on Isla Fragatas and around Isla Muisné.

A BRIEF HISTORY

Archaeological research has revealed that the country's first inhabitants were Asian nomads who crossed the Bering Strait 20,000 years ago. Over time, these groups were followed by Polynesians, who apparently crossed the Pacific Ocean by canoe and ended up on this continent. We have very little information on pre-Incan history. Excavations in the coastal region, in the modern-day provinces of Guayas and Oro, have uncovered traces of a sedentary civilization skilled in pottery techniques, which lived in the Valdivia region 4,000 years ago. Furthermore, human bones found here, most notably brachycephalic skulls, are believed to be those of the first people to have practised pottery in South America. Moreover, in the province of Manabi, on the Santa Elena peninsula, archaeologists have found pottery fragments attributed to the Machalilla culture and dating back to 1,500 B.C.

Eleventh century vestiges indicate that two tribes with a relatively developed social structure stood out from the others: the Caras, who had settled on the Pacific coast, and the Quitus, who lived in the mountains. The Caras easily conquered the Quitus and integrated them into their tribe. In the early 13th century, a new tribe of warriors, the Puruhás, appeared in the southern part of the country. The marriage of a Puruhá prince and a Shyri princess united the two kingdoms.

The Arrival of the Incas

The Incas, for their part, had been living in the Peruvian Andes since the 11th century. In the late 15th century, led by their sovereign, Túpac Yupanqui, they decided to extend their empire

The Incas

Starting in the 12th century, this people formed a vast empire known as Tahuantinsuyu, a Quichua word meaning "the four directions of the world". The Inca empire stretched along the Andes mountain range from Chile to modern-day Colombia. It was ruled by an emperor believed to be a direct descendant of Inti, the Sun God; this divine connection entitled him to the powers of an uncontested monarch. His people approached him with great veneration, fear and humility, and he only communicated with others through an intermediary, never looking at the person before him. Always surrounded by an escort, he was carried about on a richly decorated litter drawn by men. Incan society was based on a rigid social structure that included privileged classes: the nobility, made up of the Inca's male descendants and war chiefs, and the priests, essentially the sacrificers and other dignitaries of the solar cult. The *ayllu*, the basic unit of Incan society, formed an extended family grouped into a village, and was the civilization's true economic nucleus. War booty plundered from the neighbouring peoples was distributed among the various classes of Inca society. The conquered peoples were torn away from their land, transplanted to other parts of the empire to prevent any attempt at rebellion, enslaved and finally assimilated.

onto Ecuadoran territory. They were briefly halted by the Shyris in the north. In 1493, Túpac died and was succeeded by his son, Huayna Cápac, who defeated the Shyris, extending his empire to the Colombian border. Hoping to strengthen his kingdom, he married the daughter of a deposed king, Princess Paccha, who bore him a son, Atahualpa. This union brought about a series of changes: the centre of power was Cuzco, the conquered provinces were governed by means of a bureaucratic system, and use of the Quichua language became obligatory throughout the kingdom. Furthermore, an irrigation system was set up and new foodstuffs, such as potatoes and peanuts, began to be grown. To ward off any attempt at rebellion in remote, newly colonized regions, the Incas separated entire populations. Tribes living in Quito were thus moved to Cuzco in order to undermine their confidence.

In the early 16th century, the Europeans colonizing the Caribbean islands unwittingly unleashed a terrible smallpox epidemic, which spread into the heart of the empire, wiping out large numbers of Incas, including Emperor Huayna Cápac. The empire was thus divided between his two sons, with Huáscar taking over the south, Atahualpa the north. Neither of the two was satisfied with his inheritance, and a merciless, fratricidal war broke out between Atahualpa, the bastard, and Huáscar, the legitimate son. After several years of fighting, Atahualpa and his men succeeded in invading Peru from Quito, and crushed Huáscar and his troops near the town of Ambato (central Ecuador) in 1532. Atahualpa thus became the king of a

---

Quichua

Quichua was the official vernacular of the Inca empire (Tahuantinsuyu). With the arrival of the conquistadors, Spanish soon became the country's major language. Although the use of Quichua diminished considerably, the language did not disappear altogether. Today, it is spoken only by Amerindian communities living on the high plateaus of the Andes in Ecuador, Peru, Bolivia and northern Chile. Still, in those places where it is commonly spoken, Quichua is enjoying something of a revival. Some Quichua words, such as condor, poncho and puma, have been incorporated into the English language.

---

crippled and more or less divided empire.

In the meantime, in the early 16th century, a rumour that aroused a great deal of interest spread all the way to Panamá. According to reports, there was an empire overflowing with riches south of the isthmus. Its name: Eldorado. A few adventurers and sailors tried vainly to find it.

In 1524, Francisco Pizarro and Diego de Almagro became fascinated with the idea of conquering such an empire, and succeeded in convincing Father Hernando de Luque to finance their costly and perilous expedition. Unfortunately, after a brief stay on the Colombian coast, they found nothing but some hostile natives and forests strewn with swamps. A second expedition was carried out at the end of 1526. Guided by Pizarro, the Spanish sailed along the Pacific shoreline and dropped anchor at the mouth of the Río San Juan, in Colombia. Pizarro sent his captain, Bartolomé Ruiz de Andrade, ahead as a scout. Ruiz and his men continued along the Pacific coastline and landed at Esmeraldas on September 21, 1526. It was thus Bartolomé Ruiz who first set foot on Ecuadoran soil. Ruiz named the area Bahía de San Matteo, as September 21 is St. Matthew's day. He was greeted by the natives, who gave him gifts as a sign of welcome and a token of friendship. He continued his voyage southward and was no doubt the first European to cross the equator in the Pacific. Farther south, he met men decked out in gold and beautiful fabrics, sailing boats made of balsa wood, then spotted the snowy peak of the Chimborazo volcano.

Satisfied with his discoveries, Ruiz backtracked and rejoined Pizarro in Colombia. Unfortunately, Pizarro received an order to return to Panamá with his troops. At that point, he took out his sword, drew a line in the sand, and told his men that anyone who didn't want to continue the expedition was free to go back to Panamá. He warned them, however, that those who did would be derided, tried and perhaps even thrown in prison, while those who crossed the line to follow him would become rich and famous. Thirteen soldiers accepted the challenge. This tale has survived the centuries and is now known as "Los trece de l'Isla de Gallo".

Pizarro and his 13 men sailed southward along the coast and landed at Tumbes, a Peruvian town located south of the present-day border of Ecuador and Peru. The Europeans were given a warm reception by the natives, who presented them with jewels, gold and fabrics. They found the coveted Inca empire in the midst of a crisis, and realized that the peoples colonized by the Incas had only recently been subjugated. Delighted, Pizarro returned to Spain toward the end of 1528 with a great deal of information on this enigmatic land and the offerings he had received. His goal was to convince the king of Spain that El Dorado might be there. He was locked up for disobeying orders and unpaid debts, then summoned to appear before King Charles V, who granted him the right to govern the territory to be conquered.

The Spanish Conquest

After planning his expedition carefully, Pizarro set sail with the firm intention of colonizing the territory and carrying off the possessions of the so-called kingdom; he landed at Tumbes, a village he had visited on his first voyage. He was accompanied by just 300 men, about 60 cavalrymen and nearly 200 foot soldiers.

In the meantime, Atahualpa had emerged victorious from his duel with Huáscar in central Ecuador and was walking peacefully to Cuzco. News of the mysterious strangers' arrival on the coast spread quickly by word of mouth, and soon everyone was talking about the Spaniards. Pizarro decided to travel farther south, to Cajamarca, to meet Atahualpa, who greeted him amicably at first. However, realizing how outnumbered he was, Pizarro took

fright and convinced himself that it would require both force and cunning to conquer the Inca empire. He decided to lay a trap for Atahualpa by setting up a meeting with him. When Atahualpa and his men arrived, they were ambushed by Pizarro and his troops, who seized the opportunity to capture the Incan ruler. In the hope of saving his own life, Atahualpa made a deal with Pizarro: in exchange for his freedom, he would fill a room in his house with several dozen tons of gold. The amount has probably been exaggerated by the oral tradition, but it is still an indication of how much of the precious metal the Incas had. To the Spaniards' delight, the room was slowly filled with gold. One day, however, a rumour reached Pizarro's ears: the Incas were gathering secretly and preparing a counter-attack to liberate Atahualpa. Furious, Pizarro reneged on his promise and instead of setting Atahualpa free, set up a puppet court to try him. The verdict was bitter: he was condemned to be burnt at the stake. Atahualpa was terrified of being cremated, because his body would be completely destroyed; he therefore converted to Catholicism and was strangled instead. He died on August 29, 1533.

Word of Atahualpa's death spread all the way to Europe, and many people were outraged by the cowardly, dubious manner in which he had been executed. However, the gold and other treasures of the Inca empire arrived shortly after the news, making it easier for people to forget about Atahualpa's demise.

Although his leader was dead, the brave and loyal General Rumiñahui continued fighting the Spanish and succeeded in destroying the town of

Cajamarca. Atahualpa's corpse was exhumed and brought back to Quito to be reburied. Meanwhile, two Spanish battalions were sent to conquer Quito, as well as the rest of Ecuador. The race was on: Sebastián de Benalcázar, Pizarro's faithful lieutenant, led an expedition from Peru, while Pedro de Alvaro headed for the northern part of Ecuador from Guatemala. Pizarro managed to convince Alvaro to give up and return quietly to Guatemala in exchange for a large sum of money.

Atahualpa

The son of Huayna Cápac and his wife, a Shyri princess, Atahualpa was crowned king of the Incas after defeating and killing his half-brother Huáscar in a war of succession, and became the last emperor to rule over his people. His reign came to an end with the arrival of the Spanish conquistadors, led by Francisco Pizarro. He was captured and held for a huge ransom. Once this was paid, Pizarro betrayed him, christened him and killed him in 1533.

In the meantime, the Cañari and Puruhá Amerindians, eager for vengeance, joined forces with the Spanish to fight the Incas. The conquistadors still faced a number of obstacles, however. The sky-scraping Andes Cordillera towered over the plains from east to west, protecting the most populated part of the country. The Spanish also came to learn about *soroche*, better known as mountain sickness. The devastated villages and burnt lands left over from the war between the two brothers made it difficult for the Spanish to get fresh supplies along the way. Finally, when they reached Quito in 1534, they found the city completely destroyed, as the Incas had preferred to level it rather than let it fall into Spanish hands.

On December 6, 1534, the city rebuilt by the Spanish was christened Villa de San Francisco de Quito. Rumiñahui launched a counter-attack, and though he put up a fierce fight, he fell into a trap and was captured. Blinded by greed, the conquistadors tortured him so that he would reveal where the Incas hid their gold. Rumiñahui refused to yield and was finally killed. The following year, Benalcázar founded the city of Guayaquil, located on the Costa 416 kilometres from Quito. Twice destroyed by the Incas, the city was reconstructed a third and final time by Francisco de Orellana.

In 1540, Pizarro put his brother Gonzalo in charge of the city of Quito. The next year, Gonzalo Pizarro and Francisco de Orellana led an expedition to the Oriente (Amazonia) in search of Eldorado. In March 1541, the men climbed down from the high plateaus of the Andes and slowly made their way into the depths of the luxuriant tropical forest, where it rained continually and they had to clear a path with their swords. A good number of them succumbed to mysterious illnesses. Orellana, realizing that the mission wasn't progressing and that supplies were running low, offered to scout ahead along the waterways. Bitter, tired of waiting and believing that Orellana had deceived him, Pizarro decided to return to Quito. Meanwhile, Orellana and his men, failing to find enough food or gold, followed the Río Napo and the Amazon to the Brazilian coast, thus becoming the first Europeans to cross the South American continent.

Francisco Pizarro (1475-1541)

A Spanish conquistador who took part in numerous expeditions in the South Seas, Pizarro served under Vasco Núñez de Balboa when the latter crossed the Darién isthmus (Panamá) and discovered the Pacific Ocean in 1513. Later, he became fascinated by Hernando Cortés's fabulous exploits in Mexico. In 1520, although he was already 45 years old at the time, he found himself driven by the desire to make new discoveries and wanted to accomplish a feat on a par with those of Cortés and Balboa. With the help of Diego de Almagro, he decided to try to conquer Peru for King Charles V of Spain. After a few fruitless attempts, he succeeded in vanquishing the Inca empire and killing the Inca Atahualpa after betraying him and having him baptized. In 1541, shortly after putting his ex-partner, Almagro, to death, Pizarro himself was killed by Almagro's son, Diego el Monzo.

Over the following years, Ecuador was crippled by internal fighting, as some money- and power-hungry conquistadors were ready to do anything to achieve their ends. At the time, the economy was based on gold and silver mining. However, once the gold supply had been exhausted, the Spanish turned their interest to the fertile land surrounding the Avenida de los Volcanes, which was perfect for farming. In order to meet the needs of the empire, the Spaniards set up the *encomienda* system, under which labour was provided by natives working in absolutely atrocious conditions.

The *encomienda* system was intended to reward Spanish soldiers and encourage them to settle on Ecuadoran lands. It was a form of feudalism, under which each soldier was granted a parcel of land and control over all the natives living on it. Unfortunately, this "control" took on the form of punishment, and spawned all sorts of injustices. In addition to working the land, the Amerindians were exploited by the Spanish in other areas of activity as well (household work, mining, etc.). This deplorable practice survived all the way into the 20th century; today, it is better known as the *hacienda* system. The *encomienda* system angered the king of Spain, because it made it harder and harder for him to collect taxes owed to him. He thus decided to send over some representatives to abolish the practice.

In addition, slaves were brought over from Africa to work on the cacao plantations on the Costa. Soon afterwards, various animals, most notably the cow, the mule, the horse and the pig, were introduced into the country by the conquistadors. Next, the first banana plantation in South America got off to a good start, and numerous factories were set up to meet the huge European demand for textiles.

In an effort to manage his overseas colonies better, the king of Spain created viceroyalties. The empire of Tahuantinsuyu was gradually supplanted by the viceroyalty of Peru and by Lima.

The late 16th century saw the arrival of a number of religious orders, such as the Dominicans and the Franciscans, and later the Augustinians and the Jesuits. Numerous missions were established in Amazonia in the hope of

Important Dates in the History of Ecuador

Late 15th century: From their base in the Peruvian Andes, Túpac Yupanqui and his army decide to extend the Inca empire onto Ecuadoran territory.

1493: Death of Túpac Yupanqui. His son, Huayna Cápac, succeeds him and extends the Inca empire to the Colombian border.

1527: Death of the Inca Huayna Cápac.

1530-1532: A war of succession breaks out between Huayna Cápac's two sons, Huáscar and Atahualpa. The latter crushes his brother's troops.

1530: Conquistador Francisco Pizarro lands in Tumbes, in northern Peru.

1532: Pizarro and his men lay a trap for Atahualpa and take him prisoner in Cajamarca, Peru.

1533: Atahualpa is assassinated.

1534: Sebastián Benalcázar founds the city of Quito on December 6.

1541: Francisco de Orellana sets out in search of El Dorado. He finds no gold, but is the first European to navigate the full length of the Amazon, all the way to the Atlantic Ocean.

1563: Quito becomes the seat of an *audiencia real* (a court of justice also holding political powers), supervised by the Spanish Crown.

1736: French geodesist Charles Marie de La Condamine arrives in Ecuador.

1801: German scientist and famous traveller Alexander von Humboldt arrives in Ecuador.

1812: The country's first constitution, which is never implemented.

1822: On May 24, General Sucre defeats the Spanish in the Battle of Pichincha. At General Simón Bolívar's instigation, the Audiencia Real de Quito joins Venezuela, Panamá and Colombia to form the Republic of Gran Colombia.

1830: The Audiencia Real de Quito declares its independence and adopts the name "Ecuador"; General Juan José Flores becomes the country's first president.

1832: The Galápagos Islands become part of Ecuador.

1835: Charles Darwin comes to the Galápagos Islands for a five-week stay.

1852: Abolition of slavery.

1860: Gabriel García Moreno comes to power in Ecuador.

1875: Gabriel García Moreno is assassinated.

1897: Eloy Alfaro becomes president of Ecuador.

1908: Inauguration of the railroad between Quito and Guayaquil.

1912: Eloy Alfaro is assassinated.

1941: The Peruvian army invades southern Ecuador.

1942: Under the Protocol of Rio de Janeiro, Ecuador loses a large portion of its territory to Peru.

1945: Ecuador becomes a member of the United Nations.

1967: Discovery of oil in Lago Agrío, in Amazonia.

1969: Ecuador joins the Andean Pact. The other members are Colombia, Chile and Peru. This association favours free trade among these countries.

1987: A large earthquake ravages the Quito region and damages some of the buildings in the city's historic centre.

1990: June uprising of native communities throughout the country over territorial claims.

1992: Sixto Durán Ballen becomes president of the republic.

1994: In June, another general native uprising.

1995: Friction at the Peruvian border in early January.

1996: Populist Abdala Bucarán Ortiz is brought to power, along with the country's first woman vicepresident, Rosalia Ortega.

1997: Abdala Bucarán Ortiz and Rosalia Ortega are dismissed by the parliament in favour of Fabian Alarcón.

converting the Amerindians. This led to the construction of small villages on the edge of the Oriente. The Amerindians put up a ferocious resistance; villages were destroyed and all their inhabitants killed. After a few fruitless attempts, the missionaries had no choice but to give up and return to their monastery in Quito.

Less than 30 years after it was founded, Quito became a province known as an "Audiencia Real", subordinate to the viceroyalty of Lima—a state of affairs that lasted for nearly three centuries. Numerous colonial churches and towns were erected during this period. Many have survived to this day, and contain religious masterpieces by artists of the Quito School. This school, created by a large group of native artists, such as Miguel de Santiago and Hernando de la Cruz, greatly influenced many European artists, as well as American baroque art. The most striking examples are found in the towns of Quito and Cuenca. The labour was provided exclusively by Amerindians, who had to work in often inhuman conditions under the direction of the Spanish. This led to a substantial number of Amerindian uprisings. The Audiencia Real also had to fend off numerous attacks by English and Dutch pirates, who sailed along the Pacific shoreline looking for gold and silver. At the same time, a tax increase on merchandise and various foodstuffs further angered the natives, who demonstrated their displeasure all over the country.

In 1736, King Louis XIV of France assigned two teams of scientists to determine the validity of Newton's theory that the earth is slightly flattened at its poles. The first expedition was led by French geodesist and naturalist Charles Marie de La Condamine. He arrived in Ecuador accompanied by three cartographers and six other scientists sent to conduct a series of experiments, with the goal of measuring the length of a degree of the meridian, a few kilometres north of Quito. A second team, led by French mathematician Pierre Louis Moreau de Maupertuis went to Lapland to try to determine whether the planet really was flattened-out at the poles. It took him barely two years to confirm Newton's hypothesis, while La Condamine's team had to combat the Amerindians and the freezing temperatures of the Andean peaks for five long years before reaching the same conclusion as Maupertuis. Furthermore, German naturalist and geographer Alexander von Humboldt arrived in Ecuador toward the end of the 18th century and carried out numerous climatological, geological and botanical studies.

Independence

In the early 19th century, echoes of the victories of the French and American Revolutions and Napoleon's invasion of Spain made their way all the way to Quito, along with certain new trends of thought. These events prompted members of the Creole oligarchy, led by Marqués de Selva Alegre, to take over the city of Quito on August 10, 1809 in the hope of liberating their country from Spanish control. The attempt was a bitter failure, and the siege of Quito lasted just over three weeks; still, it paved the way for independence. Thirteen years later, on May 24, 1822, the Pichincha volcano was the scene of the decisive battle. With the help of Simón Bolívar, Venezuelan general Antonio José Sucre succeeded in

Alexander von Humboldt (1769-1859)

From June 1799 to August 1804, Alexander von Humboldt travelled over 10,000 kilometres in North, Central and South America, including some particularly dangerous regions, and introduced the public to numerous discoveries theretofore unknown to Europeans. He conducted a great deal of geographical, botanical and climatological research. On December 8, 1801, Humboldt landed in Ecuador, where he struck up a friendship with Carlos Montúfar, son of the governor of Selva Alegre, an important figure in the struggle for independence. Humboldt described the ruins of the Inca empire and succeeded in measuring and identifying the cold ocean current of the Pacific that flows along the coast of South America and now bears his name. He proved that the American continent was older than commonly believed; counted over 400 terrestrial volcanoes, including 18 in Ecuador; listed an incredible number of plant and animal species and frankly denounced the atrocities committed during the colonization of the South American continent.

liberating Quito from Spanish domination.

The Audiencia Real de Quito joined its neighbours to the north, Venezuela, Panamá and Colombia, to form the Republic of Gran Colombia, but proclaimed its independence in 1830, at which time it adopted the name Ecuador. However, independence did not bring about national harmony immediately. General Antonio José Sucre was assassinated, leaving the country under the military leadership of General Juan José Flores, whom many suspected of having played a role in Sucre's murder. Vincent Rocafuerte took over as president at the end of Flores's term, but the general returned to power from 1839 to 1845.

The country had a whole string of presidents from 1845 to 1860. José María Urbina abolished slavery in 1852. The period between 1860 and 1875 was dominated by a single man, Gabriel García Moreno. Perceiving that Ecuador was going through a crisis, he turned to Catholicism to unify the country. He also introduced and developed an education system and established such institutions of higher learning as the Escuela Politécnica Nacional (the national polytechnic school). He undertook the construction of the railroad between Quito and Guayaquil, thus linking the Costa and the Sierra. Still, his bellicose character and religious fanaticism bothered many Liberals, who ended up assassinating him in 1875. Twenty-two years later, in 1897, the country's first Liberal president, Eloy Alfaro, was elected. A true man of action, he finished the railway line between Quito and Guayaquil and inaugurated it in 1908; introduced the first divorce laws in Latin America and abolished the death penalty. In 1911, after a period of strained relations with his own party, he was forced to resign. After a few months of exile, however, he returned to power. A civil war broke out, and Alfaro was arrested and imprisoned, then finally killed during a riot in Quito on January 28, 1912. Between 1925 and 1948, Ecuador experienced a period of economic and political instability, during which some 20 presidents held office.

Taking advantage of the Ecuadoran government's weak state, Peru invaded the southern part of the country in 1941. At the end of the war, a part of the Amazon was annexed to Peru under the Protocol of Rio de Janeiro. Today, Ecuadorans are vehement about their claim to this territory. One need only glance at a map made in Ecuador to see that the borders shown on it are not the same as those on maps published elsewhere. According to the United Nations, the country covers a total area of 270,670 square kilometres. This number is hotly contested by the Ecuadorans, who assert that another 174,565 square kilometres belong to them.

In 1964, the first agrarian-reform law was passed. Unfortunately, the lands granted to the natives were located at high altitudes and were difficult to farm. The year 1964 was also marked by the founding of a native federation (the Shuars).

Three years later, in 1967, black gold was discovered in a part of the country occupied only by a small town called Lago Agrío. Scores of entrepreneurs flocked to the source of their future wealth, and with them came a highly contagious form of corruption. With the arrival of trucks and bulldozers bearing the torch of unbridled capitalism and the resulting invasion of the modern world, the Amazon forest shrank at an astonishing speed, forcing the people, plants and animals that had always lived there into a smaller and smaller space. The magnificent riches of the Ecuadoran subsoil were drained by oil-

Simón Bolívar

This illustrious general, born in Caracas (Venezuela) in 1783, has earned a permanent place in history as the first person to try to consolidate the countries of Latin America into one nation. After waging a long battle against Spanish domination, he succeeded in liberating Venezuela, Colombia (which at the time included present-day Panamá) and Ecuador. With these victories under his belt, he founded the Republic of Gran Colombia (encompassing all the aforementioned countries), and became its president. The first Panamerican Congress was held in Panamá, but Bolívar, in spite of his military success, could not manage to keep the country unified. Driven to despair, he died in Santa Marta (Colombia) in 1830. Bolívar is considered a true hero, and places all over Latin America bear his name.

industry giants like Texaco-Gulf, Maxus, Elf, Occidental, Arco and Petroecuador.

After a long period of dictatorship, the military agreed to give up the power they had usurped and allow the country to return to democracy following the adoption of the 18th Constitution of the Republic in 1978. Democrat Jaime Roldos Aguilera was elected president in 1979. He started off his term by launching a literacy campaign and was not afraid of international, and particularly American, opinions of his views. For example, he sided with the Salvadorans and backed the Sandinistas in Nicaragua. On May 22,

1981, he expelled the Summer Linguistic Institute from the country. The institute was a North American association that purported to be working in various religious domains, but was actually conducting industrial and economic espionage. On May 24, 1981, Independence Day in Ecuador, his term came to a tragic end when he was killed in an airplane crash. This accident raised some questions, as a few months after Roldos's sudden death, General Omar Torrijos, a friend of the former president's who opposed Ronald Reagan's ideas, also died in a plane crash.

Oswaldo Hurtado Larrea took over the presidency until 1984. In the meantime, the plunge in oil prices slowed the country's economic growth. León Febres Cordero was in power from 1984 to 1988. His term was punctuated by failures: he was unable to negotiate an agreement with foreign creditors in order to reduce his country's foreign debt, and his government's image was sullied by corruption scandals, as well as a military rebellion in 1987. The next president was Rodrigo Borja, who remained in office until 1992; like his predecessor, he was very unpopular with Ecuadorans, whom he left with one of the highest debts per capita in all Latin America.

The year 1990 was marked by the national Amerindian uprising in June. Native communities throughout the country gathered along the Pan American highway and blocked traffic for several days with felled trees and big rocks to show how angry and dismayed they were about the land claim issue. A number of demonstrators also occupied the Iglesia de Santo Domingo in colonial Quito. The military

stepped in to stabilize the situation. Elected on August 10, 1992 under the banner of the Republican Unity party, Sixto Durán Ballén was urged to take action by the International Monetary Fund (IMF), then imitated most other countries on the continent by prescribing some drastic medicine for the Ecuadoran economy. While these austerity measures did enable Ecuador to regain control of part of its debt, they also had serious repercussions on the poorest communities in the country, whose purchasing power went down yet another level. Nearly four years to the day after the national Amerindian uprising of June 1990, the natives surprised the Ecuadoran people by blocking the country's main road, the Pan American highway, once again. This time, too, the army had to intervene in order to restore order.

The beginning of 1995 was marked by the mobilization of armed Ecuadoran and Peruvian troops in the Amazon, in a disputed border zone (340 km^2) in the Condor cordillera. This area, located some 500 kilometres south of Quito, in the northernmost part of Peru, is part of the territory that Ecuador and Peru have been quarrelling over since the signing of the Protocol of Rio de Janeiro on January 29, 1942. The discovery of gold and oil deposits in the area was the source of this new conflict. The Protocol of 1942 put an end to a border war that had broken out in January 1941. Under the treaty, Peru was granted the larger part of the disputed territory, but Ecuador was never entirely satisfied with the terms, at least as far as part of the border (about 80 km) was concerned. There has thus been an ongoing controversy over the demarcation of the border in a hard to reach, mountainous area located in the heart of the Amazon jungle.

This conflict elicited strong reactions on the international scene, and peace negotiations were begun by the very sponsors who had cosigned the Protocol of 1942: the United States, Argentina, Brazil and Chile.

While the beginning of 1995 was marked by external problems, the end was marked by accusations of embezzlement levelled against ex-Vice President Alberto Dahík. In October 1996, Dahík and his family fled to Costa Rica.

Populist Abdala Bucarám Ortiz's ascension to power gave rise to questions and concern. He took office on August 10, 1996 for a four-year term with the country's first female vice president, Rosalia Ortega, and bears the unflattering nickname *"el loco"* (the madman). Bucarám was already a controversial figure and had been accused of nepotism. He improved his image during the Rio Summit in Cochabamba, Bolivia, where, for the first time, he met his Peruvian counterpart, Alberto Fujimori. Bucarám wanted to introduce social reforms; indeed, during his candidacy, he promised voters that he would be the "president of the poor". The beginning of 1997 was shrouded by controversy and confusion. Congress dismissed Abdala Bucarám Ortiz and named Fabian Alarcón, the President of the Assembly, in his place. A climate of uncertainty pervaded the entire country as Abdala Bucarám Ortiz, Fabian Alarcón and Rosalia Ortega all laid claim to the presidency for three days. Finally, on February 11, 1997, Fabian Alarcón was elected interim president of Ecuador until August 10, 1998.

POLITICS

Ecuador's first constitution was written in 1812 and underwent numerous modifications over the years. A new constitution, which went into effect in 1978, defines the country as a democratic republic. Since 1979, all citizens aged 18 or over have been able to vote freely for the candidate of their choice. The presidency is won by obtaining over 50% of the votes. The president and vice president are elected for a four-year term.

The country is divided into 21 provinces, each with a governor named by the president of the republic. Furthermore, each province is subdivided into urban and rural districts known as *cantones*.

THE ECONOMY

Before the explosion of the petroleum industry, farming was the mainspring of the country's economy. The discovery of black gold in 1972 led to a decade or so of economic reshuffling that negatively affected many other areas of activity, most importantly agricultural production. During the 1980s, the drop in oil exports on the international market, combined with the 1987 earthquake, had a devastating effect on the country's economy. The earthquake destroyed several oil pipelines, forcing the government to suspend its petroleum exports for nearly a year. Furthermore, the discovery of oil in Amazonia disrupted the lifestyle of the Amerindian communities in the Oriente, and the encroachment of the modern world began to threaten their existence.

Ecuador thought its vast oil resources would enable it to generate prosperity, wipe out its debt and stabilize the country. It is estimated, however, that the oil reserves will be exhausted around 2010, thereby plunging the country into economic ruin.

Today, oil is still the country's principal source of revenue, but the farming industry is growing. With its fertile land and varied climate, Ecuador has a great deal of agricultural potential. The farming industry employs 40% of the working population and provides more jobs than other areas of activity. Most of the farms in Ecuador are located on the Costa. The country's main crops are bananas, oranges, wheat and coffee. Banana exports account for nearly half Ecuador's foreign sales. Thanks to its forests, the Costa is the world's leading producer of balsa wood. Other natural resources include the vast quantities of fish and seafood along the Pacific coast and out to the Galápagos Islands, which have enabled the country to become one of the top producers of farmed shrimp in the world.

THE ECUADORANS

Over 40% of the country's 11.5 million inhabitants are Amerindian, and nearly 50% mestizo. Only 10% of the population is white. The majority of Ecuador's multiethnic population lives along the coast or in the Andes, in the valleys and on the high plateaus. The rest of country's residents live in the east, in the region known as the Oriente. The various Amazon peoples have a great deal in common, not only where their ancestral traditions and belief systems are concerned, but also in regard to the problems they are facing today. Their differences are subtle, and defining and explaining them adequately would require a precise anthropological study far beyond the bounds of this guide. The Sionas, Secoyas, Cofans, Shuars, Achuars, Huaranis and Quichuas all live in the Amazon region.

Language

The official language of Ecuador is Spanish, which is spoken by over 90% of the population. About 10% of the country's Amerindians still speak Quichua, but they generally understand Spanish well.

A Few Ecuadoran Expressions

There are many charming, typically Ecuadoran expressions. As soon as you arrive, you'll notice that many words are pronounced differently depending on the region. On the Costa, the endings of certain words change and sometimes even disappear. This is true of *buenos días* and *a las ordenes*, which are often pronounced *bueno día* and *a la orden* there.

chevere	great, fantastic
luego	later
sigue sigue lo mas	keep going
campesino, indegena	country person, Amerindian
¿como le va?	How are you?
a la orden	at your service

THE ARTS

Art in Ecuador is as rich and colourful as the flora and fauna. In colonial times, the city of Quito, sometimes justly called the Florence of the Americas, was the birthplace of a school of sacred art known as the Escuela de Quito (Quito School).

Born in Gand in 1495, Fleming Jocke Ricke belonged to the Franciscan order when he founded the country's first school of fine arts in Quito in 1524. Under his direction, many Amerindians began to express themselves through art. During the 17th and 18th centuries, guided and influenced by the religious orders that came to the country one after the other under the conquistadors, Ecuadorans began carving wood and stone and working gold. They proved to be remarkably talented, creating veritable works of art that can be found in the country's numerous religious sanctuaries. The value of these architectural pieces was recognized in 1978, when UNESCO designated Quito's colonial centre a World Heritage Site.

The best-known artists are Manuel Chili, whose pseudonym, Caspicara, means "wooden head"; Miguel de Santiago and Bernardo de Legarda. Still, most of the artists of the Quito School will forever remain anonymous.

Painting

Miguel de Santiago was born in Quito in 1633 and died in 1706. The illegitimate son of Lucas Vizuete and Juana Ruíz, he bore the name of his adopted father, Hernando de Santiago. No one knows who taught him to paint.

Santiago comes from the oldest line of colonial mestizo painters. His credits include a series of paintings on the life of St. Augustine, executed for the Augustinians, and another on the miracles of the Virgin of Guadalupe (1700), for the Guápulo monastery. He worked for the Franciscans throughout his lifetime.

Santiago was considered a genius of colonial painting, as he was an unparalleled draughtsman with a very spare style. His paintings are closely linked to the Spanish tradition represented by Zurbaran, Murillo and Ribera. Still, modern critics sometimes remark upon his lack of originality and the fact that his work does not have a distinctly American quality about it.

Santiago's nasty character made him the subject of a number of anecdotes. According to one, he killed a model who was posing for him for a painting of Christ on the cross. This painting was mysteriously stolen shortly after 1895...

Miguel de Santiago's disciples were Nicolás Javier Goribar, his daughter Isabel and Barnabé Valenzuela.

19th-century Painters

Antonio Salas (1780-1860)
A disciple of Samuel Samaneigo and Bernardo Rodríguez, Salas was the heir to the traditions of colonial painting. He witnessed the transition from colonial rule to republicanism. Salas painted such heroes of independence as Bolívar and Sucre, but also tackled religious subjects. He was the father and

teacher of an entire dynasty of famous 19th-century painters.

Rafael Salas (1821-1906)
The son of Antonio Salas, he was awarded a grant, through the agency of President Gabriel García Moreno, to master his art in Europe. An excellent portraitist and one of the country's leading landscape painters, he is considered one of the three artists most representative of Ecuadoran academicism. He was an excellent portraitist and one of the country's leading landscape artists.

Ramón Salas (1815-1905)
Another of Antonio Salas's sons and one of the pioneers of a school of painting that aimed to portray the manners and customs of the time. He also painted the occasional miniature, portrait and sacred piece. The Museo de Arte Moderno, the museum of modern art, has a few interesting examples of his "manner paintings".

Luis Cadena (1830-1889)
One of Antonio Salas's disciples, Cadena travelled to Chile, where he met Monvoisin. After that, President Robles arranged for him to receive a grant to study in Italy. Upon his return to Ecuador, he became the director of the Escuela de Bellas Artes, the national school of fine arts. He made a name for himself by painting portraits that exemplified the academic standards of his day.

Juan Manosalvas (1837-1906)
Manosalvas received a grant from Gabriel García Moreno's government to study in Rome in 1871. Upon his return, he became a professor at the Academia de Bellas Artes, the academy of fine arts. He was the third academic painter of his time to make a name for himself and trained the following generations of painters.

Rafael Troya (1845-1920)
One of Luis Cadena's disciples, Troya started out his career by working for scientists Reiss and Stubel, with whom he travelled the country, carefully studying the landscape without "destroying the fundamental shapes of nature". A great landscape artist with an eye for spacial harmony, he also introduced human forms into his compositions.

The Origins of Amerindian Painting

The triumph of the liberal revolution in 1895 was paralleled by the gradual secularization of the society, which was accompanied by a number of social reforms. Thanks to these, the 20th century saw a slow increase in public awareness of the social and cultural realities in Ecuador.

Up until the beginning of the 20th century, Ecuadoran art simply imitated European works. Purely decorative, it was intended to satisfy the demand of the conservative upper classes. The intellectuals of the 1930s, who were influenced by a new ideology, believed that it was essential to break with the classical and romantic cannons, and to use this new vision to ask more profound questions linked to the problem of identity (who are we?).

"Indigenism" may be defined as a movement in the visual arts that strives to reclaim the Andean indigenous experience, drawing inspiration from a European pictorial language (impressionism, cubism, expressionism, etc.).

Although they were also influenced by Mexican mural painting, the artists of this period studied the indigenous world in all its isolation and tragedy. To do so, they exaggerated natural forms and distorted the figures who appeared in their works.

Precursors of Change

Pedro León (Ambato 1894-1956)
León made the transition from academicism to indigenous painting. He identified first with impressionism and the work of Cézanne, then later adopted indigenous themes. His most famous painting is *Cangahua* (1940).

Camilio Egas (Quito 1889-1961)
Egas was the first painter to associate himself with the movements in fashion in Europe at the time (1911). He solemnly devoted himself to indigenous painting, using a realistic technique. He was awarded the Mariano Aguilera prize for his *Retrado de Mujer* (Portrait of a Woman, 1923). On a trip to New York in 1927, he fell under the spell of expressionism (*La Calle 14*; 14th Street, 1937). Up until the 1940s, he was influenced by hyperrealism (*Desolacion*; Desolation, 1949). Egas created an extremely varied body of work and enjoyed a great deal of prestige in cultural circles, even long after his death. He exiled himself in France for several years, then returned to Ecuador, where he worked until his death in 1961.

Victor Mideros (Ibarra 1888-Quito 1969)
A disciple of Rafael Troya, Mideros was one of a number of Ecuadoran painters who moved from academicism to a more spiritual style. He was awarded the Mariano Aguilera prize on two occasions.

Indigenist Painters

José Enrique Guerrero (Quito 1905-1988)
Guerrero made the transition from impressionism to expressionism. He strove to depict a landscape characterized by the heaviness of its atmosphere and its coarse features (*Quito Horizontal*).

Leonardo Tejada (Latacunga 1908-)
Tejada developed the indigenous theme with a more lyrical eye, dealing with subjects such as popular art and folklore (*Cuentayo*).

Eduardo Kingman (Loja 1913-)
One of the leading figures in the indigenist movement, Kingman has been most strongly influenced by Mexican muralists. His style is characterized by clearly outlined figures, with a focus on faces and hands. His major works include *La Visita* (The Visit) and *La Sed* (Thirst). *Les Guandos* (1941), in which he denounces the social condition of the indigenous people and their relationship with the manager of the *hacienda*, is definitely his masterpiece. Kingman's paintings bear witness to the oppression and suffering of the Amerindians.

Diogenes Parades (Quito 1910-1968)
Parades began his career as a realist, but later adopted the theme of his generation. In order to denounce the tragedy of the indigenous people, he produced hideous images by using earthy colours that create a dramatic atmosphere. One example of this period is *La Tormenta* (The Storm).

Oswaldo Guayasamín (Quito 1919-)
Guayasamín is the most universal of all Ecuadoran painters. He first attracted attention by winning first prize at the Third Latin American Biennale in Barcelona for a piece from a series entitled *Huaycayñan* (Path of Tears). Afterward, he painted a series called *La Edad de la Ira* (The Age of Anger), in which he expresses the pain and tragedy of contemporary man. He produced another series of paintings on Quito and still another on tenderness. He also executed a number of murals in Ecuador and abroad (the Palacio del Gobierno, the Consejo Provincial de Pichincha, the Casa de la Cultura and Madrid's Barajas airport).

Contemporary Painting

In South America, the word "contemporary" refers to painting from the 1950s onward. The pioneers of contemporary painting, particularly abstraction, were Alberto Coloma Silva, Manuel Rendón Seminario and Araceli Gilbert.

Manuel Rendón Seminario (1894-Portugal 1982)
The undisputed father of Ecuadoran abstract painting, Seminario settled in Ecuador in the 1930s, and stirred up quite a commotion. He was trained as a painter in Paris, and despite his extensive education, was overlooked by contemporary society, which preferred the figurative style of Guerrero, Guayasamín and D. Paredes. He won first prize at the Latin American Biennale in 1951 and 1954.

Araceli Gilbert (Guayaquil 1914-)
Gilbert is both a painter and a sculptor. At the height of the indigenist movement, he followed in the footsteps of Manuel Rendón and turned to geometric abstraction, then shifted to kinetic art. He started gaining public recognition and earning respect in artistic circles in the early 1960s, winning the October Salon (1960) and Mariano Aguilera (1961) prizes.

Contemporary Painters

Estuardo Maldonado (1930-)
A painter and sculptor, Maldonado belonged to the group of artists that typified the sixties generation. This avant-garde group, VAN, opposed the figurative painting of the indigenists, claiming that their painting and the principles upon which it was based had remained superficial, and that their art had become elitist. Maldonado studied fine arts in Guayaquil and travelled to Europe (Paris). At first, he created geometric arrangements of pre-Columbian signs. He also produced works of sculpture, using a sheet of stainless steel. Like other painters of his generation, he updated pre-Columbian and ancestral signs by placing them in a distinctly contemporary environment.

Anibal Villacis (1927-)
A self-taught artist, Villacis travelled to Paris, where he was influenced by numerous people, primarily Canogar and Tapies. He was awarded the international first prize at the Latin American Independence Show in 1972. He is linked to the group VAN through his pre-Columbianist themes. His paintings feature carefully worked textures and thick surfaces with calligraphic patterns borrowed from archaeology and folklore.

Enrique Tabara (1930-)
Tabara started off as an expressionist of the indigenist generation, but soon moved on to abstraction. He aligned himself with the pre-Columbianists (VAN), using textures and calligraphy borrowed from pre-Hispanic ceramics and rendering them into the contemporary pictorial language. Feet and legs take the place of pre-Columbian language and become repetitive elements, while at the same time symbolizing his painting; today, his research focuses on magic and fetishism.

Oswaldo Viteri (1931-)
A self-taught painter, Viteri was awarded several mentions at the 6th Biennale in Sao Paulo (1961) and the 2nd Biennale in Cordoba (1964). Working within the abstract movement, he favours distinct shapes and geometric compositions. Like other painters, he tackles the theme of identity, but he is particularly interested in experimenting with materials (impasto and textures).

Luis Molinari (Guayaquil 1929-1994)
Molinari studied in Buenos Aires (1951-1960), Paris (1960) and New York (1967). He was the successor of Araceli Gilbert's geometric abstraction. Later, after being influenced by the New York art scene, he turned to kinetic art and optical effects (op art).

Nelson Román (Latacunga 1943-)
Román was one of four artists, the others being Washington Iza, Ramiro Jácome and José Unda, who imposed their poetic style on the seventies generation. This generation of painters returned to figurative art, not in the indigenist style, but rather through hideous images whose magical atmosphere is tinged with horror, irony

and coarseness, and which aim to denounce social injustice and thereby subvert the system. A sense of dread pervades his paintings, which feature dramatic skies, phantasmagorical groups of people and nightmarish creatures. He later took to depicting scenes of folklore and magic.

Gonzalo Endara Crow (1936-1996)
Crow started out by creating hideous images, but then discovered magic realism. He depicted tranquil landscapes featuring a combination of the simplicity of daily life and the magic of the supernatural. To do so, he painted blue horses, strange-looking birds and giant eggs and apples. He made the cover illustration for Gabriel García Márquez's novel *Cien Años de Soledad* published in English as *One Hundred Years of Solitude*. Later, he transferred his landscape themes to the Costa, painting iguanas, fish and other similar creatures evocative of the magic realism of the tropics.

Miguel Betancourt (Quito 1958-)
Betancourt is one of Ecuador's successful young painters. His work falls in the tradition of abstract expressionism. Two other important painters of the new generation are Luigi Stornaiolo and Marcelo Aguirre.

Sculpture

In the 17th century, a great sculptor from the Quito School, Manuel Chili, enjoyed considerable renown, although the dates of his birth and death are unknown. His major pieces are on view in the Iglesia San Francisco and the Catedral. The mestizo artist Bernardo de Legarda, another great sculptor from the Quito School, left his mark on the 18th century. His most important work is definitely the superb reredos in the Capilla de Catuña.

Literature

Very few Ecuadoran writers have managed to gain recognition outside of the country. Still, Ecuador has produced a number of noteworthy poets and authors.

Strongly influenced by European models, the Creole bishop Gaspar de Villaroel (1587-1665) was one of the first people to make a name for himself in the narrative genre. Eugenio Santa Cruz y Espejo (1747-1795) was a philosopher, journalist and author of satirical, anti-establishment books, and also wrote the country's first journalistic publication, *Primicias de la Cultura de Quito*.

At the dawn of the 19th century, poet José Joaquín Olmedo, greatly inspired by classical lyricism, composed his *Canto a Bolívar*. Later, Juan León Mera (1832-1894) depicted the lifestyle of 19th-century Amerindians in his book *Cumandá*; he also wrote Ecuador's national anthem. Juan Montalvo, for his part, used his pen to protest García Moreno's regime.

The novel *Huasipungo*, by Jorge Ycaza (1906-1979), details the atrocities inflicted on the Amerindians, who gradually claimed rights of ownership over their land. This book was translated into English as *The Villagers* and is considered one of the masterpieces of Latin American literature. A must for anyone wishing to learn more about the class struggle in Ecuador.

Music

Ecuadoran music derives its influences from Amerindian and European civilizations. Pre-Columbian instruments included flutes and percussion instruments made with shells and bones. Later, string instruments like the guitar, the harp and the violin were introduced by the Spanish. All these contributions greatly influenced Ecuadoran music as we know it today. It is most often heard in *peñas*, where both young and old come to dance to the sounds of Ecuadoran folk music; the best-known are in Quito and Otavalo.

The Colonial Flute

The flute is one of the oldest wind instruments. There are four different kinds: the recorder, the transverse flute, the straight flute and the double flute.

Transverse flutes are made with several materials, such as reeds and metal, have six holes and are painted differently according to the tribe to which they belong.

The fife and the *rondador*, the equivalent of the panpipe (shepherd's pipe or syrinx), also fall into the flute category.

Panpipes

The first panpipe was made with reeds of various lengths and circumferences tied together with plant fibres. Over time, the instrument became associated with the Greek god Pan, who supposedly created it out of passionate love for the nymph Siringa; it is thus referred to in certain places as the *siringa* (syrinx). In Ecuador, it is known as the *rondador*.

The **panpipe** is a wind instrument with an extremely soft sound. It comes in all different sizes, from tiny ones with only eight pipes to big ones with 20, 30 or more.

The tiny **pentaphone panpipe**, which has five sounds, is used in certain places in Imbabura only once a year, as it is considered a ritual instrument. It is used in the festivities held during the autumnal equinox (September), when locals pay homage to the sun.

The **large panpipe** has six sounds and is used by some Amerindians to practice their scales.

There are also **reed panpipes**, the traditional pipes made of bone, wood, feather shafts or reeds and strips of leather.

he **condor-feather panpipe** is made up of feather shafts of various lengths,

attached side by side with a delicate wire.

he **double panpipe** can be played by two people. It is an Ecuadoran *rondador* with a series of up to 40 tubes of increasing size. The large *rondador* is obviously of secular, popular origin.

Andean horns are bull's horns with a thin reed attached at the tip, from which the sound is emitted.

The **marimba** has keys of various sizes made with the wood of palm trees. The resonance chamber is made up of pieces of bamboo positioned like a panpipe under each key; the sound is created by hitting them with two or more sticks, also made of palm-tree wood and covered with several layers of rubber at the tips. The instrument sits on two supports known as *burros*. The marimba is tuned by binding the laths tightly together with linen strings. When they play the marimba, the mestizos of Esmeraldas form a traditional orchestral ensemble that usually includes a bass drum, four *guasás* and two *cununos*.

PRACTICAL INFORMATION

Ecuador has something for nearly every style of travel, from luxurious comfort to rough adventure. Whatever your preference, planning ahead and being prepared for the unexpected is always a good idea. This section is intended to help you organize your trip to Ecuador by providing general information and practical advice.

Please note that all prices in this guide are in U.S. dollars.

ENTRANCE FORMALITIES

Before leaving home, be sure you have the official documents that will allow you to enter and leave Ecuador. Though the requirements may seem lax, without the proper documents you will not be able to travel within the country. Safeguard these documents and always have them on your person.

Since entrance formalities can change without warning, be sure to verify that the requirements mentioned below still apply before your trip.

Passport

Travellers from Canada, the United States, Great Britain, Australia and New Zealand entering Ecuador must have a passport that is valid for the length of their stay in their possession at all times. This is the only officially accepted form of identification.

Bring a photocopy of the important pages of your passport with you, as well as any other crucial documents (driver's license, health insurance, etc.), and leave copies with someone at home. Also take note of your passport number and its expiry date. This will make it easier to replace any official documents that might be lost or stolen.

In the event that you lose an important piece of identification, contact your country's consulate or embassy (see below).

Tourist Card

Besides your passport, you must have a tourist card (*tarjeta de turismo*) to enter and exit the country. In most cases, this card is issued by your travel agent, when you're checking in at the airport or on the plane. The card allows all visitors (Canadians, Americans, British, Australians, New Zealanders) to remain in the country for 60 days. The airfare or package price usually includes the cost of the card, which is $10. The card must be turned in upon departure, so remember to hang on to it. Keep it in your passport.

Visa

Canadian, American, British, Australian, and New Zealand travellers do not need a visa to enter Ecuador. Other travellers should check with the Ecuadoran embassy or consulate in their country to see if they need a visa. This visa costs $30 and is valid for three months.

Departure Tax

Everyone leaving Ecuador must pay a departure tax of $25 (the most expensive in South America with Peru). If you are leaving by air, the payment is made at the airport, when you check in. Be sure to have this amount in cash ($ or sucres), credit cards are not accepted.

Customs

Those entering the country may have in their possession one litre of alcohol, 200 cigarettes and $100 worth of goods (besides personal items). Drugs and firearms are of course forbidden.

EMBASSIES AND CONSULATES

Foreign Embassies and Consulates in Ecuador

Embassies and consulates representing your home country can provide valuable assistance in the event of health emergencies, legal problems or the death of a travel companion. Only urgent cases are dealt with, however. Visitors are responsible for any costs incurred as a result of services provided by these official bodies. You can also receive mail here.

Austria
Embassy: Calle Veintimilla 878 at Amazonas, Quito, ☎ (02) 503-456.

Belgium
Embassy: Calle Juan León Mera 863 at Wilson, Quito, ☎ (02) 545-340, ⌨ 507-367.
Consulate: Calle Lizardo García and Vélez, ☎ (04) 454-429.

Canada
Consulate: Avenida 6 de Diciembre 2816 at James Orton, Quito ☎ (02) 543-214.
Consulate: Calle Córdova 810 at Victor Manuel Rendón, 21st Floor, Guayaquil, ☎ (04) 563-580 or 566-747, ⌨ 314-562.

Colombia
Embassy: Avenida Colón 133 at Amazonas, Quito, ☎ (02) 553-263.

Germany
Embassy: Avenida Patria at 9 de Octubre, Edificio Eteco, 6th floor, Quito, ☎ (02) 232-660.

Great Britain
Embassy: Avenida González Suárez 111 at 12 de Octubre, Quito, ☎ (02) 560-309.

Italy
Embassy: Calle la Isla 111 at Albornoz, Quito, ☎ (02) 561-077.

Netherlands
Embassy: Avenida 12 de Octubre 1942 at Luis Cordero, Quito, ☎ (02) 229-229.

Peru
Consulate: Avenida Colón at Amazonas, Edificio España, Quito, ☎ (02) 520-134.

Spain
Embassy: Calle La Pinta 455 at Amazonas, Quito, ☎ (02) 564-373.

Switzerland
Embassy: Avenida 3617 at Juan Pablo Sanz, Edificio Xerox, 2nd Floor, Quito, ☎ (02) 434-948, ⌨ 449-948.
Consulate: Avenida 9 de Octubre 2105 at Tulcán, Guayaquil, ☎ (04) 453-607, ⌨ 394-023.

United States
Embassy: Avenida 12 de Octubre at Patria, Quito, ☎ (02) 560-309.

Ecuadoran Embassies and Consulates Abroad

The main function of consulates is to issue official documents (visas, immigration papers etc.), but they also often have a department dealing with tourism inquiries, and will send information brochures and pamphlets to you free of charge.

In Australia
Ecuadoran Embassy: 405 Burk St., 2nd floor, Melbourne 3000, Victoria, Australia, ☎ (03) 600-0866, ⌨ (03) 600-0414.

In Belgium
Ecuadoran Embassy: Chaussée de Charleroi, 70, 1060 Brussels, ☎ 537-9193, ⌨ 537-9066.

In Canada
Ecuadoran Embassy: 50 O'Connor Street, suite 1311, Ottawa, Ontario, ☎ (613) 563-8206, ⌨ 563-5776.
Ecuadoran Consulate: 1010 Rue Sainte-Catherine Ouest, suite 440, Montréal, Québec, ☎ (514) 874-4071, ⌨ 563-5776.
Ecuadoran Consulate: 151 Bloor St. W., suite 470, Toronto, Ontario, M5S 1S4, ☎ (416) 968-1286 or 968-2077, ⌨ (416) 968-3348.
Ecuadoran Consulate: 9032 Lyra Place, Burnaby, British Columbia, ☎ (604) 420-7767.

In Germany
Ecuadoran Embassy: Koblenzer Str. 37, 5300 Bonn 2, Deutschland, ☎ 352-544 or 352-545, ⌨ 228-361.

In Great Britain
Ecuadoran Embassy: Flat 3B, 3 Hans Crescent, Knightsbridge, London SW1X 0LS, ☎ (071) 584-1367 or 584-2648, ⌨ (071) 823-9701.

In Italy
Ecuadoran Embassy: Via Guido d'Arezzo 14, 00198 Roma, Italia, ☎ (06) 854-1784 or 854-6185, ≈ (06) 845-1434.

In the Netherlands
Ecuadoran Embassy: Prinsengracht 278, 1016 HJ Amsterdam, ☎ (3120) 252-830, ≈ 626-5326.

In Spain
Ecuadoran Embassy: Principe de Vergara 73, Piso Séptimo, 28006 Madrid, España, ☎ 562-7215 or 562-7216, ≈ 561-3067.

In Switzerland
Ecuadoran Embassy: Helvetiastrasse 19-A, 3005 Berne, Switzerland, ☎ (031) 351-1755 or 431-755, ≈ (031) 351-2771.

In the United States
Ecuadoran Embassy: 2535 15th St., N.W., Washington, D.C. 20009, ☎ (202) 234-7200, ≈ (202) 667-3482.
Ecuadoran Consulate: 800 Second Ave., Suite 501, New York, N.Y. 10017, ☎ (212) 808-0170 or 808-0171, ≈ (212) 808-0188.
Ecuadoran Consulate: 612 North Michigan Ave., suite 718, Chicago, IL 60611, ☎ (312) 642-8579.
Ecuadoran Consulate: 548 South Spring St., suite 602, Los Angeles, CA 90013, ☎ (213) 628-3014 or 628-3016, ≈ (213) 628-3805.

ENTERING THE COUNTRY

By Air

Most European airlines that offer flights to Ecuador do so via the United States or through another Latin American country.

There are no direct flights from Canada to Ecuador. You must first fly to the United States or Latin America and from there get a flight to Quito or Guayaquil.

The following airlines have flights to Ecuador: Ecuatoriana from New York to Quito and from Miami to Guayaquil; KLM from Amsterdam to Guayaquil; Lufthansa from Frankfurt to Quito via Bogota; Saeta from New York to Quito; Continental Airlines from Houston to Quito and Guayaquil; American Airlines from Miami to Quito and Guayaquil.

Airports

Most visitors arrive in Ecuador by plane. The country has two international airports. The **Aeropuerto Mariscal Sucre** is located north of the city of Quito, while the **Aeropuerto Simon Bolívar** is located in the city of Guayaquil.

Airline Offices

American Airlines: Avenida Amazonas 367 at Robles, Quito, ☎ (02) 561-144.

Avianca: Avenida 18 de Septiembre at Amazonas, Quito, ☎ (02) 508-843, ≈ (02) 502-746.

Continental Airlines: Naciones Unidas at Avenida Amazonas, Edificio del Banco de la Previsona, Quito, ☎ (02) 461-485.

Ecuatoriana: Avenida Colón at Reina Victoria, Quito, ☎ (02) 563-003 or (02) 563-891, ≈ (02) 563-920.

Iberia: Avenida Amazonas 239 at Jorge Washington, Quito, ☎ (02) 560-456 or (02) 546-547, ⌨ (02) 566-852.

KLM: Avenida Amazonas 3617 at Juan Pablo Sanz, Quito, ☎ (02) 455-233, ⌨ (02) 435-176.

Lufthansa: 18 de Septiembre 238 at Reina Victoria, Quito, ☎ (02) 541-300.

Saeta: Calle Santa María at Avenida Amazonas, Quito, ☎ 542-148.

Overland

From Peru: Buses cross the Ecuadoran border at Huaquillas and Macará. Tensions have been high at various points along this border during the whole month of January for a few years now, in remembrance of a border conflict in 1941. War broke out between Ecuador and Peru in January 1995, in a 340-square-kilometre, contested border zone in northern Peru, proving that the situation is far from being resolved. If possible, avoid crossing the border during this period.

From Colombia: Buses cross the Ecuadoran border at Tulcán.

The border is open between 6am and 8pm. The offices close between noon and 1pm or 2pm, depending on which day it is.

INSURANCE

Health Insurance

Health insurance is the most important type of insurance travellers can get. A comprehensive health insurance policy that provides a level of coverage sufficient to pay for hospitalization, nursing care and doctor's fees is recommended. Keep in mind that health care costs are rising quickly everywhere. The policy should also have a repatriation clause in case the required care is not available in Ecuador. As patients are sometimes asked to pay for medical services up front, find out what provisions your policy makes in this event. Always carry your health insurance policy with you when travelling to avoid problems if you are in an accident, and get receipts for any expenses incurred.

Theft Insurance

Most residential insurance policies cover a percentage of personal belongings against theft if the items are stolen outside the country. If you plan to travel with valuable objects, check your policy or with an insurance agency to see if additional baggage insurance is necessary. To file an insurance claim for a theft incurred while on holiday, you will need a police report from the country you are visiting.

Cancellation Insurance

This type of insurance is usually offered by your travel agent when you purchase your air tickets or tour package. It covers any non-refundable payments to travel suppliers such as airlines, and must be purchased at the same time as initial payment is made for air tickets or tour packages. Trip cancellation insurance comes into effect if a traveller has to call off a trip for valid medical reasons or because of a death in the family. This type of insurance can be useful, but weigh the likelihood of your using it against the price.

Life Insurance

By purchasing your tickets with certain credit cards you will get life insurance. However, many travellers already have another form of life insurance and do not need extra insurance.

HEALTH

Ecuador is a wonderful country to explore; however, travellers should be aware of and protect themselves from a number of health risks associated with the region, such as malaria, typhoid, diphtheria, tetanus, polio and hepatitis A. Cases of these diseases are rare but there is a risk. **Travellers are therefore advised to consult a doctor (or travellers' clinic) for advice on what precautions to take.** Remember that it is much easier to prevent these illnesses than it is to cure them and that a vaccination is not a substitute for cautious travel.

Illnesses

Please note that this section is intended to provide general information. If you are travelling with prescription medication, bring the prescription as customs officials may ask to see it.

Malaria

Malaria (paludism) is caused by a parasite in the blood called *Plasmodium*

sp. This parasite is transmitted by anopheles mosquitoes, which bite from nightfall until dawn. The parasite is present year round in Ecuador, below 1,500 metres of altitude, in the rural and urban zones of the Pacific coast and the Amazon Basin. There is no malaria risk in Quito and its surrounding area, or in the more visited mountainous areas of the centre of the country. The Galápagos Islands are free of malaria.

The symptoms of malaria include high fever, chills, extreme fatigue and headaches as well as stomach and muscle aches. There are several forms of malaria, including one serious type caused by *P. falciparum*. The disease can take hold while you are still on holiday or up to 12 weeks following your return; in some cases the symptoms can appear months later. While most people recover from malaria, it is important to take all possible precautions against the disease. A doctor can prescribe anti-malarial medication to be taken before and after your trip (various types exist, depending on the destination, length of trip, your physical condition, etc.). Since the parasite that causes malaria is constantly evolving, anti-malarial medication is not foolproof. As much as possible, travellers should avoid getting bitten by mosquitoes (see section on mosquitoes, p 45).

Yellow Fever

Like malaria, yellow fever is transmitted by infected mosquitoes. The illness often passes unnoticed, but if symptoms do appear they will do so three to six days after infection, and include fever, headaches, vomiting, back aches and muscle cramps. The symptoms usually do not last long and vary in intensity. An effective vaccination against yellow fever, best taken before departure, is available; consult your physician. Once again, as the vaccine is not 100% effective, it is important to avoid getting bitten by mosquitoes (see section on mosquitoes, p 45).

Hepatitis A

This disease is generally transmitted by ingesting food or water that has been contaminated by faecal matter. The symptoms include fever, yellowing of the skin, loss of appetite and fatigue, and can appear between 15 and 20 days after infection. An effective vaccination is available. Besides the recommended vaccine, good hygiene is important. Always wash your hands before every meal, and ensure that the food and preparation area are clean.

Hepatits B

Hepatitis B, like hepatitis A, affects the liver, but is transmitted through direct contact of body fluids. The symptoms are flu-like, and similar to those of hepatitis A. A vaccination exists but must be administered over an extended period of time, so be sure to check with your doctor several weeks in advance.

Dengue

Also called "breakbone fever", Dengue is transmitted by mosquitoes. In its most benign form it can cause flu-like symptoms such as headaches, chills and sweating, aching muscles and nausea. In its haemorrhagic form, the most serious and rarest form, it can be fatal. There is no vaccine for the virus, so take the usual precautions to avoid mosquito bites.

Typhoid

This illness is caused by ingesting food that has come in contact (direct or indirect) with an infected person's stool. Common symptoms include high fever, loss of appetite, headaches, constipation and occasionally diarrhea, as well as the appearance of red spots on the skin. These symptoms will appear one to three weeks after infection. Which vaccination you get (it exists in two forms, oral and by injection) will depend on your trip. Once again, it is always a good idea to visit a travellers' clinic a few weeks before your departure.

Diphtheria and Tetanus

These two illnesses, against which most people are vaccinated during their childhood, can have serious consequences. Thus, before leaving, check that your vaccinations are valid; you may need a booster shot. Diphtheria is a bacterial infection that is transmitted by nose and throat secretions or by skin lesions on an infected person. Symptoms include sore throat, high fever, general aches and pains and occasionally skin infections. Tetanus is caused by a bacteria that enters your body through an open wound that comes in contact with contaminated dust or rusty metal.

Soroche (mountain sickness)

Dizziness, headaches, loss of appetite and vomiting are the major symptoms of *soroche*. The cause is simply a lack of oxygen; your system does not have a chance to produce the excess of red blood cells required to oxygenate the blood at higher altitudes. The best treatment is rest. In Quito, the worst you'll experience will probably be a headache. Take an aspirin, avoid cigarettes and alcohol, and take it easy. If the symptoms persist, however, it is a good idea to head downhill. Your breathing will be easier. If you plan on spending time at higher altitudes than Quito, spend a few days in the city to allow your system to adjust.

Never take any sleep-inducing medication, which slows down your breathing and thus your oxygen intake. *Soroche* can affect anyone, young or old, even those in top physical shape. Anyone who heads quickly to over 2,400 metres is at risk.

Rabies

Since the end of the 1980s, more than 120 cases of rabies have been reported in Ecuador. The risk is thus very real. This illness is usually transmitted by dog bites. Though there have been many educational campaigns, many dogs remain un-vaccinated. Bats, squirrels and wolves can also carry the disease.

The virus, which is transmitted by the saliva of the infected animal, attacks the nervous system and ultimately the brain. Symptoms include violent fits and localised paralysis. The illness can be fatal. Luckily, it only develops after a few weeks. If you are bitten, wash the wound, consult a doctor immediately and notify the police.

The conventional treatment involves several painful injections in the stomach spread over several days. Many clinics in Quito offer this treatment.

Other illnesses

Cases of illnesses like hepatitis B, **AIDS** and certain venereal diseases have been reported; it is therefore a good idea to be careful. Remember that condoms are the best protection against these illnesses.

Fresh water is often contaminated by an organism that causes **schistosomiasis**. This infection, which is caused by a parasite entering the body and attacking the liver and nervous system, is difficult to treat. It is therefore best to avoid swimming in fresh water.

Remember that consuming too much alcohol, particularly during prolonged exposure to the sun, can cause severe dehydration and lead to health problems.

Insufficiently treated water, which can contain disease-causing bacteria, is the cause of most of the health problems travellers are likely to encounter, such as stomach upset, diarrhea or fever. Throughout the country, it is a good idea to drink bottled water (when buying bottled water, make sure the bottle is properly sealed), or to purify your own with iodine or a water purifier. Most major hotels treat their water, but always ask first. Ice cubes should be avoided, as they may be made of contaminated water. In addition, fresh fruits and vegetables that have been washed but not peeled can also pose a health risk. Make sure that the vegetables you eat are well-cooked and peel your own fruit. Do not eat lettuce, unless it has been hydroponically grown (some vegetarian restaurants serve this type of lettuce; ask). Remember: cook it, peel it or forget it.

If you do get diarrhea, soothe your stomach by avoiding solids; instead, drink carbonated beverages, bottled water, or weak tea (avoid milk) until you recover. As dehydration can be dangerous, drinking sufficient quantities of liquid is crucial. Pharmacies sell various preparations for the treatment of diarrhea, with different effects. Pepto Bismol and Imodium will stop the diarrhea, which slows the loss of fluids, but they should be avoided if you have a fever as they will prevent the necessary elimination of bacteria. Oral rehydration products, such as Gastrolyte, will replace the minerals and electrolytes which your body has lost as a result of the diarrhea. In a pinch, you can make your own rehydration solution by mixing one litre of pure water with one teaspoon of sugar and two or three teaspoons of salt. After, eat easily digested foods like rice to give your stomach time to adjust. If symptoms become more serious (high fever, persistent diarrhea), see a doctor as antibiotics may be necessary.

Nutrition and climate can also cause problems. Pay attention to food's freshness, and the cleanliness of the preparation area. Good hygiene (wash your hands often) will help avoid undesirable situations.

Mosquitoes

A nuisance common to many countries, mosquitoes are no strangers to Ecuador. They are particularly numerous during the rainy season. Protect yourself with a good insect repellent. Repellents with DEET are the most effective. The concentration of DEET varies from one product to the next; the higher the concentration, the longer the protection. In rare cases, the use of repellents with high concentrations (35% or more) of DEET has been associated with convulsions in young children; it is therefore important to apply these products sparingly, on exposed surfaces, and to wash it off once back inside. A concentration of 35% DEET will protect for four to six hours, while 95% will last from 10 to 12 hours. New formulas with DEET in lesser concentrations, but which last just as long, are available

To further reduce the possibility of getting bitten, do not wear perfume or bright colours. Sundown is an especially active time for insects. When walking in wooded areas, cover your legs and ankles well. Insect coils can help provide a better night's sleep. Before bed, apply insect repellent to your skin and to the headboard and baseboard of your bed. If possible, get an air-conditioned room, or bring a mosquito net.

Lastly, since it is impossible to completely avoid contact with mosquitoes, bring along a cream to soothe the bites you will invariably get.

The Sun

Its benefits are many, but so are its harms. Always wear sunscreen. Many creams on the market do not offer adequate protection; ask a pharmacist. Too much sun can cause sunstroke (dizziness, vomiting, fever, etc.). Be careful, especially the first few days, as it takes time to get used to the sun. Take sun in small doses and protect yourself with a hat and sunglasses.

First Aid Kit

A small first aid kit can prove very useful. Bring along sufficient amounts of any medications you take regularly; it can be difficult to find certain medications in small towns in Ecuador. Also, bring a valid prescription in case you lose your supply. Other medications such as anti-malaria pills and Imodium (or an equivalent), can be hard to find in Ecuador. Finally, don't forget self-adhesive bandages, disinfectant cream or ointment, analgesics (pain-killers), antihistamines (for allergies), an extra pair of sunglasses or contact lenses and medicine for upset stomach.

CLIMATE AND PACKING

In Ecuador, the word "climate" takes on a whole new meaning. Because of its position on the equator and its steep terrain, the country presents a variety of climates, which change over short distances depending on the altitude. Basically, the year is divided into two seasons. Winter, which is hot and humid, extends from December to May, while summer, much cooler, extends from June to November. Nevertheless, depending on their geographical location on the equator, the northern regions of the Costa see average temperatures around 27°C. The southern Costa is crossed by the cold Humboldt Current, which leads to cooler temperatures. Heading east, the hot, humid and rainy climate of the Oriente causes average temperatures between 24°C and 28°C. The temperature in the Sierra is much lower due to the higher altitude; on average it fluctuates between 14°C and 18°C. Finally, the Galápagos Islands enjoy a dry and temperate climate throughout the year.

Thus, what type of clothing you bring depends entirely on which region you will be visiting. Generally speaking, however, loose-fitting cotton clothing is best. Wear shoes rather than sandals when exploring the Sierra, as they will protect you from cuts that could get infected. If you plan on doing any hiking in the mountains, be sure to bring along proper hiking boots and warmer clothes. For cooler evenings, a long-sleeved shirt or jacket will come in handy. A small umbrella or raincoat will protect you from showers. In fact, clouds routinely take over clear blue skies causing surprise rainstorms. Women in miniskirts are frowned upon, except on the beaches of the Costa. Bring a few fancier items for nights out as many places have dress codes. The Amazon region is characterized by its hot, humid and rainy climate. Bring casual, comfortable clothes that dry quickly if you are heading to this part of the country. For more information on packing for a trip in the Oriente, see p 248.

WHEN TO GO

The high season in Ecuador runs from the end of May to the end of August and from the middle of November to the end of January. If you plan on visiting during these periods be sure to reserve well in advance, especially if you are heading to the Galápagos Islands or the Oriente. The beaches of the Costa are literally overrun by vacationing Ecuadorans in February and March. Also, the numerous religious and commemorative holidays throughout the year can often bring everything to a standstill. For example, the long parade to the Cisne sanctuary in Loja renders the streets in this area completely impassable. Finally, the tensions that flare up along the border between Peru and Ecuador during the month of January make this an area to be avoided for security reasons.

A Packing Checklist

- insect repellent
- insect coils
- sunscreen
- first-aid kit (see Health , p 46)
- flashlight
- sunglasses
- hat
- walking shoes
- light wind-breaker
- plastic sandals for shower and beach
- "ziplock" plastic bags (for wet bathing suits, documents, sea shells, etc.)
- mosquito netting (if you plan to travel outside large cities)
- water purification system (iodine tablets, water purifier, etc.)
- travel laundry line or bungee cord

- earplugs (for noisy hotel rooms or long bus and boat trips)
- pocket knife and plastic plate (for preparing your own fruit and vegetables)
- extra pair of glasses or contact lenses

SAFETY AND SECURITY

Unlike other countries in Latin America, Ecuador is not a dangerous country, but here as anywhere theft is always a possibility. Thieves' favourite haunts include markets and the *terminal terrestre* (bus station), as well as poorly-lit streets and parks. The crime rate is rising in certain major cities, particularly Guayaquil, Esmeraldas and Manta, along with a few neigh-bourhoods in Quito.

Never accept food or drinks from strangers. You run the risk of waking up in a strange place with no luggage and no money. If you rent a car, do not drive at night. Most roads are not lit, and Ecuadorans have a tendency to drive very fast. The Pan American highway and the highway between the Costa and the Sierra via Santo Domingo de Los Colorado are particularly dangerous at night. These roads are winding, and visibility is reduced at higher altitudes. Also, the road between Quevedo and Guayaquil is often a playground for thieves.

Despite all this, the likelihood that you will be robbed is small. Remember that to the majority of Ecuadorans, even your everyday possessions (particularly things like cameras, leather suitcases, video cameras, and jewellery) represent a great deal of money. A degree of caution can help avoid problems. For example, do not wear jewellery, keep your electronic equipment in a nondescript shoulder bag slung across your chest, and avoid revealing the entire contents of your wallet when making a purchase.

A money belt that goes under your clothes can be useful for hiding money, traveller's cheques and passports. Follow the "never all the eggs in one basket" principle: put your money in many different places, so that if any one bag is lost or stolen, you have not lost everything. Always carry on your person emergency funds and important documents. Remember, the less attention you draw to yourself, the less chance you have of being robbed.

Avoid bringing anything of value with you to the beach. However, if you must, keep a close eye on it. Some hotels have a safe where you can leave your valuables.

Women Travellers

The question of women travelling on their own is never black and white, as what one woman considers offensive, another may not even notice. Generally, it is important to remember that you are in a Latin American country, and the cultural rules are not the same as in Western Europe or North America. A woman alone will attract plenty of attention, and there will invariably be a wave of comments as she walks down the street. However, this attention is not generally aggressive, and ignoring it is the best reaction. Observe the basic safety rules for of all foreign travellers, and you should not have any problems. Be careful what you wear and avoid questionable or poorly-lit areas. If you're travelling in the Costa, do not

stroll along the beach after nightfall. Also, bring along your own sanitary products, as it may be difficult to find them outside major cities like Cuenca, Guayaquil and Quito, and local stores simply might not carry your favourite brand.

Homosexuality

Being openly gay or lesbian in Ecuador is not the best idea for the traveller. Homosexuality is formally forbidden by the State and can lead to imprisonment. There a few clandestine gay bars in Cuenca, Guayaquil and Quito, though they are difficult to find.

For more information on gay life in Ecuador contact fedaeps@orlando. ecx.ec.

TRANSPORTATION

By Car

Distances can be considerable in Ecuador, especially since, though most highways are in good condition, it is impossible to go any faster than 40 kph on the smaller roads. It is therefore very important to plan your itinerary well, above all to avoid driving at night.

Renting a Car

Renting a car in Ecuador is easy. Most of the major car-rental agencies have offices in the country. Expect to pay on average $40 per day (plus about $0.12 per kilometre in certain cases) for a small car, not including insurance and taxes. A four-wheel-drive vehicle is

Table of Distances (km)

Ambato									
40	Baños								
306	309	Cuenca							
288	288	250	Guayaquil						
251	291	557	535	Ibarra					
47	87	353	335	204	Latacunga				
231	271	537	515	20	184	Otavalo			
136	176	442	420	115	89	95	Quito		
52	55	254	233	303	99	283	188	Riobamba	
376	416	682	660	125	329	145	240	428	Tulcán

more expensive, between $50 and $70 per day. This last option is worth serious consideration if you plan on taking the smaller roads. Choose a car in good condition and one that is relatively new. A few local companies charge less, but their vehicles are often in much worse shape. When renting, be sure to take sufficient insurance to cover the costs of an accident. A $1,000 down-payment is often required (in cash or by credit card). Before signing the rental contract, ensure that the method of payment is clearly indicated. Remember that when you sign, your credit card must cover not only the rental cost but also the insurance deductible. Certain credit cards (gold cards) automatically insure you against vehicle theft or a collision, but they often do not cover four-wheel-drives.

Foreign driver's licenses are valid in Ecuador.

Driving and the Highway Code

Though it can be very practical to have your own set of wheels to take you off the beatenpath, we do not recommend driving in Ecuador. With all due respect to Ecuadorans, we must admit that they have a tendency to drive dangerously fast, and though the highways and main roads are generally in good condition, the Pan American highway is winding, sometimes slippery and an accident waiting to happen. And despite the fact that there is no shoulder, traffic still runs at a fair clip. The occasional pothole here and there is a problem. Then there is the rock 'n' roll passing style: if you're lucky the car behind you will give a few warning honks on the horn before he pulls out face to face with the oncoming traffic to pass you! The lack of lighting, the steep mountain terrain and the poor signage of Ecuadoran roads make driving at night something to be avoided. Not to mention that some cars don't have headlights...

Driving on the secondary roads is a whole other can of worms. These are often gravel roads; some are paved, and most are pockmarked with potholes of all sizes. Traffic moves slowly. Also, animals of all kinds, but mostly dogs, are continually crossing the road. Our canine friends, for some reason, feel the need to chase after all cars, all the while foaming at the mouth and barking wildly. The best course of action for travellers in this case is to slow down and continue on their merry way to the din of barking dogs.

Small villages line these secondary roads, and drivers must be careful of the numerous pedestrians. Speed bumps have been placed in village streets to slow down drivers. Unfortunately, these are poorly indicated; they are usually located on the way into town. Roads signs are also few and far between (there are no speed limit, stop or yield signs). Thus, to find your way around, the only alternative is to ask directions from the locals.

Traffic is heavy in Quito and Guayaquil, where drivers dodge dangerously in and out of traffic. The elementary rules of the road as travellers may know them are nonexistent, and use of the turn signal has been replaced by a constant and repetitive leaning on the horn. Few drivers check their blind spot before passing. Furthermore, pedestrians must be especially careful when crossing the street, for just because the light is red does not mean the cars will stop.

Finally, never leave your car unattended. Try to pick a hotel with a private parking lot. What's more, many Ecuadorans will offer to watch your car during your absence. Accept on good faith, but only pay once you return and only pay one person. This service usually costs about 1,000 sucres.

Car Service

In certain regions of the country, particularly the Costa, young Ecuadorans will offer to wash your car; sometimes they'll even do it without asking you. Of course, they expect a little something for their trouble. Even if you don't or didn't want your car washed, it is better to pay them (and avoid a scratched car or worse). Expect to pay about 1,000 sucres.

Police

Police and military checks along the highway are routine to monitor drivers. Officers have the right to stop anyone who breaks one of the rules of the road, or simply to check their papers. Be sure to always have your passport or a photocopy certified by your embassy or consulate. Otherwise, you will have trouble proving your identity, which can cause trouble. Generally speaking, officers are obliging, and will help out if you have car trouble. In an emergency dial **101**.

Gas

Gas (petrol) stations are located throughout the country and prices are relatively reasonable. Few stations accept credit cards.

By Taxi

Taxis are available in most medium-sized towns and of course in the major cities. The cars are often quite old, but will get you where you are going. In most cases, the fare is determined by a meter, though it can be set in advance. If you set the price ahead of time, be clear on what it includes before accepting, and only pay at the end.

Shared Taxis

In shared taxis (*taxis ruta*) the fare is shared by all the passengers even if they have different destinations. These are found mostly in Guayaquil.

By Bus

The whole country is well served by a fair number of bus companies. Almost every city has a *terminal terrestre* where all buses arrive and depart from. The bus is therefore an efficient and economical way of getting around. To take a bus, simply go to the local *terminal terrestre* or hail one from the side of road. Buses stop frequently and are often very crowded. Nevertheless, it is possible to buy your ticket in advance at the *terminal terrestre*. This is a good idea if you're taking a long trip; tall people can thus avoid getting stuck in the seat over the wheel. Remember that the back seats do not always recline and offer a much bumpier ride, thanks to the less than perfect road conditions. Finally, the majority of buses do not have toilets.

Some companies have relatively comfortable, air-conditioned buses complete with a movie. Stops are less frequent and things move a lot faster. The price is slightly higher; however, for long distances the time saved more than outweighs the extra cost.

In more remote regions, trucks and other vehicles often take on extra passengers for a few sucres.

By Plane

Interior flights are a practical and relatively economical way to visit the country. A flight from Quito to Cuenca takes about 30 minutes and costs only about $30. Owned by the State but run by the military, **TAME** is the largest airline offering domestic flights in Ecuador. It flies to most of the major cities in the country. **SAN** and **SAETA** also offer flights within Ecuador. The prices and departures are similar.

TAME: Avenida Amazonas at Colón, 6th Floor, Quito, ☎ (02) 509-375, ⇆ 561-052
Calle Colón 1001 at Rábida, Quito, ☎ (02) 554-905.

SAETA: Calle Santa María at Avenida Amazonas, Quito, ☎ (02) 542-148.

SAN: Calle Santa María at Avenida Amazonas, Quito, ☎ (02) 564-969, ⇆ 562-024.

By Train

Travelling by train is one of the most interesting and pleasant ways to see the country, albeit one of the slowest. There are only three regular routes: Alausí to Durán, Ibarra to San Lorenzo and Quito to Riobamba. The trip from Alausí to Durán is considered by many to be one of the most spectacular train rides in the world. Thousands of tourists take it each year. The train from Quito to Riobamba crosses the Andes through luxuriant vegetation,

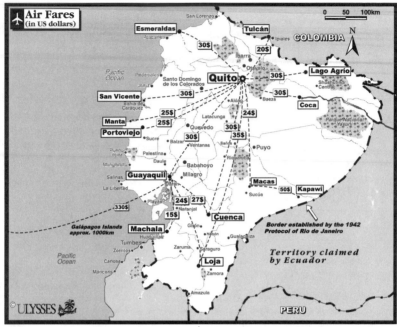

allowing passengers to admire magnificent landscapes along the way. Unlike the other two routes, the trip from Ibarra to San Lorenzo is not by train but by *autoferro*, an old schoolbus mounted on the rails.

The best seats are on the roofs of the trains or *autoferros*. Departures are once daily, and tickets are purchased at the station on the day of departure. Arrive early as space is limited.

Route	Fare	Travel time
Quito-Riobamba	$8	5-7 hours
Ibarra-San Lorenzo	$10	8-12 hours
Alausí-Durán	$8	10-12 hours

Hitchhiking

If you have time, it is possible to hitchhike your way around. People are friendly and like talking to strangers, but usually expect a small payment. Of course, a certain amount of caution is advised. Women travelling alone should not hitchhike. Given the low cost of a bus ticket, hitchhiking should really be a last resort.

TOUR COMPANIES

When planning a trip to Ecuador (or to almost anywhere else, for that matter), travellers have to decide what they have in mind, and this in turn will determine whether a tour package or independent travel is more suitable.

Those who are interested mostly in relaxing by the beach will often end up staying at the same hotel and in the same area for most of their visit, and this is where it makes the most sense to consider buying an air-and-hotel package, which in some cases costs only slightly more than air fare alone. Some of these packages are based on the all-inclusive formula, with meals, drinks and certain activities included in the price. While this is useful in controlling costs, it may lock you into taking nearly all your meals at hotel buffets whose offerings may soon induce boredom. Air-and-hotel packages usually can be bought only through travel agencies or, in some cases, from the tour divisions of airline companies.

For visitors who plan to move around within Ecuador, the options are package tours, independent travel or a combination of the two. Often access to remote areas like the rainforest, the mountain highlands and national parks or contact with Amerindian communities is limited to those who are part of a tour group. Such tours do not only cater to older or less-experienced travellers. They generally provide well-planned itineraries, comfortable vehicles and lodgings, and an overall sense of security. Drawbacks include very limited flexibility and being stuck in the same surroundings with the same group. Travel agencies in your country can often, though not always, provide information on escorted tours.

Independent travel will appeal to many visitors because it allows almost infinite flexibility in the choice of itineraries and a sense of freedom that no package tour can offer. Travellers also have considerable leeway in choosing accommodations and meal arrangements that suit their budgets and tastes. However, as mentioned above, many remote areas are inaccessible to independent travellers for security and ecological reasons. Travelling independently does require communications skills (see Glossary section, p 299), an ability to deal with the unexpected, and a willingness to put up with occasional inconveniences or discomfort.

Even some independent-minded travellers may want to consider combining package tours with do-it-yourself travel. One possibility is to arrive independently in Ecuador and buy a multi-day tour from a local tour company to see a few of the main sights or perhaps to experience adventure travel in some of the less accessible regions of the country.

Below are the addresses of tour agencies that organize excursions into various regions of the country and walking tours of various cities.

Metropolitan Touring: Avenida Amazonas 339, Quito, ☎ (02) 560-550, ⇌ 564-655, www.ecuadorable.com, info@ecuadorable.com; represented in the United States by Adventure Associates, 13150 Coit Road, Suite 110, Dallas Texas, 75240, ☎ 1-800-527-2500, ⇌ (972) 783-1286.

Nuevo Mundo: Avenida Coruña 1349 at Orellana, P.O. Box 402-A, Quito, ☎ (02) 552-617, ⇌ 565-261, www.venweb.com/ec/nmundo.htm, nmundo@uio.telconet.net; represented in the United States by Big Five Tours & Expeditions, 819 South Federal Hwy, Suite 103, Stuart, Florida 34994, ☎ (561) 287-7995, ⇌ (561) 287-5990 and by International Expeditions, One

Environs Park, Helena, Alabama 35080, ☎ (205) 428-1700, ⌨ (205) 449-3712.

Sierra Nevada: Calle Juan León Mera 741 at Ventimilla, Quito, ☎ (02) 553-658, ⌨ 659-250

Safari: Calle Calama 380 at Juan León Mera, Quito, ☎ (02) 552-505, ⌨ 220-426, admin@safari.ecx.ec.

Surtek: Avenida Amazonas at Ventimilla, Quito, ☎ (02) 561-129,

Pamir Adventure Travel: Calle Juan León Mera 721 at Ventimilla, Quito, ☎ (02) 547-576, ⌨ 542-605

Crater Tours: Calle Calama 161 at Diego de Almagro, Quito, ☎ (02) 545-491, ⌨ 554-503.

Latin American Travel Consultants

This organization publishes an interesting quarterly information bulletin on South and Central America. Subjects like safety, health, weather, travel costs, economics and politics are discussed. A subscription costs $39 US per year. You can also request information on a particular country, which will be sent to you by fax or by e-mail ($10). For more details contact them at the following address: P.O. Box 17-17-908, Quito, Ecuador; ⌨ (02) 562-566, lata@pi.pro.ec, www.amerispan.com/latc or www.greenarrow.com/latc.htm.

South American Explorers Club

This non-profit organization was founded in 1977 in Lima, Peru. A second office in Quito opened in 1989.

The headquarters, however, are located in New York State. The club was founded to help anyone planning a trip to South America, in particular Ecuador, whether for biological or anthropological research or for adventure or activities (mountain climbing, river rafting, etc.). Membership fees are $40 per person or $60 per couple per year, and include the quarterly magazine as well as access to all sorts of information: topographical maps, geological maps, road maps, a library and travel reports written by other members. Members also have the use of storage space for their hiking equipment, camping gear and backpacks. Personal mail and e-mail can also be sent to the club. Finally, the club is an excellent place to meet other travellers and form groups for excursions. Non-members are welcome, but out of respect for members are requested not to linger too long. The staff is young, friendly and dynamic.

In Quito: Calle Jorge Washington 311 at Leonidas Plaza, ☎ and ⌨ (02) 225-228, explorer@saec.org.ec. Open Mon to Fri 9:30am to 5pm.

In Lima: Avenida República de Portugal 146 at Breña, ☎ (14) 314-480, montague@amauta.rcp.net. Open Mon to Fri 9:30am to 5pm.

In the United States: 126 Indian Creek Road, Ithacam NY 14850, ☎ (607) 277-0488, ⌨ 277-6122, explorer@samexplo.org, www.samexplo.org. Open Mon to Fri 9:30am to 5pm.

MONEY AND BANKING

Currency

The currency in Ecuador is the **sucre.** The bills come in denominations of 50,000, 20,000, 10,000, 5,000, 1,000, 500, 100 sucres and occasionally in 50, 20, 10 and 5 sucres. Coins come in denominations of 1,000, 500, 100, 50, 20, 10, 5 and 1 sucres.

At press time $1US = 3,920 sucres.

The prices quoted in this guide are in American dollars, as the basic value of goods and services tends to remain stable, though local prices may fluctuate.

Banks

Banks are usually open weekdays from 9:30am to 1pm. They are found in all the major cities and towns. Most will exchange US dollars; fewer exchange travellers' cheques or other foreign currencies. Always carry some cash.

Casas de Cambio or Exchange Offices

Exchanging money on the street is illegal. In certain cities, locals will offer to exchange your American dollars, but it is safer to use the services of specialist since there are many counterfeit bills in circulation.

Casas de cambio are open from Monday to Friday, from 9am to 6pm and occasionally on Saturday from 9am to 1pm. They usually offer better rates than the bank and the service charge is included.

To get the best rate it is always preferable to exchange your money in a big city like Quito, Guayaquil or Cuenca.

American Money

American money should be the currency of choice for travellers to Ecuador. It is easy to exchange and enjoys a better rate than other currencies.

Travellers' Cheques

Though travellers' cheques are the safest way to carry money, they are not always easy to exchange. They are sometimes accepted in restaurants, hotels and certain shops, and are generally easy to cash in banks or exchange offices. Keep a list of your cheque numbers separate from your cheques so that they can be cancelled and replaced if they are lost or stolen. Always carry some cash.

Credit Cards

Visa and MasterCard are useful in many larger establishments in the cities. Do not rely solely on credit cards as many small merchants do not accept them. Once again, even if you have a credit card and travellers' cheques, always carry some cash. If you plan on visiting the Galápagos Islands, note that many places do not accept Visa. For some unknown reason, MasterCard is virtually the only credit card accepted.

Exchange Rates

$1 CAN	= $0.71 US	$1 US =	$1.40 CAN
1 £	= $1.62 US	$1 US =	0.62 £
$1 Aust	= $0.81 US	$1 US =	$1.24 Aust
$1 NZ	= $0.69 US	$1 US =	$1.44 NZ
1 guilder	= $0.53 US	$1 US =	1.88 guilders
1 SF	= $0.70 US	$1 US =	1.43 SF
10 BF	= $0.29 US	$1 US =	35 BF
1 DM	= $0.57 US	$1 US =	1.74 DM
100 pesetas	= $0.72 US	$1 US =	140 pesetas
1000 lire	= $0.61 US	$1 US =	1637 lire

$ **1US = 3,920 sucres**

TELECOMMUNICATIONS

Mail

There is a post office in every city. Some hotels can also mail your letters and sell you stamps. Wherever you send your mail from, expect it to take quite a while to reach its destination. The postal service is a bit slow. If you have something urgent to send, use the fax service at EMETEL. Stamps are sold in post offices and in certain shops.

Telephones and Faxes

International and local calls can be made from **EMETEL** offices, which are located in almost every city or in the major hotels. Calling overseas is easy from these offices. It also saves you the extra huge fees that hotels usually charge. You don't need to collect your change either, since the lengthof your call is recorded by computer and you pay at the counter afterward the call. EMETEL also offers fax service. You must pay cash, except in hotels. Public telephones are rare; a few can be found in major cities, airports or universities. A few EMETEL offices sell *fichas* (tokens) for local calls. A minimum of three minutes is charged for international calls.

Three minutes to North America costs about $9, to Europe about $12.

The international country code for Ecuador is **593**. The EMETEL personnel will explain in Spanish, or maybe in broken English, how to call overseas from Ecuador.

Telephone Numbers and Area Codes

Telephone numbers in Ecuador have six digits. Below is a list of the provinces and their corresponding area code. Only use the area code when calling from outside the area you are trying to reach.

Pichincha and Quito: **02**
Bolívar, Chimborazo, Cotopaxi, Pastaza and Tungurahua: **03**
Guayas: **04**
Galápagos, Los Ríos and Manabí: **05**

Carchi, Esmeraldas, Imbabura, Napo and Sucumbios: **06**
Azuay, Cañar, El Oro, Loja, Morona Santiago and Zamora Chinchipe: **07**

ACCOMMODATIONS

Lodging possibilities in Ecuador vary widely depending on where you are. Generally speaking, you must add 20% to room prices in major hotels. It is also the norm to leave a few sucres per day for the maid (at the end of your stay).

Most major hotels accept credit cards; smaller hotels usually do not.

Accommodation Rates and Taxes

The rates listed in this guide are for double occupancy, and do not include the sales tax, though many of the smaller hotels include the tax in their prices. Some establishments charge per person, others per room. This is a consideration when you are travelling alone, as you often have to pay a large price for a large room if there aren't any singles. Prices given are meant as a guide; individual rates are subject to change.

Hotels

Hotels rooms can be found in just about every town in Ecuador. The quality and comfort of these rooms varies from one town to the next, but it is generally easy to find a room to suit you. Some budget hotels are not strong on cleanliness, which is one reason to always ask to see the room first. Also, depending on the region, check if the room has hot water, mosquito netting

and a fan. Note that on market days, the best hotels are usually full. To avoid an upset, reserve in advance or arrive the day before the market.

Motels

Motels are dubious places where the rooms are often rented out by the hour and amount to little more than houses of ill-repute.

Apart-hotels

Apart-hotels are like hotels in that they offer all the services, but like apartments because rooms include kitchenettes equipped with dishes and utensils. This is a very economical option for longer stays.

Cabañas

Cabañas differ little from hotels, except that rooms are often located in small, individual pavilions or cabins. They are generally inexpensive and sometimes include a kitchenette.

Bed & Breakfasts

Very few people have adapted their homes to receive guests. The level of comfort varies greatly from one place to the next. These rooms usually do not have private bathrooms.

Lodges

Lodges are found mainly in the tropical rainforest of the Oriente, on private property close to a national park or reserve. They are generally not accessible to independent travellers; to stay in a lodge you must purchase a package from a tour company. Such packages usually include full board and a tour of the park or reserve. The Oriente chapter of this guide provides more information on lodges.

Youth Hostels

There are very few youth hostels in Ecuador. Quito and Guayaquil each have a few.

Camping

Camping is permitted in certain national parks.

 RESTAURANTS

Restaurants serving all sorts of fare, from local to international, abound near the major tourist sites. Service is always very courteous and thoughtful, whether you're in a fine restaurant or a small eatery. A 20% tax is added to the price of the meal. Prices mentioned are for a meal for one person, not including drinks and tax.

$	$6 and less
$$	between $6 and $12
$$$	more than $12

Tipping

A delicate subject indeed. Whether at a hotel or a restaurant, clients and staff alike do not agree on the amount of tip to be left. In restaurants, certain patrons believe they should give 15% of the bill before tax, while waiters and waitresses say this is a minimum amount and that it should be based on the bill after tax. Another example is on the better cruise boats, where some of the best guides work, offering better service than elsewhere. This service should be rewarded, especially when you consider that many guides live on pitiably small salaries and rely on tips to survive. Basically, if you can afford to treat yourself to a cruise or a fine meal in a restaurant, you can afford to leave an appropriate tip.

ECUADORAN CUISINE

Ecuadoran cuisine varies from one region to the next. One constant, however, is the abundance of fresh fruit all year long: oranges, *murucuyás* (passion fruit), papayas, bananas and watermelon are just a few examples. Tourist towns offer dishes tourists know (pizza, hamburgers, etc.) as well as regional Ecuadoran specialties. Delicious Creole dishes are also common. In the Sierra, chicken, pork and beef are prepared in a variety of ways.

The Costa is washed by the waters of the Pacific Ocean, and as expected a huge variety of fish and seafood figure prominently on the menus in this region. *Cebiches* (or *ceviches* depending on the place) are deliciously prepared by most restaurants in the Costa. Ecuadorans and Peruvians both claim to have invented this tasty, traditional dish of lightly-cooked seafood or fish marinating in an acidic mixture of onion and lemon and accompanied by corn. Be careful, however, as the lightly-cooked fish in *cebiche* can contain parasites that a tourist's digestive system simply cannot handle.

The Costa also boasts numerous banana plantations that grow many different types of this fruit. These are prepared in a variety of ways depending on their ripeness.

Vegetarian Cuisine

If you follow a macrobiotic diet, you'll have to put it on hold while in Ecuador. If your diet is based on milk products, however, you shouldn't have any trouble. Large cities like Cuenca, Quito and Guayaquil have vegetarian restaurants. Occasionally the definition of vegetarian is somewhat softened to include fish and chicken dishes. In more remote villages, even if the menu does not list vegetarian dishes, it is usually possible to politely make a special request.

Small Gastronomical Glossay

Aji: very spicy condiment
Ajo: garlic
Almuerzo: lunch
Arroz: rice
Café sin leche: black coffee
Café con leche: coffee with milk
Carne: meat
Cerveza: beer
Cena: supper
Chancho: pork
Comida: food
Cuy: whole guinea-pig on a spit, slow-cooked over an open fire
Chifa: Chinese restaurant
Desayuno: breakfast
Empanadas: small, cooked corn patties stuffed with onions, meat, chicken or vegetables

Encocado: fish mixed with coconut milk
Huevos revueltos: poached eggs
Huevos fritos: fried eggs
Huevos duros: hard-boiled eggs
Hornado: suckling-pig
Jugo: juice
Leche: milk
Legumbres: vegetables
Llapingachos: potato, cheese and corn dish
Locro: potato- and milk-based soup
Mantequilla: butter
Pimienta: pepper
Pato: duck
Pavo: turkey
Pollo: chicken
Postre: dessert
Queso: cheese
Res: beef
Sal: salt
Seco: fried meat
Ternera: veal
Verde: dried banana chips
Vino: wine

Typical Ecuadoran Recipes

Muchines de Yuca
Grate a medium-sized yucca and combine with an equal amount of grated cheese; add salt, one chopped onion and an egg; form small bite-size pieces and fry them in butter or oil.

Fritada
Cut 1.5 kg of pork (preferably chops) in pieces; season with salt, oregano and cumin; add three or four large garlic cloves. Season the meat the night before or at least six hours before cooking; cook in a frying pan with a bit of water. Once the water evaporates add some oil and brown the meat.

Alcoholic Beverages

Though there is no comparison with European beers, there are two locally brewed beers: Club and Pilsener. Another local option is a mixed drink called *aguardiente*, made with sugar cane and spices.

 # SHOPPING

Native Markets

Ecuador has a rich tradition of crafts that has continued for centuries. These creations can now be found in the public markets of villages along the Andean cordillera. The most famous of these is certainly the market in Otavalo (see p 110); other, lesser-known ones are just as interesting. These markets are the social gathering places of the Andean people. During the day, clothing, mats, fruit, flowers and animals liven up the streets, offering a picturesque show unique to Latin America. Try to arrive the day before market-day because the best hotel rooms fill up fast.

These countless markets attract scores of craftspeople, farmers, shoppers and tourists come to sell and buy a multitude of different goodies. Besides the traditional craft items like mats, ponchos, scarves and other exotic clothing and accessories, you'll find all sorts of local animals, living and dead, here to satisfy the most eccentric of consumers. The treatment of certain animals may seem cruel and shocking to travellers; just remember that you are in a foreign country where the established practices and norms differ from those of another cultural context. If this disparity bothers you and you don't want to be shocked, simply avoid this part of the market, which on the whole will surely prove most fascinating.

A Few Souvenir Ideas

Some markets specialize in certain types of crafts. Among the more famous are Cotacachi, north of Otavalo, which specializes in leather and leather goods; the market in Santonio de Ibarra, which specializes in woodworking and carving, and the market in the village of Chordeleg, near Cuenca, which boasts a good selection of silver items.

Other ideas include Panama hats for hat lovers and Otavalo woolens for those who aren't allergic to wool. Those with more sensitive skin might prefer the much finer alpaca woolens.

Bargaining

Bargaining is part of the fun of visiting the markets. More often than not, a cheaper price can be negotiated. Remember, however, that natives depend on the sale of their goods to survive. If you have no intention of buying something, don't bargain just to see how far you can go. Furthermore, some people don't realize that they may actually be haggling over what amounts to a couple of dollars, a nominal sum for a tourist, but quite a lot of money to a local vendor.

Major Markets

Monday: Ambato (see p 139)
Tuesday: Guano (see p 144), Latacunga (see p 137), Riobamba (see p 144).
Wednesday: Cuenca (see p 220), Riobamba (see p 144), Saquisilí (see p 135), Tulcán (see p 116).
Saturday: Cotacachi (see p 113), Guano (see p 144), Lacatunga (see p 137), Otavalo (see p 110), Riobamba (see p 144).
Sunday: Cuenca (see p 220), Pujilí (see p 137), Sangolquí (see p 109).

MISCELLANEOUS

Religion

The majority of Ecuadorans consider themselves Catholic (about 95%). In essence, as in many Latin American countries, Catholicism has occupied a very important place in the history of Ecuador, from colonial times to the present day. Today, however, there are fewer and fewer of practising Catholics in the major cities, though the religion continues to inspire a vibrant tradition and remains popular in rural and Andean regions. During certain of the traditional religious holidays, Holy Week for example, all economic activity can come to a halt.

Electricity

Electrical appliances run on an alternating current of 110 volts (60 cycles), just as in North America. European travellers will need both a converter and an adapter with two parallel flat pins for any appliances they plan to bring along.

Drugs

If you are travelling with prescription drugs, bring the prescription in order to justify their presence in your luggage.

Drugs are easy to find in Ecuador. If you plan on enlivening your trip with a bit of haschich or marijuana, or some other illicit substance, we would like to remind you that many North Americans and Europeans with the same idea now languish in prison in Quito. This would definitely put a damper on your trip, so think twice. Police and dogs regularly check the luggage of passengers passing through Guayaquil.

If you would like to pay a visit to these unfortunate detained souls who are always happy to receive visitors, here are the addresses:

Penal García Moreno (prison for men) is open for visiting hours from 10am to noon and from 2pm to 4pm on Wednesdays, Saturdays and Sundays. This prison is located in a questionable neighbourhood, so do not bring any valuables with you. It is in the "El Tejar" area, not far from Plaza San Francisco. From the plaza, head south of Calle Sebastian de Benelcazar to Calle Vincente Rocafuerte, then turn right towards Mont Pichincha. The Penal García Moreno is about six blocks up on the right.

Carcel de las Mujeres (prison for women) is open for visiting hours from 10am to 4pm on Wednesdays, Saturdays and Sundays. This prison is located in a relatively safe part of town. Take any bus heading north on

Avenida 6 de Diciembre toward the "El Inca" neighbourhood, and get off at Avenida El Inca. Next, head east to Calle de la Toronjas. Turn left. The prison is on your right, about one block away.

N.B. If you do visit these prisons, bring along some reading material, food and toiletries (soap, toothpaste, sanitary napkins, etc.).

Time Zones

Ecuador is five hours behind Greenwich Mean Time. There is, however, no daylight savings time. Consequently, in the spring and summer, Ecuador is one hour behind the east coast of North America, two hours ahead of the west coast, seven hours behind continental Western Europe and six hours behind the United Kingdom. The rest of the year, the country is on the same time as North America's east coast, three hours ahead of the west coast, seven hours behind continental Western Europe and six hours behind the United Kingdom.

Weights and Measures

Officially, Ecuador uses the metric system. The following conversion table may be useful, especially since many products, such as gasoline, are sold by Imperial measures.

Weights
1 pound (lb) = 454 grams (g)
1 kilogram (kg) = 2.2 pounds (lbs)

Linear Measure
1 inch = 2.2 centimetres (cm)
1 foot (ft) = 30 centimetres (cm)
1 mile = 1.6 kilometres (km)
1 kilometres (km) = 0.63 miles
1 metre (m) = 39.37 inches
Land Measure
1 acre = 0.4 hectare
1 hectare = 2.471 acres

Volume Measure
1 U.S. gallon (gal) = 3.79 litres
1 U.S. gallon (gal) = 0.83 imperial gallon

Temperature
To convert °F into °C: subtract 32, divide by 9, multiply by 5
To convert °C into °F: multiply by 9, divide by 5, add 32.

OUTDOORS

Ecuador's natural attractions are extremely rich and so diversified that one word, "ecotourism", springs inevitably to mind. Unfortunately, there is no single definition of "ecotourism", and every tour operator seems to want to use it to mean whatever they like.

Not so long ago, ecologists were thought of as a group of dreamers in search of the Holy Grail. Today, the word "ecology" is on everybody's lips and resounds in fields other than tourism. Thus, for some years now, tourism, in general, has been making way for ecotourism.

Ecotourism, or "Green Tourism", if you prefer, is becoming more fashionable over the world. Exotic images spring immediately to mind: animal photo safaris; hiking through luxuriant forests crisscrossed by streams, where the flora and fauna have evolved so fantastically as to seem unreal... Ecotourism essentially means getting off the beaten path; above all, though, it is synonymous with "respect for nature".

Ecotourism, or Green Tourism

Ecuador is truly a dream location for ecotourism enthusiasts. To this day, there is nowhere else in the world like the Galápagos Islands, with their remarkable flora and fauna. In the Amazon region, the Reserva Faunística Cuyabeno and the Parque Nacional Yasuní shelter rare jewels of nature under their umbrellas of rich tropical vegetation.

In order to preserve this ecological heritage, which is, admittedly, essential to future generations; it is imperative to refrain from sullying and destroying the remarkable biological diversity of this small but magnificent Andean country. The discovery of petroleum in the Amazon has already lead to the destruction of acres of forest and to the pollution of the environment. Numerous animal and vegetable species have disappeared as a result of human encroachment, while others are on the verge of extinction. Indigenous tribes have been reduced to the pitiable status of circus animals for the benefit of unthinking tourists in search of the exotic. The Galápagos Islands must limit the number of visitors in order to protect the fragile ecosystem of the archipelago. In spite of this restraint, certain pathways in this marvellous, insular world are beginning to be dangerously over-trodden.

Protecting nature also means opposing destructive improvements and thoughtless gestures that are made sometimes. At the risk of seeming terribly moralizing, we must remind visitors that it is very important, if not imperative, to obey certain rules:

• Do not discard trash or garbage, because it pollutes the environment.

• Do not make fires in parks or nature reserves because it destroys the forest.

• Do not feed the animals.

• Do not buy souvenirs made from animal skin or feathers, because it encourages killing of animals by smugglers.

• Do not hunt animals. If a guide suggests a meal be made from an animal he will kill, refuse categorically.

• Out of respect, ask permission before taking photographs of people.

• Do not visit the Huaorani Amerindians. They want nothing whatsoever to do with outsiders. Visiting them increases the friction between the modern world and their culture, and reduces them to the status of a pathetic spectacle.

• Bring as few plastics bags as possible, because more often than not they are forgotten; and whether they remain buried forever underground or are left on the surface, they are not biodegradable and pollute.

• Use biodegradable soaps and shampoos.

Hiking and Climbing in the Andes

Ecuador is crossed by majestic mountain chains, making it a dream spot for anyone who wants to climb to their summits. Graced by five peaks, the volcano of Chimborazo, 6, 310 m in height, presents an interesting challenge for experienced climbers. Parque Cotopaxi harbours one of the highest active volcanoes in the world. Its nearly perfect symmetrical cone attracts a significant number of visitors every year. Considered the most accessible volcano, Tungurahua is, in its turn, an excellent place for novice climbers.

In recent years, increased interest in climbing in the Andes has led to a proliferation of tour companies and mountain guides. Be careful! Many of these people are simply not qualified to do this type of work. To attract customers, they offer expeditions at ridiculously low prices. However, they have no knowledge of safety practices in mountain climbing, don't know how to use the necessary equipment, and

Colonial witness of a prosperous era.

Iglesia de la Compañía de Jesús, a mystical sanctuary.

The colourful clothing of a former time.

wouldn't know how to react if a problem should arise along the way. They can barely be counted on to know the correct route to get to the top of the mountain. Unfortunately, the inexperience of these pseudo-guides causes accidents, some fatal.

After a series of accidents, the mountain guides decided to correct the situation by forming ASEGUIM, Asociación de Guias de Montaña *(in Quito, Calle Juan Larrea 657 at Rio de Janeiro, ☎ (02) 568-664)*. Located near the Parque El Ejido, this association aims to educate would-be guides about he dangers that await them. Also, in conjunction with foreign consulates and embassies, it organizes rescue operations for people who become lost in the Andes.

There were two fatal accidents in the mountains of Ecuador in 1996. Around the end of July, a tourist from the Spanish province of Basque died while descending the side of the Cayambe volcano. Less than a week later, a French tourist was also killed, after having conquered the summit of Mount Iliniza. In both instances the tourists were accompanied by other mountain climbers but didn't have a guide. Since mid-century, about eighty fatal accidents have occurred in the country's high mountain ranges. For your own safety, consult a specialized tour company to obtain the services of an experienced guide. Be wary of so-called guides who can't prove their competence or aren't recommended by a reputable company. For a short list of recommended companies and guides, see p 75.

PARKS AND NATURE RESERVES

Ecuador has six national parks, three ecological reserves, two wildlife reserves, two recreational parks and one biological reserve. Networks of trails in each place allow you to discover its rich and varied fauna and flora. Here is a list of all the parks and nature reserves. A detailed description of each can be found further along in the guide.

National Parks: Parque Nacional Sangay (see p 146), Parque Nacional Machalilla (see p 196), Parque Nacional Cotopaxi (see p 145), Parque Nacional Yasuní (see p 255), the Galápagos Islands (see p 263) and Parque Nacional Podocarpus (see p 227).

Ecological Reserves: Reserva de Churute (see p 196), Reserva Ecológica Cotacachi-Cayapas (see p 118, 166) and Reserva Ecológica Cayambe-Coca (see p 119).

Wildlife Reserves: Reserva Faunística Cuyabeno (see p 256) and Reserva Faunística Chimborazo (see p 147).

Recreational Parks: Parque de Recreación El Cajas (see p 227) and Aera Nacional de Recreación el Boliche (see p 145).

Biological Reserve: Reserva Biológica de Limoncocha (see p 256).

The majority of these places can only be visited if accompanied by guides. If you intend to make them part of your itinerary, be forewarned that many unqualified people offer their services as guides or representatives of specialized tours organizers (see p 75).

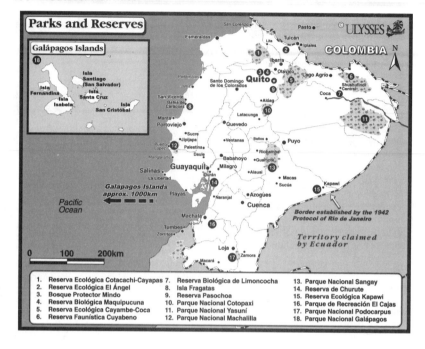

Parks and Reserves

Galápagos Islands

COLOMBIA

Galápagos Islands approx. 1000km

Pacific Ocean

Border established by the 1942 Protocol of Rio de Janeiro

Territory claimed by Ecuador

0   100   200km

1. Reserva Ecológica Cotacachi-Cayapas
2. Reserva Ecológica El Ángel
3. Bosque Protector Mindo
4. Reserva Biológica Maquipucuna
5. Reserva Ecológica Cayambe-Coca
6. Reserva Faunística Cuyabeno
7. Reserva Biológica de Limoncocha
8. Isla Fragatas
9. Reserva Pasochoa
10. Parque Nacional Cotopaxi
11. Parque Nacional Yasuní
12. Parque Nacional Machalilla
13. Parque Nacional Sangay
14. Reserva de Churute
15. Reserva Ecológica Kapawi
16. Parque de Recreación El Cajas
17. Parque Nacional Podocarpus
18. Parque Nacional Galápagos

When planning a visit to these national parks and reserves, make sure that the guide has a valid certificate attesting to his competence. The guide should be associated with an accredited company that holds a permit allowing access to the park.

Over the past few years, many misinformed tourists have been swindled. For example, several companies do not have access permits for the Parque Nacional Yasuni. Consequently, they offer tourists cut-rate excursions and bring them south of the park on the Río Cononaco. The unsuspecting tourists believe they have visited the park itself.

 BIRD-WATCHING

Every year, many birders are attracted to Ecuador by the great variety of avian species. Nearly 2,000 have been identified across the whole country. Several locations have what it takes to satisfy just about anyone's curiosity. Over the years, the Hotel Tinalandia (see p 168), about 15 kilometres from Santo Domingo, has become a favourite meeting place for birders. In fact, over 150 subtropical bird species can be spotted here. Bird-watching fanatics can visit the Reserva Biológica Macipucuna or the Bosque Protector Mindo, both just a few hours from Quito. The Amazon Basin (Oriente) and the Galápagos Islands also harbour many species of rare birds.

 RAFTING

In Ecuador, the rivers flow from high Andean peaks through magnificent canyons to verdant tropical forests. In recent years, rafting has become more and more popular with tourists visiting Ecuador. The rivers range from Class I to Class IV, allowing travellers to choose appropriately. Before setting off on an excursion like this, take the time to choose a serious, competent company. Don't forget that a good reputation is often synonymous with safety, and your life may depend on the competence of your guide. December to May are the best months to shoot the rapids.

 SNORKELLING

Snorkelling equipment is really quite simple: fins, a mask and a snorkel. With no required course, snorkelling is still one of the most interesting of all outdoor activities, allowing everyone access to the beauty of the underwater world. The Galápagos Islands offer remarkable sites for enjoying snorkelling. Since it is sometimes difficult to rent equipment in the Costa, it's best to bring your own.

 SCUBA DIVING

The best place for scuba diving is some 1,000 kilometres to the west of the continent in the seas surrounding the Galápagos Islands. Some would say the islands are a bit too far away, but they really are worth the trip. It is, however, necessary to have taken lessons and hold an up-to-date certificate. In Puerto Ayora, on Isla Santa Cruz, a local business, Galápagos Sub-Aqua, offers the necessary course. Others towns on the Costa also have excellent spots for diving. Wherever you go, make sure you are accompanied by qualified people whose equipment is in good condition.

  ## SURF- AND SAIL-BOARDING

Beginners who want to enjoy these two sports to the fullest will find some windswept bays on the Pacific coast in the vicinity of Montañita (see p 190).

 ## DEEP-SEA FISHING

Most of the large, coastal tourist centres, like Salinas and Playas, offer deep-sea fishing excursions. It's a nice way to get out onto open water and enjoy the beauty of the ocean. It's also a good way to get to know the different types of fish that are caught in Pacific waters. Equipment and advice are furnished on board.

 ## CYCLING

The roads in Ecuador are not ideal for cycling. Given that the highways have no bicycle lanes and the secondary roads are dotted with holes, a mountain bike would be the most practical. Nevertheless, cycling is still a pleasant way to explore the country. Extreme caution is necessary, however, because the drivers go fast and don't always obey traffic laws. In Quito, some companies organize bicycle excursions to certain isolated regions of Ecuador (see p 91).

 ## HORSEBACK RIDING

In certain regions of the country, particularly in the high Andean plateaus, the inhabitants get around on horseback more often than otherwise. Since the roads are narrow and unpaved, it is a most agreeable means of transportation. Visitors can sample the pleasures of riding too, because many hotels and tour companies offer excursions on horseback.

 ## SWIMMING

The beaches on the Pacific coast can not compare to the white, sandy beaches of the Caribbean. However, some of them are very nice for swimming and relaxing. The beaches between Muisné and the Bahía de Caráquez (see p 193), while not yet very developed, are nonetheless interesting.

 ## SOCCER OR *FÚTBOL*

Fútbol is, without a doubt, the most popular sport throughout Ecuador. The young, and the not so young, play it with passion. It is possible to attend weekend *fútbol* matches in the cities of Quito or Guayaquil. In Quito, *fútbol* games take place in the Estadio Atahualpa *(Avenida 6 de Diciembre at Naciones Unidas)*.

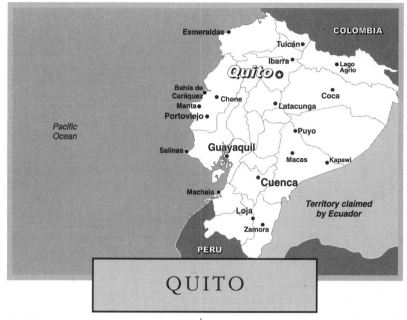

QUITO

A s soon as the airplane carrying you to Quito breaks through the clouds and mist of the highlands, you'll realize that this is no ordinary capital. Arriving in Quito by day, it is impossible not to be fascinated by the extraordinary setting of this city, surrounded by majestic volcanoes that seem to be either guarding it or just waiting for the right moment to bury and destroy it. Quito is located a few kilometres south of the equator, the imaginary line that divides the earth into two hemispheres at 0°0' latitude; it is perched at an altitude of 2,850 metres, making it the second highest capital in South America after La Paz, Bolivia, and the third in the world, Lhasa, the religious capital of Tibet, being the first.

Though it looks Spanish now, the area now known as Quito was inhabited by numerous tribes in the past. Among these were the Incas, who completely

destroyed it before the conquistadors could get their hands on it. Under Rumiñahui, the Incas waged a merciless war against the Spanish, and preferred to raze their own city rather than hand it over to the invaders; when the Spanish got to Quito, the ruins were still smoking.

Although Quito was razed by the Incas, its colonial core was reconstructed in an opulent style and given a certain splendour befitting its role as a capital city. It was officially founded on December 6, 1534 by Sebastián de Benálcazar for the Spanish crown. The new arrivals breathed new life into the town, and the Spanish world supplanted the Inca world.

Colonial Quito is crisscrossed by narrow streets. Candles and holy images are sold in front of the city's numerous religious sanctuaries, whose entrances are crowded with pilgrims. The many colonial buildings perpetuate the memory of the Spanish era and lend the area a charm conducive to daydreaming and poetic inspiration. The churches are full of priceless art, and in some of those decorated in the flamboyant baroque style, the attention to detail is pushed to an almost impossible extreme. Thanks to its architectural riches and impressive number of museums and churches, Quito's colonial core was added to UNESCO's list of World Heritage Sites in 1978 and declared part of the State Cultural Heritage in 1984. The Iglesia de la Campañia de Jesús, the Iglesia y Convento de San Agustín and the Plaza San Francisco are but three examples of the outstanding colonial monuments found here. Most of the colonial architecture is the work of artists from the Quito School. It should be noted that the city's historic core is still undergoing major restorations, as many sites were severely damaged by the 1987 earthquake.

In 1563, about 30 years after it was founded, Quito was elevated to the rank of Audiencia Real, which further strengthened the Spaniards' dominant position over the next three centuries. At the time, the Spanish colonies were divided into viceroyalties, each under the authority of a viceroy to whom the King of Spain delegated his royal power. The Audiencia Real de Quito was originally connected to the viceroyalty of Lima, but because the two capitals were so far apart, it was decided, in the late 17th century, that the Audiencia Real de Quito would thenceforth be a dependency of the viceroyalty of New Granada (modern-day Colombia). A century and a half later, Quito was liberated from Spanish control following the famous Battle of Pichincha (1822), in which Venezuelan General Antonio Sucre crushed the colonial troops. The Audiencia Real de Quito then joined Gran Colombia, which encompassed modern-day Colombia, Venezuela and Panamá. This union only lasted a few years; in 1830 Quito declared its independence from Gran Colombia and became the capital of Ecuador (the country wasn't actually named Ecuador until one year later).

Over the past 30 years, the population of the country's cultural hub has risen from 200,000 to nearly 1,300,000.

FINDING YOUR WAY AROUND

The city of Quito stretches over 30 kilometres, and is 10 kilometres across at its widest point. It is divided into two distinct sections, modern Quito and colonial Quito. Modern Quito is characterized by glaring social inequality, with the lofty silhouettes of opulent, well-protected mansions; shopping malls and banks side by side with working-class neighbourhoods. By contrast, the historic centre of the city, to the south, consists mainly of poor neighbourhoods. As in the rest of Latin America, the Pan American highway runs through the country from north to south, taking on the name Avenida 10 de Agosto as it passes through the capital. The streets are commonly labelled *Avenidas* or *Calles*. *Avenidas* are main arteries and generally run north-south, perpendicular to the *Calles*. It should be noted that a good number of Quiteños don't know the names of their own city's streets, so it can be useful to remember the name of a public building (a church or a hotel, for example) located near the street you're looking for. Furthermore, El Centro (colonial Quito) is easy to

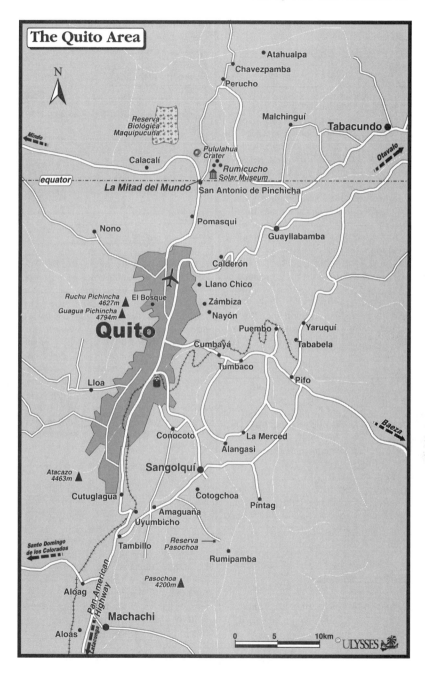

The Quito Area

N

Atahualpa
Chavezpamba
Perucho

Reserva
Biológica
Maquipucuna
Malchinguí
Tabacundo

Mindo

Pululahua
Crater
Calacalí
Rumicucho
Solar Museum

equator
La Mitad del Mundo
San Antonio de Pinchicha

Otavalo

Nono
Pomasqui
Guayllabamba

Calderón

Ruchu Pichincha
4627m
El Bosque
Llano Chico

Guagua Pichincha
4794m
Zámbiza
Nayón

Quito
Puembo
Yaruquí
Tababela

Cumbayá

Tumbaco

Lloa
Pifo

Baeza

Conocoto
La Merced
Alangasi

Atacazo
4463m
Sangolquí

Cutuglagua
Cotogchoa
Píntag

Amaguaña
Uyumbicho

Santo Domingo
de los Colorados
Tambillo
Reserva
Pasochoa

Rumipamba

Pasochoa
4200m

Alóag
Pan-American Highway

Machachi

Aloas

0   5   10km

© ULYSSES

explore on foot but can be dangerous, especially at night.

From the Airport

The small **Mariscal Sucre** airport is located north of the city, on Avenida Amazonas. When you step out of the airport, you'll be greeted by countless taxi drivers eager to offer their services. They should charge you between three and four dollars to take you to your downtown hotel. If a driver demands twice as much, ask another one. If you're on a tight budget, the bus is the most economical option. Go straight to Avenida 10 de Agosto with your baggage and catch a bus heading south. Of course, the bus is likely to drop you off a few minutes' walk from your hotel. Furthermore, if you have several bags, bear in mind that there is little storage space on these vehicles.

By Car

We do not recommend driving in Quito: you'll waste a lot of time in traffic jams, not to mention navigating your way around the city and finding parking. Furthermore, Ecuadorans drive dangerously fast and don't always respect international rules of the road. By renting a chauffeured automobile at the Akros hotel (see below), you can avoid all the headaches of driving and still enjoy the freedom of getting around by car.

Car Rental Agencies

Budget rent-a-car: Avenida Colón at Amazonas, ☎ 548-237 or 237-026

In the Akros hotel: Avenida 6 de Diciembre 3986, ☎ 430-610, ⌨ 431-727 (chauffeured cars).

Ecuacar: Avenida Colón at Amazonas, ☎ 529-781.

Aeropuerto Mariscal Sucre, ☎ 459-052.

Hotel Colón Internacional, ☎ 525-328, ⌨ 562-705.

Avis rent-a-car: Avenida Colón 1741 at 10 de Agosto, ☎ 550-238 or 550-243.

By Bus

Buses are easy to spot and fall into three different categories of comfort, *selectivo*, *ejecutivo* and *popular*, whose set fares are 50¢, 40¢ and 25¢ respectively. It is highly advisable to spend the extra 15¢ or 25¢ and take the *selectivos* or the *ejecutivos*, which are decidedly safer and more comfortable. You hand in your ticket when you get off. Be careful: the buses do not come to a complete stop to let people on and off, but simply slow down. If you have a lot of baggage, it is better to take a taxi, as the buses are often packed.

Bus Terminal (*terminal terrestre*)

The bus station is located in the southernmost part of Quito, at the corner of Calle Maldonado and Cumandá, right near the Plaza Santo Domingo. This is the terminal for buses serving almost all towns and villages in the country. Many bus companies have employees who roam the halls of the station calling out names of destinations, in search of potential

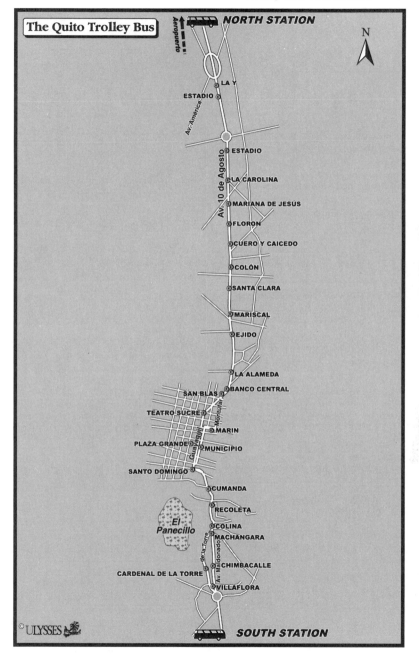

customers. You can get to the terminal by taking the new trolley bus; get off at the Cumandá stop.

By Train

The train station is located a few kilometres south of colonial Quito, just past the bus terminal. In principal, the train leaves the station every Saturday morning at around 8am and goes as far as Riobamba. Tickets cost about $10 apiece and may be purchased at the station from Friday morning onwards.

By Trolley Bus

The electric trolley bus system was set up in 1996 to alleviate the growing pollution problem caused by the city's scores of buses. In all, there are 54 trolley buses with a total capacity of about 6,000 passengers. The trolley buses travel north-south and vice-versa. The set fare is 30¢.

By Taxi

Taxis abound and the fares are affordable by North American and European standards. Depending on the distance, you generally won't have to pay more than $4 or $5. The fares go up a little after nightfall. It costs about $50 to hire a driver for the entire day. You can call Tele Taxi *(☎ 220-800)* 24 hours a day.

? PRACTICAL INFORMATION

Area Code

The area code for Quito is 02.

Tourist Offices (CETUR)

Calle Eloy Alfaro 214 at Carlos Tobar, ☎ 225-190 and 507-560.

Calle Venezuela at Mejía, ☎ 514-044.

Aeropuerto Mariscal Sucre, ☎ 246-232.

Latin American Travel Consultants

P.O. Box 17-17-908,
☎ 562-566
latc@pi.pro.ec
http://www.amerispan.com/latc   or
http://www.greenarrow.com/latc.htm

This organization publishes a very interesting quarterly information bulletin on South and Central America, dealing with subjects such as safety, health, temperature, travel costs, the economy and politics. A yearly subscription costs $39. The organization will also fax or e-mail you information on a particular country for $10.

South American Explorers Club

This non-profit organization was founded in Lima, Peru in 1977. A second office opened in Quito in 1989. The headquarters are in New York State, however. The club's goal is to help anyone wishing to travel in South

America, especially in Ecuador, be it to conduct biological or anthropological research or to enjoy outdoor activities (mountain climbing in the Andes, river rafting, etc.). It costs $40 per person or $60 per couple to join the club, which buys you a subscription to the club's quarterly magazine and access to the club's information resources (topographical, geological and road maps; library; travel reports written by other members). Members are also provided with storage space for their hiking equipment, tent and backpack, and can have letters and e-mail sent to the club's address. The South American Explorers Club is an excellent place to get a group of people together for an excursion. Non-members are welcome, but, out of consideration for members, are politely requested not to dawdle about the premises for too long. The staff are young, friendly and energetic.

In Quito: Mon to Fri 9:30am to 5pm; Calle Jorge Washington 311 at Leonidas Plaza, ☎ and ⊷ 225-228, explorer@saec.org.ec

In Lima: Mon to Fri 9:30am to 5pm; Avenida República de Portugal 146 at Breña, ☎ 314-480, montague@amauta.rcp.net

In the United States: Mon to Fri 9:30am to 5pm; 126 Indian Creek Road, Ithaca, NY 14850, ☎ (607) 277-0488, ⊷ 277-6122, explorer@samexplo.org, http://www.samexplo.org

Tour Companies

Even if you are an independent traveller, taking an organized tour with a local company does have its advantages. A tour can be your only means of reaching remote places like the rainforest, the high mountains or the Galápagos Islands. You might even decide to take a city tour to learn more about the architecture or different neighbourhoods. Here is a list of tour companies based in Quito.

Metropolitan Touring: Avenida Amazonas 339, ☎ 560-550, ⊷ 564-655.

Nuevo Mundo: Avenida Coruña 1349 at Orellana, P.O. Box 402-A, ☎ 552-617, ⊷565-261, nmundo @uio.telconet.net.

Sierra Nevada: Calle Juan León Mera 741 at Veintimilla, ☎ 553-658, ⊷ 659-250.

Safari: Calle Calama 380 at Juan León Mera, ☎ 552-505, ⊷ 220-426, admin@safari.ecx.ec.

Surtek: Avenida Amazonas at Veintimilla, ☎ 561-129.

Pamir Adventure Travel: Calle Juan León Mera 721 at Veintimilla, ☎ 547-576, ⊷ 542-605.

Crater Tours: Calle Calama 161 at Diego de Almagro, ☎ 545-491, ⊷ 554-503.

Telephone Centres (EMETEL)

Avenida 10 de Agosto at Colón.

Calle Benalcázar, between Mejía and Sucre.

Avenida 6 de Diciembre at Colón.

At the *terminal terrestre* (bus station).

Airlines

Air France: Avenida 18 de Septiembre at Amazonas, ☎ 524-201, ⇌ 566-415.

TAME: Avenida Amazonas at Colón, 7th floor, ☎ 509-375, ⇌ 561-052. or
Calle Colón 1001 at Rábida, ☎ 554-905.

SAETA: Calle Santa María at Avenida Amazonas, ☎ 542-148.

SAN: Calle Santa María at Avenida Amazonas, ☎ 564-969, ⇌ 562-024.

Ecuatoriana: Avenida Colón at Reina Victoria, ☎ 563-003 or 563-891, ⇌ 563-920.

Avianca: Avenida 6 de Diciembre 511 at 18 de Septiembre, ☎ 508-843, ⇌ 502-746.

Iberia: Avenida Amazonas 239 at Jorge Washington, ☎ 560-456 or 546-547, ⇌ 566-852.

KLM: Avenida Amazonas 3617 at Juan Pablo Sanz, ☎ 455-233, ⇌ 435-176.

Exchange Offices
(Casas de cambio)

Casa Paz: Avenida Amazonas at Robles, ☎ 563-900 or 564-500 or
Avenida Amazonas 379 at Jaramillo Arteaga, ☎ 516-844.

Ecuacambio: Avenida de la Rebública 192 at Almagro, ☎ 540-148 or 543-575.

Multicambio: Avenida Colón at Reina Victoria, ☎ 561-734.

Maps

Instituto Geographico Militar: Calle Paz at Mino, ☎ 522-066. Detailed maps of the country are available here.

Libri Mundi (see p 100) also sells maps.

Camera Repairs

Finding a place to get your camera repaired in Ecuador can be quite an adventure. There's only one name you need to remember: the Centro de Mantenimiento Fotografico (CEMAF). Gustavo Gómez, the repairman, can work miracles on cameras and lenses. Edificio Molina Of 1, near Parque El Ejido on Calle Asunción 130, at the corner of Avenida 10 de Agosto. The place looks a bit dilapidated, but the service is friendly and efficient.

Post Offices *(Correo Nacional)*

Calle Colón at Reina Victoria.

At the airport.

Avenida 9 de Octubre at Eloy Alfaro.

Avenida 12 de Octubre at Fosch.

Avenida Naciones Unidas at Japón.

Calle Benalcázar 688 at Chile.

Laundromats

Lavandería Lavalimpio: Calle Tamayo 420 at Roca.

Lavandería Opera de Jabón: Calle Joaquin Pinto 325.

Lavandería Modernas: Avenida 6 de Diciembre 2400 at Colón.

Laviseca: Calle Luís Cordero at Tamayo.

Pharmacies

Fybeca: Calle Venezuela at Bolívar.
or
Avenida 6 de Diciembre at Checoslovaquia
or
Avenida Amazonas (facing Plaza de Toros).

Farmacía Alaska: Calle Venezuela at Rocafuerte.

Hospitals

Hopital Voz Andes: Calle Juan Villalengua 263 (some doctors speak English), ☎ 241-540.

Metropolitano: Avenida Mariana de Jesús at Occidental, ☎ 431-457.

Spanish Courses

Spanish courses are available at a number of well-established language schools in Quito. This is an excellent environment in which to learn a foreign language and familiarize yourself with a new culture. The programs are extremely varied and can last anywhere from a single week to several months. Here are a few schools you might try:

Academis de Español Equinoccial: Calle Roca 533 at Juan León Mera, ☎ 525-690, ⚲ 529-460 eee@eee.org.ec.

Academia Latinoamericana de Español: Calle José Queri at Eloy Alfaro, ☎ 452-824, ⚲ 433-820 latinoa1@spanish.com.ec

Amazonas: Calle Jorge Washington 718 at Amazonas, Edificio Rocafuerte, 4th floor, ☎ and ⚲ 504-654.

American Spanish School: Calle Carrión 768 at 9 de Octubre, ☎ and ⚲ 229-165, jproano@serv1.telconet.net.

South American Spanish Institute: Avenida Amazonas 1549 at Santa María, ☎ 544-715, ⚲ 226-348 mlramire@srv1.telconet.net

Estudio de Español Pichicha: Calle Xaura 182, between Lizardo García and Foch, ☎ 452-891, ⚲ 601-689.

Instituto Superior de Español: Calle Ulloa 152 at Jeronimo Carrión, ☎ 223-242, ⚲ 221-628 Institut@superior.ecx.ec

Experiment in International Living: Calle Hernado de la Cruz 143 at Avenida Mariana de Jesús, ☎ 229-596.

EXPLORING

Tour A: Modern Quito ★★

The numbers following names of attractions refer to the map of modern Quito.

Modern Quito's attractions include half a dozen museums, a park, a lookout and a few other points of interest.

A former botanical garden, **Parque El Ejido ★ (1)** is the largest green space in downtown Quito. Many artisans come here on weekends to display their paintings and various other creations beneath the foliage of century-old trees. A commemorative statue of Eloy Alfaro, President of the Republic from 1897 to 1901 and from 1907 to 1911, stands in the middle of the park. Unfortunately, it is dangerous to walk in this park after dark.

Located east of Parque El Ejido and erected in 1944, the **Casa de la Cultura Ecuatoriana Benjamín Carrión (2)** *(Avenida Patria at Avenida 12 de Octubre, ☎ 565-721 or 565-808)*, with its giant, circular, glass façade, is considered the country's most important cultural centre. It contains numerous exhibition and conference rooms, and its second floor is occupied by the **Museo de Música y Arte Moderno José Joaquin Pinto ★** *($1.25; Tue to Fri 10am to 6pm, Sat and Sun 10am to 2pm)*, named after a celebrated Ecuadoran painter. This museum, frequented mainly by Ecuadoran students, displays 19th-century Ecuadoran works focussing on religious themes, as well as portraits of famous figures painted around 1822,

the year of independence. Joaquin Pinto (1842-1906) lived at a time when the country was undergoing great upheavals. A self-taught painter, he constantly strove to surpass himself. He is considered the finest Ecuadoran painter of the 19th century, thanks to his individual style, wide range of themes and varied pictorial techniques (oil, watercolour, pastel, charcoal, pencil and engraving). His scientific mind led him into a close collaborative relationship with French researcher Auguste Cousin, author of *Faune malégologique de la République de l'Équateur*, a monumental contribution to the pool of knowledge about Ecuadoran mollusks, for which Pinto provided the illustrations. Perhaps the most important segment of this remarkably prolific artist's body of work is his depiction of Ecuadoran customs, which reflects the many facets of daily life here.

The Casa also houses the **Museo de Instrumentos Musicales Pedro Pablo Traversari ★★★**, on the third floor, as well as the **Eugenio Espejo** library. The Museo de Instrumentos Musicales Pedro Pablo Traversari, the second largest museum of its kind in the world and the largest in the Americas, displays over 4,000 musical instruments from all over the world. The museum was named after the son of an Italian who immigrated to Ecuador around 1895 and worked for Eloy Alfaro as a music instructor. Inaugurated around 1980, the museum exhibits all sorts of instruments from the colonial and pre-Columbian eras, including some that belonged to nomads who lived in this region in 10,000 B.C. Instruments used by tribes now living in Ecuador are also on display. At the **Museo Indígena**, on the

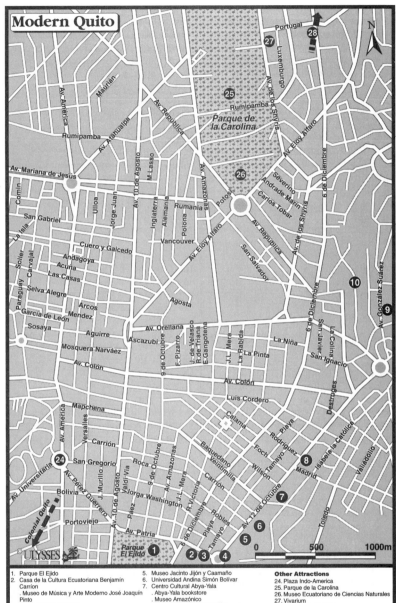

Modern Quito

Colonial Quito

N

© ULYSSES

0   500   1000m

1. Parque El Ejido
2. Casa de la Cultura Ecuatoriana Benjamín Carrión
    . Museo de Música y Arte Moderno José Joaquín Pinto
    . Eugenio Espejo library
    . Museo de instrumentos musicales Pedro Traversari
    . Museo Indígena
3. Museo del Banco Central del Ecuador
4. Museo Arqueológico Hilde y Eugen Weil Bauer
    . Centro de Investigaciones Arqueológicas
5. Museo Jacinto Jijón y Caamaño
6. Universidad Andina Simón Bolívar
7. Centro Cultural Abya-Yala
    . Abya-Yala bookstore
    . Museo Amazónico
    . El Centro de documentación
    . Isona
8. C.E.F.A. (Centro de exposiciones y ferias artesanales)
9. El Mirador
10. Iglesia de Guápulo

Other Attractions
24. Plaza Indo-America
25. Parque de la Carolina
26. Museo Ecuatoriano de Ciencias Naturales
27. Vivarium
28. Museo Guayasamín

same floor, visitors can see a collection of traditional clothing of various kinds.

Adjacent to the Casa de la Cultura Ecuatoriana Benjamín Carríon, the **Museo del Banco Central del Ecuador ★★★ (3)** *($3; Tue to Sun 9am to 4pm; Avenida Patria, between Avenida 6 de Diciembre at Avenida 12 de Octubre, ☎ 223-259)*, the largest museum in Ecuador, illustrates the history of the country in chronological order, from the arrival of the first inhabitants to the modern era, with the help of three floors of impressive pre-Columbian art collections, works of sacred art dating from the colonial era, and paintings and furniture from various periods. The museum also contains a magnificent gold mask personifying the sun worshipped by the Incas, the adopted emblem of El Banco Central del Ecuador.

Turn right toward Avenida 12 de Octubre.

The **Museo Arqueologico Hilde & Eugen Weil Bauer (4)** *(free admission; Avenida 12 de Octubre at Calle Ladron de Gueverra, cater corner to the American embassy; ☎ 230-577)* belongs to the **Universidad Católica del Ecuador** and displays a large collection of archaeological objects, including hatchets and stones discovered in the eastern part of the country by Eugen and Hilde Weil Bauer, a German couple who took an interest in Ecuadoran archaeology. When her husband died in 1986, Hilde Weil Bauer donated their unique collection to the Pontificia Universidad Católica del Ecuador. Open to the public since April 13, 1988, the museum will probably move in 1997, in order to become part of the Museo Jacinto Jijón y Caamaño (see below).

The **Centro de Investigaciones Arqueológicas**, on the third floor of the same building, is an eminently didactic place; all the rooms contain maps, photographs and all sorts of documents and resources that enable visitors to better understand and situate the archaeological objects found along the coast, in the Cordillera and in the eastern part of the country.

When you leave the museum, turn right and follow Avenida 12 de Octubre to the gates of the campus of the Pontificia Universidad Católica del Ecuador. Turn right, then left, and go to the fourth floor of the building.

The **Museo Jacinto Jijón y Caamaño ★ (5)** *(50¢; Mon to Fri 9am to 4pm; ☎ 529-260 or 529-270)* is a small, private, institutional museum containing numerous masterpieces of colonial and republican art dating from the 17th, 18th and 19th centuries, as well as a small gallery devoted to archaeology and certain pre-Incan cultures.

It is worth noting that the library of the Pontificia Universidad Católica del Ecuador is one of the most extensive in the country.

Go back to Avenida 12 de Octubre and turn right.

On your right as you walk away from the university campus, shortly after Calle Carrión, you'll see the **Universidad Andina Simón Bolívar (6)**, which has only been open since September 23, 1993.

Next to the university, the **Centro Cultural Abya-Yala (7)** is dedicated to researching and fostering indigenous cultures through various publications. It contains the **Abya-Yala** bookstore, the **Museo Amazónico, Isona** and **El Centro de documentación** *(50¢; Mon to Fri 9am to noon and 2pm to 6pm; Avenida 12 de Octubre 1430 at Avenida Wilson, ☎ 506-267 or 562-633)*. The documentation centre has over 15,000 volumes devoted to the many native cultures of the Americas, while the museum aims to heighten public awareness of the Amazonian peoples and their way of life. Items displayed include pottery and clothing. The bookstore sells volumes on the natives' history, alternative medicine, anthropology and mythology. Isona is devoted to the promotion and sale of music from Ecuador and elsewhere in Latin America.

When you leave, turn right and head north.

The **C.E.F.A. (Centro de exposiciones y ferias artesanales) (8)** *(free admission; Tue to Sat 9am to 6pm and Sun 9am to noon; Avenida 12 de Octubre 1738 at Avenida Madrid, ☎ 225-464 or 503-873)* is a place where Ecuadoran artists can exhibit their work free of charge. Sculptures, paintings, musical instruments and clothing are all displayed here.

Continue to the end of Avenida 12 de Octubre, turn left on Avenida Colón, walk past the Hotel Quito, then turn right on Avenida González Suárez.

You will find yourself at the **mirador** ★★★ **(9)**, which commands a spectacular view of the eastern cordillera. On cloudless days, the Cayambe (5,740 m) and Puntas (4,450 m) volcanoes can be seen clearly. It was from here that Francisco de Orellana launched his famous expedition to the Amazon in search of

El Dorado. There is a small trail studded with steps leading to the **Iglesia de Guápulo**. Attacks on tourists are common here, so it is better to take a taxi or the bus to the church rather than venturing down on foot.

The **Iglesia de Guápulo** ★★★ **(10)** *(in the hollow of the eastern cordillera, a few kilometres from the Hotel Quito)* was erected in 1649 in honour of the Virgin of Guadalupe. During May, many pilgrims come to this shrine to pay homage to the Virgin. The grey stone façade, which dates from 1693, the year the church was finished, was built by Fray Antonio Rodríguez, Quito's first Franciscan architect. Beautiful retables adorn the niches inside the church, and the pulpit, by Juan Bautista Menacho, is rightly considered one of the loveliest in all South America. The tall, elegant stained-glass windows that top the entablature diffuse the light warmly inside. The church and the sacristy both contain paintings by Miguel de Santiago and Nicolás Javier de Goríbar.

Tour B: Colonial Quito ★★★

The numbers following the names of attractions refer to the map of colonial Quito.

This tour focuses mainly on the treasures of colonial Quito. Roaming the streets of old Quito will enable you to admire Ecuador's rich architectural heritage. Many of these buildings bear the scars of time, having been damaged by earthquakes at one time or another. Not surprisingly, therefore, the various architectural styles characteristic of the 16th, 17th and 18th centuries are often juxtaposed on the city's religious monuments. The church interiors were decorated by artists from the Quito School. The true value of these architectural treasures was finally recognized when the historic centre of the city was placed under the care of UNESCO and designated a World Heritage Site. It should be noted that most of the churches in the colonial centre often have irregular hours. Furthermore, some of them are still undergoing repairs for damages caused by the 1987 earthquake, and might be closed during your stay in Quito.

At the corner of Calle Luís Sodiro, facing **La Alameda** park, stands the **Iglesia El Belén ★ (1)**, also known as the **Capilla El Belén**. It was here that Father Juan Rodríguez led the midnight mass of Christmas 1534, the first mass to be celebrated in Quito. A number of paintings by artists from the Quito School adorn the interior.

Opposite the church, climb the stairs leading up to **La Alameda ★ (2)**, the oldest park in Quito. Its origins date back to 1749, in the days when the Spanish used to let their horses graze here. It now has an artificial lake crisscrossed by canals, and is also home to the oldest astronomical observatory in the Americas. Built in 1868 by ex-President Gabriel García Moreno, this facility was considered by many contemporary astronomers to be the finest of its time. In the centre of the park are several statues erected in memory of members of the French scientific expedition in which Charles Marie de La Condamine took part. These scientists were assigned to verify Newton's hypothesis that the earth was slightly flattened at each pole.

Walk down Calle Guayaquil (Sabaña Santa) to Calle Flores, at which point you'll enter the colonial area. To fully appreciate its beauty—and for your own safety—keep your eyes peeled! You'll notice that most of the houses here have tall, wide doors, built so that horses and carts loaded with all sorts of provisions could pass through. The Spanish would then let the animals roam freely in La Alameda park.

The **Teatro Sucre**, located on the **Plaza del Teatro ★★ (3)**, was built in 1878. One of the major cultural centres in the country, it contains public concert halls and conference rooms. A monument to General Sucre, who is shown accompanied by freedom, symbolized by a young woman breaking her chains, adorns the façade of the theatre. This is not, however, the original monument, which showed Sucre proudly crushing a lion, the symbol of Spain, beneath his foot.

Take Guayaquil to Calle Chile.

The **Iglesia y Convento de San Agustín ★★★ (4)** *(Calle Chile at Calle Guayaquil)* were designed by architect Francisco Becerra, whose other credits include the cathedral in Puebla, Mexico. The church was begun in 1581 and completed in 1617. It has three naves; the main nave is crowned by a false vault with intersecting ribs, while the lateral naves are topped by raised vaults. The façade is flanked by stone columns and adorned with four animal figurines symbolizing the four Evangelists (Saints John, Matthew, Mark and Luke), while the interior is a curious mixture of Gothic Revival and Moorish styles. The walls are covered with works by Miguel de Santiago. Unfortunately, the church is presently closed for restoration, and it is not yet known when the work will be completed.

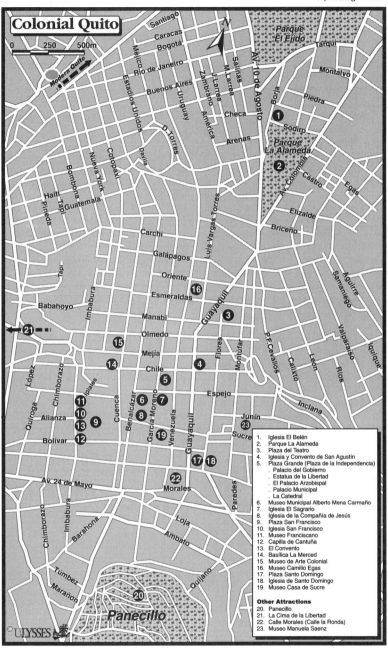

Colonial Quito

0   250   500m

Modern Quito

Santiago
Caracas
Bogotá
Río de Janeiro
Méjico
Estados Unidos
Buenos Aires
Uruguay
Salinas
J. Larrea
M. Larrea
Zambrano
América
Checa
Arenas
Av. 10 de Agosto
Boria
Montalvo
Piedra
Sodiro
Parque
El Ejido
Tarqui
D. Torres
Dávila
Cotopaxi
Nueva York
Bombona
Haití
Tapi
Pineda
Guatemala
Parque
La Alameda
Av. Colombia
Castro
Egas
Elizalde
Briceño
Carchi
Galápagos
Oriente
Esmeraldas
Babahoyo
Tapi
Imbabura
Manabí
Olmedo
Mejía
Chile
López
Chimborazo
Ipiales
Quiroga
Alianza
Cuenca
Benalcázar
García Moreno
Venezuela
Bolívar
Av. 24 de Mayo
Chimborazo
Imbabura
Barahona
Trúmbez
Marañón
Loja
Ambato
Morales
Paredes
Quijano
Luis Vargas Torres
Guayaquil
Flores
Montúfar
P.F.Cevallos
Calixto
León
Ríos
Iquique
Valparaíso
Samaniego
Aguirre
Espejo
Inclana
Junín
Sucre
Guayaquil

Panecillo

© ULYSSES

1   ●1
2   ●2
3   ●3
4   ●4
5   ●5
6   ●6
7   ●7
8   ●8
9   ●9
10   ●10
11   ●11
12   ●12
13   ●13
14   ●14
15   ●15
16   ●16
17   ●17
18   ●18
19   ●19
20   ●20
21   ●21
22   ●22
23   ●23

1. Iglesia El Belén
2. Parque La Alameda
3. Plaza del Teatro
4. Iglesia y Convento de San Agustín
5. Plaza Grande (Plaza de la Independencia)
    . Palacio del Gobierno
    . Estatua de la Libertad
    . El Palacio Arzobispal
    . Palacio Municipal
    . La Catedral
6. Museo Municipal Alberto Mena Carmaño
7. Iglesia El Sagrario
8. Iglesia de la Compañía de Jesús
9. Plaza San Francisco
10. Iglesia San Francisco
11. Museo Franciscano
12. Capilla de Cantuña
13. El Convento
14. Basílica La Merced
15. Museo de Arte Colonial
16. Museo Camilio Egas
17. Plaza Santo Domingo
18. Iglesia de Santo Domingo
19. Museo Casa de Sucre

Other Attractions
20. Panecillo
21. La Cima de la Libertad
22. Calle Morales (Calle la Ronda)
23. Museo Manuela Saenz

You can, however, visit the gallery in the **Convento** *(50¢; schedule varies)*, where magnificent gilt frames set off a series of paintings executed in 1656 by Miguel de Santiago after Dutch artist Schelte Bolswert's engravings showing the life and miracles of San Agustín. The **Sala Capitular ★★★**, adjacent to the Convento, dates from 1741-1746. It is rectangular, and its sloping coffered ceiling has a Renaissance design, complete with canvases and painted medallions. It was here that Ecuador's first declaration of independence was signed on August 10, 1809. The remains of various heroes of the war of independence are interred beneath the centre of the Sala Capitular. There is a ladder leading down to the tombs, but unfortunately there's no electricity down there!

When you leave, turn right on Calle Chile, into the heart of colonial Quito.

Better known as the **Plaza Grande ★★★ (5)**, the **Plaza de la Independencia** is where the city of Quito was founded. Here, as in all colonial cities in Latin America, you'll find the city's major traditional monuments, the seats of civil, religious and municipal power in the colonial era.

To the west stands the **Palacio del Gobierno ★★**, the government palace and headquarters of the present President of the Republic, Fabian Alarcón. It was built in the 18th century and was the seat of the Audiencia Real (meaning a royal court of law was located here). Take a look at the soldiers standing guard; their 16th-century uniforms are those worn by Ecuadoran troops in the famous Battle of Pichincha (1822). The balustrade of the exterior gallery was imported in 1890 by the then president

Antonio Flores. It was once part of Paris' Tuileries, burned a century earlier during the French Revolution. Inside the presidential palace, visitors can admire a magnificent collection of paintings by celebrated Ecuadoran artist Oswaldo Guayasamín depicting the adventures of Francisco Orellana exploring Amazonia.

Standing proudly in the middle of the square is the **Estatua de la Libertad ★**, a commemorative monument covered with symbols. It was erected in 1909, in memory of the first cry for independence, 100 years earlier. Made of bronze and marble, this statue shows, among other things, a fleeing lion wounded by an arrow, symbolizing the departure of the Spanish, as well as a condor breaking a chain between his legs, evoking the liberation of the people of Ecuador.

On the north side of the square, **El Palacio Arzobispal ★** was built in the 17th century then restored in the 20th. Its ornamentation and architecture are neoclassical in style.

The modern silhouette of the recently built **Palacio Municipal** rises up on the east side of the Plaza del Teatro. This concrete structure is much less elegant than the other buildings on the square, but at least it is a more functional public edifice for the city employees who work there.

The **Catedral ★★★** (Basílica San Pedro) was erected in the 16th century, but has had to be renovated on numerous occasions over the centuries; the resulting integration of a variety of architectural styles is interesting. The building has three naves separated by lancet arches. The main nave is set off by a Mudejar-style ceiling, and the lateral naves are topped by a single-sloped roof. In 1797, the cathedral was damaged by an earthquake, and only the oldest section and the wooden parts of the structure survived. The Catedral contains remarkable paintings by artists from the Quito School, including one of Caspicara's masterpieces, *La Sábana Santa* (*Descent from the Cross*), above the altar. The mortal remains of General Antonio Sucre and General Flores lie in a small chapel.

Rumour has it that the weapons of the Spanish soldiers who fought between 1534 and 1822 are buried under the **Plaza de la Independencia**.

Continue your tour by heading west on Calle Espejo.

The **Museo Municipal Alberto Mena Caamaño ★ (6)** *(free admission; Tue to Fri 9am to 4:30pm, Sat 9am to 1:45pm; Calle Espejo 1147 at Calle Benalcázar, ☎ 210-863)*, set up inside a former barracks next to the **Palacio del Gobierno**, displays works of art, antique furniture and a collection of weapons from the colonial era. In the basement, life-sized wax statues have been used to re-create the murder of several patriots by royalists disguised as Franciscan monks on August 2, 1810.

Retrace your steps, then turn right on Calle García Moreno (or Calle de las Siete Cruces).

The **Iglesia El Sagrario ★★ (7)** *(Calle García Moreno and Espejo)*, a former chapel that was once an outbuilding of the adjacent **Catedral**, was severely damaged by an earthquake in 1987. According to the inscription on the portal, the church was begun in 1669 and completed in 1706. Built of beautifully cut grey stone, it has three naves. The arch in the centre of the portal is flanked by Corinthian columns. The façade is neoclassical in style, and some magnificent frescoes of the archangels, by Bernardo de Legarda, were discovered inside during a recent restoration project. Bernardo de Legarda was a mestizo Ecuadoran artist who lived in Quito in the 18th century. Though first and foremost a sculptor, he was also a painter, silverer and gilder. Drawing his inspiration mainly from religious themes, he created several major works, which can be viewed in various religious buildings in colonial Quito, two examples being the decoration of the dome of El Sagrario and the retable of the Capilla de Cantuña.

Continue on the same street to Calle Sucre.

Next, you'll see the **Iglesia de la Compañia de Jesús ★★★ (8)** *(Calle García Moreno at Calle Sucre)*, considered one of the most spectacular 17th-century religious buildings in South America. Inside, over four tons of gold glitter away, illuminating the walls, doors, altar and ceiling with their reflections. Begun by the Jesuits in the early 1600s, the church was completed in 1774. The façade is made of volcanic stones carved in a baroque style. Although the church was seriously damaged by fire while being restored in February 1996, it is still open to the public.

Walk up Calle Sucre to Calle Cuenca.

The **Plaza San Francisco ★★★ (9)** is laid out around a fountain and surrounded by several buildings of historical interest: the **Iglesia San**

Iglesia San Francisco

Francisco, the **Museo Franciscano**, the **Capilla de Catuña** and the **Convento**. This famous square, whose construction was begun shortly after Quito was founded on January 25, 1535, is the city's largest grouping of colonial buildings and remains one of the finest ensembles of religious architecture in South America.

The **Iglesia San Francisco** ★★★ **(10)** was designed by Francisco Becerra, the renowned architect of the Puebla cathedral in Mexico. This monastery church was begun in the late 16th century and completed in 1623. The façade of the Iglesia San Francisco and certain doors of its outbuildings offer a fascinating panorama of Renaissance architecture. The church is made up of a single-span nave, a transept of equal width and several magnificent side chapels connected to one another by Mudejar-style arches. The building was originally graced with a splendid Mudejar-style coffered ceiling. Unfortunately, two centuries ago, a fire destroyed everything but the parts corresponding to the choir of the transept. The statue of Our Lady of Quito on the high altar is a perfect example of the Quito School. The remarkable baroque-style walls and ceiling are painted with scenes from the lives of St. Peter and St. Paul.

The **Museo Franciscano** ★★★ **(11)**, adjacent to the church, boasts an impressive collection of paintings, sculptures and works of art from the Quito School.

The **Capilla de Cantuña** ★★★ **(12)** was named after the man who built it, Francisco Cantuña, an Amerindian. According to legend, Cantuña had promised to finish the chapel by a certain date. Fearing he wouldn't be able to meet the deadline, he sold his soul to the devil in exchange for a guarantee that he would complete the work on time. He later regretted making the pact, however, and started praying for his soul. When the chapel was inaugurated, one stone was missing; Cantuña was saved, for the devil had not finished his work. Another legend has it that the chapel was financed by hidden Inca gold. The building has a single nave and contains magnificent works by artists from the Quito School. Among the more noteworthy of these is the main retable, a richly carved piece by Bernardo de Legarda.

Built under the supervision of Franciscan monk Fleming Jocke Ricke, the **Convento** ★★ **(13)** became, over the following centuries, an important studio for the Quito School, where natives could express their artistic impulses. Ricke is also recognized as the first man to have planted wheat in Ecuador. Inside the monastery, magnificent paintings depict scenes from St. Francis's life. The cloister, for its part, features numerous Doric columns.

As you leave, turn left and walk through the little market on Calle Cuenca to Calle Chile.

The **Basílica La Merced** ★★★ **(14)** *(Calle Cuenca at Calle Chile)* owes its existence to José Jamie Ortiz. The last church to be erected during the colonial era, in the early 18th century, it is different from the others in that it was entirely built by the Spanish. According to legend, the Virgin of La Merced protects the residents of Quito from earthquakes and volcanic eruptions. The basilica contains many works by artists of the Quito School. Noteworthy examples include the high altar, the spectacular paintings by Victor Mideros and a very pretty canvas by Goríbar. The building has a tall tower topped by a heavy bell and a clock, which was made in London in 1817 and is the oldest in Quito. The bell has only been rung once, as the vibrations damaged the tower! The façade of the basilica is baroque in style, while the ceiling is adorned with hollow mouldings dating from the 17th century.

The monastery, for some unknown reason, contains a non-religious monument—a statue of Neptune set in the middle of the fountain in the cloister.

Continue on Calle Cuenca to Calle Mejía.

Laid out on two floors of a pretty colonial house, the **Museo de Arte Colonial** ★★★ **(15)** *($1; Tue to Fri 10am to 6pm, Sat 10am to 3pm, Sun 10am to 2pm, closed Mon; Calle Cuenca 901 and Mejía, ☎ 212-297)* boasts an interesting collection of paintings and sculptures from the 16th, 17th and 18th centuries. The 16th-century paintings are static and characterized by a great deal of ingenuity; the 17th, by dark colours and somewhat austere scenes based on themes of Spanish origin; the 18th, by greater movement and lighter, more luminous colours, with a particular emphasis on white, green, blue and red. The museum's most famous sculpture is without a doubt Manuel Chili's *Resurrected Christ*, representing Jesus's triumph over death. The detail on the hair and teeth is exquisite. Manuel Chili, also known as Caspicara, was one of the most important Ecuadoran sculptors of the 18th century, and is renowned for his finely detailed miniatures.

Turn left on Calle Mejía, left again on Calle Venezuela, then right on Calle Esmeraldas, which will take you to Calle Luís Vargas Torres.

The **Museo Camilio Egas** ★ **(16)** *(Tue to Fri 9am to noon and 3pm to 6pm, Sat 9am to 1pm; Calle Venezuela and Esmeraldas, ☎ 514-511)* bears the name of a modern Ecuadoran painter who spent several years in France then returned to Quito. The museum displays many of the Egas's paintings and is quite interesting, even if you know little about his art. Camilio Egas lived from 1889 to 1962.

Go back to Calle Venezuela and turn left. Turn left again on Calle Simón Bolívar and continue to Calle Guayaquil.

The **Plaza Santo Domingo (17)** is sure to catch your attention; in front of the church, a monument shows General José Antonio Sucre pointing proudly with his right hand to the Pichincha volcano, where he won the battle that brought about the end of Spanish domination once and for all on May 24, 1822. The **Iglesia de Santo Domingo** ★★ **(18)** houses one of the oldest altars in the Republic. The statue of the Virgen del Rosario, a gift from Charles V of Spain, is a must-see.

The **Museo Fray Pedro Bedón** ★★ *($1.50; Calle Flores, Mon to Fri 9am to 12:30pm and 1pm to 6:30pm, Plaza de Santo Domingo)* stands beside the monastery of the Iglesia Santo Domingo. The primary goal of this little museum is to explain the history and expansion of the Dominican order in the Americas and elsewhere in the world. Visitors can admire a considerable number of oil portraits and sculptures of saints who belonged to the order, including St. Dominic de Guzmán, St.

Catherine of Sienna, St. Vincent Ferrer and St. Thomas Aquinas. Also on display are a number of representations of the Virgin Mary (the Virgin of the Eucharist, the Virgin of the Rosary, etc.).

A number of these works, namely those of European origin, are attributable to Francesco Guerini (18th-century Italian painter) and Pedro de Mena (17th-century Spanish sculptor). Works by artists from the Quito School include paintings attributed to Brother Pedro Bedón (17th century), Miguel de Santiago (17th century), Manuel Samaniego (18th century), as well as sculptures by Father Carlos (17th century) and Bernardo de Legarda (18th century).

While touring the museum, you can read brief biographical profiles of important members of the order, including Brother Bartholomé de las Casas (1474-1566), celebrated defender of natives and the "first European to denounce the injustice of the colonial system..." (Enrique Duseel), Brother Pedro Bedón (Quito 1555), painter, politician, theologian and defender of natives and founder and director of the Brotherhood of the Rosary (a brotherhood is a group of devoutly religious people who profess to observe the laws of the Church).

Finally, the museum exhibits various objects that belonged to the monastery of Santo Domingo and were used by the order over the centuries, for example, a 19th-century rosary made of shells and silver, 18th-century books owned by the Brotherhood of the Rosary and 18th-century vestments embroidered with gold and silver.

Go back to Calle Simón Bolívar and turn right on Calle Venezuela.

Since 1978, the **Museo Casa de Sucre** ★★ **(19)** *($1; Tue to Fri 8am to 12:30pm and 1:30pm to 4:30pm, Sat 8am to 1pm; Calle Venezuela 573 and Sucre,* ☎ *512-860)*, owned by the army, has occupied the former home of Venezuelan general José Antonio Sucre, who served under Bolívar and is renowned for his famous victory in the Battle of Pichincha. Though Sucre stayed here for barely 10 months, the museum displays documents, clothing, weapons and flags that belonged to him; some items were used during the Battle of Pichincha. The second-floor furnishings are replicas of the originals.

Other Local Attractions

Overlooking Quito from a height of 3,200 metres, the **Panecillo** ★★★ **(20)** is a giant copy of the Virgin of the Immaculate Conception, created by Bernardo de Legarda. It dominates the city and offers a spectacular view of the surroundings. To the west, you'll see the site of the famous Battle of Pichincha. A long flight of stairs starts right near the Chimbacalle station and ends at the Panecillo. Unfortunately, knife attacks on tourists are common along this route, so it is wise to get a small group together and share a taxi.

La Cima de la Libertad ★★ **(21)** *(schedule varies)* is a museum perched at an altitude of some 3,000 metres on the side of the Pichincha volcano, on the very site where General Sucre won the historic battle for the independence of Ecuador on May 24, 1822. An arms museum and an enormous mural commemorate the event. The view is quite simply stunning.

Theoretically called **Calle Morales, Calle la Ronda** ★★★ **(22)** *(between Calle García Moreno at Calle Venezuela, right near Avenida 24 de Mayo)* is the oldest colonial street in all of Quito. Numerous balconies adorn the traditional houses along this charming, narrow, little street, once the site of an native marketplace. Unfortunately, tourist attacks are common here after dark.

The **Museo Manuela Saenz** ★ **(23)** *($1; schedule varies; Calle Junín 710)* is set up inside a pretty colonial house. Laid out on three floors, it displays letters exchanged by Simón Bolívar and Manuela Saenz, born in Quito on December 1795, as well as paintings, weapons and other objects. Saenz was Bolívar's mistress and muse. After his death, she exiled herself to Paita, in northern Peru, where she died on November 23, 1856, at the age of 61.

The **Plaza Indo-America (24)** *(opposite the Faculty of Administrative Sciences of the Universidad Central de Ecuador and the Teatro Universidad)* pays tribute to the aboriginal chiefs of all countries in Latin America. Among other things, visitors will find a statue of Atahualpa's famous general, Rumiñahui (meaning "stone-face" in Quichua; when you see it you'll understand why!).

The four-kilometre-long **Parque de la Carolina** ★ **(25)**, welcomes *pelota de guante* enthusiasts on Saturdays and Sundays. This modern version of pelota is similar to volleyball, but is played with teams of three. Near the centre of the park is an immense cross commemorating the pope's visit on January 30, 1985. On weekends, the park is very popular with families eager to get a bit of fresh air and enjoy some exercise (jogging, aerobics, etc.). An artificial lake lies in the park's hollow; unfortunately, it is very polluted. Parque de la Carolina even has a gardening club for those wishing to learn about horticulture.

The **Museo Ecuatoriano de Ciencas Naturales** ★ **(26)** *(25¢; Calle Rumipamba 341 at Avenida de los Shyris, ☎ 449-824)* is located in the park. A small, non-profit museum, it exposes visitors to Ecuador's wealth of biological, geological and palaeontological resources. Items on display include numerous maps, stuffed and mounted animals and butterflies.

Those who haven't had a chance to visit the Oriente can stop by the **Vivarium** ★★ **(27)** *($2; Tue to Sun 9am to noon and 3pm to 6pm; Avenida de los Shyris 1130 and Portugal, ☎ 230-988, ⇌ 448-425, touzet@orstom.ecx.ec)*, home to numerous reptiles and amphibians from all over South America.

The **Museo Guayasamín** ★★★ **(28)** *(free admission; Mon to Fri 9am to 12:30pm and 3pm to 6:30pm, Sat 9am to 12:30pm; Calle José Bosmediano 543, ☎ 446-277)* is located in the Bella Vista neighbourhood, in the northern part of town. To get there, take bus #3, destination Bella Vista. This museum, the former home of celebrated contemporary painter Guayasamín, houses an impressive collection of paintings and ceramics, as well as numerous copies of archaeological and colonial pieces, executed by the artist himself.

OUTDOOR ACTIVITIES

 Cycling

Bike Rental Shops

The following shops rent out bicycles and organize group outings to picturesque parts of the country, led by official guides.

Pedal Andes
P.O. Box 17-12-602
☎ 220-674
explorer@saec.org.ec

Aventura Flying Dutchman
Calle Foch 714 and Juan León Mera
☎ 542-8806 or 449-568
↵ 567-008

Rent Bike Biciteca
Avenida Brasil 1612 and Edmundo Carvajal (near the El Bosque shopping centre)
☎ 241-687

 Rafting

Many rafting outfits simply don't take adequate safety measures. Don't hesitate to ask a lot of questions, and don't forget that while there are many of these enterprises, they are not all equally reputable. We have spoken with many guides who have never been certified or otherwise trained in river rafting. The price difference is not that significant. Do some research before making a decision; your life could depend on it.

Here are a few outfits that can help you organize a rafting trip in the greater Quito area:

Row Expediciones
Calle Salazar Gómez 144 and Martínez Mera
☎ and ↵ 458-339
rafting@row.ecx.ec

Row Expediciones makes it possible for visitors to explore some of the wildest rivers in the country. A variety of excursions are offered on rivers ranging from Class I to Class V. The professional, bilingual, certified guides are trained in first-aid. The groups are generally small, and all outings include meals. A day costs about $70, two days about $140.

Sierra Nevada
Calle Pinto 637 at Avenida Amazonas
☎ 553-658
↵ 554-936

This outfit offers more or less the same services as Row Expediciones.

 ACCOMMODATIONS

The city of Quito has scores of hotels and all sorts of other accommodations. The hotels in modern Quito are by far the safest and best equipped.

Modern Quito

The **Hostal Tatu** *($8 bkfst incl.; sb, ℂ, ℜ; Avenida 9 de Octubre 275 and Jorge Washington,* ☎ *544-414 or 236-699)*, near Parque El Ejido, has large, clean and simply laid-out rooms containing several beds. Guests are welcome to use the kitchen.

The **Hostal Eva Luna** *($6 per person; tv, sb, ℂ, hw; Calle Roca at Avenida Amazonas, ☎ 234-799)* is a pleasant little hotel for women only, located in the heart of modern Quito, just steps away from the luxurious Alameda Real. It has rooms with four or six beds apiece, and can accommodate a total of up to 14 women. Guests can even use the kitchen and do their laundry here. The bedspreads, made of traditional fabrics from Otavalo, will keep you warm during the cool Andean nights. The hostel also has a terrace with a table and chairs, where you can relax after touring the city. The place is run by the tour company next door, Safari, so guests are always kept well-informed of the various excursions available, most of which are geared to ecotourism. Finally, guests are welcome to come and go as they please. Rates vary according to the length of your stay.

The **Alberque Juvenil Mitad del Mundo** *($7 per person bkfst incl.; sb, ℜ; Calle Pinto 325 and Reina Victoria, ☎ 543-995)* rents out slightly Spartan but very economical common rooms containing two to four beds. International Youth Hostel card holders receive a modest discount.

El Cafecito *($12; sb, ℜ; Calle Luís Cordero 1124 and Reina Victoria, ☎ 234-862)*, a small cafe and a small hotel rolled into one, is an economical option for budget-conscious travellers. Very well-located, it is popular with backpackers who enjoy chatting and exchanging travel stories. Good vegetarian food.

In the same vein, **The Magic Bean** *($7 per person; sb, ℜ; Calle Foch 681 and Juan León Mera, ☎ 566-181)* is a pleasant · little restaurant (see p 96)

with a few modestly decorated rooms. This is one of the best low-budget establishments in Quito. The staff are young and friendly, and guests can have e-mail sent to them here.

The **Posada del Maple** *($15; pb, ℜ, ℂ, tv; Calle Rodríguez at Avenida 6 de Diciembre, ☎ 237-375)* has clean, safe, no-frills rooms. The service is friendly, and guests are welcome to use the kitchen. Popular with tourists.

The seven little rooms at the **La Estancia Inn** *($15; pb, tv, ℜ; Calle Wilson 508 and Diego de Almagro, ☎ 235-993, ≈ 568-664)* offer good value for the money. Though hardly luxurious, they are comfortable, clean, reasonably priced and well-located. Friendly service.

In the centre of modern Quito, the **Alston Inn Hotel** *($25; tv, hw, ℜ, pb; Calle Juan León Mera 741 and Baquedano, ☎ and ≈ 521-587, 229-955 or 508-956)* has simple rooms, as well as laundry service. However, the noise of cars and passers-by might bother you if you're staying in one of the front rooms. The little restaurant looks out onto Calle Juan León Mera, so you can do some people-watching while you eat.

Located in the northern part of town, the **Hotel Zumag International** *($25; pb, tv; Calle Mariana de Jesús at Avenida 10 de Agosto, ☎ 232-450 or 526-578, ≈ 504-070)* has somewhat sombre, austere rooms, but some of them offer an interesting view of the Pichincha volcano.

Located right near the Vaca Ortiz hospital and the offices of the Fundación Macipucuna, the Scandinavian hotel **Rincón Escandinavo**

($25; ℜ, pb, hw, tv; Leonidas Plaza and Baquerizo, ☎ 222-168 or 540-794, ≈ 222-168) has 25 clean, quiet, fully equipped rooms with hardwood floors and all the comforts. Italian restaurant on the premises.

The **Hotel Ambassador** *($25; ℜ, tv, pb, hw; Avenida 9 de Octubre 1052 at Avenida Colón, ☎ 561-777 or 562-054, ≈ 503-712)*, located near the EMETEL, has clean, spacious rooms with wall-to-wall carpeting; unfortunately, they have definitely seen better days. Restaurant and private parking for guests.

Right near the French embassy, the **Hostal Plaza Internacional** *($28; ℜ, pb, hw; Leonidas Plaza and 18 de Septiembre, ☎ 549-937 or 522-735, ≈ 505-075)* is a converted colonial house. It rents out small, well-kept rooms that are warmly decorated with antiques and still have their original woodwork. The polyglot manager is very obliging.

The 35 rooms at the **Hotel Embassy** *($30; pb, hw, tv; Calle Presidente Wilson 441 at Avenida 6 de Diciembre, ☎ 561-990, ≈ 563-192)* are outmoded but clean and safe.

Just steps away from bustling Avenida Amazonas and Parque El Ejido, the **Rincón de Bavaria** *($30; tv, pb, hw, ℜ; Calle Gral Páez 232 and 18 de Septiembre, ☎ 509-401)* offers spacious, clean and simply decorated rooms.

The **Café Cultura** *($50; pb, hw, tv; Calle Robles 513 and Reina Victoria, ☎ and ≈ 224-271, sstevens@pi.pro.ec)* is a very pretty colonial house with 16 rooms, which are generally occupied by a slightly bohemian international clientele. The rooms are clean and

decently furnished, but if you don't mind spending six dollars more, opt for the suite, which is bathed in pastel colours, adorned with antique furniture and opens onto an immense balcony. Perfect for a romantic stay.

A pretty colonial house whose charm has been remarkably well preserved, the **Hostal Palm Garten** *($50; ℜ, pb, hw, tv; Avenida 9 de Octubre 923 and Luís Cordero, ☎ 526-263 or 523-960, ≈ 568-944)* has about 20 clean, inviting, tastefully furnished rooms, some with a balcony.

The **Hotel Santa Barbara** *($53; tv, pb, hw, ℜ; Avenida 12 de Octubre 2263 and Coruña, ☎ 225-121, ≈ 564-382)* is a converted colonial house containing 16 clean rooms with hardwood floors; some also have a balcony. Ask for a room with a view of the Pichincha volcano. Guest parking lot.

Located steps away from the South American Explorers Club, the **Amarantha Internacional** *($56; tv, ℜ, pb, ◉; Leonidas Plaza 194 and Jorge Washington, ☎ 543-619 or 508-887, ≈ 560-586)* is an apart-hotel with 19 bright, spacious suites, all equipped with a kitchenette with pots and pans and dishes.

The **Hotel República** *($60; tv, pb, hw; Calle República and Azuay, ☎ 436-391 or 436-553, ≈ 437-667)* is a little farther from the colonial centre, but located in a safe, quiet neighbourhood. The rooms are well kept, but the decor is very nondescript.

The **Hotel Tambo Real** *($78; ℜ, hw, pb, tv; Avenida 12 de Octubre and Patria, ☎ 563-820, ≈ 554-964)*, located opposite the Casa de la Cultura Ecuatoriana, has 90 clean, spacious rooms; ask for one with a view of the Pichincha volcano. Some have a minibar and a kitchenette. Twenty-four-hour room service.

The owner of the **Hotel Chalet Suisse** (*$80;* ℜ *pb, hw, ctv; Calle Reina Victoria and Calama,* ☎ *562-700 or 563-966,* ≈ *563-966)*, Jean-Pierre Magnena, is the ex-president of the hotel-keepers' association of the province of Pichincha. All the rooms are charming and well-equipped, complete with a minibar. Some have a bidet. The restaurant has a good reputation.

The recently built **Hotel Sebastián** (*$83;* ℜ*, pb, hw, ctv; Calle Almagro 822 and Luis Cordero,* ☎ *222-300 or 223-400,* ≈ *222-500)* belongs to the owners of the Nuevo Mundo tour company (see p 75). The rooms are equipped with a small heater and are bright, tastefully furnished and embellished with warm colours. In addition to having a good restaurant, the Sebastián is one of the few hotels in Ecuador to filter its tap water. The staff are friendly and obliging, and can easily help you organize excursions all over the country. With its central location and high-quality facilities, this is undoubtedly one of the best hotels in Quito.

Though the rooms at the **Hotel Quito** (*$95; pb,* ≈*, ctv,* ℜ*, hw; Avenida González,* ☎ *544-600 or 544-514,* ≈ *567-284)* are all comfortable, their appeal lies mainly in how quiet they are and the stunning view they offer of the Guapulo valley. Ask for one at the back; the rates are the same, and the view is decidedly more interesting. There's a pretty outdoor pool where guests can cool off after touring the city.

The **Alameda Real** (*$95;* ℜ*, ctv, pb, hw; Calle Roca 653 at Avenida Amazonas,* ☎ *562-345,* ≈ *565-759)* is located a stone's throw away from Avenida Amazonas and Parque El Ejido. Its rooms, dressed up with pastel colours and equipped with a minibar, will satisfy even the most demanding tourists. The lobby has pretty fountains that spurt up alongside a cascade of greenery.

The **Hotel Colón** (*$100;* ℜ*, ctv, pb, hw; Avenida Amazonas and Patria,* ☎ *560-666,* ≈ *563-903)* is a large establishment that offers all the comfort of a top-notch hotel. Some rooms afford a pretty view of Parque El Ejido. A non-smoking floor, a casino and a discotheque can all be found on the premises.

The **Hotel Akros** (*$125; ctv, pb, hw,* ℜ*; Avenida 6 de Diciembre 3986,* ☎ *430-610,* ≈ *431-727)* will appeal to business travellers and vacationers alike. The rooms are bright, spacious, elegant and bathed in pale colours. All the bathrooms are large, modern and equipped with a telephone. The hotel also has an excellent restaurant, a parking lot and a chauffeured car-rental service. The staff are attentive and will make every effort to ensure that your stay is as pleasant as possible.

Located north of Parque de la Carolina, a few minutes from the airport, the **Holiday Inn** (*$170; ctv,* ⊛*, pb, hw,* ℜ*; Avenida Los Shyris 1757 and Naciones Unidas,* ☎ *445-305 or 251-666,* ≈ *251-958 or 445-180, www.crowneplaza.com)* is a symbol of the ongoing American invasion of Ecuador. This top-notch establishment only has suites and is equipped with conference rooms, a bar, a restaurant, an exercise room and a whirlpool bath.

It was clearly designed for business travellers.

If you have money to burn and are looking for real luxury, the **Oro Verde** *($240; hw, pb, ctv, ≈, △, ℜ; Avenida 12 de Octubre 1820 and Luis Cordero,* ☎ *566-497 or 567-128,* ⊷ *569-189)* is an absolutely top-flight establishment. It is very well kept and prides itself particularly on its attentive service. The rooms are bright, well-equipped and spotless. Guests enjoy access to four excellent restaurants, three non-smoking floors, a casino, a swimming pool, a sauna, a gym and a squash and racquetball court. What more could you ask for? Oh, yes: a doctor is available on the premises 24 hours a day.

Colonial Quito

Most hotels in the colonial centre offer only the basics, and not all are as clean as one might hope. If you're looking for comfort and luxury, you're better off staying in modern Quito.

The rooms of the **Hotel Santo Domingo** *($6; Plaza Santo Domingo)* are some of the cheapest in town, but also some of the least charming. They will suit travellers who aren't very demanding as far as comfort is concerned and don't plan on spending the day inside.

If you're looking for affordable accommodations near the *terminal terrestre* (bus terminal), try the **Hotel Juana de Arco** *($8; Calle Rocafuerte 1311 and Maldonado,* ☎ *214-175)*. The rooms are spartan but fine for one night.

Located near the Alameda park, the **Residencial Marsella** *($9; sb, ℜ; Calle Los Ríos 2035 and Julio Castro,* ☎*515-884)* has relatively clean rooms, as well as a terrace and a restaurant.

The **Hotel Gran Casino Internacional** *($10; Avenida 24 de Mayo and Loja,* ☎ *514-905, 216-595 or 214-502)* has basic rooms that sometimes look as if they could use some cleaning, but will fill the bill for adventurous travellers on a shoestring budget. This place is very popular with backpackers.

For a few dollars more, you can stay in one of the relatively clean, affordable rooms at the **Hostal Huasi Continental** *($12; pb, hw; Calle Flores 332 and Sucre,* ☎ *517-327)*, near Plaza Santo Domingo.

Right near the Plaza del Teatro, the **Hostal La Casona** *($20; pb, ec, tv; Calle Manabí 255,* ☎ *514-764,* ⊷ *563-271)* offers laundry service and clean, charming rooms laid out around an inner court. Definitely one of the best deals in colonial Quito.

 RESTAURANTS

Like the hotels, the best dining establishments in town are concentrated in modern Quito, which has all sorts of restaurants for every taste.

Modern Quito

El Maple *($; Calle Páez 485 and Roca,* ☎ *520-994)*, set up inside a house, is a vegetarian restaurant that serves generous portions at economical prices, which vary according to what's on the daily menu. The woodwork lends the place a cozy touch.

The **Taco Factory** *($; Calle Foch 713 and Juan León Mera, ☎ 543-956)* is a small Mexican restaurant that serves excellent homemade tortillas at affordable prices. Friendly service and an unpretentious decor.

El Arabe *($; Calle Reina Victoria 627 and Carrión, ☎ 549-414)*, a restaurant run by Algerians, is the perfect place to tuck into a *shawarma*, a *shish taouk* or a *falafel* before continuing on your way. Friendly service and mouth-watering food.

Chapati *($; Calle Calama and Diego de Almagro, ☎ 521-244)* is another good local restaurant that serves a wide variety of dishes geared to vegetarian tastes. Friendly, courteous service. Try the carrot juice!

El Holandez *($; Calle Reina Victoria 600 and Carrión, ☎ 522-167)* is sure to please visitors looking for delicious, varied vegetarian food. The menu lists Indian-, Thai- and Japanese-style dishes. The place also has a terrace for outdoor dining.

The friendly atmosphere of the **Art Forum** *($; Calle Juan León Mera 870 and Wilson, ☎ 544-185)* cafe attracts intellectuals and students, as well as local shopkeepers who enjoy honing their conversation skills; as for tourists, they come here to relax and catch their breath.

The **Tex-Mex** *($$; Calle Reina Victoria 847 and Wilson, ☎ 527-689)* occupies an old colonial house whose interior walls are bathed in warm pastel colours. The place serves a good choice of Mexican dishes, such as tacos, enchiladas and burritos. Friendly service.

The little restaurant at the **Café Cultura** *($$; Calle Robles and Reina Victoria, ☎ 224-271)* is a good place to grab a quick bite to eat between two local attractions or to enjoy a relaxed conversation over a cup of coffee or tea. The atmosphere is informal and the service friendly. There are a few vegetarian dishes on the menu.

The **Magic Bean** *($$; Calle Foch 681 and Juan León Mera, ☎ 566-181)* has quickly become a mainstay with the bohemian crowd. It is one of the few places in Ecuador where you can enjoy a good organic salad. Known for its wide choice of crepes, it also serves excellent espresso. The outdoor seating area provides a place for customers to relax and exchange travel stories.

The **Bambú Bar** *($$; Calle Diego de Almagro 2213, ☎ 543-107)* serves a delicious *aguacates* (tomato and avocado) soup, as well as tasty empanadas. A good place for lunch.

Every Sunday, the restaurant at the **Hotel Colón Internacional** *($$; Avenida 9 de Octubre 1052 at Avenida Colón, ☎ 561-777)* serves an excellent brunch that will satisfy even the heartiest appetite.

The bottles of wine lined up along the wall are the main attraction at the **Rincón del Gaucho** *($$; Calle Diego de Almagro 422 and Lizardo García, ☎ 547-846 or 223-782)*, a small Argentinian restaurant. Tasty international cuisine with a good selection of meat dishes.

El Cebiche *($$; Calle Juan León Mera 1232 and Calama)* proves that it is possible to savour excellent *cebiche* in Quito. Simple, unpretentious decor.

The wide choice of pizza served at the **Pizza Hut** *($$; Calle Espejo 847 at Calle Guayaquil)*, a member of the American chain, attracts both Ecuadorans and tourists who need their fix of North American food.

If you'd prefer to try an Ecuadoran-style pizza, head for **El Hornero** *($$; Calle Veintimilla at Avenida Amazonas)*.

With its first-class meat dishes, the **Shorton Grill** *($$; Calle Calama 216 and Diego de Almagro)* ranks as one of the best grills in town. Not for vegetarians.

Recognized by carnivores as one of the best places in town for grilled food, **La Casa de Mi Abuela** *($$$; Calle Juan León Mera and La Pinta, ☎ 230-945)* is set up inside an old house and devotes itself exclusively to the careful preparation of positively delectable steaks. Generous portions.

Set up inside an old colonial house, **La Querencia** *($$$; Avenida Orellana 155 and 12 de Octubre, ☎ 229-993)* is in competition with La Choza (see below) to serve the best traditional Ecuadoran food in town. It combines an inviting atmosphere with marvellous local cuisine. Its à la carte selections and enviable table d'hôte have earned it unanimous approval.

La Choza *($$$; Avenida 12 de Octubre, ☎ 507-901)*, opposite the Oro Verde hotel, serves delicious traditional Ecuadoran cuisine in a comfortable setting reminiscent of days gone by. A popular breakfast spot.

Located north of town, the **Taberna Piedmonte** *($$$; Calle Arosemena Tola 173 and Eloy Alfaro, ☎ 433-607)* offers an interesting selection of traditional Italian dishes. The service is amicable, discreet and efficient. Just the place for a business dinner or a romantic meal for two.

The service at the **Vecchia Roma** *($$$; Calle Roca 618 and Juan León Mera, ☎ 565-659)* is courteous and very attentive, while the delicious menu is composed of Italian dishes. The countless empty wine bottles hanging from the ceiling lend an original touch to the decor.

Besides its tasty dishes, the restaurant on the top floor of the Hotel Quito, **El Techo del Mundo** *($$$; Avenida González 2500, ☎ 567-284 or 230-300)*, offers a stunning view of the city.

El Tártaro *($$$; Calle Calama 153 at Avenida 6 de Diciembre, ☎ 230-936 or 528-181)* caters mainly to businesspeople looking for good, simple, international cuisine.

Le Chalet Suisse *($$$; Calle Calama 312 and Reina Victoria, ☎ 562-700)* has a sizeable following of patrons who appreciate well-presented Swiss cuisine. In addition to the usual fondues, it serves a good number of meat-based dishes in creamy, highly-seasoned sauces. Friendly, attentive service.

The **Rincón de Francia** *($$$; Calle Roca 779 and 9 de Octubre, ☎ 232-053 or 554-668)* is the good old French restaurant where members of polite society come to indulge in the sin of gluttony. The menu lists numerous meat dishes prepared according to marvellous recipes from France. The service is unostentatious and a bit slow.

Los Redes de Mariscos *($$$; Avenida Amazonas 845 and Veintimilla)* belongs to the same people as the chic Mare Nostrum (see below). The quality of the seafood is equally high here, but the decor and the service are more informal. There is a small outdoor seating area for guests wishing to enjoy their meal on bustling Avenida Amazonas.

As indicated by its name, **La Casa China** *($$$; Calle Luis Cordero and Tamayo)* is a chic oriental restaurant that serves good Szechuan and Cantonese dishes.

If you're looking for a Japanese restaurant, go to **Fudji** *($$$; Calle Robles)*, which, in the opinion of many Quiteños, serves better food than Tanoshii, the restaurant in the Oro Verde (see below). Located cater corner to the Café Cultura, it is one of the most highly reputed restaurants in town.

If Fudji is full, head to the Oro Verde hotel, whose Japanese restaurant, **Tanoshii** *($$$; Avenida 12 de Octubre 1820 and Luís Cordero, ☎ 566-497 or 567-128)* is sure to satisfy you.

Even if you're a little far from the coast, you can still tuck into some excellent fish and seafood dishes at **Mare Nostrum** *($$$; Calle Foch 172 and Tamayo, ☎ 237-236)*. The main building has a fireplace and pretty stained-glass windows that diffuse the light warmly. The food and service are impeccable.

El Mesón de la Pradera *($$$; Orellana at Avenida 6 de Diciembre, ☎ 504-815)* is recognizable by its flags flapping in the wind. Set up inside a cozy, beautifully renovated colonial house, it

is one of the most highly rated establishments in town. The walls are wainscotted, and three fireplaces warm up the atmosphere. The menu features a number of traditional Spanish veal, beef, seafood and chicken dishes.

At the restaurant in the **Akros** *($$$; Avenida 6 de Diciembre 3986, ☎ 430-610)* hotel, a pianist tickles the ivories during your meal to help you forget about the bustling activity on Avenida 6 de Diciembre. Meat, fish and poultry dishes all figure on the menu.

Le Gourmet *($$$; Avenida 12 de Octubre 1820 and Luis Cordero, ☎ 566-497 or 567-128)* is one of the four restaurants in the luxurious Oro Verde hotel. The elegance of the setting, the attentiveness of the waiters, who could hardly be more discreet, and the unique, inventive menu make this one of the best dining establishments in town.

Colonial Quito

Right next-door to the Cueva del Oso restaurant, **La Cafetería la Zamba Teresa** *($; Calle Chile and Venezuela, ☎ 583-826)* is the perfect place to sip a cup of coffee or tea before continuing your tour of colonial Quito.

The restaurant in the **Gran Casino** *($; Avenida 24 de Mayo and Loja)* is a good choice for a quick, simple, inexpensive snack.

The small, modestly decorated restaurant **El Crillo** *($$; Calle Flores 825 and Olmedo)* serves a wide variety of meat and chicken dishes.

Located at the corner of the Plaza Grande, **La Cueva del Oso** *($$; Calle*

Chile and Venezuela, ☎ *583-825)* occupies a colonial house with very high ceilings. The dishes are delectable and elegantly presented. Folk musicians liven up the atmosphere in the evening. Meat, poultry and seafood flavoured with herbs and spices.

ENTERTAINMENT

Come evening, you can find a number of nightclubs with a very distinctive atmosphere in Quito. Known as *peñas*, these places feature traditional music played on Andean instruments (pan flutes, etc.), whose lively style is characteristic of Ecuadoran culture. Three of the most popular *peñas* are **El Rincón Andino** *(Calle Luis Cordero and 6 de Diciembre)*, **La Peña Ñucanchi** *(Avenida Universitaria 496 and Armero)* and **La Peña del Castillo** *(Calle Calama 270 and Reina Victoria)*.

Rumours *(Calle Juan León Mera and Veintimilla)* is a popular place where travellers come to chat quietly over drinks.

The **Reina Victoria** *(Calle Reina Victoria 530 and Roca)* is a charming little bar that tries to recreate the atmosphere of an English pub with its dart boards, fireplace and simple food. One of the few places in Quito where you can enjoy a good imported beer.

If you're looking for somewhere to have a beer while playing pool or darts, head to the **Ghoz Bar** *(Calle La Niña 425 and Reina Victoria)*. Varied music and a crowd made up of both tourists and locals.

The **No Bar** *(Calle Calama, between Juan León Mera at Avenida Amazonas)*, not to be confused with the Ghoz Bar,

is a small, unpretentious bar that caters to both tourists and locals, who sit around tables and exchange travel stories over cold beer.

The bar **Papillon** *(Calle Diego de Almagro and Santa María)* is very popular with young backpackers. The music is loud and varied, and the place is filled with smoke.

Every Wednesday and Friday evening, the **Teatro San Gabriel** *(Avenida America and Mariana de Jesús; for reservations,* ☎ *506-650 or 464-780)* presents folk ballet shows, during which 60 dancers and musicians let loose on stage.

Movie Theatres

Cinéma Benalcázar
Avenida 6 de Diciembre and Portugal

Cinéma Colón
Avenida 10 de Agosto and Colón

Cinéma Fénix
Avenida 6 de Diciembre and Luís Cordero

More often than not, these three theatres show American movies.

For a unique and perhaps more interesting selection, inquire at La Casa de la Cultura.

SHOPPING

Among the many shops in Quito that specialize in Ecuadoran, Bolivian and Peruvian crafts, a few stand out for the quality of their products. Furthermore, unlike the vendors at the public markets, these places take credit cards.

Centro Artesanal
Calle Juan León Mera 804
☎ 548-235

Galeria Latina
Calle León Mera 833
☎ 540-380 or 540-998

La Bodega
Calle Juan León Mera 614

Olga Fisch's Folklore
Avenida Colón 260

Fundación Sinchi Sacha
Calle Reina Victoria 1780 and La Niña
☎ 230-609

Casa Indo Andina
Calle Roca 606 and Juan León Mera

Handicrafts Otavalo
Calle Sucre 255

Productos Andinos
Calle Urbina 111 and Luis Cordero

Bustling **Avenida Amazonas** is punctuated by peddlers displaying their wares.

The **Ipiales** *(Calle Chile)* market is held every day in colonial Quito. You'll find all sorts of handicrafts, clothing and sundries.

One store, which didn't yet have a name when we were in town, is definitely worth checking out for its wide variety of reasonably priced **musical instruments** (guitars, flutes,

etc.). In colonial Quito on Calle Flores 654, at the corner of Calle Chile, ☎ 225-591.

Quito has several modern shopping centres that are sure to please homesick travellers, these include **El Bosque** (north of town, Avenida Occidental) and **Multicentro** (Avenida 6 de Diciembre and La Niña).

Bookstores

Libri Mundi has the largest selection of travel guides and literature in Ecuador, including a good number of books written in English, French and German.

Main store
Calle Juan León Mera 851 and Veintimilla
☎ 234-791 or 529-587

In the Hotel Colón
☎ 550-455

In the Oro Verde hotel
☎ 567-128 or 566-497

South American Explorers Club
Calle Jorge Washington 311 and Leonidas Plaza
The club sells a variety of new and used travel guides.

Abya-Yala
Avenida 12 de Octubre 1436
This store has a large number of books on the peoples of Ecuador.

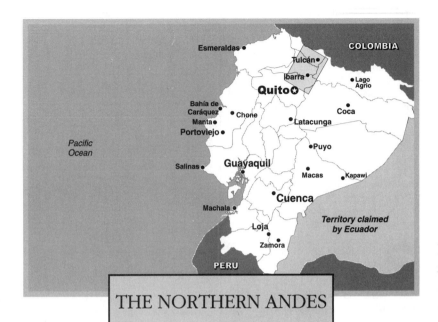

Esmeraldas •

Tulcán •

Ibarra • •
Quito ◉

•Lago
Agrio

COLOMBIA

Bahía de
Caráquez •
Manta •
Portoviejo •
• Chone

Pacific
Ocean

• Coca

• Latacunga

•Puyo

Salinas • **Guayaquil**

• Macas

•Kapawi

Cuenca

Machala •

*Territory claimed
by Ecuador*

Loja •

Zamora •

PERU

THE NORTHERN ANDES

T he region north of Quito harbours a great many attractions, as spectacular as they are unexpected, and an abundance of beautiful landscapes. Once past Quito, travellers have a date with history - the history of the middle of the world. In fact, not far along the route, a monument designates the very spot at which French scientist Charles Marie de La Condamine and his colleagues calculated the curvature of the earth. For its part, the Pan American highway leads to the village of Calderón, known for the production of original figurines called *masapáns*, made of a baked mixture of flour and salt; the highway then rambles along its mountainside route before descending into the magnificent valley of Guayllabamba. Little by little, the mountains spread apart, opening up to the sky. At this point, weather permitting, the third highest summit in the country, Cayambe, is visible,

rearing on the horizon and culminating at an altitude of 5,790 metres. This volcano offers much to gratify experienced climbers. The road forges on, into a region whose main attraction is the celebrated market of Otavalo (unquestionably the most popular in the country), which is held every Saturday, in addition to the regular markets of the surrounding little native villages. These markets are privileged locales where numerous artisans who produce Panama hats, jewellery and other trinkets prized by travellers congregate. In fact, tourists bring home crafts like trophies, using them to add a touch of originality with exotic undertones to their home decorating. From here, the Imbabura and Cotacachi volcanoes are impossible to miss, corralling Otavalo and reflecting their majestic silhouettes in myriad neighbouring lakes. Next come a few large towns and small villages, such as Cotacachi and San Antonio de Ibarra, whose townspeople sculpt wood with surprising dexterity and are admirable leather workers. A little further along, the quiet town of Ibarra is also the point of departure of the famous *autoferro* (a bus that circulates on railroad tracks), which conducts travellers to San Lorenzo on the Pacific coast. Next, as it progresses northward, the road gradually descends, the flora changes slightly and another pleasant surprise awaits: the valley of Chota, a veritable piece of Africa lost in the Andes. Continuing along, the route winds up at Tulcán, gateway to Colombia.

FINDING YOUR WAY AROUND

The towns and attractions north of the Ecuadoran capital are easily accessible. In fact, many bus routes travel the Pan American highway in the direction of these towns. Travellers who plan to rent a car and explore the area on their own will be pleased to know that the Pan American highway spans the country from north to south and that the great majority of towns in this region are linked by it. Moreover, this central axis is in excellent condition year-round.

Pomasquí

By Bus

From Parque Hermano Miguel in Quito, many buses circulate on Avenida America, heading ultimately to La Mitad del Mundo but crossing the little village of Pomasquí along the way. The trip costs about $0.25 and takes a little under one hour.

La Mitad del Mundo

By Bus

From Parque Hermano Miguel, many buses circulate on Avenida America, heading to La Mitad del Mundo. The trip costs about $0.25 and takes a little under one hour.

Rumicucho

By Bus

Many buses head to the little village of San Antonio from Quito. From there, walk about four kilometres north or take a taxi.

The Pululahua Crater

By Bus

From Quito, take a bus to San Antonio. From there, take a taxi or try to find a bus that is headed toward the crater.

Calderón and Guayllabamba

By Bus

Buses leave the *terminal terrestre* in Quito regularly in the direction of Calderón and Guayllabamba by way of Avenida 10 de Agosto.

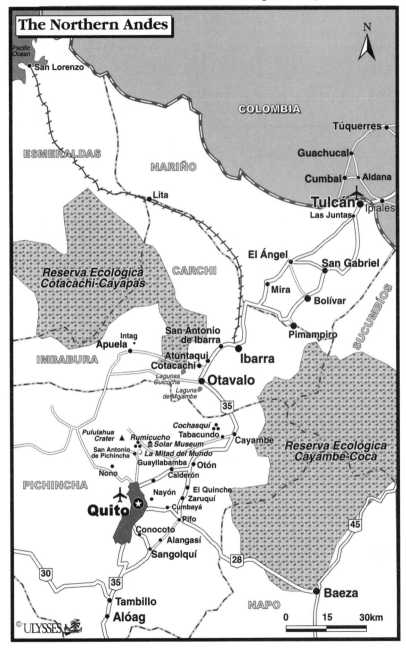

The Northern Andes

Pacific Ocean

San Lorenzo

COLOMBIA

Túquerres

ESMERALDAS

NARIÑO

Guachucal

Cumbal • Aldana

Lita

Tulcán • Ipiales

Las Juntas

El Ángel

San Gabriel

Reserva Ecológica Cotacachi-Cayapas

CARCHI

Mira

Bolívar

Apuela • Intag

San Antonio de Ibarra

Pimampiro

IMBABURA

Atuntaqui

Cotacachi

Ibarra

Lagunas Guicocha

Otavalo

Laguna del Mojambe

35

Cochasquí

Tabacundo

Cayambe

Reserva Ecológica Cayambe-Coca

Pululahua Crater

Rumicucho

Solar Museum

San Antonio de Pichincha

La Mitad del Mundo

Guayllabamba

Otón

Nono

Calderón

PICHINCHA

Nayón

El Quinche

Zaruquí

Quito

Cumbayá

Pifo

Conocoto

Alangasí

Sangolquí

28

45

30

35

SUCUMBÍOS

Tambillo

Alóag

NAPO

Baeza

0   15   30km

© ULYSSES

N

El Quinche

By Bus

From Quito, buses take a little under one half-hour to reach El Quinche.

Sangolquí

By Bus

From Quito, the bus ride to Sangolquí takes about 20 minutes.

Los Tolas Cochasquí

By Bus

Many buses headed north from Quito conduct travellers very near to the pyramids. Ask the driver to drop you at the side of the road. From there you must walk between 10 and 15 minutes.

By Taxi

From Guayllabamba, a taxi costs about $15.

Cayambe

By Bus

Many buses circulate from Quito in the direction of Cayambe. The trip lasts about one hour and costs a little under $2.

Otavalo

By Bus

A great number of buses travel the Pan American highway from Quito or from Tulcán in the direction of Otavalo, but only the companies Transportes los Lagos and Transportes Otavalo drop passengers right in the town. The fare costs about $2 and the trip takes about two hours. Other bus lines drop passengers off along the Pan American highway, and from there Otavalo is about 10 minutes away on foot. On Saturday, buses leave practically every 20 minutes. The *terminal terrestre* is on Avenida Abdón Calerón at Bolívar.

By Train

The Ecuagal tour company provides transportation between Otavalo and Ibarra for the sum of $10. Departures are Saturday mornings at about 11am; the duration of the trip is one hour and 30 minutes. As well, depending on the number of passengers, the company provides links between Otavalo and San Lorenzo, and Ibarra and San Lorenzo; departures are the last Sunday of every month at about 7:30am. Tickets cost $30 and $25 respectively. For information in Quito: Avenida Amazonas 1113 at Pinto, ☎ 02-229-579 or 02-229-580, ≠ 02-550-988. Ask to speak to Hébert.

Peguche

By Bus

Some buses leave Otavalo in the direction of Peguche for about $0.25. It is also possible to walk from Otavalo to Peguche by following the railroad toward the forest, and then turning left onto a dirt road that leads to the Peguche falls. From there, the village is about one kilometre away. The hike takes about one hour.

Iluman

By Bus

Buses from Otavalo conduct passengers to Iluman for the modest sum of $0.25.

Cotacachi

By Bus

Many buses travelling north from Quito, Otavalo or Tulcán carry passengers to Cotacachi.

San Antonio de Ibarra

By Bus

A great many buses leaving Otavalo or Ibarra provide regular service to San Antonio de Ibarra.

Ibarra

By Bus

Practically every hour, several buses from Quito circulate in the direction of Ibarra. The trip takes about three hours and costs a little under $2. From Otavalo, buses travel to Ibarra every hour for the modest fare of $0.30. There are three *terminals terrestres*: Calle Pedro Moncayo at Flores, on Calle Velescaat Boria and close to the obelisk.

La Esperanza

By Bus

From Ibarra, many buses serve La Esperanza for the sum of approximately $0.50.

El Ángel

By Bus

Buses leave Quito almost every hour for El Ángel. The trip is about four hours and costs approximately $2.60.

Tulcán

By Bus

Several buses from Quito and Otavalo circulate in the direction of Tulcán. From Quito, plan for about five or six hours travel time and a fare of $4. The *terminal terrestre* is situated about four kilometres south of the city.

By Plane

The airline TAME provides regular flights from Quito to Tulcán, Monday through Friday. Planes take off at about noon; one-way fare is approximately $20. The airport is a few kilometres north of Tulcán.

PRACTICAL INFORMATION

Calderón

Telephone centre (EMETEL): Facing the central park, on the main street.

Cayambe

Telephone centre (EMETEL): Between Calle Sucre and Restauración.

Otavalo

There is no official tourist bureau in Otavalo, but many agencies that organize excursions to the surrounding villages and national parks also provide tourist information. However, a great number of these are involved in illegal business dealings.

One reliable tour company is **Zulaytur** *(Calle Colón at Sucre, 3rd floor, ☎ (06) 921-176, ⇌ 921-176)*. Zulaytur is owned by Rodrigo Mora, who works in collaboration with Club Aventure in Montreal. As well as providing tourist information free of charge, the agency organizes anthropological and sociological excursions, such as home visits. Through these outings, Mora is attempting to educate tourists about the lifestyles of native people, their education, their religious beliefs, as well as the social and political organizations of their communities. In addition, his agency organizes trips throughout the region: to Lagunas de Mojanda, to Gruta de la Paz and to the *fralejones* of Reserva Ecológica El Ángel.

Telephone centre (EMETEL): Avenida Abdón Calerón, between Jaramillo and Sucre.

Banking: Cambios S.A., Calle Modesto Jaramillo at Pasaje Saona or Calle Sucre at Colón.

Mail: Inside the municipal building, on Calle García Moreno, facing the central park.

Cargo: To send packages by air, contact Ecuador Cargo System I.A.T.A., Calle Sucre 1208, between Morales and Salinas, ☎ and ⇌ (06) 921-088.

Pharmacy: Farmacía la Dolorosa, Calle Calderón at Bolívar.

Laundry: Lavandería, Calle Roca 942.

Saeta Office: Calle Sucre 1005, ☎ (06) 921-819.

Language School: Instituto Superior de Español, Calle Sucre 1110 at Morales, 3rd floor, ☎ (06) 922-414, ⇌ 922-415.

Ibarra

Telephone centre (EMETEL): Calle Colón at Olmedo.

Autoferro: At the end of Calle Chica Narvaez, facing the obelisk.

Banking: Imbacambios, in the WAY shopping centre, Calle Oviedo at Bolívar, 3rd floor, ☎ (06) 955-129 or 958-749; Banco Continental, Calle Olmedo and Colón.

Telephone centre (EMETEL): Calle Sucre 448 at García Moreno.

Mail: Calle Salinas 664 at Oviedo,

Tulcán

Tourist office (CETUR): Calle Pichincha, between Sucre and Bolívar.

Telephone centre (EMETEL): Calle Olmedo at Ayacucho, at the *terminal terrestre*.

Banking: Calle Sucre at Avenida 10 de Agosto; Casa Paz, Calle Ayacucho at Bolívar.

Mail: Calle Bolívar at Junín.

Border crossing: The Colombian border is open from 6am to 8pm; on some days the offices are closed between noon and 1pm or 2pm.

Colombian Consulate: Calle Bolívar at Bocaya.

 EXPLORING

Pomasquí

Two kilometres before Mitad del Mundo, Pomasquí is a little village of no particular appeal that travellers tend to pass through without even noticing. Nonetheless, those who do stop can admire the interior of its church, which houses a hundred-year-old tree-trunk in which is sculpted *El Señor del Arbol* ★, an original and ancient representation of Christ. The many miracles attributed to him by local oral tradition are illustrated in paintings displayed around the sculpture.

La Mitad del Mundo ★★

Fifteen kilometres north of Quito, at an altitude of 2,483 metres, a little lane is bordered by busts of the European and Ecuadoran scientists who participated in the research and many expeditions undertaken to verify Newton's hypothesis regarding the flattening out of the earth at its poles. It leads to a commemorative, and not a little unusual, monument. For almost 20 years, **La Mitad del Mundo** ("the middle of the world") has stood here, marking the exact location of the equatorial line as calculated by Charles Marie de La Condamine and the members of the French geodesic mission in the middle of the 18th century. Visitors to this site can have the unique experience of placing one foot in the southern hemisphere and the other in the northern hemisphere.

Housed inside the monument is the **Museo Etnográfico** ★ *($0.50; Tue to Sun 10am to 5:30pm, ☎ 527-077)*. Spanning three floors, this museum retraces the histories of the different ethnic groups that today make up the population of Ecuador. Many handicrafts, musical instruments and items of clothing may be viewed.

Facing the monument is a tourist complex built according to the plans of a mock colonial town, with no residents. There are many souvenir shops, some art galleries, an EMETEL,

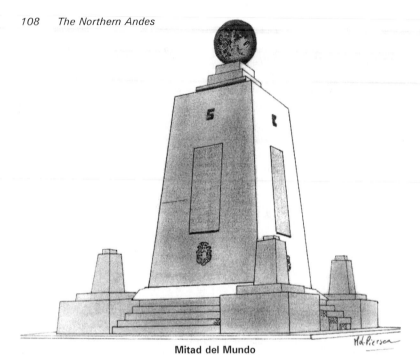

Mitad del Mundo

little fast-food stands and two quality restaurants.

West of the monument of La Mitad del Mundo, a little building encloses a superb **model reproduction of colonial Quito** *($0.50; Mon to Sun 10am to 5pm)*.

Just near the Mitad del Mundo, in the small village of San Antonio, the **Solar Museum ★★** is unjustly ignored by travellers and tour companies. In our opinion, this little museum is much more significant than the Museo Etnográfico, inside the monument of the Mitad del Mundo, because it displays astronomical exhibitions. Constructed by Luciano Andrade Marín on the equinoctial line, it houses maps of the sky, models and other interesting objects, including a fascinating sundial that indicates the time and the month.

The museum curator is Mr. Oswaldo Muñoz of the Nuevo Mundo tour company (see p 75).

Rumicucho

Rumicucho is a small archaeological site comprising pre-Columbian ruins evocative of ancient military citadels, about four kilometres from the little village of San Antonio de Pichincha. The surrounding scenery is much more engaging than the ruins themselves.

The Pululahua Crater ★★

Situated about five kilometres from La Mitad del Mundo, the impressive crater of Pululahua is eight kilometres in diameter and has a mirador that offers an altogether spectacular view into the depths of the ancient volcano, which was still active as recently as the turn of the century. Some people have settled here and peacefully cultivate the crater's arable soil. Unfortunately, the show is sometimes spoiled by clouds obstructing the field of vision. A little trail leads down to the bottom of the crater. A warning to anyone interested in taking this hike: the descent should only be undertaken by those in excellent physical condition.

Calderón

Situated 30 kilometres north of Quito, Calderón is a small, quiet town, that comes to life for the occasion of its Saturday and Sunday **markets.** Calderón is equally known for its popular and unique figurines, collectively known as *masapáns.* These statuettes, made of a composite of salt and flour which is baked in the sun or in an oven and then hand-painted, are curiosities whose mysterious origins reside perhaps in the custom of making offerings on the Day of the Dead. These local, popularly inspired, family-made crafts generally involve finely worked, minutely detailed decorative elements that are combined to form dolls, pendants, brooches or other curios. Among the *masapáns* shops worth mentioning are Folklore Artístico, Figuras de Masapán *(Calle Carapungo 745,* ☎ *822-470)* and, just opposite, Artesanía Carapungo, Figuras de Masapán *(Calle Carapungo,* ☎ *822-476).* On November 2nd, the Day of the Dead, townspeople dress up in bright colours, attend mass, and then visit their ancestors at the cemetery to discuss their lives and their aspirations.

Guayllabamba

The little town of Guayllabamba sits in the magnificent valley of its namesake river. Many fruit trees, such as avocado, ornament the landscape. There is nothing particularly noteworthy here except the beauty of the scenery, which leaves admirers agape.

El Quinche

El Quinche is located about five kilometres southwest of Guayllabamba. Its church houses a wooden statue of the virgin who bears the name of the town, Nuestra Señora de El Quinche, sculpted by the artist Diego de Robles at the very end of the 1500s of the virgin who bears the name of the town, Nuestra Señora de El Quinche. Many pilgrims come venerate the virgin for the numerous miracles attributed to her. The church also houses a few paintings illustrating the most famous of these miracles, as well as other paintings and sculptures by artists of the Quito School.

Sangolquí

Continuing southward, you'll reach Sangolquí, a major Andean town with a population of about 35,000. Despite its numbers it is reasonably quiet, although it comes to life for the busy Sunday **market.** Thursday, there is a second **market**, which, while smaller than the other, also attracts a few curious visitors.

The Pyramids of Cochasquí ★★

A few kilometres from Guayllabamba and exactly five kilometres from the equinoctial line is the archaeological site of Cochasquí, the origins of which date as far back as A.D. 150. Archaeologists report that the site was probably constructed by the civilization of the Quitus-Cara, but that much later, around the 15th century, it was occupied by the Incas before finally falling into the hands of the Spanish conquerors. The site includes 15 truncated pyramids, nine of which possess ramps accessing their apexes and providing a view of the ensemble, laid out in the form of a *T*. The *T*-formation combines two significant elements: the vertical line, called *pa*, signifying life; and the horizontal line, called *tum*, signifying death. The two names fuse to form the word tumpa, which means, tomb, resting-place of the dead. As well, 15 funerary tumuli were also found among these pyramids. The level where the pyramids are truncated essentially corresponds to the height of the tumuli of the Pyramids of Egypt.

An additional curiosity is that the site is aligned with other archaeological sites and natural features such as the volcano Cayambe; the cylinder of Puntatzil, at the foot of the volcano; Cerros de la Marca and Rumicucho. These natural and archaeological landmarks thus form an imaginary line, traditionally known as *Inti-Yan*, or *Camino del Sol*. This expression means "the road of the sun", which is to say the path that the sun took 2,000 years ago during the March and September equinoxes. Observers of the sun and astronomers of the era had thus already determined that the equator passed through this region. They were not far off, because astronomical measurements made 2,000 years later demonstrated that the equator passes just five kilometres south of this site.

Cayambe

Right near the equinoctial line, Cayambe was established at the foot of the volcano of the same name. Situated in the **Reserva Ecológica Cayambe-Coca ★★** (see p 119), the **Volcán Cayambe ★★★** represents an appealing challenge for experienced climbers. During his passage through Ecuador, the famous German traveller Alexander von Humboldt described this volcano as an eternal natural monument. Dairy products and the fabrication of cookies called *bizcochos* make up the essential economic activity of the town.

Otavalo ★★★

Every Saturday, Otavalo becomes one of the liveliest villages in Ecuador, thanks to its celebrated **market**, a succession of brightly coloured stalls displaying woollen and textile products identified the world over with Otavalo. In addition to textiles, an unlimited variety of crafts at modest prices, such as Panama hats, jewellery, assorted ceramics and other trinkets are also sold here, making this locale very popular with tourists. Most prices may be haggled over; indeed, Otavaleños seem to obtain particular pleasure from the game of selling. Skilled entrepreneurs, they seem to possess an innate gift for commerce.

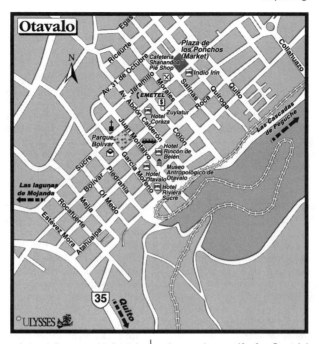

The origins of the delicate and minutely detailed work of Otavaleños weavers, descendants of the Cara people, date back to well before the Spanish subjugation of the Incas. Before being colonized by the Incas, the Caras were established in Otavalo and in the surrounding little villages, where they created clothing that they traded with the peoples of the Oriente and the Costa. Later, the Incas were themselves colonized and exploited by the Spanish. Over the centuries, scores of weaving shops sprang up, and native people were forced to work over 100 hours per week under insupportable conditions, in order to submit to the demands of Spanish colonial management. This unfortunate apprenticeship nonetheless permitted Otavaleños to develop a unique weaving technique. At the beginning of the 20th century, a weaver decided to take up the motif of a Scottish tweed then in fashion. He was so successful that the products of Otavalo have since become renown on a global scale. Otavaleños, who travel the world year round marketing their products, are easily recognized. Men generally wear hats and have long braided hair. Their dress is made up of white pants and shirts, navy ponchos and sandals. Women are distinguished by the many brilliant glass-bead necklaces they wear and by long shawls that cover their heads and shoulders. They also wear sandals and long, dark blue skirts.

The fashion of native peoples was imposed as a uniform by Spanish colonizers, especially hacienda owners (private plantations), who wanted to differentiate themselves from local residents.

Today, it is above all the women who preserve and maintain the traditional lifestyle, which is most noticeably expressed in dress.

For their part, men have replaced the traditional clothing with more modern, Western dress. The long braid is a symbol of virility in men, and cutting it was a form of punishment in the past. In general today, indigenous people who travel to Quito in search of employment do not wear traditional clothing because, to increase the likelihood of landing a job, it is better to be taken for a mestizo than a native.

The densely wooded **Parque Bolívar** may well bear the name of a Venezuelan, but here, as opposed to most parks in the world, there are no busts of Spanish or European heroes, but rather one of an almost unknown native person: Rumiñahui, Atahualpa's second in command.

On the third floor of the Hostería Los Andes, the **Museo Antropológico de Otavalo** *(Calle Juan Montalvo at Roca)* exhibits an interesting collection of archaeological objects, including a 28,000-year-old human skull.

The Fiesta de San Juan is held annually, from June 22nd to 27th, and Otavalo is famous for the festive flair it displays during this period. The Fiesta is the occasion for parades and dances in the streets of the city, Lago San Pablo becomes the competition waters of regattas, and cockfights provide exciting entertainment for native people. The Fiesta de San Juan is one of the oldest traditional cultural expressions not only of Otavalo, but throughout the Andes. Essentially the festival of San Juan is a sort of tribute to nature, through which appreciation is expressed for the fecundity of the earth and the abundance of the corn harvest. The festival begins the 22nd of June with a ritual bath. Celebrants seek out a spot in the mountains that has sufficient water to purify their bodies, souls and minds, and provide the strength to resist fatigue during the days of revelry to come. After the ritual bath, groups of natives divide up and go to traditional little villages, dancing from house to house. During the course of the festival, natives consciously mix traditional rituals with religious ceremony proper to Catholicism. In doing so, men and women wear costumes in a manner that ridicules mestizos, whites, the army and all those who symbolize some form of oppression in their eyes. The last two days are the setting of a competition consisting of violent battles to determine which community is strongest. Unfortunately these fights often take place when natives are in a state of advanced inebriation, and it is not rare for them to degenerate into bloody confrontations that end in injury and sometimes even death.

A little later, from September 3rd to 14th, native people celebrate another annual festival, the Fiesta del Yamor, when folk dance and music groups liven up the streets of the city. Be aware that during these periods of merrymaking, natives drink more than they customarily do, and unfortunately these drinking sessions sometimes degenerate into violent brawls.

The area surrounding Otavalo suggests many appealing excursions. There is a series of little lake-side villages that are popular with travellers, for example.

Just before Cotacachi-Cayapas park is a little reserve called **Intag** (see p 118),

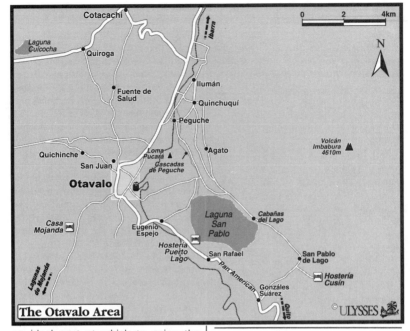

The Otavalo Area

© ULYSSES

an ideal spot at which to enjoy the outdoors in an attitude of genuine respect for the natural environment.

Peguche

A few kilometres northeast of Otavalo, this quiet little town possesses two friendly little hotels and attracts numerous visitors to its waterfalls, **Las Cascadas de Peguche ★★**. Visitors can relax and admire the falls, which flow with effervescent water, and swell with foam, through the hollows of enchanting eucalyptus groves. Many people visit the falls every week, and unfortunately, many of them leave behind their waste, enough that the spot is beginning to be shockingly polluted. If you bring food with you, please carry out your trash. Aside from tourism, Peguche earns some revenue from the sale of textiles.

Cotacachi ★

Located about 15 kilometres north of Otavalo, this city is known for its tradition of skilled leather work. Many shops border the main streets. Cotacachi also attracts travellers with limitless budgets, who come to savour the delectable dishes at the marvellous restaurant of Hostería La Mirage. Just outside the city, **Reserva Ecológica Cotacachi-Cayapas** (see p 118) appeals to outdoors types.

San Antonio de Ibarra ★

About 20 kilometres north of Otavalo, just before Ibarra, the tiny village of San Antonio de Ibarra is populated by excellent woodworkers. Numerous little shops are gathered around the central square, where artisans proudly display their creations. The most popular shop, and probably the most expensive, is without doubt the **Galería de Arte Luis Potosí** (☎ 932-056).

Ibarra ★

Popularly known as the white city, the capital of Imbabura owes its nickname to the many white houses that are scattered throughout its territory. The municipality holds so tenaciously to its reputation that owners of houses in the older section of town that are not painted white are required to pay a fine. Founded in 1606, the town is crossed by the Río Tahuando, and was nearly destroyed by the earthquake of 1868. Those hoping to avoid the teeming and overly touristy activity of Otavalo often choose to stop here and stroll in the streets of this peaceful little city of slightly outdated colonial charm.

In general, travellers come to Ibarra to board the **autoferro** ★★ (a bus mounted on railway tracks), which conducts them to San Lorenzo, a hot, humid little town on the Pacific coast that owes its popularity to the *autoferro*. Not so long ago, the sea provided the only access to this maritime port aside from the *autoferro*. A road built in 1995 now joins Ibarra and San Lorenzo. The city possesses very few attractions, but is enlivened by the sounds of traditional harmonies and rhythms that are the irresistible pulse of the entire population of the Costa. The *autoferro* begins its journey at an altitude of over 2,200 metres, crosses luxuriant forests and many waterways, runs alongside sugar-cane plantations and steep mountains, and finally reaches the Pacific coast. For a panoramic view of the passing scenery, the best seats are on the roof of the *autoferro*! Generally, the *autoferro*

leaves Ibarra every two days, but the schedule is subject to change. Arrive early, as there is but one departure, at about 7am, and seating is limited. Tickets are sold starting at 5am, and the trip can last between seven and 12 hours. The route is occasionally temporarily obstructed by animals or small rockslides. Have no fear though - the train travels at low speeds, giving passengers all the time in the world to soak up the landscape. Return to Ibarra by train is possible, or travellers can continue on their way, visiting the villages and beaches of the Costa south of San Lorenzo (see p 160). Currently, the Ibarra-San Lorenzo service is suspended, but the Ecuagal tour company (see p 104) assures the link to San Lorenzo with its own, private *autoferro*.

Parque La Merced houses a little museum and a pleasant church, **Iglesia de la Merced**, inside which is displayed a representation of the Virgin, Virgen de la Merced, who is venerated for having performed many miracles. The stone façade of Iglesia de la Merced comprises three vaulted archways supported by Corinthian columns.

Parque Moncayo distinguishes itself with a lovely cathedral, and is embellished with many trees. This is an excellent spot for a break from sightseeing or travelling.

A monument in memory of Simón Bolívar stands proudly on **Plazoleta Boyaca**, honouring the hero's victory at the battle of Ibarra, July 17th, 1823.

Adjoining the cathedral of Santo Domingo, the little **Fray Bedón museum of religious art** *($1; schedule varies)* exhibits paintings executed by artists of the Quito School.

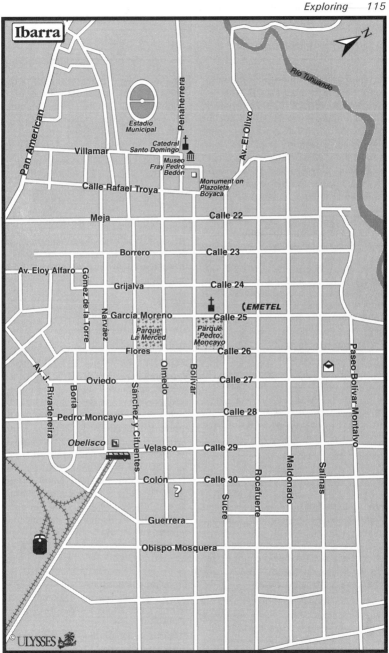

Ibarra

Río Tahuando

Pan American

Estadio Municipal

Peñaherrera

Villamar

Catedral Santo Domingo

Museo Fray Pedro Bedón

Av. El Olivo

Calle Rafael Troya

Monument on Plazoleta Boyacá

Meja

Calle 22

Borrero

Calle 23

Av. Eloy Alfaro

Gómez de la Torre

Grijalva

Calle 24

Narváez

García Moreno

Calle 25

EMETEL

Parque La Merced

Parque Pedro Moncayo

Flores

Calle 26

Olmedo

Bolívar

Av. J. Rivadeneira

Oviedo

Calle 27

Borja

Paseo Bolívar-Montalvo

Pedro Moncayo

Calle 28

Sánchez y Cifuentes

Obelisco

Velasco

Calle 29

Colón

Calle 30

Sucre

Rocafuerte

Maldonado

Salinas

Guerrera

Obispo Mosquera

ULYSSES

La Esperanza

Situated seven kilometres from Ibarra, at an altitude of about 2,700 metres, the quiet little village of La Esperanza is in a particularly charming state of tranquil harmony with the surrounding wilderness. The spot is popular with backpackers, who like to stop over and while away the hours at their leisure. Infrastructure is summary, but there is a friendly little hotel.

The valley of Chota

North of Ibarra, the pleasures of discovery become more varied. The road heaves up mountainsides, then descends again to an altitude of about 1,500 metres. Meandering aimlessly along, travellers arrive in the valley of Chota, the arable land of which is almost entirely devoted to fruit plantations, a piece of Africa on Ecuadoran soil. The region is peopled by descendants of black slaves who were sent from their native lands in Africa to work Jesuit-owned sugar-cane plantations in the 18th century.

Mira

Mira is a mountain town nicknamed "the balcony of the Andes". Leaning against the slopes of the Andean cordillera, it provides a splendid view over the entire surrounding countryside. It is here that eucalyptus leaves are transformed into bank notes.

El Ángel

Situated at an altitude of approximately 3,000 metres, the little village of El Ángel is the home town of José Franco, the artist responsible for the unusual creations in the cemetery of Tulcán. The village also serves as the entrance to the El Ángel ecological reserve.

La Gruta de la Paz

Situated one hour, 30 minutes from Tulcán by bus, Gruta de la Paz is a lovely cave that shelters a sculpture of the Virgin Mary.

Tulcán

Perched at 2,960 metres above sea level, Tulcán is the highest city in Ecuador. Seven kilometres from the border, it is the northern gateway between Ecuador and Colombia and a major drug-trafficking centre. The teeming, bustling city is even more dynamic on the occasion of its weekly Saturday **market**. As well, **markets** animate the streets of the city on Thursday and Sunday. Near Parque Isidro, there is a fascinating **cemetery ★★★** *(Calle Cotopaxi and Ambato)* that encloses a sculpted boxwood tree, representing the town's principal attraction.

Crossing the Border

From Tulcán travellers can take a bus to the border, at a place called **Rumichaca**. Once there, travellers must have their passports validated with an

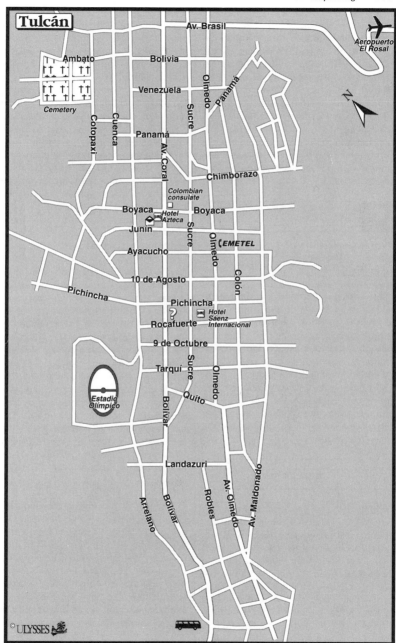

Tulcán

Av. Brasil

Aeropuerto
El Rosal

Bolivia

Ambato

Cemetery

Olmedo

Panamá

Venezuela

Sucre

Cotopaxi

Cuenca

Panamá

Av. Coral

Chimborazo

Colombian
consulate

Boyaca

Boyaca

Hotel
Azteca

Junín

Sucre

Olmedo

(EMETEL

Ayacucho

Colón

10 de Agosto

Pichincha

Pichincha

?

Hotel
Sáenz
Internacional

Rocafuerte

9 de Octubre

Sucre

Tarquí

Olmedo

Estadio
Olímpico

Quito

Bolívar

Landazuri

Av. Olmedo

Av. Maldonado

Robles

Arrelano

Bolívar

© ULYSSES

exit stamp at the Ecuadoran immigration office. Then they are required to walk 200 metres to the Colombian immigration office and have their passports checked again. After these formalities are completed, two options present themselves. Travellers may take a taxi to the Colombian city of Ipiales; the trip cost 400 pesos per person and other travellers are always open to sharing the ride. Otherwise it is about a 30-minute walk along a bumpy road to Ipiales.

 PARKS

Reserva Ecológica Cotacachi-Cayapas ★★

The Reserva Ecológica Cotacachi-Cayapas stretches over more than 304,400 hectares and is home to numerous animal species, such as condors, falcons, deer, wolves and rabbits, which roam the park through fauna that varies according to altitude. This reserve is difficult to reach and is only accessible via the Sierra or the Costa. Moreover, it is practically impossible to enter by one region and leave by another.

Intag ★★

Administered by a likeable and dynamic couple, Carlos Zorilla and Sandy Statz, Intag, a small private reserve, covers about 500 hectares on the western slopes of the Andes, north of the little village of Apuela, and just before the Reserva Ecológica Cotacachi-Cayapas. This is an ideal spot for nature lovers who wish to distance themselves from the beaten path and the tourist hubbub of Otavalo and its surroundings. There are many trails to discover, running slightly willy-nilly through a forest inundated by clouds and set amid a web of rivers, and leading to isolated little villages. The forest provides a habitat for many exotic animals, including ring-eyed bears, howler monkeys, ocelots, jaguars and pumas. Also found here are toucans and yellow-eared parrots, the latter being on the verge of extinction. It is possible to hike from village to village for several days, but there are no tourist facilities in most places, excepting those villages linked to main roads. Travellers who choose to visit these isolated villages are advised to bring tents and sleeping-bags.

Carlos Zorilla is a full member of a regional nature conservation organization which he himself co-founded to promote tourism as an intermediate solution to the issues of mining development, illegal hunting and deforestation. As an example of illegal hunting, it is not rare for poachers kill the bear for its gall-bladder. As an alternative source of income, tourism has a beneficial influence throughout the region surrounding Intag. The environmental organization for the protection of nature is called DECOIN (Defensa y Conservación Ecológica de Intag) and keeps a small office in Apuela.

In the aim of minimizing the negative effects that tourism can have on the ecology of the reserve, its owners accept only a limited number of groups per year. The groups must be made up of about six people and stay for a minimum of two nights. Intag receives only people who have reserved places in advance, because, as a result of the couple's involvement in environment issues, they must sometimes absent themselves from the reserve to travel throughout the country. Those interested in this experience should send their reservations in writing, and well in advance, as the mail service is slow: Intag, Casilla 18, Imbabura, Otavalo, Ecuador. Budget for about $40 per person, including bed and full board

Note that meals served at Intag are strictly vegetarian, with lots of dairy products and eggs; no chicken or red meat.

Reserva Ecológica Cayambe-Coca ★★

Founded in 1970, the Reserva Ecológica Cayambe-Coca encloses the **Volcán Cayambe ★★★** and the surrounding high Andean plateaus. It is spread over an area of 400,000 hectares, from the peaks of the Andes to the Amazonian piedmont, and shelters birds of prey (falcons and condors), wolves and foxes, as well as rather unique flora. Many lakes are scattered over the territory of the reserve, permitting fishing enthusiasts to catch some of the trout that teem in their waters. Tourist infrastructure is minimal, which explains the small number of people who visit. At 5,790 metres, the Volcán Cayambe is the third-highest peak in the country. This volcano is definitely not a training ground for novice hikers. The route to the summit is strewn with crevices, making access particularly difficult. At about 5, 000 metres, there is a rudimentary shelter, poorly insulated and without toilets. Consult a good tour company before venturing onto Cayambe (see p 75).

Lakes

The region around Otavalo is strewn with lakes, each as resplendent as it is distinct, which seduce visitors. A few of these are listed below.

The **Lagunas de Mojanda ★★★** are about 15 kilometres from Otavalo via a rough and climbing dirt road. On foot the ascent takes about one hour. When the sky is clear, the summit of the mountain offers visitors a splendid view over the western cordillera, the Volcán Cayambe and the little villages nestled in the valley. The lakes, of a wild beauty, remain free of hotel and restaurant development. There is but a simple shelter in which to pass the night. As well, the lakes are excellent for trout-fishing. A taxi from Otavalo costs about $7 one-way to the Lagunas.

Laguna Cuicocha ★★★ lies at a little over 3,000 metres of altitude in an old crater about 10 kilometres west of the Volcán Cotacachi. The Laguna is part of the Reserva Ecológica Cotacachi-Cayapas. The view of the lake and its environs is altogether engrossing. Two small volcanic islets seem to float at the centre of the crater, although access to these is forbidden due to scientific studies that are being carried out on them. Boats may be rented to explore the lake (about $16), whose waters are fed by the run-off of melting snow from Cotacachi. A little restaurant permits travellers to satisfy their appetites, all the while observing the lagoon.

Majestic **Lago San Pablo ★** is located a few kilometres south of Otavalo and offers vacationers numerous aquatic-sport possibilities. Sightings of wagtails in the reeds are frequent.

Lago Yahuarcocha ★ was nicknamed "the lake of blood", because a great number of Cara Amerindians were once massacred here while attempting to resist the Incas. At the end of the battle, the bloodied bodies of the defeated were thrown in the lake, changing the colour of the water. This grim past is well gone by, and the charms of this lake, surrounded by beautiful scenery, can now be appreciated. A car racecourse encircles the lake.

Reserva Ecológica El Ángel ★★

Administered by INEFAN, the Reserva Ecológica El Ángel was created in 1992 and stretches over about 15,700 hectares, with altitudes varying from 3,400 metres to over 4,000 metres. The principal attraction of this reserve is unquestionably the *parámo*, which shelters strange plants called *fralejónes*. These plants are covered in little hairs that protect them from the wind, ice and sun. The Zulaytur tour company organizes excursions in the reserve. For information contact Señor Rodrigo Mora, in Otavalo, Calle Colón at Sucre, 3rd floor, ☎ and ✉ (06) 921-176.

 ACCOMMODATIONS

Guayllabamba

The **Hostería María José** (*$12; pb, hw, △; Guayllabamba via Tabacundo on the Pan American highway)* is in a very peaceful setting. Honey is sold here. The rooms are small but clean.

Cayambe

Kept in an old house constructed about 70 years ago, the **Hostal Cayambe** (*$7; Calle Ascázubi at Bolívar,* ☎ *361-007)* faces Banco del Pichincha. The congenial welcome of the hosts makes up for the small dimensions of the modestly decorated rooms.

Located on the way out of the city, the **Hostería Napoles** (*$16; tv, hw, ℜ, pb; Pan American highway North,* ☎ *361-388 or 361-366)* has many small, cosy, pleasant *cabañas* decorated with interior brick walls. Parking is available to guests.

Otavalo

The heart of tourism in the northern Andes, Otavalo offers travellers accommodation options for every taste and every budget. Most hotels are at most 10 minutes on foot from the market, but, for those seeking a little peace and quiet, a few quality hotels are located a little outside the city, near Lago San Pablo or on the road that leads to Las Lagunas Mojanda. For travellers who are planning to visit the Saturday market, it is preferable to arrive in the city two days ahead of time and early in the morning to choose accommodations, because on market-day the best hotels often post no vacancies.

The **Residencial Santa Martha** (*$4; hw mornings only, sb; Calle Colón 704 at 31 de Octubre)* offers small, simple rooms adjoining a shared bathroom. Friendly staff.

The **Residencial Colón** *($4; hw, sb; Calle Colón 713, between 31 de Octubre and Ricaurte, ☎ 920-022)* provides unceremonious shelter for those seeking inexpensive rooms.

In a converted colonial house, the **Residencial Le Rocio** *($6; hw, pb; Calle Morales at Miguel Egas, ☎ 920-584)* proposes clean, very simply decorated rooms. Ask for a room with a view of the volcano. The cordial staff provides laundry service.

Just near the poncho market, the **Hotel Indio** *($6; pb, hw; Calle Colón at Sucre)*, not to be confused with the more stylish Indio Inn (see below), is a small, inexpensive establishment without any special charm that rents clean rooms. The personnel is friendly and welcoming.

The cramped rooms of the **Hostal Residencial La Cascada** *($8; hw morning and night; Calle Cristóbal Colón at Sucre, ☎ 921-165)* and **Hostal Los Pendoneros** *($8; ℜ; Avenida Abdón Calderón 510 at Bolívar, ☎ 921-258)* have little character and are certainly lacklustre, but they are adequate for travellers who wish to stop over for one or two nights.

For the same rate, opt instead for the hotel **Riviera Sucre** *($8; Calle García Moreno 380 at Roca, ☎ 920-241)*, in a comfortable colonial house with clean, very spacious, airy rooms with hardwood floors. Some rooms also have balconies. Guests can wash their clothes next to a garden ornamented with giant cacti, plants and flowers, and there escape from the tourist din of downtown. The staff is very friendly and obliging, and can help organize excursions in the area. This is the perfect spot for travellers with limited budgets who seek quality lodgings.

A lovely, hundred-year-old house, the **Hotel Otavalo** *($12 pb, $11 sb; ℜ, hw; Calle Roca 504, between Juan Montalvo at García Moreno, ☎920-416)* numbers among the better hotels in town. Its rooms, of unequal dimensions and decorated in diverse styles, are laid out around large interior courtyards separated by archways. Insist on seeing the room before making a choice.

There are two hotels called Indio in the city. The **Indio Inn** *($12; pb; Calle Sucre 1214 at Salinas, ☎ 920-004)* is without doubt the better of the two and is considered one of the best establishments in the city. It has 31 rooms distributed on three floors, all of them clean and well-maintained, but those with balconies seem to be a bit noisy. Light sleepers should opt for rooms opening onto the interior court.

The **El Cacique** *($16; pb, ℜ, hw, ctv; Avenida 31 de Octubre 900, between Calle Quito and the Pan American highway North, ☎ 921-740, ≈ 920-930)* hotel offers an excellent price/quality ratio for the thrifty. The rooms are decorated with wall-to-wall carpeting, provided with small chests of drawers, and equipped with little windows for aeration. The amiable owner is named Luis Cabascango.

El Cacique Real *($16; pb, hw; facing the El Cacique hotel)*, owned by Luis' brother, is a modest establishment with rooms similar to those at the hotel El Cacique.

Located just near the central park, the **Rincón de Belén** *($16; ℜ, hw, tv, pb;*

Calle Roca 820 at Juan Montalvo,
☎ *and* ⌐ *921-860)* hotel offers clean, modern rooms decorated with wall-to-wall carpeting. A parking lot is available to guests.

For a few dollars more, opt for the largest hotel in town, the **Hotel Coraza** *($22; pb, hw, ℜ; Calle Abdón Calderón at Sucre,* ☎ *921-225,* ⌐ *920-459)*. Situated right downtown, a few minutes' walk from the market and just next door to S.I.S.A., it rents about 40 clean, modern, bright and safe rooms.

In our opinion, the hotel **Ali Shungu** *($60; ℜ, pb, hw; Calle Quito at Egas, Casilla 34,* ☎ *920-750)* is the best place to stay in the city. The establishment has been open for a little over five years and, year after year, attains an excellent standard of quality. The owners, Margarita and Francisco, are a friendly American couple who warmly welcome tourists and are especially considerate of their needs. In the aim of preserving a friendly ambience conducive to relaxation, they turn away groups in preference to independent travellers. The 16 rooms of the hotel are spotless, each decorated with care and furnished with taste. Two suites were recently added for families. Each of these comprises two rooms, a sound system, cassettes, books, a refrigerator and a balcony. A lovely, bucolic garden is kept in a large interior courtyard in which guests are free to lounge. Folk music shows are presented on weekends. The staff is courteous, likeable and efficient. Travellers who come to Otavalo by car can make use of a private parking lot, guarded by three fierce dogs that dissuade the most brazen of thieves. For a light additional fee, travellers may be met at the airport.

Isolated on the slopes of the Andes, accessible by a rough road eight kilometres before Lagunas de Mojanda, the hotel **Casa Mojanda** *($70 1/2b; ℜ, pb, hw; Apdo Postal 160, Otavalo,* ☎ *731-737,* ⌐ *922-969, mojanda@srvl.telconet.net)* is a veritable little mountain paradise owned by an affable couple: Betty, an American, and Diego, an Ecuadoran. The rooms are all bright and equipped with antique furniture, and offer an altogether incredible view of the mountains. Some of the rooms have fireplaces in which logs crackle softly and flames dance on the hearth. There is a play room for the entertainment of children and the peace of mind of parents, where videos may also be viewed. Six horses are available on hire for outings in the region. For the rate of $25 per person, including breakfast and lunch, travellers may stay in a large dormitory comprising five very comfortable bunk-beds, two showers and a bathroom. In addition, the hotel possesses an excellent restaurant which prepares strictly vegetarian meals (there is not even any white meat on the menu) according to the inspiration of the day. The dining-room is decorated with a fireplace, and the view of the nearby landscape is superb. Weather permitting, guests may see the Volcán Cotacachi. A taxi from Otavalo costs about $2 for a five-minute trip.

Camped proudly on the shores of Lago San Pablo, 5.5 kilometres south of Otavalo, the hotel **Puerto Lago** *($55; ℜ, pb, hw; Sector San Rafael, south of Otavalo,* ☎ *920-920,* ⌐ *920-900)* is watched over in the north by the Volcán Imbabura, in the west by Cotacachi and in the south by Mojanda, and itself offers a superb view out over the lake. All of the rooms are warmed by fireplaces. Some look out onto the lake, while others have views of the volcanoes. The hotel has its own boat for touring the lake. Moreover, this is a great place for photographers. The hotel restaurant maintains an excellent regional reputation, and the staff is obliging. This is an ideal spot for those wishing to distance themselves from the hubbub of Otavalo.

Situated a few kilometres north of San Pablo, just before Otavalo, the **Hostería Cabañas del Lago** *($55; ℜ, pb, hw; on the shore of Lago San Pablo, ☎ 918-001, ↵ 918-108)* offers small, clean rooms decorated with brick walls and grouped next to the lake shore and a miniature golf course. Meanwhile, travellers may experience a profound sadness at the sight of some animals that are caged for the simple entertainment of the curious. Pedal-boat and jet-ski rentals are available.

Founded in 1602, the **Hacienda Cusín** *($80; ℜ, ≈, hw, pb; 10 km southeast of Otavalo, ☎ 918-003, ↵ 918-013, reservations from Quito, ☎ 243-341)* seems frozen in the 17th century. The rustic decor of this colonial house is beguiling, and the main building has preserved elements of its past, such as superb wainscotting and antiques, but an outmoded charm emanates from the 25 rooms, which are very unevenly decorated. A tree-shaded yard permits guests to escape from the commotion of Otavalo. Bicycle and horse rentals are available.

As indicated by its name, the luxurious **Hacienda Pinsanquí** *($80 or $120 bkfst incl., pb, hw, ℜ; ☎ and ↵ 920-387)* is a converted hacienda, whose foundations date back to 1790. It is situated five kilometres from Otavalo and seven kilometres from Cotacachi. The old-fashioned charm of this hotel will

doubtless please romantic souls seeking restful, select accommodations full of atmosphere. Each room is unique and pleasantly decorated with antique furniture. After outings in the surrounding area, travellers can relax in complete tranquillity in the hotel's bucolic garden, and observe llamas peacefully strolling about. Horses may be hired for pleasant excursions.

Peguche

Travellers who wish to flee the troops of tourists in Otavalo might try the pleasant little weaving village of Peguche, which possesses two friendly hotels, very popular with bohemian and international clienteles. To get there, board a bus headed toward Ibarra, and ask the driver to drop you at Peguche (about five minutes past Otavalo). Once arrived, you may either ask the locals for directions or follow the many signs posted on either side of the main street. It is possible to walk here from Otavalo by following the railway tracks; plan for about a 40-minute hike.

Just near the railway tracks, the friendly **Hostal Aya Huma** *($9 or $14; hw, sb, ℜ; P.O. Box 98, Otavalo, ☎ 922-663, ↵ 922-664)* has clean rooms, modestly decorated with regional crafts. Laundry service and Spanish courses are offered, and the staff can help organize excursions in the surrounding area. A lovely garden is kept behind the hotel, where a few hammocks are slung near a murmuring brook. The restaurant prepares delicious meals to satisfy vegetarians and carnivores alike.

The **Hostería Peguche Tío** *($14; ☎ and ↵ 922-619)* is situated a short distance from the road and offers quality lodgings slightly superior to those of Hostal Aya Huma. The central area houses a bar and a restaurant that serves a variety of local meals. On the top floor, the spectacular surrounding scenery may be observed at leisure. The rooms are in cabins behind the main building. They are simply decorated in local colours and are equipped with fireplaces to warm cool mountain nights. It is not rare for llamas to appear suddenly.

Cotacachi

Right downtown, **Le Mesón de las Flores** (*$28; ≈, ℜ, hw, pb; ☎ 915-928*) is housed in a lovely colonial home and offers small, modestly decorated rooms. The cleanliness of the establishment is irreproachable.

Situated just next door to Hostería La Mirage, the **Hostería La Banda** (*$50; ℜ, △, ☀, pb, hw; ☎ 915-176, ≈ 915-873, reservations from Quito, ☎ 02-520-698, ≈ 02-541-387*) seems to commune with nature. Footpaths have been cleared, and visitors strolling them may meet four friendly llamas. Every room is immaculate and possesses a fireplace, antique beds, a desk and a spacious chest of drawers. Whirlpools and saunas are at clients' disposal.

Discreetly nestled in the Andes about 15 minutes from Otavalo, the very romantic **Hostería La Mirage** (*$120 or $185 1/2b; hw, tv, ℜ, ≈; Avenida 10 de Agosto, ☎ 915-237, 915-077 or 915-561, ≈ 915-065; from the United States or Canada ☎ 1-800-327-3573*) melds colonial and modern architecture admirably well. It is surrounded by luxuriant greenery, meticulously kept by a staff of 12 gardeners and crisscrossed by some inviting paths. The 24 rooms vary in dimensions, are named after species of birds or flowers, and are all warmly decorated, each in a different style but similarly charming: canopy beds, colonial furniture, oriental carpets, etc. Each room is furnished with a fireplace which is lit by a staff member every night so that guests may stay warm during the cool nights of the Sierra. As well, every room includes a splendid private bathroom with a very large shower. The hotel's amenities include a heated pool and a lovely little chapel for special occasions. Horses may be rented. There is also airport pick-up service, if desired. The hotel restaurant (see p 127) is considered one of the best in the country.

Ibarra

On the way into the city, on the right, facing the Ajavi hotel, the **Hostal Familiar Imbacocha** (*$12; tv, hw, pb; Calle Cristóbal Gómez Jurado 527 at Avenida Mariano Acosta, ☎ 640-646*) offers simple but clean rooms that open onto a lovely garden that is home to hummingbirds and orange trees. The owner is friendly and welcoming. Do not be surprised, though, if you have to ring several times.

The hotel **La Casona de Los Lagos** (*$18; hw, pb, ℜ; Calle Sucre 350 at Grijalva, ☎ 951-629*) is an old, colonial-style house with clean, warm, and spacious rooms with hardwood floors. The personnel is welcoming and dynamic.

Established right downtown, the hotel **Montecarlo** (*$24; ctv, ℜ, △, hw, ≈, pb; Avenida Jaime Rivadeneira 565 at Calle Oviedo, ☎ 958-182 or 958-266, ≈ 958-182*) offers 35 modern, comfortable rooms with wall-to-wall carpeting, distributed over three floors. Sauna, whirlpool and private parking are at guests' disposal. The staff is friendly.

Situated north of the city, near the Pan American highway, the 50 rooms of the **Turismo Internacional** *($24; ℜ, △, tv, hw, pb; Calle Rafael Troya at Juan Hernandez, ☎ 952-814 or 956-331, ⌨ 956-413)* hotel are all furnished with wall-to-wall carpeting and rather plainly decorated. Travellers in need of relaxation can treat themselves to a sauna or a Turkish bath.

Situated south of Ibarra, at the entrance to the city, on the left, the **Ajavi** *($40; ℜ, ≈, tv, hw, pb; Avenida Mariana Acosta 1638, ☎ 955-555 or 955-221, ⌨ 955-640)* hotel is considered one of the best in town. Its 55 rooms are comfortable and spacious. A travel agency, private parking, laundry service, restaurant and exchange bureau, just near the reception desk, are some of the advantages of the hotel.

Popular with Ecuadorans and Colombians, the **Hostería Natabuela** *($25; pb, hw, tv, ℜ, ≈; 8 km south of Ibarra, ☎ 932-032 or 932-482, ⌨ 640-230)* provides clean, well-maintained rooms, laid out for the most part around the pool.

A few kilometres south of the city, the **Hostería Chorlaví** *($50; ℜ, ≈, △, ⊛, hw, pb; Pan American highway, ☎ 955-777 or 955-775, ⌨ 932-222; reservations from Quito, ☎ 02-522-703,* ⌨ 02-956-311) is a welcome sight to tourists in search of comfort. The spacious rooms of this former hacienda are furnished in old-fashioned style with antiques. A tennis court, squash court, sauna and whirlpool are at guests' disposal.

Tulcán

Most of Tulcán's hotels are rather dirty, noisy and charmless like the city itself. Moreover, the rates for the rooms are higher than in other cities of the Sierra.

Two blocks from CETUR, the little **Residencial Quito** *($4; sb; Calle Ayacucho 450)* rents austere and slightly sombre rooms at hard-to-beat prices. As a last resort only.

For a few dollars more, travellers may opt for the **Hotel Imperial** *($8; sb, hw; Calle Bolívar at Panamá)*. Situated two steps from the cemetery, it offers rooms that are at best simple, relatively clean and safe. Ideal for travellers with limited budgets.

The **Hotel Azteca** *($15; ℜ, ≈, pb, hw; Calle Bolívar, ☎ 981-899)* numbers among the best places to stay in the city. The rooms are spacious and clean, but the beds are not very comfortable. Weekends, its nightclub attracts a motley crew that is just a tad noisy.

Situated two steps from CETUR, the hotel **Sáenz Internacional** *($20; ℜ, pb, hw; Calle Sucre at Rocafuerte, ☎ 981-916)* offers clean, safe, well-equipped rooms.

RESTAURANTS

La Mitad del Mundo

Established 25 years ago, **Equinoccio** *($$; ☎ 394-128)* is located on the equinoctial line. Pleasant little tables are distributed over two floors. Generous portions of meat are served. Folk performances are presented on weekends.

Built in colonial style, the restaurant **Cochabamba** *($$; ☎ 394-263)* invites clients to savour fine international and Ecuadoran cuisine. The service is courteous and friendly.

Cayambe

Paradero Miraflores *($; on the Pan American highway North, as you leave the city)* is known for its excellent *bizcochos* and its homemade cheese.

Next to Banco del Pichincha, the little restaurant **Don Carlos** *($)* serves simple little *secos de pollo* and *ceviches*.

If the tasty aroma of meat sizzling on hot charcoal whets your appetite, the restaurant of the **Hostería Napoles** *($$; on the Pan American highway North, as you leave the city, ☎ 361-388 or 360-366)* lovingly prepares delicious Argentinean dishes. Do not forego the homemade cheese.

Situated just north of Hostería Napoles, the restaurant **Casa D'Fernando** *($$; Pan American highway North, ☎ 360-262 or 360-756)* lies at the foot of the Volcán Cayambe. In a cosy dining-room under a vaulted ceiling, clients can savour delicious filet mignons or marinated trout in front of fireplace.

Otavalo

Pastelería Mi Pan *($; Calle Colón at Modesto Jaramillo)* prepares delicious breads and croissants. Ideal for a quick bite between sightseeing visits or for breakfast.

The restaurant **Le Alamo** *($; Calle Morales at 31 de Octubre)* is an excellent spot for a quick no-fuss bite to eat.

The chef at the little restaurant of the hotel **El Cacique** *($; Avenida 31 de Octubre 900, between Calle Quito and the Pan American highway North, ☎ 921-740)* prepares a delicious dish of guinea-pig grilled on live charcoal.

The restaurant **Alimicuy** *($; north of the poncho market)* serves delicious banana bread as well as excellent fresh juices.

Very popular with travellers, the **Hard Rock Café** *($; Calle Quiroga 504 at Sucre)* is a good place to enjoy a snack and a conversation to the sounds of lively music.

The little restaurant **Asadero Koko Rico** *($; next to the La Cascada hotel)* serves delicious braised chicken.

Chifa Estrella China *($; Calle Colón 510 at Sucre)* specializes in the preparation of Chinese dishes.

The restaurant of the **Indio Inn** *($; Calle Sucre 1214 at Salinas)* offers typical Ecuadoran dishes such as *pollo a la brasa*.

Travellers seeking a friendly little restaurant that prepares magnificent culinary creations *à la française* will be sated at **Olivier** *($$; Calle Roca at Morales)*.

S.I.S.A. *($$; Calle Abdón Calderón 409 at Sucre)* is an establishment that comprises a pleasant little café, a restaurant, a bookstore and a crafts centre.

Facing Plaza de Ponchos, **Cafetería Shanandoa Pie Shop** *($$; Calle Salinas)* is known for its delicious homemade pies, always fresh and carefully prepared. Perfect for a quick bite at any time of day.

La Pizza Siciliana *($$; Calle Sucre 1003 at Avenida Abdón Calderón, ☎ 920-213)* proposes a vast selection of pizzas.

The fare at the restaurant of the **Ali Shungu** *($$; Calle Quito at Quiroga, ☎ 920-750)* hotel is decidedly among the best in town. The menu lists a great variety of meats and fish, as well as fine vegetarian dishes, to be savoured before a glowing fireplace. Folk performances enliven weekends. Friendly, attentive service.

On the glassed-in terrace of the restaurant of the **Puerto Lago** *($$; Sector San Rafael, south of Otavalo, ☎ 920-920)* hotel, diners savour delicious Ecuadoran cuisine in complete tranquillity, enchanted by the perpetual motion of waves on the lake. Fish, meat and poultry are on the menu.

Cotacachi

The restaurant of the **Hostería La Banda** *($$; next to La Mirage, ☎ 915-176;*

from Quito, ☎ 02-520-698) serves typical regional and international meals with a base of fruit and vegetables from the hotel garden. The dining-room is very airy. Its high, vaulted ceiling protects a lovely hardwood floor and pleasant wooden tables.

The restaurant of **La Mirage** *($$$; Avenida 10 de Agosto, ☎ 915-237)* hotel is as attractive to wealthy tourists as to the Ecuadoran middle-class. Its main dining-room is decorated with antique furniture, superb mirrors and French tables covered with linen cloths and adorned with dried flowers and copper utensils. Fine national and international cuisine is carefully prepared, and served by employees in the popular traditional dress of Otavalo. The menu features a variety of dishes, such as shrimp in white wine sauce, duck in orange sauce and chicken fricassee in curry sauce. The desserts are equally alluring, and diners have trouble resisting the delicious chocolate cake... A building with large windows was specially constructed for breakfast service, so that guests may contemplate the surrounding mountains and the many hummingbirds that come to fill up at feeders placed here and there.

Ibarra

The **Charlotte Pizzería** *($; Calle Jaime Rivadeneira at Flores)* enjoys a good reputation for its quality dishes.

The little **Café Moliendo** *($; Calle Velasco at Bolívar)* serves good coffee and offers a variety of light meals. The service is friendly.

Chifa Kam *($; Calle Olmedo at Flores)* has a reputation for the excellence of its reasonably priced Chinese dishes.

Le Delfín Azul *($; Calle Alfredo Perrez Guerrero at Olmedo)* is a small restaurant that presents a copious menu of freshly-caught fish prepared according to diners' orders.

Charlotte Steak House *($$; Avenida Jaime Rivadeneira at Oviedo, ☎ 959-793)* carefully prepares generous portions of meat.

El Mesón Colonial *($$; Calle Abdón Calderón)* offers a wide variety of meat and fish. Most of the fish on the menu is caught in neighbouring lakes.

The cuisine of the restaurant of the **Ajavi** *($$; Avenida Mariana Acosta 1638, ☎ 955-555 or 955-221)* hotel puts the emphasis on regional specialties. The menu features meat and fish prepared according to the culinary tradition of the country.

ENTERTAINMENT

Otavalo

Peñas are establishments where young and old come to waltz to the sound of Ecuadoran folk music. Otavalo has a few of these.

Peña Amauta *(Calle Jaramillo at Salinas)* and **Peña Tucano** *(Calle Morales and Sucre)* are two of the liveliest nightclubs in town.

PeñaTuparina *(Calle Morales at 31 de Octubre)* is also considered a good spot to hear Ecuadoran folk music. It is only open Friday and Saturday nights, and is mainly frequented by tourists.

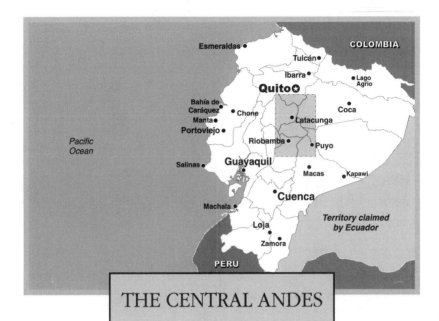

THE CENTRAL ANDES

The road that crosses the Andean cordillera was baptized the "Avenida de los Volcanes" by Alexander von Humboldt. This "avenue of volcanoes", which stretches between many majestic, snow-capped volcanoes, provides a breathtaking panorama that in certain spots takes on an inexpressible, radiant splendour and in others a keen softness, conferring on the landscapes a peaceful as much as a spectacular character that will ravish travellers who's souls are attracted to beauty as contemplation. In addition, mountaineering enthusiasts will be gratified by the presence in the region of numerous climbing possibilities, among others, Illiniza, Chimborazo, Sangay, Tungurahua, Altar and Cotopaxi. Be aware, however, that the volcano Cotopaxi, crowned with a glacial cone of almost perfect symmetry, is as magnificent to view as it is dangerous to climb. Its continuous activity represents a constant threat to neighbouring villages, which have been interred by past eruptions. At an altitude of 6,310 metres, Chimborazo is incontestably the highest summit in the country. The volcano Sangay is located in one of the least accessible regions of the country, requiring about a week of approach before it is climbed. As for Tungurahua, it constitutes an excellent training ground for climbers who would like to take on the higher Andean summits.

The region south of Quito is equally marked by the presence of picturesque little native villages that distinguish themselves mainly with their altogether charming markets, each in some manner different from the others. Exotic and distinctive souvenirs are among the treasures seasoned travellers will find on display here. The train to Riobamba offers a completely different, yet equally picturesque manner of exploring the Andean slopes. After an overnight stop, the train departs again near dawn and reaches the little village of Alausí, famous as a terminus of one of the most spectacular train routes in the world. The railroad descends the highest Andean plateaus of the Sierra and winds down to the edge of the Costa on the Pacific coast...

FINDING YOUR WAY AROUND

Reserva Pasochoa

By bus

Many buses leave Quito southward and drop passengers on the Pan American highway. Notify the driver in advance. Unfortunately it is about a five-kilometre hike to the entrance of the reserve. Departures are practically every hour, and the fare is a little under $1.

Parque Nacional Cotopaxi

By bus

Many buses leave Quito every hour and drop passengers on the Pan American highway. From there, they must walk several kilometres before arriving at the entrance to the park. The bus fare is about $1. If you miss the stop, there is another park entrance a little further south on the Pan American highway.

By train

The train from Quito enters the national park every Saturday morning. Check the schedule before leaving. The ticket is approximately $4.

Saquisilí

By bus

Many buses leave regularly from Quito and Latacunga in the direction of Saquisilí. From Quito the trip lasts a little less than three hours and costs around $1.50. From Latacunga, buses cost about $0.25 and the trip takes 30 minutes.

By taxi

It can be economical for groups to share a taxi from Latacunga. Budget for $30.

Latacunga

By bus

There is no *terminal terrestre* in Latacunga. Buses leave Quito about every hour and drop passengers at the entrance to the town, on the Pan American highway. The fare is about $1.

By train

The station is west of the Pan American highway, at the corner of Calle Julio Andrade and Avenida Aurelio Subia, behind the Hostal Quilotoa. The train usually leaves Quito Saturday morning for Riobamba by way of Latacunga. It arrives in Riobamba near the end of the morning and returns

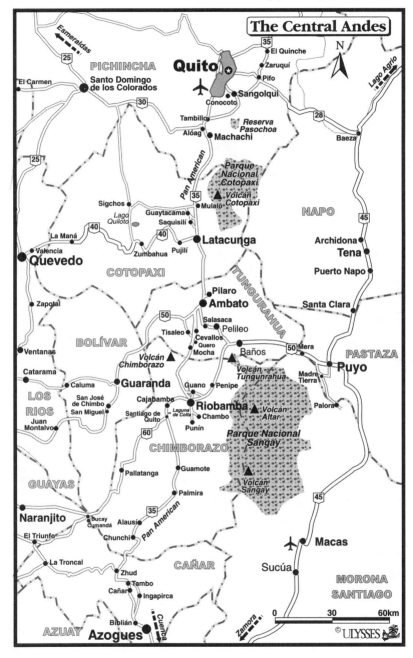

The Central Andes

N

Esmeraldas

25

El Carmen

PICHINCHA

Santo Domingo de los Colorados

30

Quito

El Quinche

Zaruquí

Pifo

Conocoto

Sangolquí

Tambillo

Reserva Pasochoa

Alóag **Machachi**

Lago Agrio

Baeza

28

25

Pan American

Parque Nacional Cotopaxi

Volcán Cotopaxi

Sigchos

Guaytacama

Lago Quiloto

Saquisilí

Mulaló

NAPO

45

La Maná

40

40

Latacunga

Zumbahua Pujilí

Archidona

Tena

Puerto Napo

Valencia

Quevedo

COTOPAXI

Zapotal

Pilaro

Ambato

Santa Clara

TUNGURAHUA

50

Salasaca

Pelileo

Tisaleo

Cevallos

Quero Mocha

Baños

50 Mera

PASTAZA

Puyo

BOLÍVAR

Ventanas

Volcán Chimborazo

Volcán Tungurahua

Madre Tierra

Catarama

Caluma

Guaranda

Guano Penipe

LOS RIOS

San José de Chimbo

San Miguel

Cajabamba

Palora

Juan Montalvo

Santiago de Quito

Laguna de Colta

Riobamba

Chambo

Volcán Altar

60

Punín

Parque Nacional Sangay

CHIMBORAZO

Pallatanga

Guamote

GUAYAS

Palmira

Volcán Sangay

Naranjito

Bucay Cumandá

35

Alausí

Pan American

El Triunfo

Chunchi

La Troncal

Zhud

CAÑAR

Sucúa

Macas

45

Tambo

Cañar Ingapirca

MORONA SANTIAGO

Biblián

Cuenca

0 30 60km

AZUAY

Azogues

Zamora

© ULYSSES

to Quito the next day at around 8am. The fare is approximately $5.

Pujilí

By bus

From Latacunga, buses travel in the direction of Pujilí every two hours and cost a little less $2.

Zumbahua

By bus

Buses shuttle between Latacunga and Zumbahua for around $1. Departures from Latacunga are almost every two hours.

Laguna de Quilotoa

By bus

Buses commute on an irregular schedule between the little village of Zumbahua and the lake. The lake is at the bottom of a volcanic crater, an approximately four-hour hike from Zumbahua, or 15 kilometres. Dress warmly for this hike, as the wind can be fierce.

Chugchilán

By bus

There are few departures from Latacunga. The trip is about three hours and the ticket price is a little less than $2.

Ambato

By bus

From Quito and Latacunga in the north, many buses head toward Ambato practically every hour, while from the south, many buses leave Baños and Riobamba, also travelling to Ambato. From Quito, the trip is close to three hours and costs roughly $2.

Salasaca

By bus

From Ambato, board any bus toward Baños. The trip lasts about half an hour.

Baños

By bus

Many buses from Quito, Latacunga, Ambato or Riobamba drop travellers in Baños. From Quito, the trip lasts slightly under four hours and costs around $3. From Riobamba it is a one-hour trip ($1). The bus terminal is located on Carretera Principal, between Calle Reyes and Maldonado.

Riobamba

By bus

Many buses guarantee a link practically every hour between Quito, Latacunga, Ambato, Baños and Riobamba. From Quito, bus fare is a little over $3 for an approximately four-hour trip. The *terminal terrestre* is located two kilometres northeast of Riobamba.

By train

Every Saturday morning, at about 8am, a train from Quito travels the length of the "Avenue of Volcanoes", conveying travellers to Riobamba. The route is very scenic and attracts foreign as well as Ecuadoran travellers with its grandiose, yet restful landscapes. The next day at the same time a train leaves Riobamba for Quito. Continuing southward, a train leaves the station in Riobamba Sunday morning at around 6am in the direction of Alausí. The fare is about $10.

Guaranda

By bus

From Riobamba or Quito, bus service provides a regular link to Guaranda. From Riobamba, the trip to Guaranda lasts two hours, 30 minutes and costs approximately $1.25. From Quito, buses charge a little over $3 for a trip of four to five hours.

Guano, Guamote and Cajabamba

By bus

From Riobamba to Guano, count on about $0.20 for a trip of about 20 minutes. To Cajabamba, the buses take just under one hour and charges a little less than $1. For Guamote, the trip is about 90 minutes and costs $1.30.

Alausí

By bus

Buses from Quito or Cuenca travel regularly in the direction of Alausí. The trip from Quito lasts about six hours and costs a little over $3. From Cuenca, count on about the same fare for a trip of about four hours.

By train

The train from Durán drops passengers in Alausí after crossing absolutely spectacular landscapes. In general, railway service is provided every day, and the ticket price is approximately $7. The trip can last between eight and 10 hours.

PRACTICAL INFORMATION

Latacunga

Telephone centre (EMETEL): Calle Quevedo Belisario at Maldonado.

Mail: Calle Maldonado at Quevedo Belisario.

Banks: The Banco de Pichincha and the Banco Popular both face Parque Vicente León.

Ambato

Tourist office (CETUR): Calle Guayaquil at Rocafuerte, next to the Hotel Ambato.

Telephone centre (EMETEL): Calle Castillo at Bolívar.

Mail: Calle Castillo at Bolívar, facing Parque Juan Montalvo.

Banks: Banco del Pacifico, Calle Cevallos at Lalama.
Banco de Guayaquil, Calle Juan León Mera 514.
Cambiato, Calle Bolívar 686.

Tour companies: Metropolitan Touring, Calle Bolívar 471 at Castillo.

Baños

Though there is no tourist bureau officially recognized by CETUR in Baños, many tour companies are prepared to furnish tourist information and even provide guide service to lead travellers to the highest Andean summits. However, be wary of con men and swindlers! Actually, for several years now, the little town of Baños has had a bad reputation, as numerous unfortunate misadventures and robberies have apparently taken place here.

Very few individuals in town have the requisite competencies to offer qualified mountain guide services. Here are the addresses of a few tour companies that can provide useful information for those travellers about to set off on mountain adventures:

Tour companies: Rainforestur, Calle Ambato and Maldonado, ☎ 740-743.

Pension Patty, Calle Eloy Alfaro between Calle Oriente and Ambato.

Willie Navarete, Calle Luiz Martínez 270.

Telephone centre (EMETEL): At the corner of Parque Central on Calle Haflants.

Mail: Facing the park, next to the EMETEL office, Calle Rocafuerte at Haflants.

Bank: Banco del Pacifico, just near the church.

Language Schools: Instituto Español Alternativo, Calle Juan Montalvo at Eloy Alfaro, ☎ and ⇌ 740-799.
Spanish School, Calle 2 at Avenida Oriente, ☎ 740-632.

Riobamba

Tourist office (CETUR): Calle 10 de Agosto at España.

Telephone centre (EMETEL): Calle Tarquí, between Calle Veloz and Constituyente.

Mail: Avenida 10 de Agosto at Calla España.

Banks: Banco Internacional, Avenida 10 de Agosto and García Moreno.

Casa de Cambio Chimborazo, Avenida 10 de Agosto at España, next to CETUR.

Tour companies: Andes Trek, Marcelo Puruncajas, Calle Colón 2225 and 10 de Agosto, ☎ 940-964, ⇌ 940-963.

EXPLORING

Machachi

Just east of the road from Quito to Machachi is the **Reserva Pasochoa**. For more information on the reserve, please see the Parks section p 145.

Mineral water comes from volcanic sources, so it is no coincidence that the little village of Machachi, in the heart of the "Avenida de los Volcanes", is the site of a Güitig mineral water bottling plant. During a visit to Ecuador it soon becomes evident that Güitig mineral water is ubiquitous in the restaurants of the greater Quito region. Rich in mineral salts, it provides the body with calcium and magnesium. Few travellers stay over in Machachi, and most pass through the village without even noticing it.

Just south of Machachi extends the **Parque Nacional Cotopaxi**. For more information on the park, see the Parks section p 145.

Lasso

Lasso is a little village of no particular appeal that owes its name to the family that resided in the area during the era of colonization. In fact, the Lasso family was so powerful that its lands extended from the town of Ambato all the way to Quito. The Hostería la Ciénega (see p 148) is still owned by the Lasso family and essentially constitutes the village's only attraction.

Saquisilí ★

About 10 kilometres before Latacunga spreads the little town of Saquisilí. Every Thursday, the town comes alive and becomes, during **market** hours, one of the most popular gathering places in the region. The market attracts fewer tourists than some others, but is more authentic: more livestock and crafts are purchased here, mainly by the native population. Some go so far as to say that this market is more interesting than that of Otavalo. For those with an affinity for the picturesque, the ambience of the Saquisilí market in itself justifies the trip.

Latacunga

About 80 kilometres south of Quito, Latacunga, capital of the province of Cotopaxi, overhangs the Pan American highway at an altitude of 2,850 metres and refuses to let go despite the destructive volcanic eruptions of Cotopaxi. Three times, in 1742, in 1768 and in 1877, the volcano has brutally awoken and poured its ravaging fury on the little town of Latacunga, obliterating it each time. The town has successfully preserved its Spanish colonial flavour, though, with its churches and white houses, built from blocks of grey Cotopaxi lava. Indeed, it is pleasant to stroll through the streets of the town centre, where a sort of torpor suffuses the colonial homes. Outside of the centre, houses have a modern look, devoid of any charm.

For travellers who plan to explore the national park of Cotopaxi, the markets of Saquisilí and Pujilí and the town of Latacunga make an attractive departure

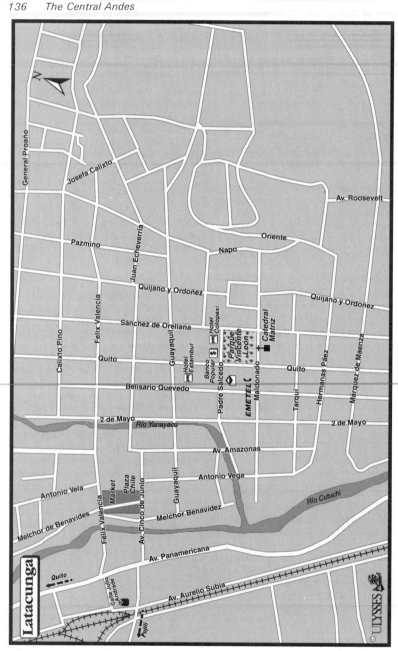

points. From Quito, the trip to Latacunga is utterly remarkable; the Pan American highway skirts the foothills of numerous volcanoes constituting, according to the designation coined by Alexander von Humboldt, the "Avenida de los Volcanes". When the sky is clear, the Volcán Cotopaxi is sometimes visible from Latacunga, its magnificent silhouette rearing on the horizon.

The Saturday **market**, held on Plaza San Sebastían, is the principal attraction in Latacunga. Merchandise of all sorts is on display - crafts (jewellery, accessories), fruits, vegetables and, of course, typical wool clothing, woven according to the technique of the artisans of Otavalo. A second **market** takes place on Tuesday and also enlivens the streets of the town. Fewer crafts are displayed, but an incredible abundance of fruits, spices and vegetables are sold.

Every year, September 24th is the celebration of **Mama Negra**, and a popular local festival in honour of the Virgen de la Merced is the scene of much rejoicing. On this occasion, in fact, the whole town comes alive in an explosion of colour and music, while a throng of costumed dancers crams the streets.

Parque Vicente León is dominated by large trees and carpeted with lovely flowers. It is the perfect spot to catch your breath before continuing on your journey. Facing Parque Vicente León stands **Catedral Matriz**. Dating from the 17th century, this neoclassical cathedral presents an interior of great sobriety, embellished with a beautiful retable. It is worth visiting.

Pujilí

About 10 kilometres west of Latacunga, the picturesque but poor village of Pujilí, cast chaotically in the Andes, comes to life for its traditional Sunday **market**. Travellers in search of a smaller, less tourist-infested market will enjoy this place. The village church, built of volcanic stone, is also quite interesting. Pujilí was gravely damaged by an earthquake at the end of March, 1996, and reconstruction is ongoing.

Zumbahua

Off the beaten path, Zumbahua is another little native village strewn in the Ecuadoran Andes some 60 kilometres west of Pujilí. It is most interesting during the picturesque Saturday **market**. As well, it is one of the rare places where llamas may still be seen. After a visit to the market, do not miss the opportunity to admire the splendid **Laguna de Quilotoa** (see p 146). Time permitting, you can take a five-hour hike to the lake from the village. Otherwise, it is possible to rent a vehicle in Zumbahua.

Chugchilán

Another charming but poor little native village, situated about 35 kilometres north of Zumbahua, past the Laguna de Quilotoa and even further off the beaten path, Chugchilán slumbers peacefully in the mountain peaks. Travellers come here to commune with nature and savour the splendid, awe-inspiring scenery. Even though Chugchilán offers little in the way of tourist infrastructure it is nonetheless an attractive departure point toward Laguna de Quilotoa and its surroundings.

San Miguel de Salcedo

Continuing southward, fewer than 15 kilometres past Latacunga, the little village of San Miguel de Salcedo presents itself as the capital of ice cream. Despite the tininess of the town, many little businesses are scattered here and there through its streets. Travellers with a sweet tooth will find this an ideal rest stop on the "Avenida de los Volcanes".

Ambato

Ambato is situated on the Pan American highway at an altitude of 2,500 metres, 140 kilometres south of Quito. No use hunting for evidence of a colonial past - the town was the unfortunate victim of the earthquake of 1949, which completely devastated it; it was later rebuilt in a modern style on its own ruins. With more than 150,000 residents, Ambato is the fourth-largest city in Ecuador. The illustrious **Fiesta de Flores y Frutas ★★★**, held every year in February, touches off celebrations in town. During this period of festivities, the streets of the city are entirely blanketed with flowers and overrun with hordes of artisans and merchants, and it is practically impossible to secure a hotel room without prior reservations. La Fiesta de Flores y Frutas was conceived after the earthquake struck the city in 1949 and inaugurated two years later, February 17th, 1951.

Ambato is also renowned as the home town of some famous individuals who each made their mark in Ecuadoran history. They include the author of the national anthem, Juan León Mera, the writer Juan Montalvo, remembered for denouncing injustices committed against the people, and Juan Benigno Vela, a politician who passionately defended the cause of the poor.

Juan León Mera was born in Ambato June 28th, 1832. During his lifetime he was known not only as the author of the national anthem of Ecuador, which he composed in 1865, but also as an autodidact, poet, writer and politician. He died at the age of 61 on December 13th, 1894.

Juan Montalvo, born in the same year as Juan León Mera but a few months earlier, on April 13th, was a famous revolutionary. Gifted with languages, he first became a polyglot by learning English, Italian, French, Greek and Latin. In 1858, he travelled to Europe, spending much time in Paris, and returned to Ecuador two years later to fiercely protest the regime of President García Moreno in his writings. Because of his dissension, he was forced into temporary exile and returned to Europe. After the death of García Moreno, he returned, settled in his native city and immediately put his pen in the service of the poor and the powerless. He died in Paris, January 17th, 1889, some hundred years after the French Revolution.

A little younger than his fellow citizens of Ambato, Juan Benigno Vela was born July 9th, 1843. He too was a liberal politician, a journalist, a great orator and an admirer of Juan Montalvo. He died in his native city in 1920, at the age of 77.

The **Museo de Fotografía Zoológica y Botánica** *(schedule varies; Calle Sucre, facing Parque Cevallos)* exhibits photographic and zoological collections with Ecuadoran themes. Innumerable stuffed and mounted animals are displayed, some of which are completely deformed and present curious morphological anomalies, and each of which represents a special case (for example, a two-headed pig). Also exhibited is a lovely collection of photographs taken at the turn of the century by an Ecuadoran Andean mountaineer.

La Quinta de Juan León Mera ★ is the former residence of the Ecuadoran writer Juan León Mera (see p 35). Footpaths descending to the Río Ambato have been maintained amid lush greenery on a surface area of five hectares. Inside the house, every room is open to the public and some of the original furniture is intact. The bedroom furniture is particularly interesting.

The **former home of the writer Juan Montalvo ★** *(Calle Montalvo and Calle Bolívar)* also merits a tour. Montalvo's original furniture and clothing are exhibited.

The **market** of Ambato, held every Monday, attracts the population of the whole surrounding area. Two other **markets**, smaller than the Monday one, take place Wednesdays and Fridays.

Salasaca

This poor little native town is about 10 kilometres from Ambato on the road to Baños and has around 10,000 residents, of whom almost 70% earn a living from craft work. These artisans' incredible dexterity, expressed particularly in the fabrication of textiles with pre-Columbian patterns, prompts comparison to Otavaleño craftsmen and craftswomen. This native community lived in Bolivia before it was enslaved and torn from its ancestral lands by the Incas in the middle of the 13th century. Salasaca distinguishes itself also by the cultural specificity of its residents, who dress in black ponchos and white pants. Some say that the sobriety of their style of dress is a symbol of respect expressed by the people of Salasaca in memory of the Inca elder Atahualpa and his heroism in the face of death.

Pelileo

Just before Baños is the little village of Pelileo, which has been utterly destroyed by earthquakes several times over the course of the centuries, most recently in 1949. Pelileo manufactures denim clothing in all sorts of styles and designs. As well, its Saturday **market** attracts a few of the curious. The road that descends toward Baños, zigzagging along the slopes of the Volcán Tungurahua, offers fantastic, simply breathtaking views.

Baños ★★★

Situated at an altitude of 1,900 metres, Baños owes its name to the hot springs that emanate from the foot of the Volcán Tungurahua. Geographically, this town of about 20,000 residents occupies a key position, on the threshold between the Oriente and the Sierra. Many travellers stop over here briefly before carrying on toward one or the other of these regions. However, it is an ideal spot to relax for a while and revel in the beauty of the lush green mountain landscape. Thanks to its location in the heart of the Andes, Baños is an excellent base from which to explore the region. Whether it is rock-climbing on the slopes of the **Volcán Tungurahua** (see p 146), visiting little native villages such as Salasaca, or simply stopping over for a few days before continuing one's journey, Baños has the attributes of a calm, safe, friendly town. On weekends the town comes to life and attracts many Ecuadorans who themselves enjoy relaxing in this privileged setting. Every year on December 15th, the town celebrates the anniversary of its founding. That day, as well as the next, a large parade is organized, and the whole town takes part, rejoicing to the rhythms of local folk music.

To relax and unwind in the **baths** of the town, it is preferable to arrive very early in the morning (5:30am or 6am) as the water is simply cleaner in the wee morning hours. The water gets dirty later in the day because of the sheer volume of bathers. All of the bathhouses open their doors at around 5am and charge admission fees of about $1.

The most popular bathhouse is certainly the **Piscina de la Virgen** *(facing the Hotel Sangay, under the huge waterfall)* which contains many pools, each maintained at a different temperature.

Next to the Piscina de la Virgen are the **Piscinas Municipales Modernas**.

The bath called **El Salado** *(a few km west of town)* is less popular with tourists but no less appealing than others.

The **Dominican church** was erected in honour of the Virgen del Agua Santa. Its interior walls are covered with paintings relating the many miracles attributed to the Virgin, and every year many Ecuadorans make a pilgrimage to this church to pay homage to her.

The **zoo** *($0.25; schedule varies)* in Baños provokes controversy and indignation. As far as we are concerned, it is inconceivable to keep so many wild animals confined for the gratification of tourists and tour operators. Others find the zoo entertaining. You may judge for yourselves...

About eight kilometres toward Puyo are the **Cataratas Agoyan**. A little further is a pleasant discovery: the trail called **Pailon del Diablo** ploughs through the forest, reaching a picturesque **suspension bridge ★★** from which the **Cataratas de Río Verde** are visible.

Riobamba ★★

Capital of the province of Chimborazo, Riobamba is approximately 200 kilometres from Quito and 300 kilometres from Cuenca, at an altitude of 2,700 metres. The annals of history record that the town was founded by Diego de Almagro in 1534. However, in 1797, a powerful earthquake entirely razed the town, which was then reconstructed about 25 kilometres east of its original location, now the site of Cajabamba. Riobamba enjoys a choice geographic situation, surrounded by magnificent summits, including the tallest volcano in Ecuador, **Chimborazo**, which culminates at 6,310 metres (see p 146). Other, similarly appealing summits are clustered in **Parque**

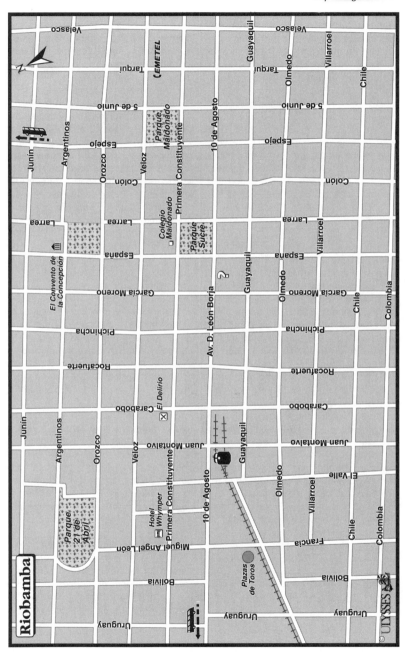

Riobamba

Nacional Sangay (see p 146), including the **Volcán Sangay** (see p 146) and the **Volcán Altar** (see p 146), to the pleasure of mountaineering enthusiasts. Before adventuring in these areas, though, travellers should consult a reliable tour company (see p 52).

A stroll through the streets of Riobamba is like travelling back in time one hundred years into the living memory of a town rich in colonial heritage and charm. Riobamba is also popular with tourists because it is the departure point of the **train ★★★** to Alausí.

The history of the railway in Ecuador goes back a little over 200 years, but its future seems rather uncertain due to an ageing infrastructure, floods and earthquakes that threaten the whole rail network, and frequent rock falls at high altitudes that sometimes obstruct the tracks. Originally, a railroad from the Sierra to the Costa was deemed necessary for the conveyance of freight. Notwithstanding the *autoferro*, a special line of buses mounted on rails that circulates on a trans-Andean route north of the capital, there is only one trans-Andean railway line in Ecuador: the Quito-Ambato-Riobamba line, with an obligatory stop in Riobamba, and then a stretch that runs Riobamba-Alausí-Guayaquil, the total distance for the two legs being 465 kilometres.

Today, while many Ecuadorans still ride the train, most prefer the roads or the airlines. The train, which travels at speeds of barely 30 kph, is generally occupied by tourists who come to behold grandiose Andean landscapes. The best seats are on the roof of the car.

The train begins its route Saturday morning in Quito, at about 8am, but by necessity stops in Riobamba. The next day, the train departs again just before dawn, between 6am and 7am. The stretch between Riobamba and Alausí is not as picturesque as that from Alausí to Bucay (on this last leg the train travels from an altitude of 2,800 metres to 300 metres over a distance of only 55 kilometres!), however, if you plan to sit on the roof of the car from the point of departure in Riobamba, dress warmly as rains are chilly and frequent and the breeze is often crisp. On the other hand, if you sit inside the car for the Riobamba-Alausí leg, chances are poor for later moving to the roof, as most places on the roofs of the cars are occupied from the beginning of the trip in Riobamba. Metropolitan Touring organizes three-day excursions combining visits to native markets, an overnight stay in Riobamba, and the trip to Bucay in the company's private car, connected to the end of the train. As well, a bus conducts travellers to Cuenca for a tour of the city and its surroundings, whence the return to Quito is by plane. Interested travellers can contact the tour company *(Quito, Avenida Republica del Salvador 970, ☎ 02-463-680, ↬ 02-464-702)*. The only drawback is that travellers may not ride on the roof of the Metropolitan car. However, once in Alausí, if there is room, you can attempt to squeeze into a spot on the roof of another car.

In front of the San Antonio de Padua church, climbing the steps that lead to **Parque 21 de Abril** *(Calle Argentinos)*, there is a superb mural illustrating the history of Ecuador through the use of figures from different historical epochs.

A Brief History of the Trans-Andean Railway

This rail link was inaugurated at the very beginning of the 20th century, in 1908, but service was interrupted after downpours flooded the region in 1983. To the great pleasure of travellers, the line was restored at the beginning of the nineties. Since then, every year, many curious thrill-seekers take the train to admire the grandiose spectacle that is the Andean landscape. After leaving Riobamba, at an altitude of 2,800 metres, the train proceeds quietly along its route to Cajabamba, where it attains 3,167 metres, descends slightly to 3,048 metres at the village of Guamote, climbs again to 3,239 metres at Palmira, and finally coasts down to Alausí, at an altitude of 2,814 metres. The train stops for 10 or 20 minutes, depending on how much freight has to be loaded, then skirts the edges of precipices, runs along steep mountainsides, coasts down the slopes of the Andes, chugs through tunnels and crosses waterways all the way to Durán, on the outskirts of Guayaquil, on the Pacific coast. The climax of the trip is incontestably when the train enters a dead-end called, "Narriz del Diablo" (Nose of the Devil), just past Alausí, where it stops, makes a very tight hairpin turn, and starts off again in the opposite direction.

Arrive early, as there is usually only one departure per day, and seating is limited. Ticket sales begin at 5am for the departure between 6am and 7am. The trip lasts 10 to 12 hours.

Around 1860, work was begun on some railroads between Quito and Guayaquil but those plans were soon abandoned. In 1895, while Eloy Alfaro was in power, Ecuador hired North American technicians with the goal of constructing what was known in that era as "the most perilous railroad in the world". A few years later, in 1899, the first kilometres of track were laid at Guayaquil. The construction was making headway, and many villages had been reached, among them Naranjito, Barraganetal and Bucay. However, as workers climbed into the Andes, they were stalled by a sizeable obstacle just before Alausí: an almost vertical wall of rock, a passage called "Narriz del Diablo". Aside from its bizarre shape and its location high in the mountains, this rocky formation is called "Narriz del Diablo" because it claimed the lives of several labourers who were working to forge ahead with the railway.

This particularly hilly leg of the railroad reached Alausí for the first time in September, 1902, and permitted travellers to contemplate the most spectacular landscapes of the entire route. Almost three years later, in July, 1905, the train reached the town of Riobamba. That same year, it attained its highest elevation, an altitude of 3,064 metres at Urbina, and reached its final destination, Quito, on June 25th, 1908.

A few years later, in September, 1915, work began on the Sibambe-Cuenca stretch, which was only inaugurated March 6th, 1965. Unfortunately service on this link was interrupted due to floods in the beginning of the nineties.

Strolling leisurely up the steps, you'll enjoy a very lovely view of the city and its surroundings on the right. If weather permits, the majestic volcanoes whose characteristic silhouettes jut from the horizon are visible, among them Chimborazo and Altar.

Colegio Maldonado holds significant appeal for history buffs. In fact, it was the setting for the signing of the first Ecuadoran constitution, in 1830.

El Convento de la Concepción ★ *($2; Tue to Sat 9am to noon and 2pm to 6pm)* has been converted into a museum and presents various sacred objects, paintings and sculptures dating from the colonial era.

Riobamba prides itself on being the birthplace of several historical figures of national importance. Among them is the scientist Pedro Vicente Maldonado, born in 1704 and deceased in 1748 at the still young age of 44 years. He assisted Charles Marie de La Condamine in his calculation of the flattening-out of the earth at its poles. Maldonado, a mathematician and geographer, was considered a great intellectual.

Every Saturday, the native **market** animates the streets of the city and attracts many local inhabitants.

Guaranda

The city of Guaranda was completely destroyed along with Riobamba by the terrible earthquake of 1797. A few years later, in 1802, a huge fire further disfigured the town's features before it was completely reconstructed. Today, having few attractions, Guaranda offers nothing in particular to travellers except its Saturday **market**. On the other hand, the bus ride to this native village passes through some truly grandiose scenery, which in itself justifies the trip.

Guano

A detour north permits travellers in search of original gift ideas to discover the expertise of the residents of the little village of Guano in making carpets of all sorts. Most shops are located around the central park and the church.

Cajabamba

This poor little native village is built on the original site of the foundation, in 1534, of the city of Riobamba, which was utterly demolished by a powerful earthquake in 1797, west of present-day Riobamba. Today the village built on those old ruins is notable for its picturesque Sunday **market**. A few kilometres from the village stands **La Balbanera** ★. Erected in 1534, this is the oldest chapel in the country.

Guamote

About 20 kilometres south of Cajabamba is Guamote, another friendly, colourful little **market** town. The town attracts many natives from the surrounding area every Thursday, who come to display and sell their craft creations amid fruits and vegetables.

Santa Teresita

Near Guano, Santa Teresita, a picturesque and typical Andean village, is worth visiting, if only for the pleasure of soaking in its hot springs with the aim of reviving the body and the spirit. The temperature of the springs is maintained around a relatively cool 20°C. Next, dress warmly, and admire in perfect calm the spectacular landscapes offered up to the eye from all vantage points in the village.

Alausí ★★★

Surrounded by magnificent mountains, Alausí is situated a little over 150 kilometres south of Riobamba and about 40 kilometres south of Guamote. Most travellers arriving in Alausí have come to take the **trans-Andean train to Durán ★★★**, a small town in the suburbs of Guayaquil. The ride from Alausí to Durán is considered by many travellers to be one of the most spectacular train trips in the world (see p 142). The **market** held every Sunday also attracts a few travellers fond of local colour.

 PARKS

Reserva Pasochoa ★★

Aside from the extinct Pasochoa volcano, the Reserva Pasochoa, situated some 40 kilometres south of Quito, shelters more than 120 bird species acclimatized to the humid tropical environment it provides. It is administered by the non-governmental organization **Fundación Natura** *(Avenida America 5653 at Voz Andes, Quito, ☎ 02-447-343)*. Admission to the reserve costs about $8. Camping is permitted for a fee of approximately $10 per night.

Parque Nacional Cotopaxi ★★★

Decreed a national park in 1975, **Parque Nacional Cotopaxi** *(admission $8)* extends over an area of more than 32,000 hectares and shelters a number of winged species, such as the condor and the hummingbird. As well, llamas, foxes, pumas and bears share the vast territory of this nature reserve.

The summit of the **Volcán Cotopaxi** was reached for the first time on November 28th, 1872, by the German Wilhelm Reiss. Since then, every year, a good number of mountain-climbers attack its near-perfect glacial cone. Although the last eruption of Cotopaxi dates back to 1882, when it destroyed a large section of the city of Latacunga, and no violent manifestations of its activity have produced themselves since then, the volcano is still active. Moderate activity was observed in 1975, expressed as wisps of smoke and a few tremors. Cotopaxi is counted among the highest active volcanoes in the world (5,897 metres altitude), and, while it has been inactive these last hundred years, it could erupt at any moment and is therefore an ever-present threat to residents of the surrounding area.

The refuge is accessible by car, but how far you get depends on the road conditions. From there, depending on your climbing experience, it is six to nine hours up to the summit.

Inside the park stretches **Aera Nacional de Recreación el Boliche ★★** *(entry included in the park fee)*. This recreational area was established with the goal of reintroducing the white-tailed deer to the park. Captive llamas may be observed here also. Among the facilities open to visitors, an information centre gives a brief overview of the flora and fauna to be found in the park. On the other hand, there is neither a hotel nor a restaurant in proximity - only a shelter is available - so those planning to stay must carry in their own food.

Laguna de Quilotoa ★★★

Perched at an altitude of almost 4,000 metres, **Laguna de Quilotoa** is a magnificent emerald-coloured lake that fills the ancient crater of an extinct volcano about 10 kilometres north of the village of Zumbahua. As well as offering a striking view of the lake, efforts to reach the perfectly circular crest of the crater are rewarded by the privilege of admiring in complete peacefulness the many snowy peaks cut out of the horizon and their perfect reflections in the lake.

Parque Nacional Sangay ★★

Parque Nacional Sangay happens to be in one of the most inaccessible regions in Ecuador. It stretches over an area of 271,000 hectares and encompasses the Sangay, Tungurahua and Altar volcanoes. The flora changes radically according to altitude and location; for example, visitors can stroll through a humid tropical forest that opens abruptly onto cold, snowy plateaus. Great numbers of amphibians and fish inhabit the park's many lakes and rivers. Be aware that a visit to this park requires good physical conditioning, a minimum stay of eight days, and necessitates a group of at least five people. Travellers planning such endeavour should consult a good tour company (see p 52).

The **Volcán Sangay ★★**, reaching an altitude of 5,200 metres, represents an appealing challenge for thrill-seekers. As the summit is approached, grumbling from the depths intensifies and the sharpening odour of sulphur teases the nostrils.

At 5,020 metres, the **Volcán Tungurahua ★★** is excellent training ground for higher climbs such as Chimborazo, which peaks at an altitude of 6,310 metres. Nonetheless, it is dangerous to venture onto it without a qualified guide.

Once named "Capac Urcu", which signifies "majestic mountain", the **Volcán Altar ★★** received its new name with the arrival of the conquistadors. It culminates at 5,320 metres and is without doubt one of the most difficult summits to conquer in Ecuador. In fact, it was not until July 7th, 1963 that a group of Italians (Mariano Tremonti, Ferdinando Gaspard and Claudio Zardini) succeeded in attaining its pinnacle. Nonetheless, patient and experienced mountaineers are rewarded for their efforts on the Altar by magnificent views of landscapes dotted with superb and mysterious lakes. In fact, each of these lakes possesses a different water colour: blue, yellow, green, etc.

Volcán Chimborazo ★★★

Even though Chimborazo (6,310 m) is not considered the tallest mountain in the world, it remains incontestably the highest summit in the Ecuadoran Andes. At one time the high summits of the Peruvian and Chilean Andean cordillera, and even those of the Himalayan range were still unknown. Beginning in 1802, Alexander von Humboldt made several attempts to reach the high icy summit of Chimborazo. Alas, he never succeeded. After many successive failures, he calculated that he had climbed the cordillera to an altitude of close to 5,880 metres. Shortly before his death, in 1859, Humboldt congratulated himself for having attained an altitude that no man before him had reached. About 20 years later, on January 4th, 1880, Edward Whymper beat Humboldt's record by being the first climber to conquer the peak of Chimborazo, at 6,310 metres.

Chimborazo rewards the efforts of those who have the courage, the patience and the temerity to ascend the slopes to its summit with superlative landscapes.

There are two shelters on the trail to the summit. The second is at an altitude of 5,000 metres and constitutes the highest shelter in the country. Before taking on Chimborazo, climbers must ensure that their cardiovascular system is acclimatized to the altitude. Take the time to stay at least four days at least 3,000 metres above sea level before hiking any higher, lest you risk suffering from *soroche* (mountain sickness).

Reserva Faunística Chimborazo ★

Situated on the slopes of majestic Chimborazo, the Chimborazo wildlife reserve is noteworthy for its many vicuñas and llamas, reintroduced with the goals of preservation and reproduction. Hummingbirds, condors and pumas also cohabit in this reserve.

Laguna de Colta ★

Just near the town of Cajabamba, a road encircles lovely Laguna de Colta and permits tranquil observation of the landscape.

 # OUTDOOR ACTIVITIES

 ## Mountain Climbing in the Andes

Here are the addresses of some tour companies in Baños and Riobamba that can furnish practical information for travellers planning to venture into the mountains; see p 75 for other companies.

Willie Navarete: Calle Luiz Martinez 270, Baños.

Rainforestur: Calle Ambato at Maldonado, Baños, ☎ 740-423.

Pension Patty: Calle Eloy Alfaro 556, Baños.

Marcelo Puruncajas: Colón 2225 at 10 de Agosto, Riobamba, ☎ 940-963, ≈ 940-963

 ## Cycling

In downtown **Baños** it is feasible to rent a bicycle and ride to the town of **Puyo**. This little trip uncovers the marvels of nature. Breathtaking landscapes, valleys, waterways, etc. offer themselves up to tour view on either side of the road. Upon arrival in Puyo return to Baños by bus, the bicycle stowed on the roof. The trip is about

60 kilometres. Below are the addresses of some places that rent bicycles.

Rainforestur: Calle Ambato at Maldonado, ☎ 740-423.

Hostal Plantas y Blancos: Calle Luis Martínez at 12 de Noviembre, ☎ 740-044.

Café Hood: Avenida 16 de Diciembre at Luis Martínez, ☎ 740-516.

 Hiking

Going south on Calle Maldonado in **Baños**, you'll find a little trail that leads to the **cross of Bellavista**. "Bellavista" means "beautiful view" and this spot is appropriately designated as the view is simply magnificent!

 ACCOMMODATIONS

Lasso

Four kilometres from the Pan American highway, a bumpy and tortuous lane, bordered on either side by magnificent, hundred-year-old eucalyptus trees of inexpressible beauty, leads to the **Hostería la Ciénega** *($50; pb, hw, ℜ; about 10 km north of Latacunga, ☎ 719-052, ☞ 719-182; reservations from Quito, Calle Luis Cordero 1442 and Avenida Amazonas, ☎ 02-541-337, ☞ 02-549-126)*. Founded more than 350 years ago, this old hacienda is rich with history and enjoys an enchanting setting in the heart of the "Avenida de los Volcanes". Unfortunately the splendour of the architecture of the main building does not extend to the rooms. The building is constructed of large stones, the interior walls are wood-panelled and the stairs are of stone. Some rooms have conserved traces of their past, but in general they are quaint, well-furnished and well-equipped. Their walls bear silent testimony to a bygone era, but murmur, to those who lend an ear, the tales of famous travellers who have stayed here, such as French scientists Charles Marie de La Condamine and German naturalist Alexander von Humboldt.

Elsewhere, horses may be rented for a tranquil promenade over the vast 10-hectare property of the hacienda. As well, hiking trails, a tennis court and a billiard room are at guests' disposal. The service is friendly but relatively slow. It is possible to visit the little markets in the surrounding area or Parque Nacional Cotopaxi. Lodging here can be an appealing experience, although a little expensive. If travelling by car from Quito on the Pan American highway, just before arriving at the little village of Lasso, a little before the Texaco gas station on the left, turn right. If you pass the station, backtrack. Buses that run on the Pan American highway drop passengers four kilometres from the *hostería*. If you choose to travel by bus, contact hotel personnel ahead of time to be picked up. Finally, the train from Quito passes every Saturday morning, but travellers are then required to walk a few kilometres to reach the hotel. Check the train schedule.

Latacunga

Hotel rooms in Latacunga are modestly decorated and offer but limited comfort and an occasional lack of cleanliness. Travellers with ampler budgets who desire a little more luxury can choose the hotels situated a little way outside the town, either south, in the town of Salcedo, at Hostería Rumipamba de las Rosas, or north, in the little village of Lasso, at Hostería la Ciénega.

Situated just near the market, the rooms of the **Hotel Cotopaxi** *($8; ℜ; Parque Vicente León,* ☎ *801-310)* lack charm to be sure, but are perfectly acceptable for one night. On the other hand, some rooms offer a lovely view of the Parque Vicente León.

The **Hotel Estambul** *($12; Calle Belisario Quevedo 7340 and Salcedo,* ☎ *800-354)* is without doubt one of the best budget hotels in Latacunga. Its rooms are clean enough, and the smiling staff can even organize excursions in the area for guests.

Facing the Cotopaxi bus cooperative, the **Hostal Quilotoa** *($12; hw; Pan American hwy,* ☎ *800-099)* offers little, noisy rooms that prove relatively clean. Its location, on the Pan American highway, is advantageous to travellers wishing to rise early to take the bus.

San Miguel de Salcedo

Upon arrival at the **Hostería Rumipamba de las Rosas** *($60; pb, hw, ≈, ℜ; Pan American highway South, 10 km south of Latacunga,* ☎ *726-128, 726-306 or 727-103; reservations in Quito, Calle Orellana 1811, Edificio El Cid,* ☎ *02-507-121 or 02-568-884)*, a charming and imposing antique cash register adorns the reception area, giving guests an idea of the picturesque, but unextravagant, style that awaits in the rooms. In fact, the walls of the rooms are all individually decorated with old-fashioned ploughing implements and other original antiques.

French-owned, this establishment is an ideal resting place, situated on the road through the Andean cordillera. Behind the hotel, a giant cactus garden is a pleasant place to stroll about after a day on a bus or climbing. Horses may be rented to explore the surrounding area. A pool and tennis courts complete the list of hotel amenities. The staff is friendly and considerate.

Zumbahua

Those who are crazy for heights and want to treat themselves to a picturesque sojourn at a reasonable price have a date at 3,854 metres with the **Cabañas Quilotoa** *($8; ℜ)*. The courteous personnel organizes excursions in the area. The cuisine is composed of traditional dishes, and the fireplace in the living room heats the cold nights of the high Andean plateaus. To reach the place, travel first to Latacunga. From there, buses leave practically every hour for Zumbahua.

Chugchilán

The Black Sheep Inn *($8; ℜ)* presents itself as just the place for travellers wishing to adventure off the beaten path in the Ecuadoran Andes. The pleasant family atmosphere is doubtless created by the warm welcome of the hosts, who will help arrange for trips to Laguna de Quilotoa or simple explorations of the region at guests' own pace. Many vegetarian dishes are prepared according to the inspiration of the day.

Ambato

Most hotels in Ambato are in the image of the town - that is to say, modern and exempt of colonial charm.

The **Hostal America** *($8; Calle Vela 737 at Juan León Mera, next to Parque 12 de Noviembre)* has small, spartan but relatively clean rooms, that are perfectly acceptable for travellers of limited means.

The **Hotel Vivero** *($14; hw, pb; Calle Juan León Mera at Cevallos, ☎ 821-100)* offers suitable, charmless, relatively clean rooms of moderate comfort, but its location, right downtown, is a considerable advantage.

Facing the restaurant El Alamo Chalet, the **Hotel Cevallos** *($15; hw, pb; Calle Cevallos at Juan Montalvo, ☎ 847-457, 824-860 or 824-877)* rents summarily decorated rooms that will satisfy travellers planning to stay one or two nights.

Situated east of the city, in the quiet residential neighbourhood of Miraflores, the **Hotel Florida** *($30; pb, hw, tv; Avenida Miraflores 1131, ☎ 843-040 or 843-074)* rents very clean but nondescript rooms.

For the same rate, the **Hotel Villa Hilda** *($30; pb, hw, ℜ; Avenida Miraflores 12 at Las Lilas, ☎ 840-700 or 845-571)* offers clean rooms that combine comfort and function. Try to choose one with a balcony offering a lovely view of the Río Ambato, ideal for sitting and resting after a day in the city.

The **Hotel Miraflores** *($30; pb, hw, ℜ; Avenida Miraflores 227, ☎ 843-224 or 844-395; reservations in Quito, Rumipamba 705 at Amazonas, ☎ 02-452-233 or 02-435-291)* offers clean, good-sized rooms that are functionally furnished but deprived of any superfluous ornamentation.

Just next to the CETUR office, a few minutes on foot from the main tourist attractions, the **Hotel Ambato** *($48; tv, pb, hw, ℜ; Calle Guayaquil and Rocafuerte, ☎ 827-598 or 827-599)* is without a doubt the best hotel in town. Its rooms prove modern, clean, and bright, and some offer a lovely view of the Río Ambato.

Baños

Baños has countless little inexpensive hotels that will satisfy travellers with limited budgets. Meanwhile, people seeking comfort and tranquillity will be happy to learn that, for a few years now, hotel infrastructure has been developing, resulting in the appearance of a few luxury hotels.

The **Hostal El Castillo** *($6; pb; Calle Luis Martínez at Santa Clara, ☎ 740-285)* rents little, quiet rooms that are perfectly acceptable for travellers of limited means.

The **Pension Patty** *($6; sb; Calle Eloy Alfaro 554)* has become, over the years, a veritable institution in Baños. Above all a meeting place for travellers enamoured with low-budget adventure, this little hotel offers simple, reasonably clean, modestly decorated rooms arranged around an interior courtyard. The owner is a mountain guide; he organizes mountain excursions and rents equipment.

The **Hostal Las Orquideas** *($6; Calle Rocafuerte at Tomás Haflants, ☎ 740-911)* is another place that will satisfy travellers of limited means. The rooms are small, and at best simple, but the staff is likeable.

The **Hospedaje Santa Cruz** *($8; pb, hw; Calle 16 de Diciembre at Montalvo, ☎ 740-648)* offers simple, cramped rooms that are a little noisy but are suitable to those with limited budgets.

Two steps from the Basílica de la Virgen, the pleasant **Banana Bar Bed & Breakfast** *($9 bkfst incl.; sb, hw; Calle 12 de Noviembre, ☎ 740-126)* is owned by the sister of Carmen, the co-owner of the Luna Runtún Resort. Here, there is a triple room, two double rooms and one room that can accommodate a family of four. The establishment offers a laundry service, and its staff is smiling and wants nothing more than to be of service. Decidedly one of the best price-quality ratios in town.

Situated next to the tour company Rainforest Tours, facing Parque Central, the **Hostal Flor de Oriente** *($15; hw, pb, ℜ; Calle Ambato at Maldonado, ☎ 740-058 or 740-717)* rents clean, well-equipped, safe rooms without any particular charm. Some rooms have balconies. Private, safe parking is available.

Without a doubt one of the most prized, economical localities in town, the **Hostal Plantas y Blancos** *($15; hw, pb, ℜ; Calle Luis Martínez at 12 de Noviembre, ☎ 740-044)* presents itself, as its Spanish name indicates, as an establishment decorated with plants that adorn the white walls of its rooms. Rigorously maintained by its likeable French owner, this establishment also possesses a pleasant rooftop terrace where guests may lounge at their leisure while watching the scenery. There is a rental service for mountain bikes, motorcycles, and even all-terrain vehicles.

The charming **Café Cultura** *($15; sb, ℜ; Avenida Montalvo at Santa Clara, ☎ 740-419)* belongs to the same owners as the one in Quito. This old colonial house offers its guests an informal and safe ambience. Although cramped, the rooms are clean and arranged around an interior courtyard embellished with a flower garden that permits guests to escape the bustle of the streets of Baños.

Situated less than five minutes by foot from the downtown market, the warm **Isla de Baños** *($20; pb, hw, ℜ; Calle Tomás Haflants 131 at Juan Montalvo, ☎ 740-315)* is owned by a friendly German couple who are happy to help with guests' plans. Distributed over two floors, its 17 rooms are clean and well-maintained, and some of them offer beautiful views of the valley of Tungurahua. A lounge that opens onto a lush exterior courtyard houses a billiard table and permits travellers to escape from the ambient hubbub. ISIC or Youth Hostel card holders are offered free breakfast.

Situated opposite the Piscina de la Virgen, the rooms of the **Hotel Sangay** *($20 or $40 bkfst incl.; pb, ℜ, hw, ◻, ≈, ctv; Calle Plazoleta Isidorio Ayora 101, ☎ 740-917, ≠ 740-056; in Quito, at the tour company Sangay Touring, ☎ 02-542-476, ≠ 02-230-738)* are distributed in two sections and are among the best in town. On one side are modern rooms, while on the other are warmer, slightly smaller rooms. This establishment provides a heated pool, a sauna, a billiard room and a ping-pong table, as well as tennis and squash courts. Moreover, the personnel organizes all sorts of excursions in the surrounding area.

Just near Isla de Baños, the **Hostería Monte Selva** *($50; hw, pb, ≈, ℜ; Calle Tomás Halflants and Montalvo, ☎ 740-566 or 820-068, ⊷ 854-685)* has 12 *cabañas* scattered on the slopes of the mountain, on either side of a stream and a stairway that runs parallel to it. All of the red-brick-walled *cabañas* are surrounded by abundant greenery and are principally designed to accommodate families or groups, offering lots of storage space yet remaining bright. An in-ground swimming pool, a bar and a restaurant are some of the luxury amenities offered at this establishment.

Situated at the entrance to the town, away form the hustle and bustle of Baños, the **Cabañas Bascun** *($35; ℜ, ◯, ≈, pb, hw, tv; ☎ 740-334)* constitutes another very pleasant place to spend a vacation. The rooms are clean, nondescript and well-maintained. This hotel benefits from excellent facilities that are sure please travellers, among them a pool, a sauna and private parking.

In an excellent location, with a likeable older couple as owners, the **Hotel Villa Gertrudis** *($35; ℜ; Avenida Montalvo 2075, ☎ 740-441, ⊷ 740-442)* is a converted old house that offers travellers slightly austere, clean and safe rooms.

The **Luna Runtún Resort** *($70, $110 with a splendid view of the valley; ℜ, hw, pb; ☎ 740-882 or 740-883, ⊷ 03-740-376 or 740-309, Runtun@ecua.net.ec)* is situated about 10 minutes by taxi from downtown, on a very bumpy road that, despite the occasional sign, seems to lead to nowhere. Fear not, this is not a hoax, and your efforts will be rewarded once you reach 2,100 metres. Once on the grounds, it is difficult to reproach this establishment, which has a choice location for a peaceful, romantic sojourn in the Ecuadoran Andes. The hotel is nestled in a spectacular setting, and its colonial architecture harmonizes marvellously with the surrounding nature. According to one of the Swiss-French owners, Olivier, while the hotel is not engaged in an ecological vocation, the proprietors are conscious of the need to preserve nature in its present state. Thus, all organic waste is composted, and glass and plastic are immediately recycled. Moreover, the owners grow their own fruit and vegetables, and use no pesticides. As well, Olivier and his wife Carmen, are actively involved in the community of Baños, teaching composting methods. Briefly put, as indicated by its advertising slogan, *"Un paraíso en las montañas"*, the *hostería* presents itself as a true mountain paradise. All of the rooms are impeccable, spacious and warmly decorated with antique furniture. There is no risk of being bothered by the irritating noise of the telephone and the television, as the rooms simply are not equipped with them. As well, the staff speaks Spanish, French, German and English, and can easily organize all sorts of excursions in the area. Finally, the magnificent view of Baños and its surroundings that may be had from some of the rooms is simply enchanting!

Riobamba

The best hotels in Riobamba are found a little outside the city.

The rooms at the **Hotel Puruhúa** *($6; Calle Daniel León Borja 4360, between Calle Valle and Juan Montalvo)* could do with a spit and polish and a bit of charm but are acceptable for an inexpensive overnight stay. Located very close to the *terminal terrestre*.

The **Hotel Internacional Segovia** *($8; pb; Calle Primera Constituyente 2228 and Espejo, ☎ 961-259)* offers austere, noisy, but nonetheless economical rooms that are perfectly suitable for adventurers.

The **Hotel Humbolt** *($15; pb, hw; Avenida León Borja 3548, ☎ 961-788 or 940-814)* rents economical, clean rooms adorned with wall-to-wall carpeting. There is a parking lot for guests, and the friendly personnel organizes excursions to Chimborazo.

For the same rate, the **Hotel Whymper** *($15; pb, hw, ℜ; Avenida Miguel Angel León 2310 at Primera Constituyente, ☎ 964-572 or 963-137, ╘ 968-137)*, situated two blocks from Hotel Humbolt, rents spacious rooms of moderate comfort. Travellers with cars can conveniently park them in the hotel's secure lot.

Situated just near Parque Sucre and less than 10 minutes on foot from the station, the **Hostal Montecarlo** *($25; pb, tv, ℜ; Calle 10 de Agosto 2541, between García Moreno and España, ☎ 960-557)* offers clean, well-equipped rooms.

Located behind Hotel El Galpón, the **Hotel Chimborazo Internacional** *($25; ≈, ℜ, pb, hw, ⌂; Calle Argentinos at Nogales, ☎ 963-474, 963-475 or 963-473)* provides modern amenities such as a pool and a discotheque, in addition to well-equipped rooms.

The **Hotel El Galpón** *($28; ≈, ℜ, pb, hw, ⌂; Calle Argentinos at Zambrano, ☎ 960-981, 960-982 or 960-983)* offers about 50 clean, modern, poorly decorated rooms, which have definitely seen better days.

For travellers wishing to distance themselves from the noise of the city, the **Hostería El Troje** *($25; pb, hw, ℜ, ≈; ☎ 960-826 or 964-572)*, situated four kilometres southeast of Riobamba, enjoys a relaxing setting; it is surrounded by eucalyptus trees and offers a welcome list of facilities, including a heated pool, a tennis court and a bar. As for the rooms, they are all clean, spacious, painted in pastel tones and equipped with comfortable beds. Some offer a lovely view of the area and are adorned with a fireplace. The personnel is friendly, the service attentive, and folk entertainment enlivens weekends.

Also located a little outside the city, three kilometres north of Riobamba, on the road to the little village of Guano, the **Hostería Abraspungu** *($30; ℜ, pb, hw; ☎ 940-820)* offers about 20 clean, bright and sizeable rooms, encircling a bucolic flower garden. The staff is friendly and considerate.

Travellers wishing to sojourn in an old hacienda converted into a hotel of note will doubtless opt for the charming **Hostería Andaluza** *($30; ℜ, pb, hw; ☎ 904-223)*, the construction of which dates back to the middle of the 16th century. Nestled at the foot of the "uncontested master" of the Ecuadoran Andes, Chimborazo, this establishment is about 16 kilometres from Riobamba, far from the hubbub of the city. Many antiques placed here and there confer on the establishment an old-fashioned air evoking the colonial era.

Guaranda

Even though the **Cochabamba Hotel** *($15; pb, ℜ; Calle García Moreno,* ☎ *981-958)* focuses more on comfort at reasonable rates than the decor, the personnel is friendly and obliging.

Without the shadow of a doubt the best hotel in town, **La Colina** *($30; pb, ℜ, ≈, hw; Avenida Guayaquil,* ☎ *980-666)* offers clean, standard rooms whose main advantage is that they offer lovely views of the surrounding area.

Alausí

Those who stop in Alausí after disembarking from the train can stay at the little, unpretentious **Americano Hotel** *($10; Calle García Moreno,* ☎ *930-159)*. Friendly staff.

 RESTAURANTS

Lasso

The chef at the restaurant of the **Hostería la Ciénega** *($$; about 10 km north of Latacunga,* ☎ *719-052; reservations in Quito, Calle Luis Cordero 1442 at Avenida Amazonas,* ☎ *02-541-337)* prepares made-to-order

fish dishes. Diners can choose from among a great variety of species that swim in the little pool situated behind the Hostería. The house duck is another recommended specialty. These meals are generally served by considerate and reserved staff in the warm main room of the restaurant, elegantly decorated in a theme dominated by wood.

Latacunga

Aside from its appealing choice of pizzas, the restaurant of the **Rodelu Hotel** *($; Calle Quito, downtown)* is an unpretentious meeting place very popular with travellers. Meat and poultry also figure on the menu.

The restaurant **Chifa Yut Wah** *($; Calle Tomás Ordónez 6973 at Quinchero)* posts a varied menu of Chinese meals to be eaten quickly in a decor that is, at most, simple.

To warm up before a trip to the market, quietly sip a coffee at **Pinguino** *($; Calle Quito)*.

Pollo Gus *($$; Pan American highway)* is a modern restaurant in flashy colours, but nonetheless is a good spot for a quick chicken meal before hopping the bus.

San Miguel de Salcedo

The restaurant of the **Hostería Rumipamba de las Rosas** *($$; Pan American highway South, Salcedo, 10 km south of Latacunga,* ☎ *726-128 or 726-306; reservations in Quito, Calle Orellana 1811, Edificio El Cid,* ☎ *02-507-121 or 02-568-884)* is a good spot to savour some Ecuadoran specialties before continuing along the "Avenue of Volcanoes".

Ambato

The restaurant **El Alamo Chalet** *($$; Calle Cevallos at Juan Montalvo)*, with its wood façade and its windows that open outward, is evocative of an old Swiss chalet. Inside, the cuisine offers, aside from traditional cheese fondue, a wide selection of meats, poultry and fish.

The friendly **Café Alemán** *($$; Calle Bolívar at Quito)* is a good spot to savour varied dishes or an evening coffee, all the while enjoying a quiet discussion.

The restaurant of the **Hotel Ambato** *($$; Calle Guayaquil at Rocafuerte, ☎ 827-598 or 827-599)* welcomes not only hotel guests, but also travellers passing through, to savour a wide variety of beef, chicken, pork and seafood dishes. The main attraction is the lovely view of the Río Ambato.

Just near the *terminal terrestre*, the modern restaurant **Pollo Gus** *($$; Calle Estados Unidos at Paraguay)* serves various chicken dishes.

Baños

Café Cultura *($; Calle Santa Clara at Montalvo)* enjoys an excellent reputation. The vegetarian dishes, the desserts, the breakfasts and the relaxed ambience that characterize this restaurant make it a popular meeting place for travellers from the world over.

Café Hood *($; Calle 16 de Diciembre at Luis Martínez)* is another spot with a good selection of vegetarian dishes. The personnel is young and friendly. Good choice of fresh juices, coffees and herbal teas. Informal, pleasant ambience.

Those wishing to savour the flavours of Italy should head next door to **Paolo's Pizzería** *($; Calle 16 de Diciembre at Luis Martínez)* where the menu features a good choice of pizzas.

Two steps from EMETEL, the little, unpretentious, family-style restaurant **Marianne** *($; Calle Luis Martínez, between Haflants and Eloy Alforo)* is owned by a French doctor named Michel. The menu offers an assortment of meat and fish.

Despite its modest setting and simple dining-room **Le Petit** *($; Calle Alfaro 246 at Juan Montalvo)* has a reputation for its quality cuisine. A wide variety of French and local specialties make up the menu.

Regines Café Alemán *($; Calle Juan Montalvo at 12 de Noviembre)* is a friendly fast-food stand offering sandwiches and good breakfasts.

The friendly restaurant **El Marques** *($; Calle Juan Montalvo at Ibarra)* serves not only varied meats prepared to your wishes, but also some choice vegetarian dishes. Particularly good is the tofu in mushroom sauce accompanied by broccoli and potatoes *au gratin*; folk musicians provide evening entertainment.

Travellers who lack the means to stay at the **Luna Runtún Resort** can at least dine at its restaurant *($$; ☎ 740-882 or 740-883 about 10 min by taxi from* *downtown)* (see p 152) and savour delicious trout prepared to their instructions and accompanied by vegetables fresh from the garden. The menu also includes delicious steak and chicken dishes. The restaurant is ideal for lunch or dinner after a hike in the mountains. The staff is friendly and the service is attentive. A terrace permits guests to enjoy peaceful, open-air dining while admiring the landscapes of the Andes.

Riobamba

Many travellers like to meet at the little restaurant **Gran Pan** *($; Calle García Moreno at Primera Constituyente)*, near Parque Sucre, for breakfast including fresh-baked bread.

Not to be confused with Cabaña Montecarlo, **Café Montecarlo** *($; Avenida 10 de Agosto at García Moreno)* is also situated two steps from Parque Sucre and constitutes a good spot for coffee or a quick bite between sightseeing visits.

Travellers appreciate the **Cabaña Montecarlo** *($; Calle García Moreno 2140)* for its good, inexpensive food. It is a very simple establishment, with cursory decoration, where the menu focuses on grilled meat dishes.

Clients who cross the threshold of the restaurant **El Delirio** *($$; Calle Primera Constituyente 2816)* cannot help but have a sense of nostalgia for the ghost of Simón Bolívar. In fact, while staying at this very spot, he composed the poem from which the restaurant takes its name, and whose words emphatically inscribed on the walls of the establishment. The menu includes a good selection of meat, poultry and fish.

The restaurant of the hotel **El Troje** *($$; 4 km away, on the road to Chambo, ☎ 960-826)* books folk groups that serenade diners on weekend evenings. The menu is unsurprising and offers satisfying meals such as beef sauteed in garlic and grilled filets of chicken.

 ENTERTAINMENT

Baños

To relax in a "retro" ambience of sixties and seventies music, **Hard Rock Café** *(Thu to Sat 8pm to 2am; Calle Eloy Alfaro at Ambato)* is an address to remember.

Just near the Hard Rock Café, the discotheque **La Burbuja** *(Thu to Sat 8pm to 2am; Calle Eloy Alfaro at Ambato)* is mainly frequented by a clientele of young tourists and locals. Varied and lively music.

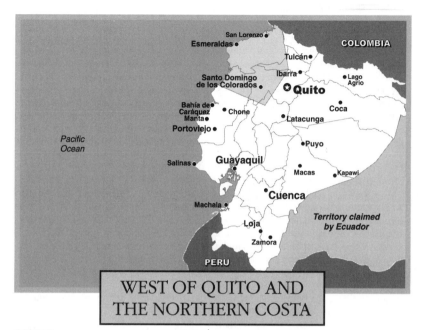

WEST OF QUITO AND THE NORTHERN COSTA

Two picturesque roads allow travellers to reach the northern Costa from Quito. These two winding roads follow a series of precipices, through the truly awe-inspiring, even astounding, scenery that only the majestic mountains that form the Andean cordilleras and the waterfalls can offer. The lower the altitude, the higher the humidity and the more tropical the vegetation. During the afternoon, however, the beauty of the landscape is, unfortunately, marred by the sudden appearance of a thick blanket of fog. This reduces visibility, hinders traffic and increases the risk of accidents. Moreover, it is important for visitors who plan on making the trip after sundown to know that, at night, there are no streetlights along these winding and even dangerous roads. Furthermore, come night-time, many trucks drive toward either the Costa or the Sierra to deliver their wares,

slowing traffic down considerably, to the extent that it builds up and vehicles are lined up for miles. Impatient drivers inevitably attempt to thread their way through the vehicles ahead of them, without knowing if another might try to manoeuvre in a similar fashion at the very same time and in the opposite direction... It is easy to imagine the dangers to which all those using this road expose themselves when subjected to such traffic conditions.

The road going north from Quito crosses the equator, goes through the little village of Calacali, then continues northwest, crossing first the Reserva Biológica Macipucuna and then the Bosque Protector de Mindo, before reaching the city of Esmeraldas. This road avoids the city of Santo Domingo de los Colorados and is a little less busy than the one going through southern Quito.

The road passing through southern Quito follows Avenida de los Volcanes, then branches off to the east to Alóa to reach the northern Costa's second largest city, Santo Domingo de los Colorados. Once there, travellers will have the choice of proceeding to Esmeraldas or heading toward Guayaquil via the city of Quevedo.

In many respects, the Costa is altogether different from the Sierra or the Oriente. Here, the picturesque Amerindian villages are replaced by equally charming fishing villages, and the grassy vegetation of the mountains gives way to a lush tropical-like vegetation. The region is populated by descendants of blacks who were uprooted from their ancestral lands in Africa and brought here as slaves long ago, as well as by mostly pure-race Amerindian peoples. The northern Costa is actually dotted with small fishing villages, dispersed along the edges of the Pacific Ocean. Like the Sierra, however, the Costa is not immune to the vagaries of Mother Nature. In 1981, for instance, a devastating earthquake and resulting tidal wave shook this region for a few moments, swallowing a number of victims for evermore, haphazardly mowed down in a terrible stampede: men, women, children, flora and fauna. This catastrophic upheaval of nature is now in the past, and life has returned to normal, at least until the next large-scale earthquake hits this region.

Most travellers go to Atacames, a very popular little village that attracts travellers and locals in search of an informal and lively atmosphere. Those who wish to avoid Atacames' noisy bustle can go farther north, to the small fishing village of Tonsúpa, or farther south, where the charming villages of Same, Tonchigüie and Muisné cling to the Pacific coast. Indeed, in every one of these villages, simply observing the fishermen spreading out their nets after a long day's work, which attracts a number of birds, against a backdrop of perpetual waves breaking and spending themselves on the sandy beach, can be very pleasant. In the simple little village of Borbón, travellers can board a small boat that will lead them into the mysterious Reserva Ecológica Cotacachi-Cayapas along the Río San Miguel's turbulent waters. Though access is difficult, this reserve remains one of ecotourism-lovers' best kept secrets. Unfortunately, this region has the highest rate of malaria in Ecuador. Consequently, visitors who wish to venture into this area should take particular care to bring anti-malaria pills.

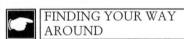

FINDING YOUR WAY AROUND

Reserva Biológica Maquipucuna

By bus

Buses do not go all the way to the reserve. They drop passengers off at the little village of Nanegal, whence they will have to take a taxi or haggle with local shopkeepers along the main road for a ride. Buses leave from Quito near the Parque Alameda at 1pm on Wednesdays, 2pm on Thursdays, 10am and 2pm on Saturdays, and 9am and 2pm on Sundays. The fare is a little under $2 for a trip lasting approximately two hours and 30 minutes. From Nanagal, a taxi will cost between $7 and $15 depending on your bargaining skills.

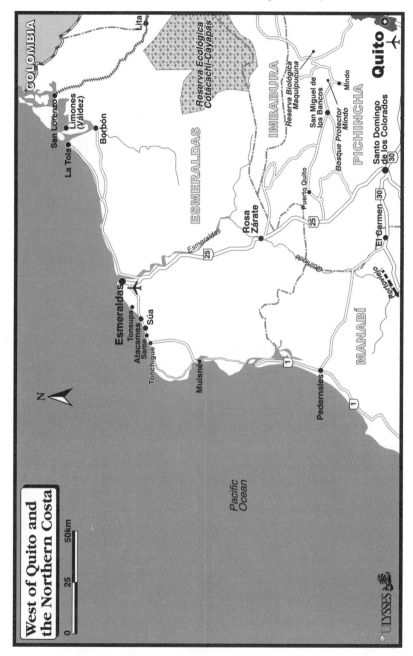

West of Quito and
the Northern Costa

0   25   50km

N

Pacific
Ocean

COLOMBIA

Lita

San Lorenzo
Limones
(Váldez)
La Tola
Botbón

Reserva Ecológica
Cotacachi-Cayapas

IMBABURA

Reserva Biológica
Maquipucuna

San Miguel de
los Bancos

Bosque Protector
Mindo

Mindo

Quito

PICHINCHA

Santo Domingo
de los Colorados

ESMERALDAS

Esmeraldas

Rosa
Zárate

Puerto Quito

El Carmen

Esmeraldas

Tonsupa
Atacames
Same
Súa
Tonchigüe

Muisne

Quitinde

Blanco

MANABÍ

Pedernales

ULYSSES

Mindo

By bus

Buses leave the capital for Mindo twice a day, in the morning and afternoon. The journey lasts around two hours and 30 minutes and costs a little under $2.

Santo Domingo de los Colorados

By bus

Numerous buses drive here from Quito on a regular basis. The trip lasts approximately three hours and costs a little over $2. Those who wish to take in the view should make the trip early in the morning. The terminal is located in the northern part of the city on Avenida de Las Tsachilas.

Esmeraldas, Atacames, Súa, Same, Tonchigüe and Muisné

By plane

TAME airlines services the city of Esmeraldas from Quito. The flight lasts approximately 30 minutes and costs around $30. A taxi to the downtown area will cost about $5. From there, a number of buses stop in the small villages south of Esmeraldas: Tonsupa, Atacames, Súa, Same, Tonchigüie and Muisné.

By bus

From Quito, several buses go to Esmeraldas. From there, another bus drives travellers toward the cities of Tonsupa, Atacames, Súa, Same and Tonchigüie. Some buses are more expensive but offer more comfort and have toilets and a television that shows American movies. Quito-Esmeraldas: prices vary from $5 to $7 for a trip lasting approximately six hours. Esmeraldas-Atacames: departures on the hour (45-minute trip for $0.50). Esmeraldas-Súa: departures on the hour (one-hour trip for $0.75). Esmeraldas-Same: departures every hour (a little under two hours for $1). The bus terminal in Esmeraldas is about two kilometres west of downtown.

Muisné

Numerous buses leaving from Quito for Muisné do not actually serve the little island, but do go through Esmeraldas. From there, another bus will drive travellers to a pier, whence a small craft will take them to the peninsula. Upon arrival in Muisné, many will be surprised to discover numerous tricycles driven by children and teenagers offering visitors transportation to the hotel for the sum of $0.50 to $1. The beach is only 15 minutes' walking distance from the pier, however, and visitors should not feel obliged to employ these tricycles.

Borbón

By bus

From Esmeraldas, buses take four hours to reach Borbón; count on spending around $3.

San Lorenzo

To reach San Lorenzo, travellers must first make their way to Esmeraldas and

The picturesque and lively Riobamba market.

Breathtaking scenery in the central Andes.

take one of the many buses heading for the little village of La Tola. From there, a boat goes to San Lorenzo. Upon arrival, many children and teenagers will offer to drive visitors to their hotel, but do not feel obliged to avail yourself of this service. Those who wish to be guided by these drivers, however, can count on spending around $0.50. Moreover, in order to avoid spending the night in La Tola (a city devoid of interest) waiting for the boat, take the early morning bus from Esmeraldas. Yet another possibility is to get to San Lorenzo by bus from Ibarra. The trip lasts approximately six hours and costs around $6.

By *autoferro*

The *autoferro* service from Ibarra (see p 114) is interrupted at present, but the Ecuagal tour company sometimes operates between Otavalo and San Lorenzo. For information, in Quito, Avenida Amazones 1113 at Pinto, ☎ (02) 229-579 or 229-580, ⌕ 550-988. Ask to speak to Hébert.

The city of San Lorenzo has recently been linked to Ibarra by a road from the Sierra to the Costa.

 EXPLORING

Mindo

The small **Reserva Biológica Maquipucuna** is only a few hours away from Quito, just before the village of Mindo. For more information, consult the "Parks" section p 165.

Clinging to the Andes, 120 kilometres northwest of Quito, the simple little village of Mindo is watered by the Río Mindo and the Río Nambillo, holding the interest of travellers with its **Bosque Protector Mindo** (see p 166), which covers approximately 19,000 hectares of territory where over 400 bird species chirp. This small market town with few facilities has approximately 3,000 inhabitants who, for the most part, make their living in forestry, which creates a conflict of interest between those who wish to protect the forest and those who exploit it.

Santo Domingo de los Colorados

This large town is located 140 kilometres west of Quito and is an important point between the Costa and the Sierra. It is at the crossroads of two major highways linking these regions. From Quito, the journey is quite spectacular. Santo Domingo de los Colorados bears the name of the Amerindians who once ruled over the region. Today, the Colorados only number about a hundred. At the time, they were distinguished by their short hair, dyed red by means of a natural colorant called *achiote*, as well as by their minimal clothing. Every year, many tourists go to Santo Domingo de los Colorados in the hopes of meeting the descendants of these famous Amerindians. Unfortunately, the gradual invasion of this land by the modern world has made it so that today, the majority of Colorados still living there wear jeans and shirts "just like everyone else" and rarely dye their hair.

The town's main attraction is its Sunday **market**. With luck, visitors will see the famous Colorados. The encroachment of the modern world has

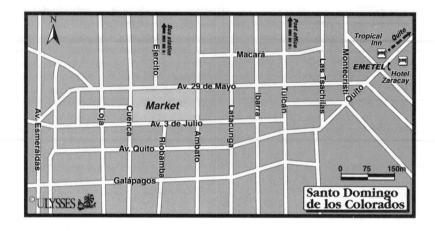

Santo Domingo
de los Colorados

virtually reduced these proud Amerindians to circus animals and robbed them of their territory and their ancestral way of life. The small neighbouring villages where the Colorados live are the best places to visit to really see them. Those who are absolutely set on taking their picture, however, should ask their permission, out of respect, before doing so. They may ask for a little money in return. Do not be cheap, and agree to their request. It is important to keep in mind, however, that these people are not tourist attractions, but women and men who, as such, deserve our respect, just like you and I...

From Santo Domingo, the road forks, heading toward either Esmeraldas or Guayaquil. On the road to Guayaquil, less than an hour from Santo Domingo, travellers will reach the **Río Palenque Science Center** ★ *(Santo Domingo, ☎ 561-646)*. This research centre aims to protect the last remnants of tropical rainforests on the west side of the Andes. Those passionately interested in ornithology will be eager to observe the 350 species of birds teeming over an area of approximately 100 hectares. Butterfly lovers are hardly left out, as around the same number of lepidopterous species have been counted there as well. The centre also has hotel facilities that, though rudimentary, can accommodate visitors: count on spending about $30 per person.

Quevedo

Situated near the Río Palenque Science Center, Quevedo is a big city animated by about 90,000 inhabitants, the vast majority of whom are of Asian origin. The city's economy is largely centred around the banana industry. Few tourists make a stop there. In fact, most quickly go on their way without taking much notice of the city.

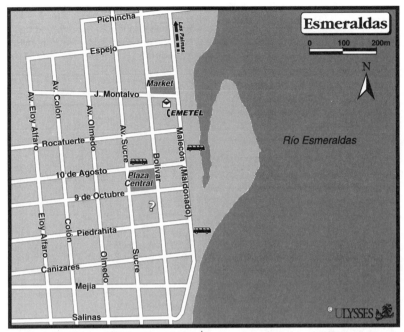

Esmeraldas

0   100   200m

N

Pichincha
Espejo
Las Palmas
Av. Eloy Alfaro
Av. Colón
Av. Olmedo
J. Montalvo
Market
EMETEL
Av. Sucre
Rocafuerte
Malecón
Bolívar
10 de Agosto
Plaza Central
(Maldonado)
9 de Octubre
?
Eloy Alfaro
Colón
Piedrahita
Cañizares
Olmedo
Sucre
Mejia
Salinas
Río Esmeraldas
ULYSSES

Esmeraldas

Unlike the population of other Ecuadoran cities, Esmeraldas' is mainly composed of descendants of black slaves who were abducted from Africa to work in sugar cane plantations. As a result, there are few Amerindians here. A port city with over 140,000 inhabitants and capital of the province that bears its name, Esmeraldas is an unattractive tropical city whose atmosphere seems troubled and rife with suspicion. Most travellers do not linger there and make haste to continue on to Atacames and its surrounding area. Esmeraldas is, however, of economic importance to the country. In fact, the trans-Andean pipeline that comes straight from the Oriente has its terminal in the southern part of this very city. This has disastrous consequences for nature, because the many oil refineries pollute the city's air and dull the brilliance of the city's once sparkling beaches and the greenery of its parks. Indeed, the verdant vegetation far from lives up to the city's name, Esmeraldas (from "emerald").

Borbón

From Esmeraldas, a sudden turn toward the north leads to Borbón. Set on the Río Cayapas, this humble little town is a small seaport whose population is mostly black. The town is hardly worth mentioning, except that this is where travellers can board a small boat for an excursion toward the Reserva Ecológica Cotacachi-Cayapas (see p 118, 166) on the tumultuous waters of the Río Miguel.

La Tola

La Tola is a small stopover village with a little over 5,000 inhabitants and offers travellers road and sea links to Esmeraldas and San Lorenzo. From this little town, in fact, travellers have the choice of taking the boat to San Lorenzo or the road to Esmeraldas.

La Tolita

At first glance, there seems to be nothing here to draw travellers. By scratching below the surface, however, it becomes apparent that this tiny island has hidden ancient origins, origins that remained undiscovered until the 20th century. In fact, one fine day, a mask worked in gold was discovered in the meanders of one the watercourses that drains the island. This mask, whose origins remain mysterious, is now the emblem of Ecuador's central bank.

San Lorenzo

This small coastal village is hot, humid, infested with mosquitos and devoid of interest except for the fact that it is the **autoferro** ★★ terminus, the famous trans-Andean train that reaches Ibarra at an altitude of over 2,200 metres. Most visitors go to San Lorenzo only to take the *autoferro* to Ibarra. At the moment, however, the service has been interrupted for an indeterminate period of time, but the Ecuagal tour company sometimes offers service from Otavalo to San Lorenzo (see p 114). The road linking San Lorenzo and Ibarra is now open and some buses follow this route.

Atacames ★★★

Situated about 30 kilometres southwest of Esmeraldas, Atacames is a small village on the Pacific coast. For the last few years, this village has become the place to stay *par excellence* for budget travellers seeking a relaxed yet lively atmosphere. Hotel facilities are still somewhat scarce, but development is proceeding at a rapid pace, to the extent that tourism is changing the face of the city along its seafront and its main street, now lined with numerous hotels and restaurants as well as bars with terraces shaded by thatch roofs.

Though the beach has been tamed in the name of tourism, the sea, for its part, refuses to yield. Every year, in fact, a number of reckless swimmers unfortunately lose their lives by underestimating the force of the powerful currents sweeping the coast in this region. Nevertheless, the beach still lends itself quite well to swimming, though it hardly compares to the magnificent white sandy beaches of the Caribbean.

As a security measure, visitors (especially women) should refrain from going down to the beach on their own after dark. Visitors should also avoid carrying valuables: it is preferable to leave these items at the hotel – if guests consider the hotel trustworthy enough, that is.

Súa ★

This little coastal village is located south of Atacames, and fishing is its principal economic activity. Súa has nothing extraordinary to offer besides its little bay, over which numerous birds fly, waiting for the fishermen to return to port with the day's catch. Visitors wishing to have a bite to eat while admiring this scene can do so, but, as you may have guessed, the menu changes from day to day, depending on the day's catch.

Same ★

This quiet little village, situated about 10 kilometres south of Atacames, has, over the last few years, seen its very first apartment complexes (condominiums) mushroom along the sea, their new owners having been charmed by the lovely, quiet beaches that border the Pacific in this area.

Tonchigüe ★

In this other little and even more developed coastal village, most inhabitants make their living fishing. It is preferable to go between 5:30pm and 6pm to witness an altogether picturesque and sometimes magical scene. This is when the fishermen return from a long day's work, as dusk quickly falls over the sea, and when their boats, illuminated by the flickering glimmer of a simple kerosene lamp, move slowly toward the coast. This procession forms a long trail of lights, mingling with the twinkling stars that light up, at the very same moment, one by one in the sky...

Muisné ★

Bathed by the waters of the Pacific, about 80 kilometres south of Esmeraldas, Muisné is a quiet little island with no cars but congested with tricycles. This island boasts often deserted and undeniably charming beaches. It is also where one of the last mangrove forests of the coastal region can be seen. Despite all this, however, travellers do not generally show much interest in this island, preferring, rather, Atacames' lively beaches and noisy discos. But beware! These long, deserted beaches can prove dangerous. It is particularly unwise to venture there alone, especially for women. Contrary to appearances, several assaults have unfortunately been reported here recently. Moreover, there are no banking institutions on the island; visitors should therefore have a sufficient amount of sucres with them before heading there.

This island's attractions are easily discovered during walks, but, visitors who prefer to take a boat around can do so as well. For more information, speak to Daniel and Barbara, a charming Swiss couple who own the Italiano restaurant (see p 173).

 PARKS

Reserva Biológica Maquipucuna ★★★

Founded in 1988, the **Reserva Biológica Maquipucuna** *($5; Calle Baquerizo 238 at Tamayo, Quito ☎ (02) 507-200 or 507-202,* ⌨ *507-201, root@maqui.ecx.ec)* spreads over 14,000 hectares of hillside territory in the Andes. It is about two hours from Quito, just north of Mindo. This reserve, a veritable sanctuary for fauna and flora, is managed by a non-profit organization seeking to protect the last remnants of cloud-forests. This forest extends from 1,200 to 2,800 metres in altitude and shelters four different ecosystems that encompass extremely diversified flora and fauna. This forest's particular characteristic is that it is constantly shrouded in clouds, creating ideal conditions for the growth of lush vegetation. These particular conditions make it the equal of a tropical rainforest because of the exceptional number of species that live here. Indeed, close to 1,200 species of plants have been counted, including no fewer than 90 species of ferns, among others. Moreover, 45 species of mammals, 370 species of birds and over 250 species of butterflies have been enumerated in this area. Most of these plant and animal species are peculiar to the region.

Different walking paths have been cleared so that visitors can explore the reserve at their own pace. Altogether, five trails totalling 10 kilometres plunge into this splendid forest, which is unlike anything else in the world.

Bosque Protector Mindo ★★★

Administered by the Los Amigos de la Naturaleza ecological group, and situated about 80 kilometres northwest of Quito, the Bosque Protector Mindo *($7)* spreads over the sides of the Pichincha volcano from 1,500 metres in altitude to a little over 4,700 metres. It covers a surface of 19,000 hectares of territory of very uneven terrain. This place is a favourite with ornithologists and nature lovers. Countless species of

birds can be observed at one's leisure: over 400 species have been enumerated! Butterflies and orchids complete the ecological wealth of this reserve. Tourist infrastructures, however, are somewhat sparse, though a few small hotels offering visitors a rudimentary comfort do exist.

Reserva Ecológica Cotacachi-Cayapas ★★

The **Reserva Ecológica Cotacachi-Cayapas** *($10)* takes its name, in part, from that of the Cayapas Amerindians, who inhabit the reserve and its surrounding area. Today, they number approximately 4,000. The Cayapas make their living off fishing and hunting, and are renowned for their remarkable dexterity in sculpting pirogues from a single log. This reserve forms a large stretch of greenery that covers 300,140 hectares from the lowlands of the Costa, at an altitude of approximately 200 metres, to the high Andean plateaus of the Sierra, situated at an altitude of over 4,500 metres. This reserve also encompasses part of the Laguna Cuicocha, located right near the small village of Cotacachi. Instituted in 1968, this ecological reserve remains less frequented by travellers because it is difficult to reach. In fact, it can only be entered from two places: either from the humble village of Borbón, whence visitors board a boat that follows the Río Miguel, or from the Sierra, near Cotacachi. The region, however, is infested with mosquitos and, for this reason, has the highest rate of malaria in all of Ecuador. Mosquitos and insects of all types abound, because most of the reserve's territory is immersed in a hot environment, indeed, a very hot and humid environment. The flora changes, of course, in accordance with the altitude. This is how visitors may get the chance to observe the effects of the striking contrasts that exist between the tropical forest and the steppe of the high Andean plateaus. Visitors will discover numerous watercourses and falls, not to mention the lakes that dot this vast, wild territory where several species of mammals such as the wolf, the sloth, the fox, the ocelot, the raccoon and the deer cohabit. Bird lovers haven't been left out either, as close to 300 species proliferate here as well. One of the best ways to visit the reserve is to stay in a lodge that is only accessible by boat, like the one situated by the Río Cayapas, known as "**Steve'Lodge**" *(about $80 per day, full-board; for reservations, contact Antonio and Judy Nagy, Casilla 5148, CCI, Quito, ☎ (02) 431-555, ⇌ 431-556, nagy@pi.pro.ec).*

Tinalandia

An old hacienda converted into accommodations with a golf course, Tinalandia is set up on a territory that covers a little over 100 hectares of forest. The proprietress, a lady of Russian origin known under the name of Tina Garzón, and her son Sergio are ardent nature lovers who, year after year, receive many bird lovers from all over the world. It is, without a doubt, one of the best places in Ecuador for bird-watching. Birders take note: over 300 species have been counted here.

OUTDOOR ACTIVITIES

Swimming

In general, the beaches of the Costa are unsupervised. Swimmers take note: be cautious and do not venture out too far.

The **Atacames beach** is not the most spectacular, but is good for a refreshing dip.

Far less developed and much calmer, the **beaches of Same** and **Muisné**, for their part, will satisfy those who wish to avoid the crowds on Atacames' beach.

ACCOMMODATIONS

Santo Domingo de los Colorados

Situated right in the middle of downtown, the **Hotel Unicornio** *($10; pb; Avenida 29 de Mayo and Ambato)* is only good for tourists who are not too demanding and have limited budgets.

For those coming from the Sierra, the **Hotel Tropical Inn** *($30; pb; tv, ℜ; Avenida Quito, ☎ 761-771 or 761-772, ⇌ 761-775)* is one of the first hotels travellers will find right upon entering Santo Domingo, on the right, west of downtown. There are 60 small, clean and carpeted but plainly decorated rooms. A private parking lot offers safe shelter for cars. The hotel's administrator also runs a parachuting school. Thrill-seekers take note.

Right near the Tropical Inn, still on Avenida Quito, on the left, is the **Zaracay** hotel *($50; pb, ℜ, ≈; Avenida Quito,* ☎ *751-023 or 754-535,* ↵ *754-535).* Behind the parking lot, watched over by an armed guard, visitors will come upon clean and modestly decorated rooms, equipped with balconies opening out on lush vegetation where a multitude of birds flutter about. Light sleepers should choose a room away from the discotheque. An inviting pool allows guests to refresh themselves any time of day.

The region's most famous hotel is perched on a hill overhanging the Río Toachi on the left, a dozen kilometres before Santo Domingo de los Colorados; it is the **Hotel Tinalandia** *($90; hw, pb, ℜ; from Quito,* ☎ *449-028,* ↵ *442-638).* Contrary to popular belief, it is not its clean, bright and spacious rooms that make its reputation, but a nine-hole golf course crisscrossed by footpaths that lend themselves marvellously to quiet bird-watching. Indeed, over 300 species of birds have been enumerated here.

Macipucuna

The **Macipucuna Lodge** *($50; full-board, sc, ℜ; reservations from Quito, Calle Baquerizo 238 at Tamayo,* ☎ *(02) 507-200 or 507-202,* ↵ *507-201, root@maqui.ecx.ec)* is reached by crossing a bridge, where visitors will discover flowers and plants arranged so as to embellish the landscape and attract birds; finally, visitors will notice a dining room in the open air adjacent to a kitchen. Behind the kitchen, a few steps will lead visitors to a bar facing four hammocks and leather and wood couches where guests can relax while quietly reading from a selection of books. Moreover, after having ordered a refreshing drink, guests will have the privilege of being soothed by the babbling of the Río intermixed with that of the birds'. A few rooms are on this same floor, the others on the upper floor. The beds are comfortable and certain rooms have large or bunk beds. The electricity is turned off at around 9pm. Meanwhile, guests can entertain themselves by playing Scrabble and checkers.

Mindo

Right before getting to the village of Mindo, travellers will notice, on the left, the simple little hotel establishment **Bijac** *($12; bc, ℜ),* which has relatively clean rooms and a friendly staff. The owner also runs the kitchen and prepares a daily menu.

The best place to spend the night in Mindo is located less than a kilometre from the village and is called **Hostería El Carmelo de Mindo** *($40; pb, hw, ℜ;* ☎ *538-756).* There are *cabañas* of different sizes, which prove quite clean, well tended and even able to accommodate small families. The staff is obliging and can help guests find guides to explore the region.

Esmeraldas

Even though the city's best hotels are here, in the northern district of Las Palmas, the establishments are, in general, a somewhat accurate reflection of the image Esmeraldas projects: noisy, rather dubious and without the least bit of charm.

Located up north, the **Hotel Del Mar** *($15; pb, ℜ; Avenida Kennedy, Las Palmas, ☎ 713-910 or 711-916)* offers modern rooms devoid of all charm, some of which overlook the sea.

Located right downtown, the **Apart-Hotel Esmeraldas** *($35; Avenida Libertad at Ramón Tello, ☎ 712-712, 728-702 or 714-714, ≈ 728-704)* is assuredly among the safest hotel establishments in Esmeraldas. Its rooms prove relatively clean and modern, but quite spartan.

The **Hotel Cayapas** *($35; hw, pb, ℜ; Avenida Kennedy at Valdez, Las Palmas, ☎ 711-022 or 711-077)*, north of the city, has rooms that are well-equipped, but devoid of any particular charm. Some have balconies.

Located north of the city, the **Costa Verde Suites** hotel *($50; hw, pb, ℜ, ≈, fan; Calle Luís Tello 804 at Hilda Padilla, ☎ 728-717, ≈ 728-716)* offers about 20 very clean rooms equipped with kitchenettes. The establishment also has a restaurant and a tiny swimming pool.

Atacames

The large majority of Atacames' hotel establishments offer little more than scant and spartan comfort. A good number of hotels do not always have running water, much less any hot water. It is important to know that the Costa's hotels adjust their prices according to the season: during the high season, from January to the beginning of April, as well as on holiday weekends, prices are increased by 10 to 20%.

The **Hotel Galería Atacames** *($10; pb, ℜ; facing the beach, ☎ 731-149)* offers small, humbly decorated rooms of somewhat questionable cleanliness, but which prove perfectly satisfactory to travellers who are not too demanding and have limited budgets. Some rooms overlook the beach.

For the same price, the **Hotel Caracol** *($10; pb, tv; on the main street toward the beach, ☎ 731-068)* has spartan rooms that are sometimes of questionable cleanliness. On the main floor, its store sells a multitude of beach-related items and other common consumer products such as sun lotion, juice and toothpaste.

The **Hotel Tahiti**'s *($10; pb; ☎ 731-078)* rooms are devoid of charm, but will amply satisfy travellers with small budgets who wish to stay by the beach.

The **Hotel y Cabañas Rodelu** *($14; tv, pb; ☎ 731-033; from Esmeraldas, ☎ 731-033 or 714-714)* is an inexpensive place for small groups to stay. Its rooms prove relatively clean and well-equipped; moreover, the bill gets reduced in accordance with the number of people.

The **Las Cabañas Caida del Sol** *($25; pb; 150 m from the beach; ☎ 731-479)* hotel establishment is kept by German-speaking Swiss people and has 10 modern and very clean rooms with matching pastel shades and bunkbeds. However, the noise emanating from the disco can, on occasion, disrupt the sleep of guests.

Lé Castell *($30; pb, ℜ, ≈; ☎ (06) 731-350, 731-542 or 731-442; reservations from Quito: ☎ 02-432-413)* rents attractive rooms with pastel-coloured aluminium roofs, which are very safe and very clean. Some rooms even border the lovely swimming pool. The other rooms are in the main building, facing the beach; these are consequently a little more noisy.

The **Villas Arco Iris** *($40; pb, ℜ; on the beach, toward the north;* ☎ *731-069)* have numerous clean little *cabañas* with thatched roofs, elevated on piles and equipped with balconies with hammocks. The *cabañas* have two beds each and are equipped with a minibar and a fridge. A small playground with swings has been put together for children. This is a good alternative for families or small groups who appreciate a pleasant and comfortable environment by the beach.

The **Hotel Castelnuevo** *($40; pb, ℜ, ≈;* ☎ *731-046 or 731-188; reservations from Quito: Calle La Niña 412 at Reina Victoria,* ☎ *(02) 232-262, 223-452 or 223-462)* is situated a few kilometres north of Atacames. It offers clean, modern and well-equipped rooms, most of which have a pleasant view of the sea. Two swimming pools and a private parking lot are available to guests.

The **Yacare** hotel *($40; tv, hw, pb, ℜ)* is located south of Atacames, by the sea. The rooms are distributed along two floors, in front of a pool with a bar that opens out on a spacious and quasi-deserted beach. The hotel also has a few small, 55-square-metre apartments containing two rooms, which are ideal for families.

Súa

The **Hotel Las Buganvillas** *($10; pb;* ☎ *731-008)* offers very simple rooms that will suit travellers with limited budgets. The place has a private parking lot for those who have a car at their disposal.

The **Hotel Súa** *($10; sb, ℜ; on the beach,* ☎ *731-004)* is run by a friendly French couple, Robert and Hélène. The hotel rents a few clean, well-kept and safe rooms, some of which offer an attractive view of the sea. Pleasant service and informal ambience.

At the city's entrance, the **Hotel El Peñon de Súa** *($15; pb, ℜ;* ☎ *731-013)* has about 20 rooms that are clean and modern, but devoid of any particular charm.

The **Hotel Chagro Ramos** *($10; pb, ℜ; facing the beach, to the right,* ☎ *731-070)* rents slightly austere rooms overlooking the sea. Its terrace and restaurant are more attractive than its rooms (see p 172).

Same

Situated on the beach, the **Hotel La Terraza** *($12, or $20 for four people; reservations from Quito: Avenida 6 de Diciembre at Juan Rodriguez,* ☎ *(02) 544-507)* is an inexpensive place that will suit travellers who are not too demanding and have restricted budgets.

The **Cabañas del Sol** *($20; pb, ℜ, ≈;* ☎ *731-151)* number 40, each able to accommodate a group of four people. This formula is an excellent choice for small groups, who will be able to enjoy the informal, tropical ambience that this tourist establishment, situated by the Pacific, strives to create.

Right next to the Cabañas del Sol, a little farther north, the **Hostería El Rampiral** *($25; pb; reservations from Quito: Avenida El Inca at Amazonas, ☎ (02) 246-341, 435-003 or 450-879)* offers 14 *cabañas*, each equipped with a fridge. Those that look out on the sea cost a little less, are made of wood, have a small balcony and a lovely view on the horizon. Those that are scattered under the shade of palm trees are more modern and more expensive.

Perched on a cliff between Same and Tonchigüe, the **El Acantilado** hotel *($30; pb, ℜ, ≈; reservations from Quito: ☎ (02) 235-034)* rents clean rooms that are plain, but offer a splendid view of the ocean and its surrounding area in return. The reception area comprises a bright dining room with a pool table, and opens out on a lovely terrace surrounding a swimming pool where a few hammocks are slung under a belvedere. A flight of stairs leads to the beach, and a parking lot is available for those wishing to park their car safely. This place is ideal for travellers wishing to escape the bustle of crowded beaches.

As its name suggests, the **Hotel Casa Blanca's** *($60; tv, pb, hw, ℜ, ≈; ☎ 731-031, 731-389, ≈ 731-096; reservations from Quito: (02) 529-317)* architecture is reminiscent of North Africa. Moreover, it is indisputably the most luxurious establishment of the region, and offers many perks that will undoubtedly please those seeking a place to stay at the beach with first-class service. Besides its private beach, four tennis courts, two clay and two concrete, allow guests to enjoy an exercise session any time of day. Those who find tennis too exerting can go play minigolf under the foliage of palm trees, after a dip in the pool or on the private beach. The rooms, for their part, are very clean, though simply decorated. Scattered throughout the surrounding vegetation, some look out on the ocean, some inland. A billiard room, a ping-pong room, a volleyball court and a private parking lot round out the facilities.

Muisné

The name of the **Paraíso** hotel *($6; sb; on the beach, to the left)* may suggest paradise, but is only so for travellers who are not too demanding when it comes to comfort and seek reasonably-priced accommodations. It does, however, offer the luxury of stretching out in a hammock and savouring a *piña colada* while contemplating the blazing sunset.

The **Cabañas Ipanema** *($6; sb; near the beach)* have absolutely nothing to do with Joâo Gilberto's lovely and romantic song, but offer 16 rustic little rooms that are safe and inexpensive. For a few dollars more, visitors can opt for *cabañas* with concrete floors, for they are a little cleaner than those with wooden floors. Service is friendly, and the place will satisfy adventurers with restricted budgets. To get there from the pier, take the road leading to the beach and turn right just before reaching the Italiano restaurant.

Those who wish to treat themselves to a little more comfort can go to the nearly **Galápagos** hotel *($14; pb, ℜ; near the beach)*, which definitely has the best rooms in the peninsula. Its 40 rooms are distributed along two floors and, though lacking in luxury, prove clean, bright, safe and comfortable.

RESTAURANTS

Santo Domingo de los Colorados

The cook at the **Hotel Tinalandia's** *($$; a dozen kilometres east of Santo Domingo de los Colorados)* restaurant prepares a large variety of meat and seafood dishes.

Note: Most restaurants in Esmeraldas, Atacames, Súa, Same, Tonchigüie and Muisné, located along the Pacific coast, a daily menu comprising a variety of fish that, as of yesterday, were still swimming in the ocean.

Esmeraldas

The **La Marimba** restaurant *($; Calle Libertad and Lavallén)* is a good place to keep in mind for traditional Ecuadoran cuisine. As a matter of course, the menu offers numerous fish and seafood dishes.

Those who wish to treat themselves to a good meal can opt for the restaurants in the **Costa Verde Suites** *($$; Calle Luís Tello 804)* and **Hotel del Mar** *($$; Avenida Kennedy)* hotels.

Atacames

Atacames' numerous restaurants are mostly gathered along or close to the beach, which is this little town's main attraction. Moreover, every night after dinner, several stands flood the main street facing the beach to sell a dessert typical of the region, called *"cocada"*. This is a little cake made of nuts, coconut and brown sugar.

The **Hotel Galería Atacames** *($; facing the beach)* has a restaurant renowned for its location. Different fish and seafood dishes appear on the menu. As an added treat, patrons also enjoy a fantastic view of the sea.

El Tiburón and **El Comedor Pelicano** *($; facing the beach)* are two other unpretentious little restaurants that will please seafood lovers.

At first glance, the **Paco Faco** restaurant's *($$; right before the beach, to the left)* façade hardly encourages customers to venture inside. Nevertheless, the throng of people who crowd the place testify to its popularity among residents. In accordance with the catch of the day, patrons will be able to savour an assortment of fish and seafood dishes prepared according to their wishes.

Those who have had their fair share of fish and seafood can go to the cosy **Pane y Vino** restaurant *($$; on the beach)*, where a variety of pizzas baked in a wood-burning oven are prepared.

Súa

Visitors can have something to eat at one of the restaurants along the beach.

The **Hotel Chagro Ramos's** *($$; facing the beach)* restaurant has a lovely view of the beach and enjoys a good reputation in the region. It offers a varied cuisine in a relaxed atmosphere. Besides the traditional fish dishes, chicken and beef are also on the menu.

Managed by a French couple, the pleasant **La bonne Bouff** restaurant *($$; on the beach)* serves, as a matter of course, delicious fish and seafood dishes, but various meat dishes with a French flavour as well.

Muisné

In addition to making excellent banana pancakes, the chef at the little **El Tiburón** restaurant *($; near the beach)* prepares fresh fish in a wonderful way.

Those who are tired of eating fish can go to the warm **Italiano** restaurant *($$; near the beach)*. Besides the Italian specialties, delicious homemade pancakes are also served here. The place is kept by a friendly Swiss couple, Daniel and Barbara.

 ENTERTAINMENT

Atacames

According to the season, various bars and nightclubs open their doors to tourists. Most of these establishments are along the beach. In addition to the **Paradisco** and the **Sanbayen** *(both on the beach)*, which promise patrons a wild night of dancing, there are many nightclubs of the same kind; the service and the summer environment are similar, but the ambience varies in accordance with the clientele that frequents them. All you have to do is to walk along the beach and choose the establishment that suits you.

Muisné

The **Bar Havana Club** *(every day from 7:30pm on; on the beach)* livens up Muisné's evenings and offers varied and entertaining music. Relaxed ambience, young mixed clientele.

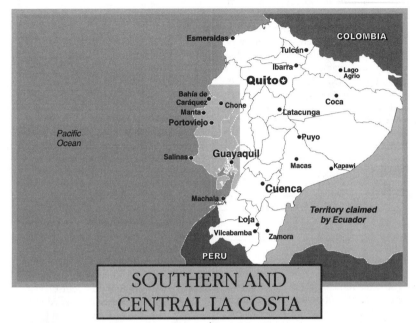

SOUTHERN AND CENTRAL LA COSTA

Often neglected by tourists who visit Ecuador, the region of La Costa, the coast, does not figure as prominently as other regions of the country in people's itineraries. Rather than descend the slopes of the Andes to the Costa, many travellers prefer to cover the high Andean peaks, forge through the mysterious Amazon, or explore the fascinating world of the Galápagos Islands. Residents of the Costa are even gibed by the people of the Sierra, who call them by the hardly flattering nickname *monos* ("monkeys"). Conversely, residents of the Sierra are considered colourless and lacklustre. Economically, the Oriente and the Costa carry more weight than the Sierra, for the former have important petroleum reserves at their disposal, while the latter benefits from numerous banana plantations and vast shrimp farms bordering the coast. The raising of these little crustaceans was undertaken in Ecuador in the mid-

1960s, but the industry only took off in the eighties. Today more than 300,000 hectares of the country's coastline are dedicated to shrimp farming. Nevertheless, global competition in this industry is fierce, and despite spectacular development, Ecuador has slipped from 1st to 3rd place, behind Indonesia and Thailand.

While the Costa is making great efforts to develop its tourism industry, outside of Guayaquil, infrastructure remains relatively limited. Without a shadow of a doubt the principal attraction of the Costa is the magnificent Parque Nacional Machalilla, but other inviting sites are unfairly overlooked by travellers. For example, a little north of Guayaquil are the charming, quiet town of Bahía de Caráquez and Isla Fragatas, both of which merit visits. As well, there are immense beaches just north of Bahía, which for the most part are pristine and are often deserted. On one of these in particular, at Punta Palmar, history buffs can enjoy the privilege of beholding La Mitad del Mundo. Fishing enthusiasts gladly travel to Salinas to cast their lines, hoping to land the catch of the day. Last but not least, just a few hours from Guayaquil it is possible to observe dolphins, those affable, irresistible mammals that delight young and old alike.

FINDING YOUR WAY AROUND

Huaquillas

By bus

From Guayaquil, the trip is about five hours and costs a little less than $4. From Machala, count on a one-hour trip for approximately $1.50. Departures are every two or three hours.

Guayaquil

By plane

The airlines, TAME, SAN, and SAETA provide several flights daily from Quito for approximately $30. A connection is available every day between Cuenca and Guayaquil for the sum of $27. From Machala, planes serve Guayaquil practically every day for roughly $15. For about $25, there is a flight to Loja. **Aeropuerto Simón Bolívar** *(☎ 282-100)* is a few kilometres north of the city, on Avenida de las Americas. A taxi from the airport costs between $4 and $5.

By bus

Many buses travel to Guayaquil from Quito. The trip is about seven hours and costs approximately $7. Buses leave Cuenca for Guayaquil practically every hour. Count on the trip lasting four hours 30 minutes and costing a little less than $5. The *terminal terrestre* (bus terminal) is situated a few kilometres from the airport.

By train

A train leaves the station in the Andean village of Alausí and arrives on the Pacific coast at the little hamlet of Durán, just near Guayaquil, from which a ferry runs to Guayaquil practically every hour from 8am to about 6:30pm. If the train from Alausí is late, you may be required to spend the night in Durán.

Car rental agencies

At Simón Bolívar airport
Budget Rent-a-Car
☎ 284-559

Avis
☎ 285-498

Hertz
☎ 511-316

Playas

By bus

Several buses leave the *terminal terrestre* in Guayaquil in the direction of Playas. Count on a two-hour trip for a little over $1.

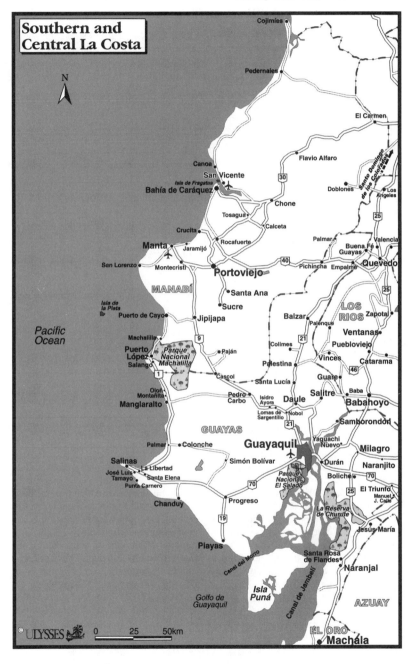

Southern and Central La Costa

N

Cojimíes

Pedernales

El Carmen

Flavio Alfaro

Santo Domingo de los Colorados

Canoa
San Vicente
Isla de Fragatas
Bahía de Caráquez

30

Doblones
Los Angeles

Chone

25

Tosagua
Calceta

Crucita
Rocafuerte

Palmar
Valencia

Manta
Jaramijó

Buena Fé
Guayas

San Lorenzo
Montecristi

40
Pichincha   Empalme
Quevedo

Portoviejo

MANABÍ

Santa Ana

25

Isla de
la Plata

Sucre

LOS
RIOS

Puerto de Cayo
Jipijapa

Balzar
Zapotal
Palenque

Pacific
Ocean

Machalilla

9

Colimes

Ventanas

Puerto
López
Parque
Nacional
Machalilla

Pajan

21

Puebloviejo

Vinces
Catarama

Salango

Palestina

Guare

46

Cascol
Santa Lucía

Olón
Montañita

1

Pedro
Carbo
Isidro
Ayora
Daule
Salitre
Baba
Babahoyo

Manglaralto

Lomas de
Sargentillo
Nobol

21

GUAYAS

Samborondón

Palmar
Colonche

Guayaquil
Yaguachi
Nuevo

Milagro

Salinas

Simón Bolívar
Durán

Naranjito

José Luis
Tamayo
La Libertad
Santa Elena

Parque
Nacional
El Salado
Boliche

70

Punta Carnero

25
El Triunfo

Chanduy

70

Manuel
J. Calle

Progreso

La Reserva
de Churute

19

Jesús María

Playas

Santa Rosa
de Flandes
Naranjal

Canal del Morro

AZUAY

Isla
Puná

Golfo de
Guayaquil

Canal de Jambelí

© ULYSSES   0   25   50km

EL ORO
Machala

Salinas

By bus

Buses for Salinas depart from La Libertad. From there, many buses travel to Salinas for the modest sum of $0.25. The trip takes about 15 minutes. From Guayaquil, buses make the two-and-a-half-hour journey to La Libertad for approximately $2.50.

Puerto López

By bus

From Salinas or Manta, the trip is about two hours and costs around $1.50.

Parque Nacional Machalilla and Isla de la Plata

If you organize a small group, you must buy your tickets at the office of the national park in Puerto López (just by the church). Budget for approximately $13 per person. The tour company Mantaraya *(in Puerto López, on Malecón, facing the three palm trees, ☎ 604-233)* organizes diving and fishing excursions on yachts to Isla de la Plata as well as expeditions in the national park. While the yachts cost a little more than other charters – about $35 per person, round-trip, excluding food and beverages, compared to between $20 and $30 per person for the least expensive boats – the crossing is more enjoyable and more comfortable, and the guides are generally more competent.

Jipijapa

By bus

From Puerto López and from Manta the trip is approximately one hour and 15 minutes and costs about $1. Departures virtually every hour.

Portoviejo

By plane

Flights from Quito are scheduled two or three times a week and cost approximately $25.

By bus

From Manta, the trip is one hour and costs $0.50; departures practically every hour. From Guayaquil, the trip is three hours and 30 minutes and costs about $3. From Bahía de Caráquez, the trip is two hours for the sum of $1; departures almost every hour.

Manta

By bus

Many buses leave from the *terminal terrestre* in Guayaquil in the direction of Manta. The trip is about four hours and costs approximately $4. From Quito, the trip takes over nine hours and the fare is a little less than $7. The *terminal terrestre* in Manta is at the corner of Avenida 24 Mayo and Avenida 8.

By plane

Flights leave regularly from Quito for Manta. Budget for approximately $25. The airport is located a few kilometres east of the city.

Bahía de Caráquez

By plane

There is an airport in the little village of San Vicente. Two or three times a week, flights are offered from Quito for the sum of approximately $30.

By bus

From Quito, the trip is close to eight hours and costs about $6.50. From Manta or Puerto López, the route travels through Portoviejo. From Guayaquil, count on a six-hour journey for about $5.50. The *terminal terrestre* in Bahía is on the Malecón at the corner of Calle Vinueza.

Isla Fragatas

This island is only accessible through the services of a tour company: Bahía Dolphin Tours *(Calle Salinas, Edificio Dos Hemisferios,* ☎ *692-084 and 692-086,* ⌐ *692-088, archtour@srv1.telconet.et)* or Guacamayo Adventures *(Avenida Bolívar and Arenas, Apartado 70,* ☎ *690-597,* ⌐ *691-412).*

San Vicente

By plane

Two or three times a week, flights are provided from Quito for the sum of about $30.

By bus

From Manta, the bus ride lasts roughly three hours and costs approximately $2.25. From Canoa, buses travel in the direction of San Vicente every half-hour for the modest sum of $0.30.

By boat

A ferry leaves the dock of Bahía de Caráquez when it is fully loaded or every half-hour. The trip is about 10 minutes and tickets for car-ferry service cost $3 (passengers travel free). Travellers on foot can board boats for the modest sum of $0.25; frequent departures.

Canoa

By bus

From San Vicente, buses travel in the direction of Canoa every half-hour for the minimal cost of $0.30. The trip takes about 20 minutes.

By bicycle

From San Vicente a very scenic road stretches 17 km to Canoa. Hiking, or renting a bicycle in Bahía, is a wonderful means of exploring the long deserted beaches along the route. Needless to say, the road provides magnificent views over Bahía and the ocean.

Pedernales

By bus

From San Vicente, tickets are $3 for a three-hour ride. From Guayaquil, count on nine hours and slightly more than $8.

Cojimíes

By bus

From Pedernales, the bus-trip lasts one hour and 30 minutes and costs about $2.

By boat

From Muisné, boats to Pedernales cost $5 and the trip is one hour and 30 minutes. The sea is sometimes rough and rain is a possibility.

 PRACTICAL INFORMATION

Huaquillas

Telephone centre (EMETEL): On the main street.

Immigration office (*Oficina de Migraciones*): On the main street; open every day, generally from 8am to noon and from 2pm to 6pm.

Machala

Tourist office (CETUR): Avenida 9 de Mayo at Pichincha.

Telephone centre (EMETEL): Avenida 9 de Octubre at Calle Vélez.

Post office: Calle Bolívar at Juan Montalvo.

Banks: Banco Continental, Avenida 9 de Octubre at Juan Montalvo.

Banco del Pacífico, Calle Rocafuerte at Tarquí.

Consulate: Peruvian Consulate, Calle Bolívar at Colón, ☎ 930-680.

Guayaquil

Tourist office (CETUR): Calle Aguirre 104 at Malecón, ☎ 328-312.

Telephone centre (EMETEL): Calle Pedro Carbo at Clemente Ballén.

Post office: Calle Pedro Carbo at Aguirre.

Banks: Banco Filanbanco, Avenida 9 de Octubre at Pichincha; VISA cash advances may be made here.

Banco de Guayaquil, Calle P. Ycaza at Pichincha; VISA card withdrawals may be made here.

Cambiosa, Avenida 9 de Octubre 113.

Cambitur, Avenida 9 de Octubre 129.

Casa de Cambios Salcedo SA, Avenida 9 de Octubre 427 at Chimborazo.

American Express, Avenida 9 de Octubre 1900 at Esmeraldas.

SAN and SEATA offices: Calle Vélez at Chile, ☎ 200-600.

Tour companies: Metropolitan Touring Calle Antepara 915 at Avenida 9 de Octubre, ☎ 320-300, ⇄ 323-050.

Canodros, Calle Luís Urdaneta 1418 at Avenida del Ejército, ☎ 285-711, ⇄ 287-651.

Ecoventura, Avenida Arosemena, ☎ 206-748, ⇄ 202-990.

Consulates: Canada, Calle Córdova 810 at Rendón, 21st floor, office 4, ☎ 563-560, ⇄ 314-562.

United States, Avenida 9 de Octubre at García Moreno, ☎ 323-570, ⇄ 325-286.

Hospitals: Clinica Kennedy, Avenida del Periodista, ☎ 286-963.

Pharmacy: Fybeca (open 24 hours), Urdesa, Avenida Victor Emilio Estrada 609 at Las Monjas, ☎ 881-444, or 381-468.

Puerto López

Telephone centre (EMETEL): On Calle Principal, next to Centro de Visitantes del Parque Nacional Machalilla. For calls within the country only.

Office of the Centro de visitantes del Parque Nacional Machalilla: Behind the EMETEL office; open from 7am to noon and from 2pm to 5pm.

Tour companies: Mantaraya, Malecón (in front of the three palm trees), ☎ 604-233.

Machalilla Tour, Malecón, ☎ 604-206.

Salinas

Tourist office (CETUR): On the Malecón.

Telephone centre (EMETEL): Calle 20 at Avenida 3.

Post office: Calle Enrique Gallo, facing Filanbanco.

Bank: Filanbanco, Calle Enrique Gallo at Las Palmas.

Tour company: Pescatour, Malecón 577 at Rumiñahui, ☎ 772-391, ⇄ 443-142.

Pharmacy: Farmacía Central, Malecón at Calle 23.

Manta

Tourist office (CETUR): On the pedestrian mall, Avenida 3, between Calle 10 and Calle 11.

Telephone centre (EMETEL): On the Malecón, at the corner of Avenida 1 and Calle 11.

Post office: Avenida 4 at Calle 8.

Banks: Cambicruz, Casa de Cambio AZ, and Casa de Cambio Delgado are all on Avenida 2.

Tour companies: Metropolitan Touring, Avenida 4 at Calle 13, ☎ 623-090.

Delgado Travel, Avenida 2 at Calle 13
☎ 620-046.

Portoviejo

Tourist office (CETUR): Calle Pedro Gual at Juan Montalvo.

Telephone centre (EMETEL): Avenida 10 de Agosto at Pacheco.

Post office: Calle Ricuarte at Sucre.

Bahía de Caráquez

Tourist office (CETUR): Malecón at Calle Arenas.

Telephone centre (EMETEL): Malecón at Calle Arenas (next to CETUR).

Banks: Filanbanco, Calle Aguilera at Malecón.

Banco Comercial de Manabí, Malecón at Calle Ante.

Post office: Calle Aguilera 108 at Malecón.

Tour companies:

Bahía Dolphin Tours *(Calle Salinas, Edificio Dos Hemisferios, ☎ 692-084 and 692-086, ⊷ 692-088, archtour@srv1.telconet.et, http//www.qni.com/~mi/bahia/bahia/bahia.html)* organizes a variety of excursions for more adventurous travellers who have slightly ampler budgets. It offers expeditions to Isla Fragatas, to the dry tropical forest, to caves, to private beaches, to Montecristi and to shrimp farms. Among the most interesting trips organized by the tour company is the one to Chirije, an ocean-front lodge where nature tourism, archaeological sightseeing, and relaxation are combined in one programme.

The archaeological site at Chirije was discovered in 1957 by Emilio Estrada, who found data in French archives on the location of the equator reported by the French mission headed by La Condamine. The mission measured zero-latitude for the first time and contributed to the establishment of the metric system. The metre, the basic unit of length in the metric system, was established through measurements of, and is defined as a fixed fraction of earth's quadrant.

Set on a deserted strip of beach just 25 minutes from Bahía de Caráquez, Chirije is over 2,500 years old. The excavation of the site's substructure was made possible by contributions from institutions such as the Natural History Museum of the Smithsonian Institute in Washington, D.C. and from private firms such as Bahía Dolphin Tours, which is largely responsible for the realization of the archaeological project at Chirije. Research continues, and volunteers benefit from the experience of working side-by-side with archaeologists as they continue to unearth ancient tombs and artifacts. A museum displays the results of work accomplished so far.

The wilderness surrounding the site is absolutely breathtaking, and permits the observation of dozens of bird species in a dry tropical forest. Available accommodations are quite comfortable, consisting of private three-to-seven-person cabins that include kitchens, bathrooms, and hot water. As many as 25 people can be accommodated in four cabins.

Guacamayo Adventures *(Avenida Bolívar and Arenas, Apartado 70, ☎ 690-597, ⇌ 691-412)* organizes a trip to suit every budget. The philosophy of the tour company is based on principles of nature conservation and ecotourism. Accordingly it proposes creative undertakings that provide an alternative to the exploitation of people, animals and ecologically threatened areas (mangrove and dry forests). The tour company also figures among the founders of the environmental school of Río Muchacho, which offers environmental studies within the domain of the national education program. For more information, or to send donations, write to Escuela Río Muchacho, c/o Nicola Mears, Darío Proaño-Leroux, Casilla 11, Bahía de Caráquez, Ecuador. The tour company organizes excursions to Isla Fragatas, Río Muchacho, and the surrounding area. It also rents bicycles, kayaks, boats and fishing tackle.

Spanish schools: For more information, communicate with Guacamayo Adventures or Academía de Español in Bahía de Caráquez *(☎ 05-633-272, P.O. Box 13-02-74 Bahía de Caráquez, Manabí, Ecuador)* or in Quito *(☎ 02-448-893, P.O. Box 17-17-21-521, Quito, Ecuador)*.

 EXPLORING

Huaquillas

The town of Huaquillas would be of little interest to travellers were it not for its geographic position. In fact, it is a dusty and charmless border town through which travellers cross to and from Peru. Try to avoid crossing the border at the beginning of January, for this is the period in which the treaty that surrounded an area of disputed territory from Ecuador to Peru was signed, and occasionally at this time of year frictions intensify to the point generating sparks. Because of this historical resentment, it is preferable to cross the border by air rather than over land.

Machala

Capital of the Oro province, Machala serves as a doorway to the Peruvian border, which is located not more than 50 kilometres from here. Founded in 1758, the town today numbers almost 200,000 residents and owes its success to the flourishing banana-cultivation industry, introduced at the turn of the century. Machala presents few tourist attractions, but may serve as a home base from which to explore the bewitching petrified forest of Puyango, the **Bosque Putrificado de Puyango** (see p 195).

Durán

The little town of Durán is renowned as one endpoint of the magnificent route of the trans-Andean railroad from Alausí to the Costa. Few travellers stop over, and they hurry through lest they end up having stay the night waiting for the train. Durán possesses only minimal facilities.

Guayaquil

According to legend, the name Guayaquil is the result of combining the name of an Amerindian monarch named Guaya with that of his wife, Quil. In 1535, one year after establishing Quito, the Spaniard Sebastián de Benalcázar attempted to found the town of Guayaquil and was unsuccessful, as the Amerindians were fiercely opposed. Instead, the credit goes to Francisco de Orellana, who is better-known for accomplishing the first continental crossing from the Pacific to the Atlantic, and who founded the city in 1538.

Built on the banks of Río Guayas, Guayaquil was once a lovely colonial port town that received merchandise from the Sierra and dispatched it to Spain. Unfortunately, over the course of repeated attacks by Amerindians, pirates and brigands, the town was razed, rifled, and pillaged.

Since the birth of this tropical city, Guayaquileños have built their houses of wood for better ventilation in an effort to allay the effects of the gusting hot air that regularly beats the whole coastal region. From December to the beginning of May, ambient heat, combined with elevated humidity levels, renders the climate suffocating and altogether unpleasant. Between May and December, the weather is just hot and humid... Over the course of the centuries, most of these houses have been ravaged many times over by violent fires and the repeated attacks of pirates that once marauded the length of the Pacific coast. For these reasons, old wooden houses are gradually being replaced by permanent modern buildings.

Old houses of Guayaquil

The economic heart of the country, capital of the province of Guayas, and one of the most important seaports in Latin America, Guayaquil is Ecuador's biggest city, with close to two million residents. One of the most striking things about Guayaquil is the mix of cultures: Amerindian, Spanish, African and Asian. It is a hot, noisy city, indeed, even a dangerous one: in the last few years violent crime and all sorts of attacks have unfortunately been more common. As a rule, the majority of travellers passing through Guayaquil quickly head to Durán to take the famous train to Alausí, or hurry to the plane that deposits them in the middle of the Galápagos archipelago. Despite all its disadvantages, Guayaquil possesses certain attributes that merit recognition.

A stroll through the trees along the **Malecón ★ (1)** offers a temporary

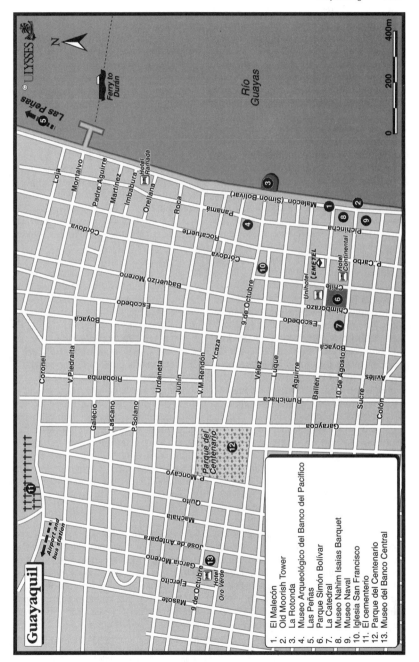

Guayaquil

Río Guayas

Ferry to Durán

Las Peñas

Airport and bus station

Parque del Centenario

Hotel Oro Verde

Hotel Ramada

Hotel Continental

Unihotel

CEMEPEL

N

ULYSSES

0   200   400m

1. El Malecón
2. Old Moorish Tower
3. La Rotonda
4. Museo Arqueológico del Banco del Pacífico
5. Las Peñas
6. Parque Simón Bolívar
7. La Catedral
8. Museo Nahim Isaias Barquet
9. Museo Naval
10. Iglesia San Francisco
11. El cementerio
12. Parque del Centenario
13. Museo del Banco Central

escape from the busy and tumultuous activity of the city and a view of the boats drifting on Río Guayas. An **old Moorish tower ★ (2)** rises proudly from the horizon, capturing the attention of passers-by with its massive silhouette and pastel colours. Unfortunately, come nightfall, the Malecón can become an arena of street crime.

At the intersection of the Malecón and Avenida 9 de Octubre is **La Rotonda ★ (3)**, of particular interest to history buffs. A circular space encloses a statue commemorating the historic meeting of Simón Bolívar and the Argentinean general José de San Martín, two very important figures in the independence of Latin American nations.

Two blocks north, **El Museo Arqueológico del Banco del Pacífico ★ (4)** *(Tue to Fri 10am to 6pm, Sat to Sun 11am to 1pm; Calle P. Ycaza 113 at Pichincha, ☎ 566-010, ext. 5390)* houses an exhibit of about 650 ceramic pieces from pre-Hispanic cultures of the Ecuadoran coast, which arouses a certain collective, national pride among Ecuadorans.

Continuing along the Malecón, you reach the popular quarter of **Las Peñas ★ (5)**, in which are located the last remaining colonial wood homes. Antique cannons point out to sea, bearing mute witness to defences mounted against pirate ships that not long ago scoured the coast. Today the neighbourhood has become an artists' enclave. Be careful! Many visitors to the neighbourhood are mugged. Moreover, it is strongly discouraged to venture onto Cerro Santa Ana (adjoining Las Peñas), as attacks on tourists are very common there.

Land iguanas bustle about under the foliage of the hundred-year-old trees of **Parque Simón Bolívar ★ (6)** *(Calle Chile and Chimborazo)*. No need to fear; despite their resemblance to prehistoric monsters and their slightly worrying expression, they are harmless, vegetarian creatures.

The foundation of the **Catedral ★ (7)** *(facing Parque Simón Bolívar)* was laid in the 16th century, but because of numerous destructions, the cathedral was not completed until much later era. Nonetheless, its Gothic Revival style is worth a gander, and romantic souls will doubtless take the opportunity to light a candle and make a wish.

Three museums are within short walking distance of Parque Bolívar, the Museo Municipal, the Museo Nahim Isaias Barquet, and the Museo Naval. At the Museo Municipal *($1; Mon to Fri 8:30am to 12:30pm and 1pm to 4:30pm; Calle Sucre at Pedro Carbo)* the public can admire, in a modern, air-conditioned locale, a variety of contemporary artwork, as well as a large guava-wood column decorated with masculine and feminine figures depicted in the positions and attitudes symbolic of fertility. There is also a diorama of a tomb composed of real bones extracted from the site at Huancavilca and artifacts meant to accompany the lost souls on their eternal journey.

On the second floor of the Filanbanco building, the **Museo Nahim Isaias Barquet ★ (8)** *(free admission; Mon to Sat 10am to 5pm; Calle Pichincha at Ballén)* was founded in honour of ex-banker and art-lover Nahim Isaias Barquet. Many years ago, he was kidnapped and then murdered by his assailants before a ransom was payed.

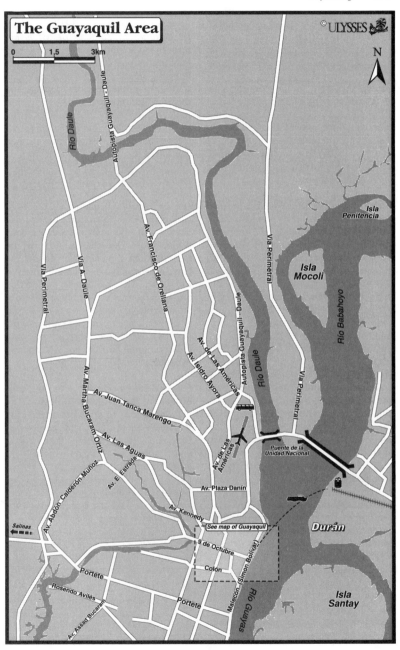

The Guayaquil Area

The museum presents an exhibition of colonial art, including polychromatic wood sculptures and oil paintings that date back to the 16th century, a period during which Amerindians, *mestizos* and people born in the country alike dedicated their work completely to the propagation of religious doctrine. Four centuries later, the perfect technique, elevated conception, and sense of drama displayed in these works continue to impress and dazzle viewers, regardless of creed.

Museo Naval ★ (9) *($0.25; schedule varies; Malecón and Sucre)* is divided into four exhibition halls and recounts the history of navigation in Ecuador from the colonial period to Independence. The museum houses paintings, historical shipboard logs, and numerous models and reproductions of antique vessels, notably the first submarine constructed in South America, the *Hipopotamo*, designed by the Ecuadoran José Rodriguez in 1838.

The **Iglesia San Francisco ★ (10)** *(Calle Chile at Avenida 9 de Octubre)* has been renovated several times since its original construction in the 18th century, but it is nevertheless worth visiting. If time does not permit a visit to the Otavalo market, take note that some Otavaleños peddle their wares next to this church.

El cementerio ★★★ (11) (the cemetery) is the preserve of countless memorials of all sorts, each more beautiful than the last, including that to the former president of the country, Vicente Rocafuerte. However, vigilance is a must here and it is preferable to visit in a group as the deserted lanes are sometimes haunted by mysterious shadows that seem to dart between the tombstones...

Parque del Centenario (12) *(Avenida 9 de Octubre at Lorenzo de Garailloa)* bisects Avenida 9 de Octubre and constitutes one of the largest parks in the city. It is wonderful spot in which to take a break from the hustle and bustle of sightseeing.

A few blocks from Parque del Centenario, the **Museo del Banco Central ★★ (13)** *(Mon to Fri 9am to 4pm; Calle Anteparra 900 at Avenida 9 de Octubre, ☎ 327-402)* presents an interesting collection of works by contemporary Ecuadoran painters. Guardian of a rich cultural heritage of some thousand archaeological pieces issued from the coastal region, the anthropological museum of the central bank proposes hands-on exploration of the past. The multimedia exhibition presents information by means of two-dimensional animation, text, speeches, ambient music, video, and comic strips, all of which elaborate on the environmental and the socio-economic aspects of indigenous societies.

For a relaxing excursion on a free day, **El Jardín Botanico de Guayaquil ★** *(situated about 15 km north of the city, ☎ 416-975)*, the botanical gardens of Guayaquil, house more than 3,000 plant species, including about 150 types of orchid.

Guayaquil is also a good base from which to explore the **Bosque Protector Cerro Blanco** (see p 196).

Playas

Also known as General Vilamil, Playas is a major resort and fishing centre some 100 kilometres southeast of Guayaquil. Many Guayaquileños have vacation homes in Playas, but during the low season (May and June) the town is very quiet. Many hotels rent rooms at reduced prices while others close up altogether. In any case, it is always possible to bargain down prices in this period. From January to April and on holiday weekends, however, the town comes alive and hotels are often completely booked up.

Playas means "beaches" in Spanish, and indeed this large village owes its name to the numerous beaches nearby, along the Pacific coast. Those who envision long white sand beaches bordering a pristine turquoise ocean will be disappointed though. Instead, however, travellers can enjoy the seascape at their leisure and observe the many balsa boats, similar to those used by natives before the arrival of Spanish colonizers, that loll on the waves. The beaches are dangerous at night.

Peninsula of Santa Elena

The annals of history tell us that Pizarro was navigating southward, in search of Eldorado, when he perceived this prominent point of the continent on the Pacific. He ordered his crew to land and collect water. The crew attempted to disembark at the spot today known as La Libertad, but the heavy swell and rocky outcrops prevented a successful landing and the crew had to move on to a calmer cove to land.

Setting foot on the peninsula, Pizarro knelt on bent knee and, holding his sword in his right hand and the standard of Castile in his left, baptised it Santa Elena, in the name of Empress Helen, mother of Constantine the Great and saint of the Catholic Church for her

dedication to the development of Christianity.

Until 1937, Santa Elena included just one district. Today it is a vast territory comprising Salinas, La Libertad, and Santa Elena proper. This region possesses vast natural resources as well as land suited to agriculture and stock breeding. The earth contains petroleum, gypsum (a mineral used in the making of plaster) and limestone, and the sea provides work for commercial fishermen and artisans. La Libertad is the economic and commercial hub of the peninsula and is therefore not particularly appealing to tourists.

Punta Carnero ★

Punta Carnero is an ideal, quiet, isolated seaside spot. This little village is signalled by the silhouettes of two quality hotels that overlook the ocean and long beaches. The sea here is particularly dangerous, though, and attempts to adventure into the water are pointless, as the threat of being swept away by the strong current is very serious. Nonetheless, the extraordinary landscape is certainly worth the trip.

Valdivia

This little village, situated about 50 kilometres north of La Libertad, is renowned as an archaeological landmark. The very oldest traces of the country's, and for that matter the continent's, original civilizations were found here. Unfortunately, most of the excavated artifacts have been moved to museums in Guayaquil.

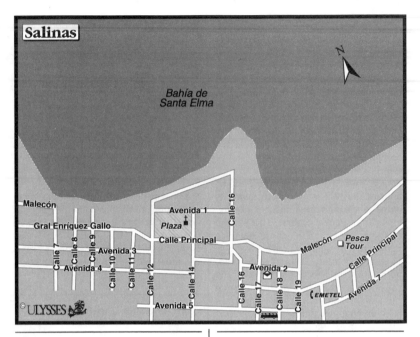

Salinas ★

About 150 kilometres west of Guayaquil and a few hours south of Puerto López, Salinas is a major resort for wealthy Ecuadorans and owes its name to the saltworks scattered throughout the area. Unlike the picturesque fishing villages dispersed the length of the Costa, Salinas has the look of a modern city of some 20,000 residents. The colonial charm of yesteryear has been replaced by the silhouettes of drab concrete hotels and apartment buildings that line the Malecón. The beach is clean and swimmable, but not particularly appealing; and even though the sea is calm, you could easily forget you are in Ecuador. Pedal-boats may be rented at the beach and the tour company Pesca Tour *(☎ 772-391, ≈ 443-142, in Guayaquil ☎ 443-365)* on the Malecón organizes ocean fishing excursions.

Montañita ★

This tiny resort town is strewn with little, economical beach-side hotels most of which close up for the low season. Montañita especially attracts surfing enthusiasts, who consider this section of the coast ideal for their sport. The area is popular with backpacking tourists.

Salango ★

Most travellers stop briefly at Salango to visit its museum *(schedule varies)*, which displays a small archaeological collection, and then satisfy their appetites at the reputed restaurant, El Delfín Magico, which is arguably more popular than the exhibition itself. The 20-minute bus ride along the coastal road linking Puerto López and Salango offers splendid views of the ocean and forest-covered hills.

Puerto López ★

A little village whose main economic activities involve fishing and tourism, Puerto López itself does not offer much to see or do, but its popularity increases every year thanks to its proximity to the entrance of glorious **Parque Nacional Machalilla** (see p 196) and **Isla de la Plata** (see p 196). Numerous are the travellers who, due to the expense of the trip, cannot visit the insular world of marvels on the Galápagos Islands and who therefore plan their itineraries around an expedition to the coastal national park of Machalilla, home to myriad animal species rarely found outside the Galápagos archipelago.

Montecristi ★

Founded in 1741, Montecristi draws the attention of travellers thanks to the skilled and versatile artisans who are based here. This little village competes with towns in the province of Azuay for the honour of being the centre of production for the best Panama hats in the world; it also produces hammocks and pottery. A group of local artisans, *Sombreros Finos Montecristi (Calle Rocafuerte 500, ☎ 606-282)*, has a little workshop just near the church, where they sell their products. Three to four metres of leaves are required to make a top-notch Panama hat. Depending on the quality, prices for the hats vary between $10 and over $75. These prices may seem high, but in Europe and North America these same

hats are sold for at least $50 and sometimes upwards of $2,000...

The village bears the additional distinction of being the birthplace of Eloy Alfaro, former Liberal-party chief of Ecuador. A bust of General Alfaro is proudly displayed in the large square facing the church. The first Liberal president of Ecuador, he is credited with the separation of the church and the school system as well as the completion of the railroad linking the coast and the highlands. The little **museum** *(schedule varies; near the church)* devoted to the life and work of this national hero houses portraits, his uniforms and a library of books that belonged to him.

La Pila

Residents of La Pila distinguish themselves through their skill in crafting faithful reproductions of pre-Columbian ceramics and offering visitors a great range of products that spreads the length of the main street. Pottery factories are situated on the neighbouring hills. The natives who originally inhabited this region have been recognized for their talent as potters of utilitarian and decorative ceramics and their creative use of form and colour.

Jipijapa

Nicknamed *La Sultana del Café* because its main activity centres around the exportation of coffee beans, Jipijapa is a large town of around 30,000 residents. It is of no particular interest to travellers; in fact, outside of coffee

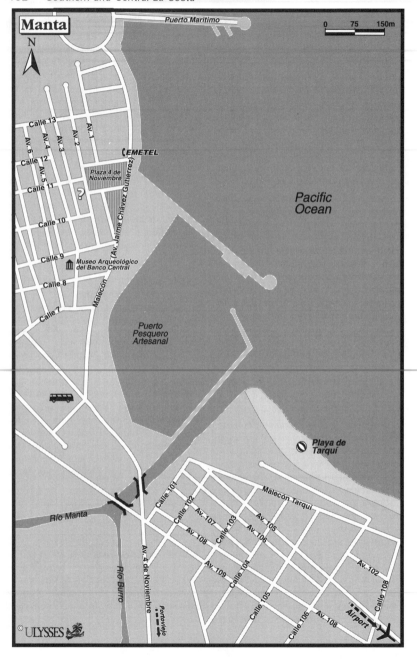

Manta

N

Puerto Maritimo

0   75   150m

Pacific
Ocean

Calle 13
Av. 6
Av. 4
Av. 3
Av. 2
Av. 1
EMETEL
Calle 12
Av. 5
Plaza 4 de
Noviembre
Calle 11
Calle 10
Calle 9
Museo Arqueológico
del Banco Central
Calle 8
(Av. Jaime Chávez Gutiérrez)
Malecón
Calle 7
Puerto
Pesquero
Artesanal

Playa de
Tarquí

Río Manta
Calle 101
Calle 102
Av. 107
Calle 103
Malecón Tarquí
Av. 105
Av. 108
Av. 106
Río Burro
Av. 109
Calle 104
Av. 102
Calle 105
Av. 4 de Noviembre
Portoviejo
Calle 106
Av. 108
Calle 108
Airport

©ULYSSES

production, there is not really anything to see.

Manta

Once known as Jocay, Manta has long been considered the capital of *manteña* culture. From about A.D. 500, the indigenous people of this region were great sailors who navigated the length of the Pacific coast on their balsa-wood boats and dominated the Ecuadoran shores until they were brought under the yoke of the Spanish by conquistador Francisco Pacheco in 1535. An important port, today Manta is a busy, noisy city that is bisected by a cove – Manta and its harbour lie to the west, and the beaches of Tarquí, which are not necessarily very inviting, to the east.

It is strongly discouraged to stroll at night in unknown or remote corners of the city. As in Guayaquil, stories of robbery and assault abound. Be careful!

The **Museo Arqueológico del Banco Central ★★** *($0.50; Mon to Fri 9am to 4:30pm; Calle 9 at Avenida 4, ☎ 622-878)* recounts the history of *manteña* culture through the ages. The figurines exhibited are representative of the anatomy of Manteños of the traditional era, with deformed skulls and large, round, hooked noses. Apparently, at a very young age, Manteño children were bound just above the eyes with a ribbon, enlarging and giving a swollen appearance to their heads, which was considered symbolic of beauty and intelligence.

Bahía de Caráquez ★★★

A little further north, Bahía de Caráquez presents an altogether more welcoming image than Manta. A large, quiet and charming village in the coastal region, Bahía de Caráquez has been attracting extra attention for the last few years because the ex-president of the country, Sixto Balén, regularly spends his vacations here. The town once played an important role in Ecuador's economy as a point of export for a large variety of products. Today it is a resort town popular with Ecuadorans and foreigners due to its lovely beaches and its proximity to **Isla Fragatas** (see p 198), which holds particular interest to bird-watchers and admirers of mangrove trees. Bahía can serve as a base from which to explore the region.

San Vicente

The little fishing village of San Vicente is situated on the other side of Bahía de Caráquez, about 15 minutes away by boat. Its economy depends on the same activities as Bahía, but its population is less affluent.

Canoa

Canoa, a little fishing village founded around 180 years ago, was partially destroyed in 1982 when the ocean current El Niño wreaked havoc all along the Ecuadoran coast. Canoa has little to offer travellers who prefer quality hotel accommodations. On the other hand, its beaches are often deserted and are devoid of tourist development,

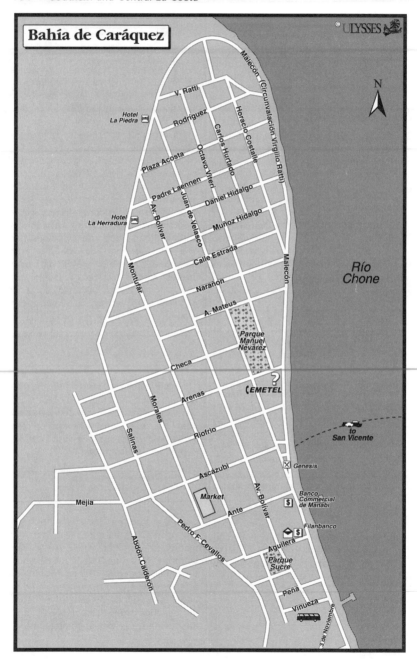

invariably pleasing those who first and foremost seek calm and tranquillity. Near the village are some caverns, in front of which blue-footed boobies are often sighted. Be careful of slippery rocks and the rising tide. It is recommended to use the services of a tour company in Bahía to travel to Canoa.

Punta Palmar ★★★

In general, historical monuments are rare in the Costa region. One exception is Punta Palmar (two hours from Bahía), which is undeniably appealing to history buffs. Due to its isolation, Punta Palmar is accessible only through guided tours organized by Bahía Dolphin Tours (see p 182) or Guacamayo Adventures (see p 183). Although it is generally accepted that La Mitad del Mundo is located north of Quito, the journal of Charles Marie de La Condamine provides evidence that the first measurement of terrestrial longitude was calculated on the Ecuadoran coast. The information furnished by the journal and the discovery of the inscription it contains prove that the metric system was invented on the coast and not in the Andes. The actual monument was constructed in 1986 with the cooperation of the French consulate in Ecuador. The inscription reads: *En homenaje a los sabios que determinaron la figura de la tierra en Ecuador en el siglo XVIII de 1736-1744 Luís Godin, Charles Marie de la Condamine, Jorge Juan, Pierre Borguer, T.V. Madondaldo,...Julio 1986.*

Moreover, the Mitad del Mundo of the Costa is a much more romantic site than the one north of Quito, given the surrounding vegetation, its seaside location and the image it conjures up of newcomers and natives together, calculating the exact spot at which the earth divides itself into two hemispheres that turn toward the unknown, limitless horizon.

Pedernales

Fewer than 10 kilometres north of Punta Palmar, Pedernales is another fishing village undergoing rapid development caused by the numerous shrimp farms along its shoreline. Pedernales possesses an infrastructure that at best can be described as summary, and nothing in particular captures the attention of tourists who, for the most part, travel right through either northward or southward.

Cojimíes

Cojimíes is a tiny fishing village with practically nonexistent tourist accommodations hardly worth mentioning, except that the town is the only significant stopover point for travellers heading to and from the little island of Muisné (see p 165).

 PARKS

Bosque Putrificado de Puyango ★★

The small petrified forest of Puyango stretches over at most 2,650 hectares, but shelters one of the largest collections of fossilized trees, plants and animals in the world. Moreover, approximately 130 bird species have been inventoried here. Numerous tour companies, among them that of the owner of Tangara Guest House in Guayaquil (see p 200), arrange excursions to the Puyango.

Bosque Protector Cerro Blanco ★

About 15 minutes from Guayaquil, the Bosque Protector Cerro Blanco *($1, $3 overnight; ☎ 871-900, ⌨ 873-528)* is spread over 2,000 hectares of dry tropical forest and offers haven to more than 200 bird species. Howler monkeys and ocelots are among the other animal species present in this protected zone. Two fields have been cleared so that visitors may observe the flora and fauna of Cerro Blanco at their leisure.

La Reserva de Churute ★

Situated 50 kilometres southeast of Guayaquil, this tropical nature reserve covers more than 30,500 hectares and protects flora and fauna including monkeys, tortoises, mangrove trees and orchids, among other species.

Parque Nacional Machalilla ★ ★ ★

The impressive Parque Nacional Machalilla *(entrance $13; for more information, contact Centro de visitantes del Parque Nacional Machalilla in Puerto López, next to the EMETEL office)* stretches over 46,700 hectares, including Isla de la Plata, and is characterized by a particular tropical environment that allows for three distinct zones of vegetation. In fact the flora of the park is dependent on three successive, completely contrasting climates: a rainy season, a dry season and an arid season. Because of this unique environment, many animal species that are indigenous to the Galápagos archipelago also inhabit this marvellous coastal park. Among these are land tortoises, land iguanas, as well as innumerable bird species, such as herons, frigate-birds and eagles. The park also includes a small archaeological museum that provides an account of the history and richness of *manteña* culture; and many spectacular beaches, among them La Playita, La Tortugita and Los Frailes. La Tortugita is interesting because of its iron-rich black sand, but the best place to swim is unquestionably Los Frailes, as it offers a superb view of the bay and the undertow here is not so strong. A loop trail crisscrosses the park over a distance of 3.7 kilometres. As well, a few austere rooms and a small campground are at the disposal of visitors who decide to stay overnight in the park.

Isla de la Plata ★ ★ ★

This magnificent island is in the domain of Parque Nacional Machalilla and floats on the ocean's surface about 30 kilometres off the coast. Travellers who lack the means to visit the celebrated Galápagos Islands can opt for a tour of Isla de la Plata. The island is home to abundant fauna, notably boobies and albatrosses (the latter are present only between April and November), which makes for fascinating visits throughout the year. On the other hand, unlike the Galápagos, Isla de la Plata is not a volcanic island. The island is believed to have broken away from the continent millions of years ago. A continental shelf remains, connecting the island to the mainland, but a bridge that was once intact has since collapsed and this land link is unfortunately below sea level.

The island is covered by two trails, of 3.5 kilometres *(punta machete)* and 5 kilometres *(punta escalera)*, respectively. It is difficult to hike both trails unless you leave very early in the morning. However, if would like to explore both trails, notify the tour company ahead of time and obtain the consent of the others in your group. It is strongly recommended to spend the night in Puerto López, since departures for Isla de la Plata start at about 7am. If you plan to travel here between June and September, it is also important to make reservations in advance, as hotels are often completely booked during this period.

Over the course of 1996, biologists observed that boobies on Isla de la Plata were nesting on tree branches. Normally the booby nests on the ground. Scientists so far conclude that rather than involving a particular sub-species indigenous to the island, the behaviour of these boobies is motivated by an instinct to protect themselves from potential predators on the ground.

Between July and October, the trip from the mainland is a wonderful whale-watching opportunity. However, in this period the sea is rougher and the wind more intense, so dress warmly. The crossing to the island takes about two hours and 30 minutes. Remember to bring water and sandwiches as there are no amenities on the island, neither hotels nor restaurants.

The boat lands at Bahía Drake, named in honour of the famous English pirate and navigator who made a career in the 16th century of plundering Spanish galleons and took refuge on Isla de la Plata. One day, he himself was attacked by other pirates attempting to seize his looted gold. Arriving at the bay of Isla de la Plata, Drake threw his treasure overboard in the hope of recuperating it later. However, he had underestimated the depth of the bay and lost his treasure forever. Oral tradition has it that no one ever saw the treasure again. The bay is named in memory of this seafarer, and the island's name, "plata", means "silver" in Spanish, evoking the wealth that lies undisturbed in the depths of the sea.

Sir Francis Drake

Born circa 1540, Sir Francis Drake was a privateer in the eyes of the English and a pirate in the eyes of the Spanish, but most importantly he was the first English navigator to circle the world. He died in 1596 fighting the Spanish.

If you would like to organize a little group, you must purchase your tickets at the office of the national park near the church in Puerto López. Budget for approximately $13 per person. The least expensive boats to the island cost between $20 and $25 per person, round-trip, excluding food and beverages. Yachts cost a little more, about $35 per person, round-trip, excluding food and drink, but the crossing is much more pleasant and comfortable, and the guides are generally more competent. The Mantaraya tour company *(in Puerto López, on Malecón, facing the three palm trees, ☎ 604-233)* organizes diving and fishing excursions to Isla de la Plata by yacht.

Frigate-bird

Isla Fragatas ★★★

Located just 15-minutes by boat from the town of Bahía de Caráquez, this little island is named for the innumerable frigate-birds that haunt its shores. While this species of seabird is also indigenous to the Galápagos Islands, there are claims that the concentration of frigate-birds is actually higher here. Ornithology enthusiasts can observe at their leisure these magnificent fishing birds that have such remarkable, distinctive sexual dimorphism. During the mating season, the giant red pouches just under the inferior mandibles of males swell to attract the attention of and seduce females. For their part, females have white throats and breasts. The most striking natural characteristic of Isla Fragatas is an exceptional concentration of mangroves, but unfortunately the proliferation of shrimp farms along the shore has caused the destruction of close to 95% of the red mangrove forest, severely reducing the nesting grounds of frigate-birds.

The island is only accessible through the services of a tour company: Bahía Dolphin Tours *(Calle Salinas, Edificio Dos Hemisferios, ☎ 692-084 and 692-086, ⇄ 692-088, archtour @srv1.telconet.et)* or Guacamayo Adventures *(Avenida Bolívar and Arenas, Apartado 70, ☎ 690-597, ⇄ 691-412)*, both located in Bahía de Caráquez.

ACCOMMODATIONS

An important detail to keep in mind concerning hotels in the Costa is to be sure that the bed is covered by a mosquito net before renting a room. The concentration of insects in the region is particularly significant and the diseases they transmit can be very serious. Mosquito netting is preferable to constant use of insect repellent, which can eventually be harmful to the skin.

Machala

Hostal la Bahía *($10; Calle Olmedo at Junín)* is decorated with little originality but is perfectly acceptable for travellers with more modest budgets.

Not to be confused with the luxurious Oro Verde, **Hotel Oro** *(30$; pb, hw, ℜ; Calle Olmedo at Juan Montalvo, ☎ 930-783, ⊷ 937-569)* is right in the centre of Machala and offers clean, simple rooms.

The rooms at the **Rizzo** *($45; pb, hw, ≈, ℜ; Calle Guayas at Bolívar, ☎ 921-511)* have certainly seen better days, but are nonetheless clean and functional. There is access to a pool, a sauna and a casino.

Flanked by a swimming pool, equipped with a gym, two restaurants and car-rental service, and offering spacious rooms complete with mini-bars, the **Oro Verde** *($100; tv, pb, hw, ≈, ℜ; Circunvalación Norte at Vehicular, ☎ 933-140, ⊷ 933-150)* is without question *the* luxury hotel in town. The personnel is friendly and efficient.

Durán

Near the station, the little hotel **La Paz** *($9; Calle Esmeraldas at Cuenca)* is popular with travellers waiting for the next day's train. Frugal shelter that is acceptable for one night.

Guayaquil

Know that staying in Guayaquil is expensive. In general, hotel prices in Guayaquil are much higher than those in Quito or Cuenca, and this holds true even when the quality of accommodation is comparable. The safest hotels are in downtown Guayaquil.

Near the *terminal terrestre* and the airport, **Ecuahogar** *($12; pb; Avenida Isidro Ayora, ☎ 248-357, ⊷ 248-341)* ranks counts among the most affordable lodgings in town. Its shared rooms and informal ambience make it a popular spot with backpackers who swap travel stories. International Youth Hostel card holders benefit from a small discount. The hotel provides a laundry service.

The 55 rooms of the **Hotel Alexander** *($20; pb, ℜ; Calle Luque 1107 between Pedro Moncayo and Avenida Quito, ☎ 532-000, ⊷ 328-474)* are austere, reminiscent of the sixties, and do not seem to have been renovated for a long time. On five floors, the rooms aim more for comfort at a modest price than decorative flair.

The **Hotel Rizzo** *($30 bkfst incl.; tv, pb, hw, ℜ; Calle Clemente Ballén 319 and Chile, ☎ 325-210, ⊷ 326-209)*, on the former site of the Hotel Continental, offers bright, modern, but simple rooms. The hotel staff are pleasant and never misses an opportunity to tell clients about the time that Pélé, the famous Brazilian soccer player, stayed here.

Another establishment situated in the heart of downtown Guayaquil, **Hotel Doral** *($30 bkfst incl.; pb, hw, ℜ; Calle Chile 402 at Aguirre, ☎ 327-175 or 327-133, ⊷ 327-088)* stands cater-corner to the EMETEL office. Its 59 rooms have certainly seen better days and could use a fresh coat of paint. If you decide to stay here, ask to see the room before renting it, as some rooms have no windows.

Just next to the Doral, the **Hotel Plaza** *($30 bkfst incl.; tv, pb, hw, ℜ; Calle Chile 414 at Clemente Ballén,* ☎ *327-140 or 327-545,* ⚏ *324-195)* has 56 austere rooms equipped with mini-bars. Some rooms enjoy a view of the iguana park.

Good deals are exceedingly rare in Guayaquil. Without question the best price/quality ratio in the city is to be found in the neighbourhood between the airport and downtown, near Colegio La Dolorosa and Iglesia Santa Gema, namely, the **Tangara Guest House** *($40-$48; Ciudadela Bolivariana, Calle Manuela Sáenz at O'Leary, P.O. Box 09-01-10275,* ☎ *284-445 or 282-828,* ⚏ *284-039).* The rooms are not all of equal dimensions, but they are all safe, well-maintained, and impeccable. A nice breakfast is available for $4, but those who prefer can keep their own provisions in the kitchen, where a refrigerator and a stove are at guests' disposal. The service is friendly and pleasant, and the owner organizes excursions in the area.

The **Hotel Sol de Oriente** *($50; pb, hw, ℜ; Calle Aguirre 603 at Escobedo,* ☎ *328-049,* ⚏ *329-352),* one of the few Asian-owned hotels in the city, offers 56 clean, functional rooms decorated in oriental style. A gym with free weights open to all guests and an aerobics room for women complete the list of amenities.

Situated near the banking district and the main tourist attractions, the **Hotel Palace** *($60; pb, hw, ℜ; Calle Chile 214 at Luque;* ☎ *321-080,* ⚏ *322-887)* is very popular with business travellers. It offers clean, spacious, comfortable

rooms at relatively affordable prices for Guayaquil.

Situated near the principal attractions, the **Hotel Boulevard** *($80; tv, pb, hw, ℜ; Avenida 9 de Octubre 432,* ☎ *562-888 or 566-700,* ⚏ *560-076)* offers very large, clean rooms equipped with mini-bars. Room service is available day and night.

If you are prepared to loosen your purse-strings, the **Hotel Continental** *($115; hw, tv, ℜ; Calle Chile at 10 de Agosto,* ☎ *329-270,* ⚏ *325-454)* is another establishment in the heart of downtown that offers clean, modern, safe rooms.

The **Hotel Ramada** *($125; pb, tv, hw, ≈, ℜ; Malecón at Orellana,* ☎ *312-200 or 311-888,* ⚏ *322-036)* stands proudly on the Malecón and has 110 carefully decorated rooms on four floors. Pool, sauna, casino and parking are at clients' disposal.

Situated behind the Catedral, **Gran Hotel** *($125; pb, hw, ≈, ℜ; Calle Boyaca at Avenida 10 de Agosto,* ☎ *329-690,* ⚏ *327-251)* counts approximately 200 cosy and spacious rooms on four floors. This establishment offers a panoply of amenities sure to please travellers for whom budgetary constraints do not apply. These include are a gym, a solarium, a sauna, squash courts and lovely cascades that quietly flow into a pool where guests can lounge and admire the view.

Facing Simón Bolívar park, the **Unihotel** *($180; pb, hw, ℜ; Calle Clemente Ballén 406,* ☎ *327-100,* ⚏ *328-352, unihotel@srvl.telcnet.net)* is situated in the UniCentro shopping centre, in the heart of the city, near the banks and the main tourist attractions. From inside UniCentro, take the elevator to the second floor. The reception desk is at the end of the hall on the left. The hotel has 134 rooms on 11 floors and most of them have been recently renovated. If you have the choice, opt for one of these, as they are brighter and rent for the same rates. Guests also have access to a gym, a sauna and a solarium.

If cost is no issue and you are looking for grand luxury, the **Hotel Oro Verde** *($240; tv, pb, hw, ℜ, ≈; Avenida 9 de Octubre at García Moreno, ☎ 327-999, ↩ 329-350)* is without question the best in Guayaquil. The rooms are impeccable, spacious and pleasantly decorated with pastel-toned fabrics. In addition, two non-smoking floors, a discotheque, three restaurants, a pool and a sauna are available to the guests. The personnel is friendly and attentive, and works hand and foot to make your stay as enjoyable as possible.

During our visit the **Colón Internacional Hilton**, located on Avenida Orellana, was under construction. Contact the Quito Hilton for more information *(☎ 02-560-666, ↩ 02-563-903)*.

Playas

The **Hotel Acapulco** *($8; sb; Avenida 2, ☎ 760-343)* rents spartan rooms of questionable cleanliness. It is one of the least expensive establishments in town and one of the least enticing.

The **Hotel Playas** *($10; pb; Malecón, ☎ 760-121 or 760-611)* constitutes a good, economical option. This recommendation is based mainly on price, as the decor of the rooms has

absolutely nothing extraordinary about it.

For a few dollars more, the **Hostería El Delfín** *($12; pb, hw, ℜ, ≡; ☎ 760-125)* offers warm, spacious rooms with hardwood floors. Ask for a room with an ocean view. Safe parking.

If you are looking for a little more comfort, try the **Hostería Bellavista** *($35; pb, hw, ≈,ℜ; about 2 km east of Malecón, ☎ 760-600)*, which offers safe, clean, modern, spacious rooms. A private parking lot is available to the clientele.

Punta Carnero

At the **Hostería del Mar** *($45; tv, pb, hw, ≡, ℜ; ☎ 775-370, ↩ 324-195)*, you can benefit from a slight discount and an absolutely spectacular view by choosing a room with a balcony looking onto the sea, but on a floor without air conditioning. A pool, a tennis court and private parking are at guests' disposal.

The **Hotel Punta Carnero** *($55; pb, hw, tv, ℜ; ☎ 775-450, ↩ 775-377)* houses about 40 large, clean rooms, most of which have ocean views. The hotel also has a pool and private parking. As well, a playground provides entertainment for children and peace of mind for parents.

Montañita

At **El Rincón del Amigo** *($8; sb, ℜ; near the beach, reservations from Quito, ☎ and ↩ 02-444-926)* the rooms are spartan, but on the other hand, the rates are hard to beat. The hotel is popular with backpacking tourists. Be sure that the mosquito net over the bed has no tears or you run the risk of having a sleepless night... Surfboards and snorkelling equipment may be rented. Friendly personnel and relaxed ambience.

People travelling in little groups interested in greater comfort can stay at the **Hotel Baja Montañita** *($40; pb, hw, ℜ; ☎ 901-218, ⇌ 901-219)*, just near El Rincón del Amigo, on the seaside. Every *cabaña* is designed to accommodate four people and boasts a beautiful view of the ocean. Amenities include a pool, a whirlpool, a restaurant and a billiard room.

About 20 minutes from Puerto López on the road between Puerto Rico and Ayangue, north of Montañita, is the ecological and tourist centre, **Alandaluz** *($5-$25; International Youth Hostel card holders benefit from a slight price reduction; sb, hw, ℜ; ☎ 604-103, in Quito, ☎ 02-542-043, ⇌ 505-084, admin@amingay.ecx.ec)*. About eight years ago, this establishment was the site of short, impromptu stopovers in simple little cabins. Today the Alandaluz centre includes about 15 rustic *cabañas* and other, cleaner, more modern, pleasantly decorated cabins, as well as about 20 rooms for travellers of all budgets. *Cabañas* with chimneys and balconies overlooking the ocean are suitable for people seeking moderate comfort, while those who simply want to stake their tents or sleep under the stars in hammocks covered by mosquito netting find this spot very gratifying. Alandaluz is an ideal place to relax for a few days and enjoy a quiet little holiday by the sea, especially if you are an ecotourism enthusiast. Water is heated with solar energy, there are compost toilets, all waste is recycled or composted and even the postcards are made from recycled paper. Little groups for excursions to Machalilla national park or to the surrounding area are easily assembled here, as the centre has its own tour company. As well, a laundry service is provided and bicycles may be rented. For all these reasons, it is distinctly more agreeable to stay at Alandaluz than in Puerto López.

The Austrian-owned **Hostería Atamari** *($60 $110; pb, hw, ℜ; in Quito Baron von Humbolt 279, Appartado 17-12-91, ☎ 02-228-470 or 02-227-896, ⇌ 02-508-369)* is about 25 minutes by bus south of Puerto López along the scenic coastal road. The establishment is not visible from the road, but two signs mark the unpaved lane that leads to the hotel. On foot, the walk is not more than 20 minutes, but you may contact the reception desk to make arrangements to be picked up. Hostería Atamari is perched on a promontory that juts into the ocean, offering spectacular views north and south. Its location, isolated from the lively little neighbouring, villages perfectly suits travellers in search of tranquillity. Cabins have up to three rooms, and are decorated with wooden furniture, knickknacks, reproductions of pre-Inca pottery and absolutely spectacular ocean views. Some open onto a balcony. A pool lies in the centre of a terrace that is ideal for sunbathing, while hammocks are slung under the roof of a covered patio where guests can lounge and admire the horizon. An isolated, slightly rocky little beach is within walking distance. Although not private, it is not largely frequented by Ecuadorans. The hotel does not organize excursions in the area, except to Isla de la Plata or Parque Nacional Machalilla.

Puerto López

Just near the EMETEL office, the **Hostal Tuzco** *($10; sb)* constitutes an economical option for backpackers. The rooms do not have much pizzazz, but are perfectly acceptable for travellers of more modest means.

Without a doubt the best hotel in town, the **Hotel y Cabañas Pacífico** *($20-$50; pb, hw; Calle Suarez and Malecón,* ☎ *604-133 or 604-147, for reservations from Manta* ☎ *614-064)* is a family hotel situated two steps from the beach and suitable for every budget. Just behind the hotel are 10 rudimentary little *cabañas* equipped with fans for less demanding travellers, while the main building has 24 rooms on three floors. The rooms are clean and spacious, but simple. A private parking lot is available and hammocks hang between the trees of an adjoining garden.

Salinas

The rooms of the **Residencial Familiar Rachel** *($10; pb, ≡; Calle 17 and Avenida 5,* ☎ *772-501)* are relatively clean and of moderate proportions. Many *comedores* and *cevicherías* are located nearby.

The rooms of the **Hotel Albita** *($10; Avenida 7 and Calle 23,* ☎ *7734-211 or 773-042)* prove to be minimally decorated; the walls seem rather bare. The showers are relatively clean but there is cold water only.

The **Hotel Contabrico** *($16; pb, hw; Calle Principal, between Calles 9 and 10,* ☎ *772-026)* is a bit out of the way, but constitutes nonetheless a nice spot for those seeking tranquillity. The hotel has a good price/quality ratio, as room rates include full board. The rooms are small, but clean and bright, and have two single beds and private bathrooms with hot water. On the other hand, there is no air conditioning, nor are there fans in the rooms. The hotel's façade opens onto a large courtyard in which hang a few hammocks.

The rooms of **Hotel Yulee** *($25; hw, ℜ, tv; Malecón and Calle 16,* ☎ *772-028)* can be furnished upon request with televisions and fans. Visa and MasterCard are accepted, but a fee of 10% is added to the bill for this service. The rooms prove generally clean and functional.

Not to be confused with the Hotel Salinas Costa Azul, which is across the street and closer to the ocean, the **Hotel Salinas** *($25; hw, pb, ℜ; Calle Gral. Enrique Gallo at Calle 27,* ☎ *772-179 or 772-993)* has cleaner rooms than this neighbouring rival.

The **Hotel Calypso** *($50; pb, hw, tv, ℜ; Malecón, junto a la Capitania del Puerto,* ☎ *772-425, 773-583, or 773-736, in Guayaquil, Antepara 802 and 9 de Octubre,* ☎ *04-281-056, 04-282-902, or 04-286-079,* ⌐ *04-282-452)* is a quality establishment that rents single, double and triple rooms and suites. A terrace provides a splendid view of the ocean and is a nice place to relax and quietly admire the landscape. A restaurant, a pool and private parking are the other services offered by the hotel.

The **Hotel Casino Miramar** *($50; pb, hw, ℜ; on Malecón,* ☎ *772-115 or 772-596)* is the largest and best-known hotel in Salinas. Its 100 rooms on three floors are all clean and functional. Colour television is an option. The single, double, triple and quadruple rooms have views either of the sea in front of the hotel, or of the large pool out back. There is a restaurant, El Velero, which serves national and international cuisine; a cafeteria, Los Helechos, and a bar, Bucarnero. For the entertainment of its guests this upscale hotel organizes a casino and a bingo game during the high season, from January to April, and on holiday weekends. Slot machines are available year round. The decor and ambience are unremarkable and the architecture of the building is reminiscent of the sixties.

Manta

The **Hostal Miami** *($10; sb; Avenida 102 at Calle 7, ☎ 611-743)* without a doubt aims to provide reasonable comfort at hard-to-beat prices, as opposed to elegance or stylishness.

The **Hotel El Inca** *($14; pb; Avenida 113 at Calle 104, Tarquí, ☎ 610-986 or 620-440, ⊷ 622-447)* rents about 20 clean, little rooms and the service is friendly. Ask for a room with an ocean view.

The **Hotel Manta Imperial** *($25 ⊗, $30 ≡; pb, tv, ≈, ℜ; Malecón near the beach, ☎ 621-955 or 622-016, ⊷ 623-016)* offers decent rooms, which are simply decorated and laid out around a pool. Some of them enjoy a nice view of the sea. The hotel is safe and has a discotheque as well as private parking.

The decor of the **Hotel Las Gaviotas** *($26; pb, tv; Malecón 1109, between*

Calles 105 and 106, Tarquí, ☎ 620-140 or 620-840, ⊷ 611-940)* is far from brilliant, but the rooms prove functional and safe. Some offer ocean views. Matching the image rooms project, the service is relatively slow and leaves a little bit to be desired.

The rooms at the **Cabañas Balandra** *($50; pb, hw, ℜ, ctv, ≡; Avenida 8 at Calle 20, ☎ 620-316 or 620-545, ⊷ 620-545)* are without a doubt the best in town. The rooms, spread over two floors, are clean, spacious and cheery thanks to exposed brick walls. They are ideal for families or small groups and are furnished with mini-bars and balconies with hammocks. In all, there are nine *cabañas* and eight suites. The hotel is very safe; a guard monitors the entrances. A pool, private parking and a cosy little restaurant are at the disposal of guests.

A member of the Swiss-German chain, the **Oro Verde** has been under construction since the end of 1996. If you foresee a visit to Manta near the end of 1997 and this luxury hotel interests you, contact one of the other members of the chain in Quito, Guayaquil, Cuenca or Machala to make reservations.

Bahía de Caráquez

Travellers with limited budgets can opt for the **Palma Hotel** *($10; sb; Calle Bolívar 914 and Arenas)*, which provides frugal shelter adequate to the needs of backpackers.

For a few dollars more, the **Bahía Bed & Breakfast** *($14 bkfst incl.; sb; Calle Ascázubi 314 at Morales, ☎ 690-146)* offers 30 rooms of differing dimensions. All are clean modestly decorated and equipped with hardwood floors; some are furnished with bunkbeds. Friendly service.

Facing the jetty, the **Bahía Hotel** *($20 $23; tv, pb, hw, ℜ; Avenida Malecón at Vinueza, ☎ 690-509 or 690-823)* offers 27 clean, modern rooms on four floors. To benefit from a discount of a few dollars, opt for a room without a fridge. Ideal for those rising early to take the boat to San Vicente.

Two steps from the Malecón and right in downtown Bahía de Caráquez, the **Hotel Italia** *($30; pb, hw, ℜ; Avenida Bolívar at Checa, ☎ 691-137, ↝ 691-092)* rents small, clean, bright, quiet, safe and well-maintained rooms. There is a little restaurant next to the reception area.

The **Casa Grande** *($50, pb/sb, tv, hw; ☎ 692-084 or 692-086, ↝ 692-088)*, is a bed & breakfast belonging to the same owners as Bahía Dolphin Tours (see p 182), provides travellers all of the domestic comforts. Its six rooms are all immaculate and bright, and can accommodate up to 18 people in all. Some of the rooms have balconies hung with hammocks that allow guests to succumb to the temptation to lounge. The rooms have superb views of the sea and dolphins have been sighted frolicking in the water, to the delight of guests. The establishment also possesses a lovely pool and terrace for unwinding after a day in town. The proximity of the ocean and downtown Bahía, and its peaceful atmosphere rank this establishment among the best hotels in town.

The **Hotel La Herradura** *($10-$45; hw, tv, ℜ; Avenida Hidalgo and Bolívar, ☎ 690-446, ↝ 690-265)* is situated north of the city and offers travellers

30 clean, suitable rooms on four floors. Some enjoy a view of the sea and are decorated with plants and antique furniture. Those with more modest budgets can stay here as less expensive rooms are also available.

The **Hotel La Piedra** *($80-$150; pb, tv, hw, ℜ, ≈; Avenida Virgilio Ratti at Bolívar, ☎ 690-780, ↝ 690-154)* is the luxury establishment in town, with pastel-toned, immaculate rooms on three floors. Ocean views are a little more expensive. Kayak and bicycle rentals are available.

San Vicente

Most of the hotels in the little village of San Vicente are on the Malecón and are accessible on foot. In general, prices rise the further north the hotel is located.

Two steps from the jetty, the **Hostal San Vicente** *($10; Malecón)* has about 25 austere rooms that are generally occupied by backpacking tourists.

Those seeking a little comfort can go to the hotel **El Velero** *($25; pb, ℜ; Malecón, ☎ 674-134, ↝ 674-301)*. It has 18 rooms, some of which open onto an interior courtyard and others which provide a view of the ocean. A few rooms can accommodate four or five people and are available to those travelling in groups. A pool and a restaurant are some of the other amenities at this hotel.

Walking distance from the jetty, the **Hotel Vacaciones** *($30; pb, hw, ℜ; Malecón, ☎ 674-116 or 674-118, ↝ 674-117)* possesses 26 clean rooms on two floors. Those closest to the pool can be a bit noisy. Among the facilities is a ping-pong room, while a mirador behind the hotel permits travellers to lounge and view the scenery.

If the Hotel Vacaciones is full, proceed on Malecón to the **Hotel Alcatraz** *($30-$60; ≈, ℜ, tv, pb; ☎ and ⊕ 674-179)*. It offers 14 *cabañas* that can each house four people. If you are only two, the staff will offer to partition off the other room, leaving you free access to the bathroom.

A little past the Alcatraz, still on the Malecón, the **Hotel Monte Mar** *($30-$60; ≈, ℜ, tv, pb; ☎ 674-197)* offers essentially the same prices as the Alcatraz, but has the advantage of being on a hill. Half its rooms enjoy a view of the sea, while the other half face the hillside and are less expensive.

Canoa

The main building of the **Hostal La Posada de Daniel** *($14 sb, $22 pb; Calle Principal, 5 streets from the beach, ☎ 691-201)* was once a hacienda and houses about five shared rooms. The complex also includes simple, clean wood cabins with palm roofs. Some of these open onto balconies and offer spectacular views of the ocean. A four-person room is equipped with a television, air conditioning and a private washroom. Hot water is available for a little less than $30. There is a bar for quiet discussions or relaxing in a hammock. Horses may be rented for a gallop along the beach.

Pedernales

The **Cocosolo** *($12-$30; Bahía, ☎ 690-531, Pedernales, ☎ 681-156, or through Guacamayo Adventures in Bahía, ☎ 691-412)* is a friendly hotel near Pedernales that offers accommodations in a dream setting facing the ocean. Warm mornings, cool evenings and spectacular sunsets render this spot irresistible. There are various lodging options, including family and single-sized cabins, and a campground for the more adventurous. A variety of excursions are organized, including the observation of monkeys in their natural habitat, a trip down the Río Cojimíes, horseback riding, and campfires. As well, the long, deserted beaches are an attraction in themselves. The hotel personnel provides service in French, English and, of course, Spanish.

 ## RESTAURANTS

As in other regions on the coast, many restaurants close down during the low season, from October to December and from May to June. However, hotel restaurants are open year round.

Guayaquil

The **UniCentro** shopping centre *($; Calle Clemente Ballén 406 and Chile)* houses affordable fast-food counters.

For those who crave North American cuisine, facing Iglesia San Francisco is a **Pizza Hut** *($; Avenida 9 de Octubre and Chile)* with a wide variety of pizzas.

Paxilandia *($; Urdesa, Calle Guayacanes and Calle Primera, in the Valmor shopping centre)* caters to vegetarian diets.

As its name indicates, **Pique y Pase** *($; Calle Lascano 1617 and Carchi)* is an unpretentious little restaurant for a quick bite. Fish and meat dishes are on the menu.

Although decoration in the little Chinese restaurant **Chifa Himalata** *($; Calle Sucre 308)* is practically nonexistent, the restaurant serves simple economical dishes. Ideal for a quick bite.

Muelle 5 *($$; Malecón and Calle Roca, ☎ 561-128)* is a small, unassuming restaurant that offers a good variety of seafood and a lovely view of boats sailing on Río Guayas.

A few steps from the Oro Verde luxury hotel, **El Caracol Azul** *($$$; Avenida 9 de Octubre 1918 at Calle Los Ríos, ☎ 280-461)* is a good spot to keep in mind for its great selection of meat and seafood dishes. Excellent quality and assorted prices.

Warmly painted in shades of purple and cream, the façade of the Mexican restaurant, **El Cielito Lindo** *($$; Urdesa, Circunvalación Sur 23, between Calle Ficus and Las Monjas, ☎ 388-426)* is evocative of traditional colonial houses. As you cros the threshold, a veritable explosion of colour comes into view, as the tables are covered with yellow, blue, green and pink cloths. The spicy and delicious cuisine matches the tone set by the decor. As well, weekend evenings are enlivened by folk entertainment.

El Mesón de la Pradera *($$$; Urdesa, Calle Bálsamos 108 at Victor Emilio Estrada, ☎ 382-396 or 382-404)* is a stylish Spanish restaurant that serves dishes of undeniable freshness. The decor is made up of antique paintings and lovely stained-glass windows that warmly refract the sunlight. Courteous and attentive service.

From the outside, the restaurant **La Parillada La Selvita** *($$; Urdesa, Avenida Olmos at Calle Brisas, ☎ 881-000)* is remarkable due to two rangy chimneys that jut from its roof. Once seated inside, you'll see that these chimneys connect to two large, open-pit ovens in which delicious meats of every variety are deliciously prepared. Large bay windows provide a beautiful panorama of the city.

The portions at **La Parillada Del Ñato** *($$; Urdesa, Avenida Emilio Estrella 1219 at Laureles, ☎ 387-098 or 888-599)* are almost as large as the restaurant itself. On entering, your gaze is inevitably drawn to the immense open kitchen and the glass counter that displays meat ready to be grilled on the spot. Sit under one of many fans that lazily stir the air overhead and sip a cool beer as you wait to be served. Pizza is served on the second floor.

The restaurant **La Nuestro** *($$; Urdesa, Avenida Emilio Estrada 903, ☎ 386-398 or 882-168)* is easily recognized thanks to a façade that recalls the older wooden houses of the city. Inside, the walls are decorated with antique paintings evocative of Guayaquil in a bygone era; traditional Ecuadoran cuisine is served here.

The plush ambience of the romantic Italian restaurant **Casanova** *($$$; Urdesa, Calle Primera 604 at Avenida*

Las Monjas, ☎ 882-475) lends itself very well to an intimate, tête-à-tête dinner date. As well as the many Italian specialties, the menu proposes a variety of fish and meat dishes. Service is attentive and courteous. The prices reflect the luxurious atmosphere of the establishment.

The cuisine at **La Trattoria da Enrico** *($$$; Calle Bálsamos 504)* is dominated by the aromas of Italy, served up in a very pleasant ambience.

Looking for a Japanese restaurant? Cost is no issue? **Tsuji** *($$$; Urdesa, Avenida Emilio Estrada 815)* has a wide selection of sushi, the sake is excellent and the staff is friendly.

Le Gourmet *($$$; Avenida 9 de Octubre at García Moreno, ☎ 327-999)*, the stylish restaurant of the Hotel Oro Verde, attracts diners for whom the high prices are of no consequence and who enjoy savouring imaginative local and international cuisines. Meats, pasta and fish are featured on the menu and are prepared in a variety of ways.

Montañita

The chef of the little restaurant at the hotel **El Rincón del Amigo** *($)* prepares a variety of typical Costa meals.

The **Alandaluz ecological centre restaurant** *($-$$)* possesses a large dining-room in which tables are arranged outdoors, facing a fireplace that is lit when brisk evening falls. The cuisine is "semi-vegetarian", which is to say there is no red meat on the menu. In addition to à la carte meals, rice and vegetables, chicken, and, of course, fish and seafood are served. The dish we recommend is prepared as

follows: the main ingredient (fish, chicken, etc.) is stuffed in a small piece of bamboo, which is closed and placed in the oven. As it cooks the food is saturated with bamboo sap, giving it a particular and enjoyable flavour.

At the restaurant of the **Hostería Atamari** *($$; about a 25-minute bus ride south of Puerto López along the scenic coastal road)* there are two adjacent dining-rooms with views over the sea: one is indoors, and the other is outdoors, covered by a palm roof. The chef concocts numerous dishes such as *lomo a la plancha*, *paella valenciana*, *pollo a la naranja*, and different types of *ceviche*. Although the menu does not include any vegetarian dishes, the cook can prepare vegetarian meals; ask your waiter.

Salango

After a visit to the little museum of Salango, do not pass up the opportunity to treat your taste buds at its wonderful restaurant, **El Delfín Magico** *($$)*. Dolphin is not on the menu, but the food is truly magical. The establishment is known for its delicious, specially prepared *spondylus* dishes. We recommend *spondylus con ajo* or *spondylus en salsa de mani*. Other fish and seafood dishes also figure on the menu.

Puerto López

Even if at first glance the decor of the little restaurant **Picantería Rey Hoja** *($; Calle Principal walking up the Malecón)* is not the most stylish in the area, the dishes are tasty and very reasonably priced. Meals are savoured on a covered terrace whose walls are decorated with assorted knickknacks. The service is quick, the juices are fresh, and the menu is similar to those of most other restaurants in the province of Manabí, which is to say, rice and shrimp, rice and fish, rice and clams, etc., all of it accompanied by bananas, of course.

The little restaurant **Carmita** *($; Malecón)* is unpretentiously decorated but is set in a particularly attractive location, providing vistas of the activity of the street and of the bay simultaneously. The food is always fresh and delicious, and the service is efficient. The house specialties include a large selection of very fresh fish and seafood prepared in a variety of different styles: *ceviche, pescado a la plancha y panada*, etc.

Spondylus *($; Malecón)* is at once a restaurant and a bar and attracts a clientele of backpackers. Informal ambience and friendly service.

The restaurant of the **Hotel y Cabañas Pacífico** *($$; Calle Suarez at Malecón,* ☎ *604-133 or 604-147)* proposes practically the same menu as other restaurants in town, served in a more modern locale for slightly higher prices. Credit cards are accepted.

Salinas

Herminia *($; Malecón and Calle 28)* is a little restaurant with an old-fashioned decor; they prepare traditional Costa dishes at very economical prices.

The chef at the restaurant **El Velero** at the **Hotel Casino Miramar** *($$; on the Malecón,* ☎ *712-115 or 772-596)* prepares a variety of fish, seafood and meat dishes.

The restaurant **Mar y Tierra** *($$; on the Malecón, just near Hotel Casino Miramar)*is surely one of the best spots in town to savour the fruits of the sea. It offers delicious seafood and fish dishes that wary according to the catch of the day. A terrace permits open-air dining.

Manta

If you are a seafood lover, the restaurants along the Malecón offer a profusion of seafood dishes.

In an unpretentious decor, **Paraná** *($; Calle 17 and Malecón)* offers delectable local cuisine. Fish, seafood and meat are on the menu.

Those looking for something other than fish or seafood can dine at **Topi, tu Pizza** *($$; Malecón at Avenida 15,* ☎ *621-180)*. On two floors, this is a delightful place to savour tasty pizza while gazing at the ocean.

Bahía de Caráquez

Genesis *($; on the Malecón)* is renowned for its excellent *ceviche* dishes at competitive prices. Sit at a table on the outdoor patio, where you can watch fishing boats bob in the water while enjoying your meal. The juices are fresh and the service is friendly.

Donatello's *($; past the terminal terrestre, on the Malecón)*: who would believe that a taste of Italy could be found in a little town like Bahía? The location is a little out of the town centre, but the food is delicious and absolutely worth the trip. After all, a little stroll after dinner is said to be a good restorative. Friendly service.

Looking to indulge and treat yourself? The hotels restaurant **La Piedra** *($$; Circunvalación at Bolívar,* ☎ *690-780)* or **Herradura** *($$; Avenida Hidalgo at Bolívar,* ☎ *690-265)* both offer fine dining.

Canoa

The restaurant **Torbellino** *($; three streets from the beach)* is a simple, rustic and unpretentious locale. The *ceviches* are sumptuous and are considered among the best in the region. The prices are comparable to those at other establishments, but the quality of the cuisine is distinctly superior.

At the restaurant-bar, **Arena** *($; on the beach)* the facilities add up to a simple thatch roof supported by a few poles. A variety of juices, cocktails and sandwiches are served. Essentially, this is an ideal spot to sip a cool drink, relax in a hammock and watch the scenery go by. The owner also sells t-shirts he designs himself. Informal and friendly ambience.

 # ENTERTAINMENT

Guayaquil

If you plan to go out after dark in Guayaquil, by all means take a taxi, as crime has unfortunately been on the rise for the last few years.

Peña Rincón Folklórica *(Malecón 208)* is the perfect spot for a colourful evening filled with dancing.

The nightclub **Amen** *(Avenida Francisco de Orellana 796)* is a good place to dance the night away. Young clientele and varied music.

The **Hotel Oro Verde** *(Avenida 9 de Octubre at García Moreno,* ☎ *327-999)* includes a bar, a discotheque and a casino among its entertainment options.

The **Hotel Boulevard** *(Avenida 9 de Octubre 432,* ☎ *562-888)* houses a discotheque and a bar.

Metropolis *(Urdesa, Avenida Victor Emilio Estrada 302)* is definitely one of the classiest clubs in Guayaquil. The music is varied, the clientele young, rich and beautiful. If you have the means, this is the place to see and be seen.

 # SHOPPING

Ocepa *(Calle Rendón 405 and Córdova)* sells a variety of crafts from the Costa, including Panama hats.

The art gallery **Man Ging** *(Urdesa, Cedros III at E. Estrada,* ☎ *884-517)* exhibits and sells the works of Ecuadoran painters.

There are two particularly interesting bookstores in Guayaquil, the **Librería Científica** *(Urdesa, Calle Luque 223 and Chile)* and the **Librería Cervantes** *(Calle Aguirre 606 and Escobedo)*.

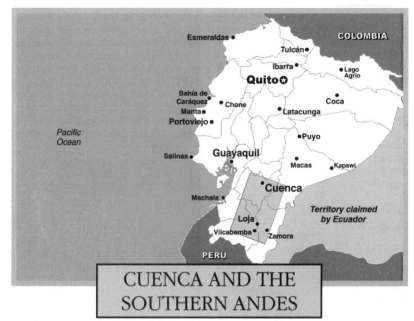

CUENCA AND THE SOUTHERN ANDES

Southern Ecuador is characterized by volcanoes that, while less imposing in size than those in the central and northern areas, are nonetheless distinctive and attractive. A bemused eye of blue sky piercing a layer of clouds beholds this land of varied mountain scenery where tumbling streams create a harmonious symphony and the singular landscape dissolves into infinity. The occasional rudimentary house, peeking above the slope of a volcano, is the only proof of the existence of humans.

Apart from the splendid landscapes that distinguish this region, it is famous for the magnificent colonial city of Cuenca, which is its heart. Visitors to the southern Andes must go through Cuenca. However, its outskirts are populated by small, picturesque, native villages that are certainly worth a visit: Gualaceo, Girón and Sígsig, for example. The villages take turns hosting weekly markets where regional artisans sell their creations. In addition, nature lovers will not want to miss the magnificent Parque de Recreación El Cajas (see p 227).

In the southern Andes, the history of the original inhabitants of this country is reflected by the unique style of the roofs of the old-fashioned little houses. The gables of most show a dove symbolising peace, a cross for protection, or an egg for fertility. Sometimes, even a cross and crescent moon may be seen. This represents the deity of the Cañaris Amerindian people who lived here before the arrival of the Incas or the Spanish. Also, the archaeological complex Ingapirca, a mute but evocative testimony to the Inca occupation, is worth studying. Further south of Cuenca, the Pan American highway travels through the Tarquí valley, rich in history and magnificent landscapes; then winds its way along stunning Andean volcanoes before arriving at Oña. This stretch of the road is worth driving for its dazzling scenery. Shortly after Oña comes the little town of Saraguro, named for the native people who populate it. The trip ends at Loja; remote and off the beaten path, the town has changed little over the years. Surrounding Loja, there are quaint little villages like El Cisne and Vilcabamba, which have a definite appeal.

FINDING YOUR WAY AROUND

Cuenca

By Plane

TAME and SAN airlines have regular flights from Quito to Cuenca every day except Sunday. TAME also flies to Cuenca from Guayaquil every day of the week. Aerogal has flights to Cuenca from Quito every day except Saturday. The price of a one-way ticket is about $30, and the trip takes about 30 minutes. The Mariscal Lamar airport is just near the *terminal terrestre*. If you plan on visiting Cuenca between June and September, be sure to reserve your tickets ahead of time because the flights are often crowded. Taxi fare from the airport to downtown is about $2.

By Bus

Many buses leave for Cuenca from Guayaquil, Quito and several villages along the Pan American highway (Latacunga, Ambato, Riobamba, Loja, etc.). The trip from Quito costs about

$8 and takes between nine and 12 hours. From Guayaquil it takes about five hours and costs about $5. From the village of Macas, sit on the left side of the bus and count on a 12 to 13-hour trip through remarkable scenery for around $7. The *terminal terrestre* is on Avenida España, about one kilometre northwest of the city centre.

Gualaceo, Chordeleg Sígsig and Paute

By Bus

Almost every hour, many buses leave the *terminal terrestre* in Cuenca heading for these four little villages. The bus trip takes about two hours and costs around $2.

Baños

By Bus

Buses leave from Cuenca for the little village of Baños almost every hour at a cost of about $1. The trip takes less than a half-hour.

Azogues, Biblían and Cañar

By Bus

Azogues is about one hour by bus from Cuenca and costs about $1 to get to. Buses leave the *terminal terrestre* every two or three hours, or as soon as they are full. The same system is in effect for buses to Biblían and Cañar.

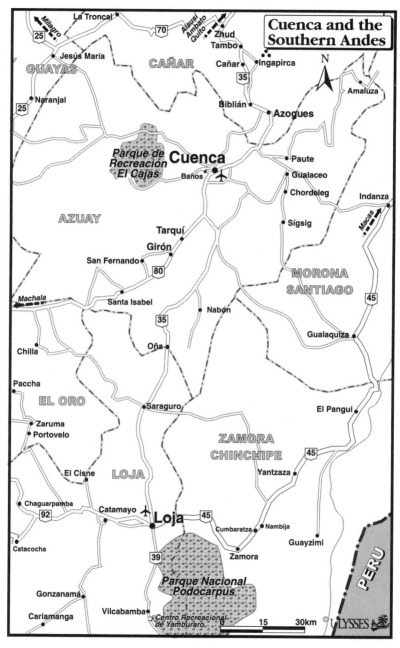

Cuenca and the Southern Andes

Milagro
La Troncal
25
Alausí
Ambato
Quito
Zhud
Tambo
Jesús María
Ingapirca
Cañar
70
Cañar
35
N
Amaluza
GUAYAS
Naranjal
25
Biblián
Azogues

Parque de
Recreación
El Cajas
Cuenca
Baños
Paute
Gualaceo
Chordeleg
Indanza
AZUAY
Sígsig
Tarquí
Girón
San Fernando
80
MORONA
SANTIAGO
Machala
Santa Isabel
Nabón
35
45
Chilla
Oña
Gualaquiza
Paccha
EL ORO
Saraguro
El Pangui
Zaruma
Portovelo
ZAMORA
CHINCHIPE
45
El Cisne
LOJA
Yantzaza
Chaguarpamba
92
Catamayo
Loja
45
Catacocha
Cumbaratza
Nambija
Guayzimi
39
Zamora
PERU
Parque Nacional
Podocarpus
Gonzanamá
Cariamanga
Vilcabamba
Centro Recreacional
de Yamburaro
0   15   30km
© ULYSSES

Tarquí and Girón

By Bus

These two small villages can by reached by bus in an hour and a half, for about $2. There is a departure every two or three hours, or when the bus is full.

Loja

By Bus

Buses leave the *terminal terrestre* in Cuenca going to Loja, with stops in Oña and Saraguro, every two or three hours. The trip from Cuenca takes approximately five hours and costs about $5. The *terminal terrestre* is on Avenida Gran Colombia at Isidro Ayora.

By Plane

The airport that serves Loja is in Catamayo, almost 30 kilometres away. TAME airlines has guaranteed flights leaving from Quito on Monday, Wednesday and Friday; and from Guayaquil on Tuesday, Thursday and Saturday. The airfare from Quito is slightly over $30; whereas, from Guayaquil, it is about $25. A taxi from the airport to downtown Loja costs about $3.

Catamayo, El Cisne and Vilcabamba

By Bus

There is regular bus service to these small towns from Loja. To get to Vilcabamba, expect to pay about $2 for a trip that takes approximately an hour and a half.

PRACTICAL INFORMATION

Cuenca

Tourist office (CETUR): Calle Hermano Miguel 686 at Córdova.

Telephone centre: Calle Benigno Malo, between Calle Sucre and Calle Córdova.

Banks: Citybank, Calle Gran Colombia 749; Banco del Pacifico, Calle Cordero at Gran Colombia; Cambistral, Calle Sucre at Cordero; Cambidex, Calle Luis Cordero 977.

Post office: Calle Gran Colombia at Borreo.

TAME: Calle Gran Colombia at Hermano Miguel, at the end of the corridor on the right, ☎ 827-609.

SAETA: Calle Sucre at Luis Cordero, ☎ 831-548.

Car rental agency: Budget Rent-a-Car, at the airport, ☎ 804-063.

Tour companies

Metropolitan Touring, Calle Mariscal Sucre 662 at Borrero, ☎ 831-185, ⊷ 842-496, see p 53.

Ecotrek, Calle Larga 7108 at Luis Cordero, ☎ 842-531, ⊷ 835-387.

Expediciones Apullacta, Calle Gran Colombia 1102 at Calle General Torres, Casilla 597, ☎ 837-815, ⊷ 837-681.

Spanish language school: Centro de Estudios Interamericanos, Calle Gran Colombia at Calle General Torres, ☎ 839-003.

Photography shop: Foto Ortiz, Calle Gran Colombia at Calle Padre Aguirre.

Laundromat: La Quimica, Calle Borrero 734 at Córdova.

Loja

Tourist office (CETUR): Calle Bernardo Valdivieso 822 at 10 de Agosto.

Telephone centre (EMETEL): Calle Olmedo at José Antonio Eguiguren.

Bank: Filambanco, across from Parque Central, between J.A. Qguigurem at 10 de Agosto.

Post office: Calle Colón at Sucre.

TAME: Calle Zamora at 24 de Mayo.

Vilcabamba

Tourist office (CETUR): Calle Diego Vaca de la Vega at Bolívar.

Telephone centre (EMETEL): Calle Bolívar at Diego Vaca de la Vega.

 EXPLORING

Cuenca

The numbers after the names of the attractions refer to the map of Cuenca.

A visit to the southern Andes region, which includes the magnificent city of Cuenca, is a must for those in search of a better understanding of the history of Ecuador. It is said that one of the main reasons the Incas extended their empire into Ecuador was the remarkable fertility of the soil. When the monarch Túpac Yupanqui and his troops crossed the northern border of Peru, they easily subjugated the peaceful native communities and conquered the rich volcanic land in the vicinity of Loja. Next, the Incas headed north to the current province of Azuay, which today includes Cuenca. Here they encountered fierce resistance from the warlike Cañaris, who defeated Túpac Yupangui and forced him to retreat to Loja to await reinforcements from Cuzco. The leader of the Cañaris became aware of the large army heading his way, and decided to join forces with the Incas rather than engage in a long, costly and futile battle. Shortly after this, Túpac Yupanqui founded an Inca city on the site of modern-day Cuenca. At that time it was named "Tomebamba" meaning "a plain as vast as the sky". History reports that Tomebamba was the equal of Cuzco. For reasons unknown today, the city was in ruins when the Spanish arrived. The city was the birthplace of another important Inca monarch, Huayna Cápac. After the death of Cápac, his two sons, Atahualpa and Huáscar, engaged in a fratricidal war of succession. Atahualpa won, and when he realized that the Cañaris had allied themselves with Huáscar, he became enraged and massacred all the male Cañaris he encountered.

When the Spanish, in their turn, landed in the vicinity, they easily convinced the Cañaris to fight at their sides.

Happy for the opportunity for vengeance against Atahualpa, they willingly aided the Spanish colonisation. The city of Cuenca was officially founded in 1557 on the ruins of the former Inca city known as "Tomebamba" by the Spaniard Gil Ramírez Dávalos. He baptized it "Santa Ana de Los Cuatro Ríos" for the four rivers that converged there: Río Machangara, Río Tomebamba, Río Yanuncay and Río Tarquí. Cuenca, the capital of the province of Azuay, is the third largest city in Ecuador with a population of 355,000. Today, the many colonial buildings that border its old paved streets give it a charming air. The city's many museums and baroque churches create a serene atmosphere that inspires reverie and recollection. Even just shopping and strolling through the innumerable crafts shops that add life to the streets could easily fill days on end. Cuenca is situated at the heart of the valley of Guapondelig. At an altitude of 2,500 metres, it enjoys a spring-like climate all year round, with relatively cool evenings and mornings.

Ecuadorans' accents differ according to their city or region. This difference is especially notable here. The Cuencanos have an image, somewhat like that of the Marseillais in France, as a people who do not really speak their language; but sing it. Cuenca has become famous in the estimation of many because of two people who were born there and were the talk of all Ecuador in 1996. The first is the distance runner Jefferson Pérez Quezada, a 22-year-old born in Cuenca, who gave Ecuador its first Olympic gold medal by running the 20-kilometre race in one hour, 20 minutes and seven seconds at the Atlanta Olympic Games. The second is Rosalía Artega Serrano, a 40-year-old native of Cuenca, who became the first woman vice-president of Ecuador.

Those in the vicinity of Cuenca on Christmas Eve have a chance to see one of the most interesting religious festivals in the country: El Pase del Niño. On this holiday, the town literally explodes into colour, music and dance. A parade of floats inspires the oohs and ahs of the townspeople and others who come from miles around.

The **Nueva Catedral** ★★ **(1)** *(Parque Abdón Calderón)* is emblematic of the city. This pink marble religious building dominates a large part of the surrounding park by virtue of its gigantic proportions. The construction of this enormous Gothic Revival cathedral began around 1880 and was never completed. Legend has it that a mathematical mistake in the original plans produced a curious result: the bells intended for the towers were at one time lined up at the entrance of the cathedral because the towers were not solid enough to support them.

Come nightfall, the huge blue domes are lit up and create an image of ethereal beauty. The interior is composed of three naves and is ornamented by a series of arches supported by columns. The floor is made with marble from Cuenca, except for the central aisle, which is paved with marble imported from Italy. The most impressive part of the cathedral is the superb canopy resting on four columns above the high altar, seemingly to shelter the crucified Christ there, marvelously sculpted of wood and covered in gold leaf. Along the walls are beautiful stained-glass windows, some imported from Europe and others made in Cuenca, that diffuse the warm glow of daylight into

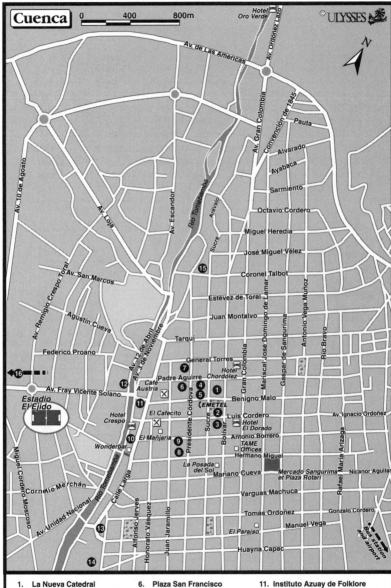

Cuenca

0   400   800m

© ULYSSES

1. La Nueva Catedral
2. El Parque Abdón Calderón
3. Catedral El Sagrario (Vieja Catedral)
4. Plazoleta Del Carmen
5. Iglesia Carmen de la Asunción
6. Plaza San Francisco
7. Iglesia de San Francisco
8. Monasterio de las Conceptas
9. El Museo del Monastario de las Conceptas
10. Museo Remigio Crespo Toral
11. Instituto Azuay de Folklore
12. El Barranco
13. Vestiges of the Inca period
14. Museo del Banco Central
15. Museo de Arte Moderno
16. Mirador Turi

Warning

For some years now, creditable sources of tourist information have warned of a shady individual who frequents the tourist district of downtown Cuenca. This man is short, about 40, has a neat appearance, speaks a little English and claims to be a homosexual businessman. He gains the confidence of single women by asking them to write a letter for him to a fictitious friend. In gratitude, he invites them to have a drink with him to celebrate his "birthday". Watch out, this man is dangerous! He is really a well-known rapist who has friends at the local police station. The author of this guide was able to determine first-hand that this individual was still operating with impunity in the city (in Aug, 1996), and was using his line on every potential victim. If he approaches you, be on your guard.

---

the cathedral. In front of the Nueva Catedral is **El Parque Abdón Calderón (2)** named after a local hero of the battle of Pichincha. A statue commemorating him at the centre of the park shows him mortally wounded, but proudly holding aloft in his right hand the flag of Gran Colombia. Apparently, he was in this position when he died...The park is highly appreciated by both tourists and local residents as a place to relax while admiring the cathedral.

Just to the east of the Nueva Catedral is **La Catedral El Sagrario Vieja Catedral (3)**, built when the city was founded. Apart from its religious purpose, it has played an essential role in the history of the country. At the time of the French geodesic scientific mission, the summit of the church served as a triangulation point in determining the height of the surrounding area. Unfortunately, tours of the interior are not permitted.

To the south of the park, lamented by both tourists and residents of the city, stands the Municipio, the poorly constructed and unsuccessful modern building that houses the municipal government offices.

Cholas

The women wearing Panama hats are called *"cholas"*. During the colonial period, in order to distinguish Spanish women of "pure" ancestry from those whose heritage included indigenous people, the later were obliged to wear Panama hats.

If, by any chance, you are feeling romantic, a short stroll from the Nueva Catedral to the corner of Calle Sucre and Padre Aguirre will bring you to the **Plazoleta del Carmen ★★ (4)** *(Calle Sucre)*, which is adjacent to the **Iglesia Carmen de la Asunción**, and is known for the picturesque flower market held there every day. Here, women called *"cholas"*, wearing Panama hats, can be found seated under parasols, selling an infinite variety of flowers. Also for sale is a unique beverage made from medicinal herbs by the clergy of the church. It is believed to be blessed with holy curative powers...

The **Iglesia Carmen de la Asunción** ★★ **(5)** shelters a truly indeterminable number of nuns; nuns are known to have arrived in Cuenca around the end of the 1600s. These pious and faithful nuns live in a closed society, completely cut off from the modern world in the silence of the cloister of the church. The door leading to the cloister is adorned with tapers and votive candles that people come to light, or to leave as offerings, as well as with flowers recently bought at the neighbouring market. Visiting the rest of the church or the cloister is not permitted. To the left of the candles, there is a closed door that has a little turnstyle in it. Here the pious leave donations of money to support the nuns, who, in return, pray for their benefactors. The church opens its doors exceptionally on Christmas day. A word to enthusiasts: the baroque architecture and the grounds are also worth a visit in themselves.

A few steps away, heading south on Calle Aguirre, the street opens into the **Plaza San Francisco (6)** *(Calle Aguirre and Cordóva)*, where numerous Otavaleños display their products of all sorts. In front of the Plaza merchants offer much more modern articles, such as jeans and toothpaste. On the other side stands the **Iglesia de San Francisco ★ (7)**, whose construction dates from the 19th century, but whose latest modifications were done in 1920. Inside, the retable, richly worked and covered in gold leaf, merits a look.

To visit one of the best museums in the city, go down Calle Juan Jaramillo to the intersection of Calle Hermano Miguel. The **Monasterio de las Conceptas ★★ (8)**, like the Iglesia Carmen de la Asunción, is not open to visitors. The monastery serves as a refuge for nuns who have chosen to live in a world of silence, apart from today's society, and to consecrate their lives to God. Visitors are, however, permitted in one part of the cloister of the monastery, in the **Museo del Monasterio de las Conceptas ★★★ (9)** *($2; Mon to Fri 10am to 4pm; Calle Hermano Miguel 633, ☎ 07-830-625)*. Admirably restored and laid out on two levels, it was inaugurated in 1986 and displays a remarkable collection of paintings, sculptures and religious folk art dating from the 17th, 18th and 19th centuries. Among other items is a rare series of photographs of the interior of the monastery and of the nuns who have chosen to live there. But the outstanding exhibit, in our opinion, is found on the second floor and is titled *"Pesebre Navideño"*. It is an immense, magnificently worked and gilded nativity scene.

In an old converted house, the **Museo Remigio Crespo Toral (10)** *(hours vary; Calle Larga 707)* recounts the history of the city in paintings, sculptures and crafts of the native peoples.

After visiting the Remigio Crespo Toral museum, go to the stairway going down to the Río Tomebamba to have a look at the **Instituto Azuay de Folklore (11)** *(Mon to Fri 8am to 6pm; Escalinita at Calle Larga)*. Artworks in every genre and from different Latin American countries found here.

Leaving the museum, continue down the stairway and go to the right as you study **El Barranco ★★★ (12)**. In Spanish the word *"barranco"* means precipice or ravine. Here, however, it designates the many old colonial houses standing on the cliff overhanging the river. Sometimes washerwomen come here to wash their clothes in the waters of the Río.

Walking back up Avenida 12 de Abril, there are a few modest **vestiges (13)** of the Inca period to be seen southwest of downtown, along the Río Tomebamba. These ruins testify, with their mixture of Inca and Cañari influences, to the Inca occupation that took place in the valley at that time.

For more information about the Inca occupation, the Cañaris and other cultures of Ecuador, continue strolling to the **Museo del Banco Central ★★ (14)** *($2; Mon to Fri 9am to 6pm; Calle Larga at Avenida Huaynac Cápac).* The archaeological and ethnological collections are particularly interesting. There are also examples of religious art and even a small archaeological site where excavations are made periodically.

Much further west, lovers of modern art will enjoy the **Museo de Arte Moderno (15)** *(hours vary; Calle Sucre at Coronel Talbot, next to the Iglesia de San Sebastián).*

In front of the church after which it is named, the **Mirador Turi ★★ (16)** overlooks Cuenca and offers a good view, not only of the city, but also of its surroundings, including the immutable, majestic and proud mountains that seem to protect it. A taxi will cost between $2 and $3, depending on your negotiation skills. For those who insist on going by foot, walk to Avenida Fray Vincente Solano and head south.

Thursdays and Saturdays are the local market days. The **markets** are at the intersections of Calle Cordova and Torres, of Calles Sucre and Padre Aguirre and of Avenida Lamar and Calle Miguel.

Gualaceo ★

Gualaceo is nestled in a magnificent valley about two hours by bus to the east of Cuenca. This very picturesque little community holds a Sunday **market** with a wide range of foods and handicrafts. Gualaceo, a little colonial town dating from the beginning of the 16th century, has marvellously withstood the wear and tear of time. The Casa Municipal deserves particular attention.

Chordeleg ★

This other little town, situated a few kilometres from Gualaceo, was formerly inhabited by the Cañari people. Shoppers go there mainly for the wealth of little boutiques along the main street that sell a variety of objects made from gold and silver. These boutiques are not only picturesque; their prices are much lower than elsewhere, and some accept Visa.

Sígsig

Other than its picturesque Sunday **market**, the little village of Sígsig has little of interest, but it does have a certain commercial appeal. Of note are the Panama hats. Despite its name, the famous Panama hat is made in Ecuador. It owes its name and its popularity to the many travellers, mostly European, who participated in excavating the Panama Canal during the last century and who adopted it. It is a light, flexible, wide-brimmed hat that protects against the rain as well as the sun, woven of several varieties of straw commonly found in Central America and in Ecuador. This hat is still very popular and sought after especially in America and Europe. In Ecuador it is produced mainly in the region of Montecristi, and is sold in the markets of Cuenca and Otavalo. In the province of Azuay, about 60% of the population weave Panama hats, but those of Sígsig are so well-known that some merchants in Cuenca prefer to buy them here.

Paute

The town of Paute is situated about 20 kilometres north of Gualaceo, stretched out in the valley of the same name, which is overflowing with fruit trees. This valley is also the site of the largest hydroelectric dam in the country, named Paute as well. Paute generates 75% of the electricity in the country. However, between the end of 1995 and March, 1996, the power plant's production was reduced to almost zero because of drought. This had disastrous consequences for Ecuador: Ecuadorans had to ration electricity. This troubling shortage happened at the same time as repetitive border conflicts between the Republic and Peru. Nay-sayers claimed that if Peruvians ever decided to invade Ecuador, all they would have to do was to bomb the power plant at Paute, and the country would be at their mercy...

Azogues

Azogues is a large town with a population of about 25,000 inhabitants. It is the capital of Cañar province and lies 35 kilometres north of Cuenca. Its name comes from the deposits of mercury found in this region during the colonial period: mercury was used to purify the gold mined by the native peoples for the enrichment of the Spanish. Azogues is known for its Saturday **market** and for its **church** ★, proudly perched on a hill and dedicated to San Francisco. It emanates a religious atmosphere that easily enchants the faithful.

Biblián

Ten minutes from Azogues, the charming little town of Biblían is spied from a distance, thanks to its magnificent **sanctuary** ★★ dedicated to the Virgen del Rocío. Sitting atop a hill, the church dominates the town and the surrounding countryside. Biblían is proud to possess and to have been wise enough to preserve its picturesque colonial streets, undeniably charming and so pleasant to walk. Though quiet during the week, it becomes busy on Saturday thanks to the weekly **market** that draws people from outlying areas.

Cañar

The poor but quaint village of Cañar is some 30 kilometres north of Azogues, near the Ingapirca archaeological complex. The little Sunday **market** adds a bit of life to this small community, but the rest of the week it dozes at an altitude of 3,100 metres, lashed frequently by wind and often rainy.

Ingapirca ★★★

Eighty-five kilometres from Cuenca and 3,200 metres above sea level, Ingapirca *($4, every day)* sits on the side of a mountain overlooking a few houses and a vast expanse of fields and pastures. History credits Ingapirca, which is over 500 years old, to Huayna Cápac. The Ingapirca archaeological site is a remarkable place that shows the dual influences of the Cañari Amerindians who used to live in this region, and of the Incas who settled here a little later. There is ample evidence that the Cañaris were the first inhabitants of the region, for example the presence of symbols like the moon, that were venerated by the Cañaris. Also, female skeletons have been discovered, one of them in a foetal position, dressed and wearing jewellery, which corresponds to the Cañari belief that death is a transition to another life. Once the Incas arrived, however, their influence was strong. Although tourists have only been able to visit this Inca archaeological site since 1966, it was first described by Charles Marie de La Condamine in 1739. Despite its modest dimensions, Ingapirca is the most important silent witness to the Inca presence in Ecuador. The ruins extend from a central platform which was probably used in worship, and is thus named "Temple of the Sun". All around it stand the ruins of many buildings; perceptible between them are steps and doorways in the trapezoidal shape typical of Inca architecture. In fact these doorways are more resistant to earthquakes than rectangular shapes. All the stones of this structure are so meticulously fitted together that at first glance there appears to be nothing between them. Looking closely, however, it becomes apparent that there is an exceedingly fine substance between the stones holding them together. Only the Temple of the Sun has withstood the test of time. The exceptional solidity of its construction is underlined by the fact that there is a substantial layer of mortar between the stones of the other vestiges of this now restored site. All around are recently discovered remains of tombs dating from the period. Ongoing periodic digs will undoubtedly uncover more. These ruins suggest a military fortress or a religious site, but their real meaning still evades historians and archaeologists, who remain perplexed and confused about them. There is no comparison between these ruins and the celebrated ruins of Machu Picchu in Peru, but they will delight fans of history and old stonework. Those not satisfied by a superficial look, who want to better understand the architecture and symbolism of the place, should go accompanied by a guide. Don't forget that Ingapirca is at an altitude of 3,200 metres. It's cold, and wind and rain are not uncommon, so dress accordingly.

The increase in tourism and interest in the archaeological site of Ingapirca permitted the opening, in 1987, of a small **museum**. Here, the history of the ruins is told and exhibits are mounted from the objects discovered on the many digs and excavations that have been done in the area.

Baños

Less than five kilometres southwest of the town of Cuenca, the simple little village of Baños is surrounded by greenery, and offers thermal spring bathing and an ambience that promotes rest and relaxation. Don't mistake it for

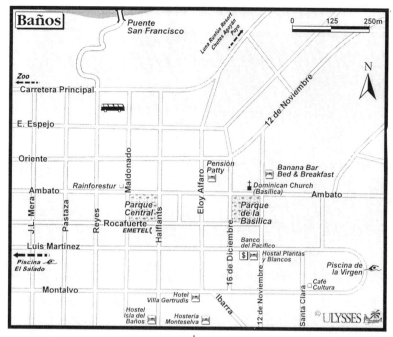

Baños

Puente San Francisco

Luna Runtún Resort
Chutes Agoyán
Puyo

0   125   250m

N

Zoo

Carretera Principal

E. Espejo

12 de Noviembre

Oriente

Maldonado

Pensión Patty

Banana Bar
Bed & Breakfast

Ambato

Rainforestur

Eloy Alfaro

Dominican Church
(Basilica)

Ambato

J.L. Mera

Pastaza

Reyes

Parque
Central

Halflants

Parque
de la
Basilica

Rocafuerte
EMETEL

16 de Diciembre

Banco
del Pacífico

Luis Martínez

Hostal Plantas
y Blancos

Piscina de
la Virgen

Piscina
El Salado

12 de Noviembre

Café
Cultura

Montalvo

Hotel
Villa Gertrudis

Ibarra

Santa Clara

Hostel
Isla del
Baños

Hostería
Monteselva

© ULYSSES

the town of the same name situated at the foot of the Tungurahua volcano (see p 146). Its white and pale blue painted church is noteworthy.

Tarquí

The village of Tarquí is set in a splendid valley to the south of Cuenca, just before Girón. An **obelisk** stands on one of its hills on the exact spot where the Peruvians were taken by surprise and besieged by the Ecuadorans during the battle of Tarquí in 1829. Soon after the defeat of the Spanish on May 24, 1822 on the flanks of the Pichincha volcano, Quito and Guayaquil were annexed by Gran Colombia. However, a few years later, in February of 1829, the Peruvians marched on southern Ecuador to expropriate it. Once in the region of Tarquí, the Peruvian army suffered a resounding and definitive

defeat at the hands of the Ecuadorans, and signed a peace treaty in the little village of Girón.

Girón

The tiny town of Girón attracts a few curiosity seekers thanks to its **museum** ★ *($1; Mon to Fri 10am to 5pm)*, erected in memory of those who fought in the battle of Tarquí, between Peru and Gran Colombia. The museum was inaugurated on February 27, 1978, which marked the bicentennial anniversary of the birth of General Sucre. Spread over two floors are weapons, clothing, flags, paintings and documents, which belonged to the combatants. Even the table on which the peace treaty was signed can be seen here.

Oña

Oña is another little town on the winding Pan American highway on the way to Loja. It doesn't offer anything special to tourists except for dramatic, extraordinary scenery. Indeed the route through Oña from Cuenca to Loja offers up what are accepted as the most spectacular of all the panoramas in Ecuador.

Loja ★

The town of Loja was founded by Captain Alonso de Mercadillo over the course of the year 1548, between the Río Malacatos and the Río Zamora. Loja, capital of the province of the same name, is one of the oldest cities in the country. It was originally built on the current location of the little town of Catamayo, but was moved a few years later to its present site. At an altitude of 2,200 metres above sea level and surrounded by majestic mountains, it enjoys a spring-like climate all year round. Destroyed more than once by earthquakes, it now has a population of about 95,000 inhabitants. Its law school was established in 1897 and is still one of the best in the republic. The town also supports two universities. Thanks to its location near the Oriente, this city is one of the favourite jumping off points for visiting the southern part of this region and the tropical rainforest around it. Because it is so remote, it attracts few tourists, but those who take the time will be rewarded. The city's cachet and ambience are particularly charming. Also, a few little villages can be visited from Loja. Of note are Vilcabamba, El Cisne, Saraguro and Catamayo. An excursion to Parque Nacional Podocarpus will delight outdoors enthusiasts.

Between August 20 and November 1, the **Catedral ★★** houses the famous little statue of the **Virgen del Cisne**, sculpted by the Spanish artist Diego de Robles near the end of the 16th century. The rest of the year, the statue is housed in the little village of El Cisne. It is displaced once a year, on August 20, and taken to Loja, 70 kilometres away, and is returned to its village of origin on November 1. Every year, this Virgin, also called *La Churona*, mobilises thousands of pilgrims from all parts of the county, and even from northern Peru, wishing to purify their consciences and renew their spiritual lives. The devotion of the believers is truly remarkable. Countless numbers of the faithful form a long procession to pick up the Virgin and carry it to Loja. The further along they are, the more heated becomes the dispute for the honour of carrying the Virgin before arrival at the destination. It is useless to try to reach El Cisne at this time of the year as the roads are completely jammed with believers.

The **Iglesia de Santo Domingo ★** and **Iglesia San Martin ★** are both worth seeing.

Three **markets** enliven the streets of the city. The most important is held on Sunday. The other two are on Monday and Saturday.

In front of the Parque Central, the **Museo del Banco Central** *(Mon to Fri 9am to 4:30pm, near 10 de Agosto)* tells the story of the city.

Hair-raising footbridge near Baños.

Catedral de Cuenca, a symbol of elegance and pride.

Natives on a pirogue in a changing world.

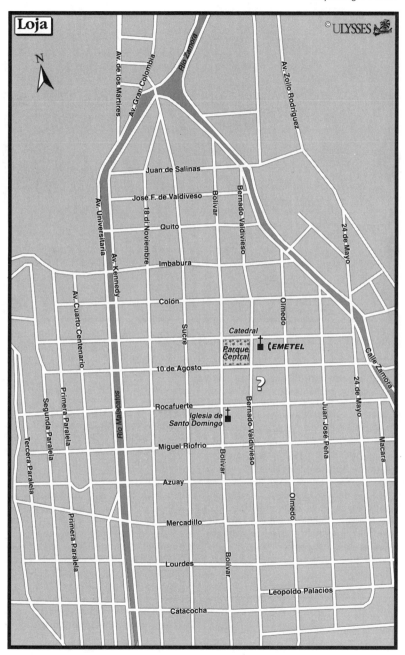

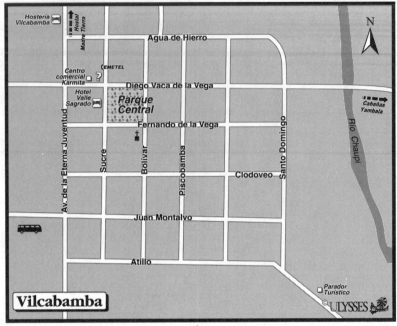

Vilcabamba

Saraguro

There are about 20,000 residents in the little village of Saraguro, which stands out mostly for its Sunday **market**. It takes its name from the Saraguro Amerindians, unfortunate victims of the Inca Empire. The Saraguros come originally from the high Andean plateaux around Lake Titicaca, within the borders of Peru and Bolivia. The men are distinguished by their sombre clothing: they wear fedora hats and short black trousers, and tie their hair back in ponytails. The women are dressed in black skirts.

El Cisne

Without a doubt, the main attraction here is the magnificent **El Cisne Gothic** sanctuary ★★, which devoutly preserves the famous Virgen del Cisne, by the Spanish sculptor Diego de Robles, except when the statue is in the Catedral de Loja, between August 20 and November 1. Adjoining the church, a museum exhibits some paintings from the Quito School. This religious building, with its impregnable appearance, seems to protect the dreams and beliefs of the region's inhabitants.

Catamayo

Catamayo is a little village of just over 10,000 residents, well-known for is many sugar plantations and as the site of the airport that serves Loja. Also, Catamayo can claim a certain amount of historical importance since it is built on the original location of Loja.

Vilcabamba ★★

Vilcabamba means "sacred valley" in Quichua. This attractive little village is pressed against a magnificent valley at an altitude of 1,600 metres. It is 40 kilometres from Loja, a few hours away by bus. Although this village was founded at the end of the 16th century, its fame dates from 1950, when much research and many publications tried to demonstrate that many of its inhabitants lived to almost 120. This phenomenon was explained largely by the influences of the climate, the pace of life, and a vegetarian diet. Since then, many people in poor health have visited this valley for a longevity cure and the hope of better health. Apparently, many have had their hopes fulfilled... The **Parque Nacional Podocarpus** (see below) and the **Centro Recreacional de Yamburaro** (see below) are near the village and are worth seeing.

 PARKS

Parque de Recreación El Cajas

This recreational area, established in 1977, spreads over 28,808 hectares at an average altitude of 3,000 metres but culminating at 4,200 metres above sea level. It contains over 200 magnificent lakes, formed by the passage of glaciers, and innumerable small ponds. El Cajas also includes unusual geological formations and is a favourite location of birders. Many trout churn beneath the surface of these teeming lakes, while numerous flocks of ducks float lightly on top. The condor and the toucan are only a couple of the winged species normally found here. As for land animals, there are foxes, gazelles and ring-eyed bears. In the domain of the *paramo*, many varieties of orchid enrich the flora. Moreover, in the interior of the park, enthusiasts of history and extinct civilizations will discover Inca ruins attesting to the presence of this people here, long ago. There is another pleasant surprise waiting inside the park, **Manzón**. It is a protected area of about 300 hectares that shelters close to 125 species of birds. A warning for birders: at the time this volume went to press, Manzón was temporarily closed to the public because of scientific studies and research on the bird populations.

Because El Cajas park is at a fairly high altitude, some people may suffer from *soroche* (mountain sickness). In addition, temperatures are cool, rain is frequent, and winds sometimes violent. Wear warm clothing. August to January is the time of year when the weather is the mildest. During this period skies are usually clear and rain is occasional. A permit is required to enter the park. It can be obtained in Cuenca at the office of the MAG (Ministerio de Agricultura y Ganadería), located at the corner or Calle Simón Bolívar and Calle Hermano Miguel. For safety's sake, it is strongly suggested, recommended really, to visit the park with a good guide. In the last few years, many people have got lost. Sadly, there have even been some fatalities.

Parque Nacional Podocarpus

This national park covers 361,340 hectares and straddles the area between the provinces of Loja and Zamora. It was created to preserve two species of angiosperms (the family of plants with visible reproductive organs and where, as opposed to gymnosperms or conifers, the seeds are contained in fruit): *podocarpus oleifolius* and *podocarpus rospigliios*. The park got its name from these two specific plant species. More than 100 lakes were created in the park as a result of the recent quaternary glaciations. Puma, foxes, toucans and parrots are only a few of the many species of rare animals that coexist in this immense park covered by lush tropical rainforest. Truly a jewel in a crown of greenery, the park shelters a great variety of plants that are as strange as they are fascinating, such as wild orchids. Access to the park requires a permit from the office of MAG (Ministerio de Agricultura y Ganadería), in Loja, on Calle Riofrío at the corner of Calle Bolívar. It costs about $20.

Centro Recreacional de Yamburaro

This little recreation centre includes a swimming pool surrounded by rich vegetation in which llamas and orchids coexist.

 ACCOMMODATIONS

Cuenca

The town of Cuenca provides numerous accommodation facilities of every possible category to satisfy any budget. Many colonial-style hotels stand right in the middle of town, making it easy to visit on foot. Others are situated near the Río Tomebamba but are still less than 15 minutes by foot from downtown. If you prefer staying out of town, there are some quality establishments that will certainly suit your needs.

The rooms at the **Hotel La Ramada** *($6; sb; Calle Sangurima 551)* are spartan and lack atmosphere, but are nevertheless among the most economical in town. As a last recourse only!

Belonging to the same owners as the hotel of the same name in Quito, **El Cafecito** *($10 sb, $14 pb; Calle Honorato Vásquez 736 at Luis Cordero, ☎827-341)* also has spartan rooms but in a safe, relaxed atmosphere. This place is very popular with backpacking tourists.

Near the Hotel Crespo, the **Residencial Siberia** *($10 pb; Calle Luis Cordero 422, ☎ 840-672)* has about 20 rather modest, but very economical rooms.

The **Hotel Milan** *($12 pb, $7 sb; hw, ℜ; Calle Presidente Córdova 899 at Padre Aguirre; ☎ 831-110 or 835-351)* is just steps away from the Mercado San Francisco and offers clean rooms with hardwood floors and a small balcony. The rooms without private bathrooms are generally just as clean as the others and will suit budget travellers. On the ground floor, a small restaurant serves quick meals to travellers on the go.

The small rooms at the **Gran Hotel** *($15; ℜ, hw, sb; Calle General Torres 970, between Calle Bolívar and Gran Colombia, ☎ 831-934 or 835-154)* will also suit the traveller on a limited budget. The hotel offers a laundry service and is near banks and the main attractions of the town.

For a few more dollars, the **Hostal Colonial**, opposite the Colegio Nacional *($18; tv, hw, pb, ℜ; Calle Gran Colombia 1013 at Padre Aguirre, ☎ 07-841-644, ≈ 825-419)*, is, as its name implies, set up in an old colonial mansion. Its rooms, clean and spacious, have large doors and high ceilings nicely decorated in warm tones where burgundy, gold and grey mix harmoniously. Six of them also boast a balcony. Excellent value for the price.

If the Hostal Colonial displays no vacancy, go to the neighbouring **Hostal Caribe Inn** *($18; pb, hw, ℜ, tv; Calle Gran Colombia 1051 between Calle Padre Aguirre and General Torres, ☎ 822-710)*, which is not that tropical in flavour but has hardwood floors or carpeted rooms. Some of them have a balcony facing the street and all are relatively clean.

The hotel **Alli-Tiana** *($20, bkfst incl.; tv, hw, pb; Calle Presidente Córdova at Padre Aguirre, ☎ 831-844 or 821-950, ≈ 821-788)* offers no-frills, very clean and well-equipped rooms. Some of them have a balcony with a nice view of the Iglesia de San Francisco, but tend to be noisy if you are a light sleeper.

Very well situated, near everything, the **Hotel Chordeleg**, *($20 bkfst incl.; tv, hw, pb, ℜ; Calle General Torres and Gran Colombia, ☎ 07-824-611, ≈ 822-536)*, a century-old colonial mansion, offers rooms laid out around an interior courtyard, some of which are very spacious and have high ceilings, while others have small but pretty balconies.

The rooms at the **Hotel Catedral** *($22; pb, hw, ℜ; Calle Padre Aguirre 817, ☎ 823-204, ≈ 834-631)* have seen better days and are in need of renovation, but are nevertheless efficient; some of them even provide a view of the cathedral. The staff is quite pleasant.

An old, fully renovated colonial house, the **Hotel Principe** *($22; ℜ, hw, tv; Calle Juan Jaramillo 782 at Luis Cordero, ☎ 821-235 ≈ 834-369)* is near the Museo del Monasterio de la Concepción and offers 30 very clean rooms, tirelessly kept-up by a pleasant and dynamic staff.

Much less charming than those of the Hotel Principe, the rooms of the **Hotel Paris Internacional** *($22; ℜ, pb, hw; Calle Sucre 678 at Borrero, ☎ 827-181 or 827-978, ≈ 831-525)* are situated a stone's throw from the former and have not withstood the test of time very well. They are nevertheless safe and well-equipped.

The **Hostal La Orquidea** *($22 to $60; ℜ, hw, tv; Calle Borrero 931 at Bolívar, ☎ 824-511, ≈ 835-844)* is a few streets away from the Nueva Catedral. It has 14 small rooms, clean but slightly dark, laid out on three levels. Those wishing for a bit of luxury can select the suite, equipped with a stove, a refrigerator and an inviting balcony.

The **Posada del Sol** *($24; hw, pb, ℜ; Calle Bolívar 503 at Mariano Cueva, ☎ 838-695, ≈ 838-995)* offers possibly the best rooms for the price in town. Here, everything smells new, or should we say old? The 12 rooms on two levels of this old, recently renovated colonial house cling to their past with their wood panelling and hardwood floors. Guests will appreciate relaxing with a book or chatting quietly by the fireplace after a busy day in town.

A renovated 200-year-old house, the **Hotel Inca Real** *($28; hw, tv, pb, ℜ; Calle General Torres 840 between Calle Sucre and Tarquí, ☎ 823-636 or 825-571, ⇆ 840-699)* has kept signs of its colonial past, as evidenced by its flower-decorated interior courtyards around which most of the 30 rooms are laid out. Some of them face the street and are obviously noisier than the others. Guests have access to a private parking lot where they can leave their car in complete safety.

Another colonial mansion transformed into a hotel, the **Hotel Internacional** *($28; hw, pb, ℜ; Calle Benigno Malo 1015 at Gran Colombia, ☎ 831-348 or 823-731)* offers 29 rooms on three levels, all well furnished, bright, nicely decorated in warm tones and with high ceilings. The staff is courteous and considerate. The hotel is a few steps away from the main attractions in town.

The **Hotel Presidente** *($28; tv, pb, hw, ℜ; Calle Gran Colombia 659 at Presidente Borrero, ☎ 831-979 or 831-066, ⇆ 824-704)* features 70 clean, carpeted, well furnished and modestly decorated rooms. Some of them have interesting views of the surrounding rooftops. Other than being close to all the principal attractions in town, this establishment has the advantage of having, on the ninth floor, above its restaurant, a terrace where guests can enjoy a sweeping panoramic view of the city.

Near the Hotel El Dorado, the **El Conquistador***($35; hw, ℜ, pb, tv; Calle Gran Colombia 643, ☎ 831-788, ⇆ 831-291)* offers about 40 clean and modern rooms, equipped with mini-bar and hair dryer, but lacking in atmosphere. The hotel has the advantage of being close to the main attractions, having private parking and a discotheque, and offering a free shuttle service from the airport.

If you travel north on the Pan American highway, about 10 kilometres from town, your attention will be drawn by an old windmill reminiscent of Don Quixote's time. The place is appropriately named **El Molino** *($50; hw, ≈, ℜ, pb; Pan American highway, north, km 7, ☎ 875-359, 875-367 or 875-358)*. Situated on the outskirts of town in natural surroundings, this renovated old hacienda with antique furniture and comfortable beds will surely please romantics in search peace and quiet. Moreover, guests have access to a lovely pool surrounded by plants and flowers.

If the location of the Oro Verde (see below) pleases, but the place itself is full or too expensive, try the friendly **Laguna Pinar del Lago** *($60; hw, tv, ℜ; Avenida Ordóñez Lasso, ☎ 837-339, ⇆ 842-833)*, built in 1996 right next door. More modest than the Oro Verde, it is nevertheless also built by a lagoon, and offers impeccable rooms for 30 dollars less.

Erected on the Río Tomebamba, the picturesque **Crespo** *($80; tvc, hw, pb, ℜ; Calle Larga 793, ☎ 831-837 or 842-571, ⇆ 839-473)* hotel boasts wood panelling, high ceilings, old furniture and vaulted passageways that bring you back to past colonial times. It is without doubt one of the most inviting establishments in Cuenca. Its 41 rooms of varied size, on four levels, are all cozy and luxurious, and the best ones offer a relaxing view of the stream. It offers an excellent restaurant, a café and a bar that are very inviting after a visit in town. The staff is efficient and welcoming and can easily organize interesting excursions in the area. A shuttle provides transportation for guests from the airport.

Despite being less charming than the Crespo, the **El Dorado** *($80; tvc, hw, pb, ℜ; Calle Gran Colombia 787 at Luis Cordero,* ☎ *831-390,* ⌨ *831-663)*, right in the middle of town, is one of the better hotels in Cuenca. This establishment has a restaurant, a café, two bars and a discotheque. Its piano-bar on the sixth floor is a great place to view the quaint rooftops of this exquisite colonial town. As far as the rooms are concerned, they are all spacious, immaculate and carefully decorated. Try to get one of the rooms with a balcony; they are soundproofed with special windows so that you can sleep peacefully. Moreover, a shuttle will pick you up at the airport, saving you cab fare. The staff is friendly and considerate.

On the outskirts of town, the **Oro Verde** *($90; tvc, hw,* △*, pb, ℜ,* ≈*;* ☎ *831-200,* ⌨ *832-849)* is without doubt the height luxury in Cuenca. Previously named La Laguna because of its location on an artificial lagoon, this establishment is now part of a German-Swiss chain that also manages hotels in Quito, Guayaquil, Manta and Machala, and caters to the most demanding travellers. Almost all its rooms and its restaurant enjoy a lovely view of the man-made lagoon situated right behind the hotel and fed by a tributary of the Río Tomebamba. It is set in the middle of a luxuriant park in which llamas and swans sometimes roam freely. The rooms are clean and carefully decorated. Rooms with wide doors suitable for wheelchair-bound guests and a non-smoking section are some of the more specialized amenities this hotel can provide. Moreover, a small playground is provided for children and an indoor pool, a gym, a hot tub and a sauna are at guests disposal. Finally, four fully-furnished and equipped apartments, complete with washer and dryer, are available for guests planning an extended stay.

Gualaceo

Travellers on a limited budget who are content with spartan but inexpensive accommodations can select the **Residencial Gualaceo** *($6; Calle Gran Colombia)*. The staff is friendly, and you're right beside the market.

The **Hosteria La Rivera** *($15; pb, hw, ℜ;* ☎ *255-052)* will interest those wishing to visit the Sunday market but wanting to avoid a right in Cuenca. The rooms are clean and simply decorated.

Those wishing for a bit more luxury will probably choose the **Parador Turistico Gualaceo** *($35; pb, hw,* ≈*, ℜ;* ☎ *and* ⌨ *830-485)*. Situated right in the middle of luxuriant vegetation and a bit on the outskirts of the village, the Parador offers 20 rooms in small, cozy *cabañas*. The hotel also has a pool, private parking and tennis courts.

Baños

The small village of Baños is so close to Cuenca that it might be more interesting for some to stay at the **Hosteria Durán** *($30; tv, hw, pb, ℜ,* ≈*; Avenida Ricardo Durán,* ☎ *892-485,* ⌨ *892-488)* rather than in downtown Cuenca. At the beginning of the century, the hotel was of more modest proportions but it has been progressively transformed into a big, full-featured tourist complex. Other than its 17 efficient and cozy rooms, you will find a pool with "hot water guaranteed" fed by thermal springs waters that must even be cooled before being supplied to the pool. A gym, tennis courts, private parking and a restaurant with an excellent reputation are among the other amenities of this establishment.

Paute

A bit on the outskirts of Paute, the **Hosteria Uzhupud** *($30; ℜ, ≈, hw, pb; ☎ and ✉ 250-329 or 250-339, from Cuenca ☎ and ✉ 806-521 or 807-784)* combines the best in tranquillity and convenience. Guests can enjoy the pool or the tennis courts or rent horses to explore the countryside. A playground has been laid out specially for the enjoyment of children and the tranquillity of parents.

Loja

Travellers seeking comfort and quiet will be a bit disappointed with the possibilities in Loja, which features mostly simple accommodations for the adventuresome on a limited budget. Nevertheless, there are some comfortable hotels, but they do not offer some of the services that one might expect from finer hotels.

The **Mexico** hotel *($5; ℜ, sb; 18 de Noviembre at Antonio Eguiguren, ☎ 570-581)* offers spartan, somewhat unclean rooms that can nevertheless satisfy travellers on a shoestring. A

restaurant of the same name is adjacent to it.

The **Hostal Londres** *($5; sb, hw; Calle Sucre 741, between 10 de Agosto and J. A. Eguiguren, ☎ 561-936)* has small, safe, lockable rooms with small balconies. The rooms have no private bathrooms, and hot showers are available only in the shared bathroom on the 2nd floor. Essentially, this rather plain hotel has hard to beat, rock-bottom rates, and its staff is pleasant.

The spartan rooms of the **Hostal Pasaje** *($5 pb, 4$ sb; Calle Antonio Eguiguren at Bolívar)* are simply decorated and have small balconies facing the rear court. The shared bathroom is sometimes cleaner than the private bathrooms and as its name implies, this hotel is perfect for the budget traveller who is just passing through.

The **Hotel Paris** *($6 pb, $4 sb; Avenida 10 de Agosto 1637, ☎ 961-639)* has unremarkable, somewhat unclean rooms. It offers electrically heated hot water for showers. This hotel will suit the adventurous and is right near the market of the Parque Central.

The **Hostal Inca** *($6; pb; Avenida Universitaria at 10 de Agosto, ☎ 961-308 or 962-478)* has very modest rooms and features a TV room. At the same corner, the **Hostal Quinara** *($10; tv, pb; Avenida Universitaria at 10 de Agosto, ☎ 570-785)* has comfortable and well-equipped rooms. The private bathrooms are charming and feature marble floors.

The rooms at the **Hotel Acapulco** *($10; ℜ, tv, hw, pb; Calle Sucre 0749 at 10 de Agosto, ☎ 570-651)* are comfortable, clean, safe and inexpensive. On the 2nd floor is a bar of the same name. Ask for a room facing the street; otherwise you might get a room with windows facing a corridor. Evenings can be a bit noisy because the rooms are located on the mezzanine, while on the main floor there is a *parqueadero* (parking lot). The hotel also features a cafeteria-style restaurant. For the budget-minded, this is a good choice.

If the Hotel Acapulco has no vacancies, the **Hostal La Riviera** *($10; ctv, hw, pb; Avenida Universitaria at 10 de Agosto, ☎ 572-863)* offers clean, well-equipped and carpeted rooms for the same price. As a bonus, you will also be nearer to the market.

For a few more dollars, right next to the river there is the **Vilcabamba Internacional** hotel *($12; pb, hw, ℜ; Calle Kennedy at Miguel Riofrio, ☎ 961-538, 962-362 or 963-393)*, where you can rent charmingly decorated, spacious, quiet and very clean rooms. The staff is very welcoming and can help you organize excursions in the surrounding area. There is a restaurant on the main floor, but the food is rather expensive.

The **El Gran Hotel Loja** *($20; hw, pb, ℜ; Avenida Iberoamérica at Rocafuerte, ☎ 562-447 or 575-200, ⌨ 575-202)* is without doubt one of the more welcoming hotels in Loja thanks to its modern, bright and spacious rooms, which are clean and well kept. The owners work closely with the Arco Iris environmental group and can easily arrange excursions for you in the surrounding countryside. A combination cafeteria and bar, the Zamorano, is open 24 hours a day.

The rooms at the **Hotel Libertador** *($20; tv, hw, pb, ℜ; Calle Colón 1431 at* Bolívar, ☎ 962-119) are situated right near the Catedral and are among the best in town. They will perfectly suit the traveller in search of some comfort. They are rather plainly decorated, but spotless. The staff is pleasant and attentive.

Opposite the Hotel Libertador, the **Hotel Ramses** *($20; tv, hw, pb, ℜ; Calle Colón 1432 at Bolívar, ☎ 560-868 or 561-402, ⌨ 578-157 or 575-827)* offers clean but rather dark rooms. If noise doesn't bother you too much, try to get one facing the street; they are larger and brighter.

Vilcabamba

Opposite the Parque Central, the **Hotel Valle Sagrado** *($5; sb; Calle Sucre)* offers many small and spartan rooms laid out around a charming interior courtyard. The staff is friendly and more than eager to help you in your endeavours.

Situated two kilometres north of Vilcabamba is a very charming inn, the **Madre Tierra** *(Prices for the rooms in the main building and in the dormitories are $9 per person and the double-occupancy cabañas fetch $12 per person. The double-occupancy cabañas have cold showers and outdoor toilets; hot showers are available inside and outside of the main building. During the low season, prices are slightly reduced. Payment can be made in American dollars or travellers' cheques or by Visa. At noon, fresh fruit juice is served. For reservations: PO Box 354, Loja, Ecuador, ☎ 673-123)*. If you enjoy tranquillity and communal living, this is the perfect place for an extended stay. The owners, a Quebecer and an Ecuadoran, built this place from scratch a little bit more than 10 years ago. There is a main building with a few rooms, a dining room and a common bathroom, and several cabins a few minutes' walk away. This complex is situated on a mountain side and offers a splendid view of the neighbouring peaks, especially at dusk. The price includes breakfast at 9am and dinner at 5pm eaten communally in the main dining room. Special meal requests can be arranged for. Most of the fruit and vegetables served, including herbs and coffee, are organically grown on the grounds of the inn, and fresh bread is baked daily on the premises. If you need your clothes cleaned, a laundry service is available at a cost of $1 per kilogram. A massage therapist visits the premises three times weekly and a one-hour massage costs $8. There are many opportunities to visit the surrounding countryside on foot with an experienced guide, or on horseback. At half past noon the bar beside the pool opens and sells beverages, sandwiches, cigarettes and fruit juices. At the end of the day, at 6:30pm, a television is installed in front of the bar and a video-movie is shown.

Cabañas Río Yambala *($5 to $15; hw, pb, ℜ; for reservations, go to the Karmita shopping centre in Vilcabamba, opposite the Parque Central or Calle Diego Vaca de la Vega, near the electronics store. Mrs. Karmita will then reach Charlie on CB and will arrange a way to get there, or Charlie will simply come and pick you up.)* The Cabañas are also known by the name of their owner, "Charlie's Cabañas". They are perched on the hills of the cordillera spanning the south of the country. Different types of *cabañas* have been built to suit individual needs. You can chose between rustic *cabañas* and more luxuriously appointed ones. All of

them offer a striking view of the surrounding mountains. This is the ideal place for anyone who wants to escape big hotels and civilization for a while. From there, excursions to the Podocarpus park and in the area of Vilcabamba can be organized. A laundry service, a sauna and a book exchange service are among the amenities available to the guests.

Situated less than one kilometre south of Vilcabamba, the **Parador Turístico de Vilcabamba** *($16; pb, hw, ℜ; ☎ 673-122, ⌨ 673-167)* offers simple, well-equipped rooms with small balconies. The staff organizes tours in the Podocarpus park and in the area of Vilcabamba.

The pleasant **Hosteria Vilcabamba** *($22; ℜ, ≈, hw, pb; approximately 1 km north of Vilcabamba, ☎ 673-131 or 673-133, ⌨ 673-167)* is situated just near the entrance of the village of Vilcabamba in relaxing surroundings. Amidst luxuriant vegetation, its very clean rooms are cozy and carefully decorated. This establishment has a pool, a bar, a restaurant and whirlpool baths.

 **RESTAURANTS**

Cuenca

Many of the restaurants in Cuenca are closed on Sunday and Monday.

El Paraiso *($; Calle Gran Colombia at Tomás Ordóñez)* claims to be one of the best vegetarian restaurants in town. Despite its modest decor, it offers delicious daily specials. It's a popular spot for breakfast.

After a visit to the Museo del Monastario de la Concepción, fans of vegetarian cuisine can go to the nearby **El Mañjaris** *($; Calle Borrero 533 at Jaramillo)*. A good choice as meatless dishes are served in the interior courtyard of a refurbished colonial house.

The little bakery **Mi Pan** *($; Calle Presidente Córdova 824)* enjoys an excellent reputation for fresh bread baked daily. It's ideal for a quick bite at the start of the day.

Close by the Nueva Catedral flies the flag of Ecuador and right next to it, that of the Netherlands, which signals the presence of **Heladeria Holanda** *($; Calle Benigno Malo 951, ☎ 831-1445)*. They serve what is probably the best ice cream in the city. Cake, coffee and tea can be savoured in a pleasant room decorated with laminated photos of Dutch landscapes.

No less charming, the little **Café Austria** *($$; Calle Juan Jaramillo at Malo)*, set in a warm, bright room with lots of wood, offers up some more of Europe. The excellent choice of cakes at the display counter is very tempting. It's the ideal spot for chatting while enjoying a cake, an ice cream or a sandwich.

The **Wunderbar** *($$; Calle Honorato Miguel at Larga)* is discreetly tucked away beside the stairway that goes down to the Río Tomebamba. This is a little coffee bar where you can have a drink or grab a quick bite in a room decorated with playbills from classic movies.

Even though the modern decor of **Chifa Pack How** *($$; Calle Presidente Córdova 772 at Luis Cordero)* is a little depressing, the chef's excellent Chinese cooking is sure to more than make up for it.

In front of the El Dorado Hotel, **La Tuna** *($$; Calle Gran Colombia)*, with its log-cabin decor, is quite picturesque. The cook prepares a vast choice of pizzas and other dishes.

The **Claro de Luna** *($$; Calle Benigno Malo 596, between Larga and Juan Jaramillo, ☎ 821-067)* is a select spot for an intimate dinner after a day in the city. The menu lists many Ecuadoran specialities.

Decorated with ceramics from Chordeleg, fabric from Gualaceo and other local crafts, the charming restaurant **Los Capulies** *($$; Calle Córdova and Borrero)* offers Ecuadoran specialities in a pleasant ambience.

The restaurant in the **Crespo** *($$$; Calle Gran Colombia at Unidad Nacional)* hotel boasts an inviting, old-fashioned dining room with a lovely view of the Río Tomebamba. The place is equally well-known for its regional and international dishes.

Every Sunday, the brunch at the Oro Verde Hotel attracts tourists and local people alike. They enjoy meat or seafood dishes, and then mull over their meal in a boat or pedalboat on the hotel's artificial lagoon, or while strolling in its mini-park. The other days of the week, the hotel's restaurant, **La Cabaña Suiza** *($$$; Avenida Ordóñez Lazo, ☎ 832-849)*, whose wooden interior and big windows evoke an old-fashioned Swiss chalet, serves delicious local and international cuisine.

The menu at **El Jardin** *($$$; Calle Presidente Córdova 723)* lists a large selection of meat and fish dishes that can be savoured quietly in one of two small dining rooms that are warmly lit by stained-glass lamps

Set in a magnificent former colonial home, whose tiled-floors reflect the sweetly romantic decor, the elegant **Villa Rosa** *($$$; Calle Gran Colombia 1222, ☎ 837-944)* is a good address to keep in mind if you have a big budget and you want to sample a variety of national and international dishes. The attentive service and the quality of the food make it one of the best restaurants in Cuenca.

Baños

The walls of the **Hostería Duran** *($$; Avenida Ricardo Durán, ☎ 892-485, ≈ 892-488)* proudly display the local marble while the menu boasts many specialities of the sweetly scented country of France.

Loja

As its name implies, the cafeteria **La Tacoteca** *($; next to the Ramses Hotel)* makes simple Mexican dishes that are perfectly adequate for a quick bite.

The **Pescadería Las Redes** *($$; Calle 18 de Noviembre 1041 at Azuay)* offers a variety of remarkably fresh fish and seafood. The staff is friendly.

Friendly staff in pleasant surroundings await you at the cafeteria-style restaurant, **Chalet Frances** *($$; Calle Bolívar 753, between 10 de Agosto and J.A. Eguiguren, in front of the main park)*. The menu includes meat, chicken and spaghetti.

In a small, unpretentious dining room, the **José Antonio** *($$; Calle Sucre at Colón)* serves what is probably the best fish and seafood in town. Shrimp and fish are prepared as you wish.

Vilcabamba

The small restaurant **Cabañas Río Yambala** *($)* can prepare a variety of vegetarian and Ecuadoran meals with advance notice.

The chic **Hostería Vilcabamba** *($$; about 1 km north of Vilcabamba, ☎ 673-131 or 673-133)* is a good place to keep in mind for a fancy night out.

 ENTERTAINMENT

Cuenca

The bar **Años 60** *(Calle Bolívar 569)* is, as its name suggests, a place where people come to drink and dance to those ever popular "retro" tunes of the sixties.

At the **Picadilly Pub** *(Calle Borrero 746 at Presidente Córdova)* tourists and locals with their singsong accent share tables and a cold beer; a variety of different tunes provide the background music.

The lively and smoky **Bla-Bla** *(Avenida 10 de Agosto)* is a favourite with Cuenca's young revellers..

The El Dorado and Conquistador hotels have nightclubs that operate at night on weekends. These places are usually frequented by people staying at the hotel in question, but there are some local people and passing tourists also.

 SHOPPING

Cuenca

Cuenca and its surroundings are famous for the excellent quality of their *sombreros de paja de toquilla,* better known as "Panama hats". The **Homero Ortega P. e Hijos Co. Ltda** *(Gil Ramírez Dávalos 386,* ☎ *823-429 or 830-560,* ⌨ *843-045 or 808-926)* factory to the east of the *terminal terrestre* is a veritable institution and lives up to its reputation. There is a guided tour of the factory that explains the hat-making process. At the end of the visit, you can buy a souvenir from the large selection of Panama hats on display. The hats that are sold here are much more expensive than those sold elsewhere in town, but Visa is accepted and their quality is clearly superior.

At **Mercado Sangurima** *(Plaza Rotarí),* you can choose from a variety of hand-crafted ceramics made in the neighbouring villages, including Saraguro and Chordeleg. The difference between them? It's simple, ceramics from Saraguro are more intricately worked than those from Chordeleg: there are more motifs and details.

Romantics won't want to miss the **Plazota del Carmen,** where a marvellous daily flower market with an infinite variety of colours and fragrances is held.

Close to the Nueva Catedral, **Kinara** *(Calle Sucre 770 at Luis Cordero,* ☎ *833-189)* sells probably the best hand-crafted art in the region. The quality of the ceramics, paintings, clothing and accessories is remarkable.

If you haven't got time to visit the famous market in Otavalo, don't worry: the market will come to Cuenca. Tireless salespeople and travellers, the Otavaleños cover the country to sell their products. While it's smaller than the one in their native village, they occupy a space in the market in Cuenca at the **Mercado San Francisco** *(just next to the Iglesia San Francisco, Calle General Torres at Presidente Córdova).*

THE ORIENTE

I t was the German botanist and geographer Franz Wilhelm Schimper who first coined the term "tropical forest" (*tropische Regenwald*). In 1898, he published a book entitled "*Plant Geography Upon Ecologist Basis*" which was translated in 1903. People have a tendency, more often than not, to confuse the term "tropical rainforest" with that of "jungle". A jungle is defined as an expanse of densely planted trees that thrive in a hot and humid climate, while tropical forests grow in a humid, tropical environment characterized by several levels of vegetation and by the presence of many species. Stretching between the tropics of Cancer and Capricorn, tropical forests cover 14% of the earth's surface, and the Oriente is but an infinitesimal part of this area.

People who have never set foot in a tropical rainforest imagine it as a place rife with phantasmagorical images of countless snakes twined round the branches of enormous trees, while pumas and jaguars frolic amidst an inextricable tangle of lianas submerged in greenery... Sorry to have to shatter any illusions, but this does not quite correspond to the world of tropical forests. This distortion of the facts is a complete fabrication stemming from the imagination of authors and further reinforced by film and television. While it is true that amidst this exuberant proliferation of greenery, the high branches of trees are strewn with lianas and covered in epiphytes, very large animals are rarely seen in this geographical region. Contrary to the Galápagos Islands, where guides can guarantee the presence of such and such a species, the Oriente is an unfathomable place, one of mystery and the unusual....

Save the rainforests!

Save the rainforests! Though we have heard this statement time and time again, its message remains very timely. Tropical forests actually play an essential role in soil conservation, atmospheric oxygenation and the regulation of rainfall, and help moderate the winds as well as the psychic equilibrium of human beings. Innumerable varieties of plants, including numerous medicinal plants whose by-products are now used to treat diseases that afflict both men and women, are to be found exclusively in tropical rainforests. For lack of money and skilled workers, the large majority of these plants have simply not been documented. It is therefore possible, and even quite probable, that remedies able to thwart the plagues that threaten plants, animals and humans lie buried somewhere in these tropical forests. Left to the mercy of numerous oil companies whose sole objective consists of increasing investors' capital, however, the Oriente's forest has been horribly mutilated and lacerated by roads leading to oil wells. The opening of these roads is also synonymous with "colonization". This causes irreparable damage and gives rise to ugly scenes before which even the most conciliatory people are unable to repress blasphemies. Besides all the knowledge that seems doomed to disappear for evermore due to the ravages of deforestation, colonists illegally capture exotic animals to sell them to the highest bidder. Dynamite is yet another poisonous legacy bequeathed by whites to Amerindians. Traditionally, natives hunt with bow and arrow, but a few of them now use sticks of dynamite to flush fish out from the rivers. The exploitation of rainforests perpetrated by the oil industry brings up worrying issues, and it is with great distress that we imagine the disastrous fate that hangs over the Oriente's still waters, where the reflection of today's storms break against the embankments of tradition...

In this setting, in fact, predators are numerous, animals hide and, despite the impressive fauna to be found here, no one is in any position to guarantee their presence, for they flee at the slightest noise. To fully appreciate a stay in the Ecuadoran rainforest, visitors must pay close attention to the slightest snapping of branches and crackling of leaves, and pay constant attention to shadows and shapes hidden among the vegetation. The breeze sometimes carries the sounds of birds, and the musical flapping of their wings cuts through the air like shadow play against a background of greenery.

For many, the Oriente evokes mysterious Amazons and the never-ending quest for El Dorado. In the Amazon, myth and reality merge under the curious gaze of the many travellers who have ventured into its depths. In 1541, while attempting to find El Dorado (the name of a mythical South American country that translates as "country of gold") and its cinnamon-covered plains, the Spanish conquistador Francisco de Orellana became the first European to sail down the Amazon and return to tell the tale. During this heroic adventure, Orellana and his men reported that they had been attacked by fierce female warriors. Hence the name of this region: Amazonia, country of Amazons. Orellana and his men's assertions were ridiculed and considered to be exaggerated fabrications by the Spaniards. Orellana returned to Amazonia in 1546 but, unfortunately, never came back.

Toward the middle of the 18th century, the French scientist Charles Marie de La Condamine travelled in Amazonia and later wrote in his journal: "*Everything led one to think that after a migration from the south to the north, female warriors would have settled in the middle of French Guyana.*"

In the beginning of the 19th century, the illustrious German adventurer Alexander von Humboldt explored the green underworld as well and wrote: "*Women weary of the state of slavery in which they were kept by men...*"

To this very day, these prudent testimonies by such credible people still go a long way in keeping travellers and historians in the dark about these mysterious Amazons, and echo the initial questions posed by Orellana and his men.

Nowadays, though the Oriente covers over half of Ecuador's total surface area, less than 10% of the country's population resides in this region. Shuars, Achuars, Huaoranis, Cofans, Secoyas, Sionas and Quichuas are among the few who do. The recent discovery of oil in Amazonia and the modern world's encroachment on this vast territory, still virgin only a few decades ago, now threatens the way of life of local native communities.

The discovery of the first oil deposits in this region of Ecuador dates back to 1967. Ever since then, the development of these deposits has experienced phenomenal growth, as the annual national yield has gone up from 1.5 million barrels in 1971 to 75 million in 1973. Today, Ecuador produces close to 400,000 barrels of oil per day, half of which is intended for exportation. Several companies, both national and foreign, drill in this region, but it is the national company Petroecuador that ensures, and has a monopoly on, its transportation and marketing. Today, a 513-kilometre-long trans-Andean pipeline with a capacity of 300,000 barrels per day links the productive region (Lago Agrío) to Esmeraldas, on the coast. In 1987, after an earthquake severely damaged it, the pipeline remained idle for close to six months. It goes without saying that such a development, after barely 25 years, did not occur without provoking great upheavals, whose first victims were Amazonia's indigenous peoples. Indeed, these people's primitive way of life, based upon an economy of subsistence in harmony with nature, is not easily compatible with this progressive invasion of the industrial world at the expense of their territory.

The Oriente is crisscrossed by many streams cascading down the flanks of the cordilleras, becoming calmer waterways as they reach its foothills and inevitably flowing into the Amazon River.

Amerindians, a people facing extinction...

During the Spanish conquest, Amazonian natives successfully repelled the invasion of their territory by conquistadors and missionaries. To the misfortune of the Amerindians, however, recent history shows that this was merely a prelude to an even more devastating offensive. In fact, the discovery of oil in 1967 has profoundly marked the history of Amerindian peoples who were forced to give in when faced with invasion by oil companies. For the natives who try desperately to preserve their culture, their rituals and their dignity, the invasion of the modern world on their ancestral land corresponds with the sounding of a sort of death knell, crushing their last hopes. The sad reality is that, much like the forests that shelter them, these Amerindians seem doomed to disappear. Their options are few: they can either become integrated into western culture, which entails losing their cultural identity, or disappear even deeper into the forest to be swallowed up for evermore...

Three-hundred and fifty kilometres wide at its mouth, the Amazon is considered, and rightly so, the planet's mightiest river. Approximately 300 billion litres of water flow from this river into the Atlantic. In the Oriente, precipitation is abundant and humidity is constant. Geographically, the Oriente is divided into two regions, the north and the south, covering five provinces. The north includes the provinces of Napo, Pastaza and Sucumbíos, while the south encompasses Zamora-Morona and Chinchipe.

 # FINDING YOUR WAY AROUND

Papallacta

By bus

Numerous buses leaving from the capital city of Quito en route to Baeza pass necessarily through Papallacta. The trip costs approximately $1 and offers the added bonus of beautiful scenery.

Baeza

By bus

For the modest sum of $1.50, visitors can enjoy a two-hour tour provided by one of the many buses running from Quito to Baeza.

Misahuallí

By bus

Several buses from Quito or Baños travel as far as Misahuallí. The journey from Quito via the city of Baños lasts about eight hours and costs around $4. To save a few hours and $1, travellers can opt for buses leaving from Quito that run through the cities of Baeza and Tena before reaching Misahuallí.

Precarious borders

Since 1822, neighbouring countries have attempted, and even succeeded in, slowly but surely usurping large portions of the Ecuadoran Amazonia, east of the cordilleras. At the beginning of the century, Brazil annexed approximately 100,000 square kilometres of Ecuador's land. Then, in 1916, Colombia took possession of yet another piece of Ecuador's territory. In 1941, Peru stationed its troops south of the Ecuadoran border, in the provinces of El Oro and Loja. Following external pressure exerted by certain countries, a treaty was signed in Rio de Janeiro, Brazil, under the aegis of the United States, Argentina, Chile and Brazil. Ecuador was thus stripped of a part of its Amazonian territory once again. Ecuador has always disputed the validity of protocol (also known as the "Rio treaty") validity, but without success. For the last 10 years, every January, on the date the famous treaty was signed, pressure mounts along the shared border. A blitzkrieg arising as recently as January 1996 attests to the fact that tensions still run high along this border.

Lago Agrío

By plane

TAME airlines has flights out of Quito once a day, toward the end of the morning, landing in Lago Agrío about 30 minutes later. The fare is around $30. There are departures every day, except Sunday. The same plane returns in the early afternoon of the same day.

By bus

The Amazonian region can be reached by overland transport in about 10 long hours. Despite the length of the trip, taking the bus, though somewhat more exhausting than flying, is much more economical at approximately $8 per person.

Coca (Francisco de Orellana)

By plane

There are planes flying from Quito to Coca. Flying time is approximately 40 minutes and the fare is around $30. There are departures every day except Sunday, but only one flight per day. The same plane returns in the early afternoon of the same day.

By bus

Buses leave for Coca on a regular basis from Quito's *terminal terrestre*. The trip is made in about 10 hours and costs around $10.

Pompeya and Limoncocha

By bus

A good number of buses go to Coca. Once there, a boat must be taken to Pompeya and Limoncocha.

Puerto Misahuallí

By bus

The bus from Quito costs around $9 for a trip lasting approximately eight hours.

Jatún Sacha

By bus

An initial trip to Tena is required. From there, many buses make their way toward the small village of Ahuano and will stop in Jatún Sacha on demand. From Tena: a 75-minute trip for the sum of $1.

Tena

By bus

Numerous buses from Quito, Baños, Riobamba, Ambato or Puyo go to Tena. From Baños, the spectacular journey lasts approximately five hours and costs around $3. From Quito, the ride takes between seven and nine hours and costs $4 to $5. From Riobamba, travellers can count on spending around $3 for a six-hour trip.

Puyo

By bus

Buses leave the cities of Quito, Riobamba and Baños for Puyo at regular intervals. From Baños, the magnificent journey lasts approximately four hours and costs around $2. From Quito, the trip takes between seven and nine hours and costs $3 to $4. From Riobamba, visitors can count on spending about $2 for the four-hour trip.

Macas

By plane

TAME airlines offers a shuttle service from Quito. There are departures on Mondays, Wednesdays and Fridays, but only one flight per day. Visitors can count on spending around $24 for a trip lasting approximately 35 minutes. Returns are on the same day, on the same plane, toward the very end of the afternoon.

By bus

The city of Macas can be reached by bus from several cities, notably Cuenca, Sucúa and Quito.

Kapawi

By plane

To reach the Kapawi complex, a plane must be taken from Quito to Macas. Once in Macas, a second, smaller plane, whose size depends on the

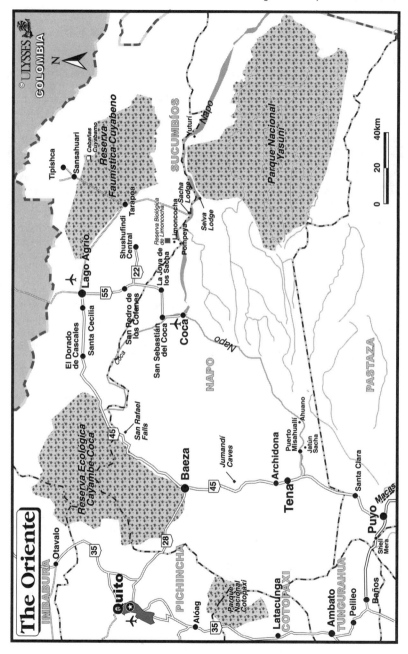

number of passengers, must be taken. This second flight costs around $100 for a return trip. Travellers fly over the Cutoukou cordillera and, to the south, can see the secondary chain of mountains whose crests line up into infinity. Up ahead, a riot of greenery speeds past. Fifty minutes later, visitors land around 30 kilometres from the Peruvian border; a river boat covers the last leg to the complex.

? PRACTICAL INFORMATION

How to organize an excursion into the Oriente

Visiting the lush Amazonian forest can be an unforgettable experience. Before embarking on such an adventure, however, visitors must understand that this region's humid and rainy climate, the innumerable insects that swarm in its midst, the limited means of transportation, the rudimentary accommodations and the exotic food can make the stay somewhat trying. Those able to cope with these conditions, though, will be amply rewarded.

Indeed, this region is rife with innumerable kinds of animals who move under its dense foliage of trees or through its watercourses. The Oriente is also renowned for its lush vegetation and, for this reason, arouses the interest of those who are attracted to nature in its primitive state.

The best way for travellers visiting the Oriente to observe its unique flora and fauna is to take accommodations in lodges, deep in the forest. These lodges are generally found on private properties in the forest, usually by the

water; they consist of individual bungalows, or *"cabañas"*, scattered about right in the middle of nature. Similarly to hotels, there are different categories of lodges, depending on the quality of services they offer as well as their facilities. These lodges are located outside Amazonian villages, at various distances by boat. As a rule, travellers cannot reach these lodges on their own, because the tour companies that manage them from the country's main cities wait until they are fully booked before starting the trip. Those who take the chance of going on their own risk being refused access. The only way to be sure of getting a place, in fact, is to purchase a package from a tour operator (see p 247). The package generally includes accommodations, a tour of the park and full board.

Nevertheless, before signing anything whatsoever, it is always very important to ask certain questions in order to avoid nasty surprises. Things to inquire about include:

● total length of stay;
● what type of accommodations (tents, lodges, hot water, private bathrooms) and available facilities;
● if food is included (full board or not);
● if access to the park is included (it is sometimes more advantageous to pay in sucres than in American dollars);
● means of transportation (bus, plane, boat);
● if mosquito nets are supplied;
● documents attesting to the guide's competence.

Visitors who are short of time can make a quick visit of the Oriente from Quito by going to the village of Baeza by the means of transport of their choice. From there, travellers can continue their journey toward Tena, then Puyo, whence they can proceed toward Baños to get back to Quito. Visitors should be advised, however, that the possibility of observing animals in the course of this trip is unlikely. Discovering fabulous scenery will, however, be compensation enough.

The Northern Oriente

Travellers who seek out the north of Ecuadoran Amazonia will be especially drawn to the two principal protected areas that occupy this territory: the Parque Nacional Yasuní and the Reserva Faunística Cuyabeno. Visitors who wish to observe animals should opt for Parque Nacional Cuyabeno. Indeed, this magnificent nature reserve will seduce visitors with the wealth and variety of its fauna and flora. The Parque Yasuní is equally interesting, but the probability of observing animals there is slimmer, because oil exploitation is, sadly, permitted there, even though the park does appear on UNESCO's list of protected sites...

These two tourist attractions are only accessible with the aid of guides. Visitors considering an excursion there should be cautious, however, because many people who are not qualified to do so act as guides or representatives of specialized tour companies. Travellers should therefore make sure that guides have valid certificates attesting to their competence. Guides must be associated with a tour company, which must hold a permit giving them access to the park.

During the course of the last few years, many misinformed tourists have been swindled. Every year, in fact, many travellers, falling victim to crooks or, quite simply, to the incompetence of their guide, return from their stay bitter and frustrated. A good number of tour companies, for example, do not hold permits to enter the Parque Nacional Yasuní. As a result, these tour companies propose excursions to tourists at a reduced price and lead their clients south of the park by travelling along the Río Cononaco. Not suspecting a thing, tourists thus believe that they have visited the park. Moreover, to save on the cost of food, many pseudo-guides feed hallucinogenic drugs known as "*yahe*" or "*ayahuasca*" to the members of their group. Last but not least, these unsuspecting visitors are further victimized by being robbed and even assaulted (especially women).

Numerous tour companies can organize excursions for travellers into Amazonia from Quito Those who plan on visiting the Oriente without using the services of one of Quito's companies, however, should make their way to Baños, Coca, Lago Agrío or Puerto Misahuallí on their own and, from there, try to gather a small group of people to share the cost of the trip and the guide.

Here are a few addresses of tour companies we recommend that operate in the north, inside the Parque Nacional Cuyabeno.

Metropolitan Touring: In Quito (see p 53).

Nuevo Mundo: Avenida Coruña 1349 at Orellana, P.O. Box 402-A, Quito, ☎ (02) 552-617, (02) 553-826 or (02) 553-818, ✆ (02) 565-261 nmundo@uio.telconet.net.

Neotropics Tours: Calle Robles 653 and Avenida Amazonas, 10 piso, of. 1006, Quito, ☎ (02) 521-212 or (02) 527-862, ≈ (02) 554-902.

Tropic Ecological Adventures: Avenida 12 de Octubre 1805 at Luís Cordero, Ed. Pallares, office 5, Quito, ☎ (02) 222-389 or (02) 508-575, ≈ (02) 222-390.

ZigZag: Calle Reina Victoria 907 at Wilson, Quito, ☎ and ≈ (02) 544-217 or (02) 561-881.

Native Life: Calle Joaquim Pinto 446 at Avenida Amazonas, Quito, ☎(02)550-836, natlife1@natlife.com.ec.

Rainforestur: Calle Ambato at Maldonado, Baños, ☎ (03) 740-423. This small but dynamic company can also organize excursions for travellers into the south of the Oriente.

The Southern Oriente

To this day, the south of Amazonia remains far less visited by travellers, undoubtedly because of the eternal border conflict between Ecuador and Peru. At the beginning of 1995, in fact, the inhabitants of certain cities were forced to evacuate for safety reasons. Nevertheless, as this conflict never quite escalates into a permanent crisis, travellers can, all the same, visit this region, which is hardly lacking in tourist attractions and has the added advantage of being situated off the beaten path. One of the main attractions of the southern Oriente is,

without a doubt, the small private reservation called "Kapawi". Those who wish to visit the Shuar native communities can make their way to the Mission de Miazal.

Before leaving for the Oriente, travellers should make sure they have received a vaccine against yellow fever, and remember to bring their anti-malaria pills.

The following is a list of tour companies working inside the Parque Nacional Yasuní and its surrounding area.

Emerald Forest Expedition: Avenida Amazonas 1023 at Joaquín Pinto, Quito, ☎ (02) 526-403

Yuturi: Avenida Amazonas at President Wilson, Quito, ☎ (02) 233-685.

For an excursion to Kapawi, contact the **Canodros S.A.** tour company *(Calle Luis Urdaneta 1418 at Avenida del Ejército, ☎ (04) 285-711 or (04) 280-173, ≈ (04) 287-651, Guayaquil, eco-tourism1@canodros.com.ec)*.

To visit a few Shuar native communities near Miazal contact **Ecotrek**, in Cuenca *(Calle Larga 7108 and Luís Cordero, ☎ (07) 834-677 or (07) 842-531, ≈ (07) 835-387)*.

The Climate

The weather is hot and humid all year round, and showers are frequent.

What to pack for an excursion into the jungle:

- Pants for arrival and departure
- Two old pairs of pants for excursions (it is inadvisable to wear jeans because they tend to be too tight and too heavy and to dry too slowly; light cotton pants are preferable)
- Three long-sleeved shirts
- Two t-shirts
- Two pairs of shorts
- Underwear and socks for every day
- Flashlight
- Hat
- Swimsuit
- Insect repellent
- Sunglasses
- Sunscreen
- Ready money (small denominations in local currency)
- Swiss Army knife
- Camera
- High speed film (400 ASA, for example)
- Pair of binoculars
- Biodegradable shampoo and soap

Baeza

Telephone centre (EMETEL): Avenida de los Quijos at Avenida 17 de Enero.

Coca

Telephone centre (EMETEL): Calle Eloy Alfaro.

Puyo

Banks: Agencia de Cambios Puyo, Avenida 9 de Octubre and Atahualpa.

 EXPLORING

The Northern Oriente

Papallacta

For an exhilarating visit, travellers can go to the small village of Papallacta, located 80 kilometres east of Quito, just slightly before Baeza. Though quiet during the week, this village comes to life on weekends, when Ecuadorans and tourists alike come to swim in the many hot springs scattered throughout the area. Also, the road from Quito has absolutely marvellous scenery.

Baeza

Baeza is accessible by taking the road going east from Papallacta. Founded in the middle of the 16th century, this quiet little village was once inhabited by Spanish missionaries who later abandoned it. The active **Reventador** volcano is quite close to Baeza. Measuring 3,485 metres in height, its distinctive silhouette looms on the horizon and can sometimes be seen on a clear day. Aside from admiring the scenery's quiet beauty, however, there is not much to see.

From Baeza, the road forks. To the south, one road leads to Tena while, to the east, the other heads toward Ecuador's tallest waterfall, **La Cascada de San Raphael ★★★**, which is over 140 metres high and whose waters eventually reach Lago Agrío.

Lago Agrío

The city of Lago Agrío was so named by American workers who came to drill for oil in the early seventies and found the area reminiscent of an American village called Sour Lake. Also called "Nueva Loja" because its first inhabitants came from Loja, Lago Agrío is the capital of the province of Sucumbíos. It was here, in this Amazonian market village, that **black gold** was discovered in 1967. At the time, Lago Agrío was just a collection of houses forming a hamlet whose population was unknown to the outside world and only linked to Quito by plane or by pirogues crossing the Río Aguarico. Since the discovery of oil, however, a 513-kilometre-long trans-Andean pipeline, starting from Lago Agrío and running through Quito before ending up in Esmeraldas on the Pacific coast, has been constructed. A bumpy and dusty road now links the city to Quito. The journey, though picturesque, takes a good 10 hours... Lago Agrío's main street, which bears the name "Avenida Quito", is the city's hub of commercial activity, but the noise, not to mention the traffic of exotic animals and the prostitution, mean that few people linger there for very long. Rather, most hasten, and with good reason, to go visit the magnificent Reserva Faunistica Cuyabeno.

Coca (Francisco de Orellana)

To the south of Lago Agrío, the small but bustling oil-producing village of Coca, with approximately 15,000 inhabitants, actually owes its growth to the discovery of black gold. This boom town also bears the name of the man who first crossed Amazonia from one end of the continent to the other. Coca, however, is a dirty place, its appearance suspect and rather dilapidated; it is a small town that does not really have any appeal in itself. Nevertheless, it is a jumping-off point for Parque Nacional Yasuní, which is renowned for its flora and fauna.

Pompeya

Pompeya is a small village situated in the middle of the Ecuadoran rainforest, a few hours by boat to the east of Coca. Pompeya's attraction lies in its proximity to an island that is overrun with monkeys.

Limoncocha

Just a very short distance from Pompeya, the small village of Limoncocha owes its popularity to its lovely lake, where a multitude of birds such as parrots, falcons and toucans cohabit. The southern part of the village is part of the Reserva Biológica de Limoncocha (see p 256).

Puerto Misahuallí

To the southwest of Coca, Puerto Misahuallí is a small village and a river port. Located at the confluence of the Río Napo and the Río Misahuallí, around 25 kilometres east of Tena, the place is very popular with travellers who go there hoping to spare themselves the cost of an excursion into the Oriente. But beware, there are many unscrupulous people posing as guides, and fraud is all too common. Visitors should be patient, and not hesitate to ask the guides many questions relating to their abilities. Ask them what itinerary they intend to follow, if meals are included and, especially, for papers attesting to their competence. This village has a few restaurants and shops at its disposal, where travellers can have something to eat and buy supplies before continuing on their way.

Jatún Sacha ★★

Dozing by the Río Napo, around 20 minutes by boat from Puerto Misahuallí, the **Fundación Jatún Sacha** *($6; it is best to reserve at least a month in advance: Jatún Sacha Biological Station, Casilla 1712-867, Quito, Ecuador,* ☎ *and* ☎ *02-441-5920, dneill@jsacha.ec)*, which was established in 1986, is a non-profit organization that seeks to protect the Amazonian forest by increasing public awareness about the dangers to which it is exposed and by promoting research with the aim of finding solutions to these problems. The territory protected by the foundation covers approximately 1,300 hectares, 70% of which consists of primary forests. Situated on the south bank of the Río Napo, less than 10 kilometres from Puerto Misahuallí, Jatún Sacha means "big forest" in Quichua. Even though many scientists and students do research on site, visitors are welcome and can sleep there as well. Jatún Sacha can accommodate about 20 visitors in four cabins equipped with bunk beds that are covered by mosquito nets. Moreover, one kilometre west of the station, there is an establishment where forestry, botany and agro-forestry research programs are carried out.

Ahuano

A tiny village buried in the stifling tropical forest, around one hour by boat from Puerto Misahuallí, Ahuano is only worthy of mention because it is the point of departure or arrival for travellers making their way to the lodges along the Río Napo.

Tena

Capital of the province of Napo and divided by the *río* that bears its name, Tena is a large village that is devoid of charm. Nevertheless, Tena is not a boom town whose existence can be attributed to the discovery of oil in the Oriente. Its origins go back to 1560, when missionaries established a mission in the area, which was very remote at the time, in order to convert natives to Christianity. The Church, however, encountered fierce resistance on the part of the Amerindian people. This explains why no trace of this past is to be found here today.

A jog to the south allows travellers to visit the city of Puyo, and to continue their journey to the village of Baños.

Archidona

Established in 1560, the little village of Archidona is worth a stop, if only to admire its church. The local **market** livens things up on Saturdays. Approximately 10 kilometres to the south of Archidona, budding speleologists will surely take an interest in the **Jumandí caves ★★**, which house bats living on stalactites and stalagmites formed over the course of the years by the infiltration of water. To explore these mysterious caves, certain important precautions must be followed. Inside, there is no electricity and it is quite cool and damp. Venturing into the caves with a partner and taking a flashlight, rubber boots as well as warm clothing is strongly recommended. An old pair of pants and an old long-sleeved shirt will serve as protection against the walls of the caves, while a hat will shield explorers from the dripping water and the bats.

The Southern Oriente

Shell-Mera

A trip to the southern Oriente can be undertaken from the small village of Baños (see p 132). From Baños, the road continues to Shell-Mera. Just before reaching the village of Mera, there is a military checkpoint, set up to monitor the comings and goings of people entering or leaving the Oriente. It is imperative for visitors to have their passport, or at least a photocopy of it, ready.

Puyo

Puyo is the capital of the province of Pastaza, where approximately 15,000 inhabitants reside. The journey by road lasts about two hours and quite spectacular landscapes can be seen along the way. There is not a lot to do in Puyo, however, and most travellers just pass through. The city has an airport.

Macas

Capital of the province of Santiago-Morona, the town of Macas is rapidly developing thanks to the discovery of a few deposits of oil. Founded by Spaniards during the 16th century, Macas is now mainly frequented by travellers en route to Miazal or to Kapawi's magnificent ecological complex in the Amazonian forest, or by those exploring the Parque Nacional Sangay or the mysterious Cueva de los Tayos, an 85-metre deep cave. This cave is a curiosity of nature that will interest amateur speleologists, and its main attraction is unquestionably the many nocturnal birds referred to as "tayos", which is how the cave came by its name. These curious birds produce an oil that serves as a combustible. Metropolitain Touring (see p 53) and Ecotrek (see p 214) organize excursions to these places.

Sucúa

The small village of Sucúa is distinguished by the existence of the Shuar Amerindians, who have created a cultural collective whose task is to preserve their habits and customs. Unfortunately, the Shuars are known for having been appalling head shrinkers. This era is now in the past, and visitors can learn more about this tribe's culture by visiting its information office *(Calle Domingo Comín and Tarqui)*.

Kapawi *(four days and three nights, $550 per person, transportation not included; Canodros S.A., Calle Luís Urdaneta 1418 at Avenida del Ejército, ☎ 04-285-711 or 04-280-173, ✆ 04-287-651, ecotourism1@canodros.com.ec, http://mia.lac.net/canodros, Guayaquil).* If the word "ecotourism" piques your curiosity or sparks your imagination, it takes on a whole new meaning here. Isolated from the tourist crowds, off

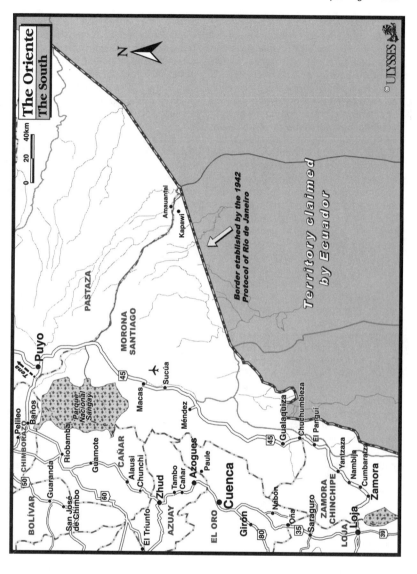

The Oriente
The South

N

0 20 40km

© ULYSSES

Border established by the 1942
Protocol of Rio de Janeiro

Territory claimed
by Ecuador

Amauantai
Kapawi

PASTAZA

MORONA
SANTIAGO

Puyo

Tena

Pelileo
Baños
CHIMBORAZO

Parque
Nacional
Sangay

45
Sucúa
Macas

Méndez

Gualaquiza
Chuchumbleza
El Pangui

Riobamba
Guamote
CAÑAR

Alausi
Chunchi

Tambo
Cañar
Zhud

Paule

Azogues

Cuenca

45

Yanitzaza
Namblja

Guaranda

San José
de Chimbo

BOLÍVAR

50

60

El Triunfo

AZUAY

EL ORO

Girón

80

Nabón
Oña

35

Saraguro

ZAMORA
CHINCHIPE

Cumbaratza
Zamora

Loja
LOJA

39

the beaten path and only accessible by plane and boat, this magnificent complex lies isolated in the southern Amazonian forest, very close to the Peruvian border, on a territory that is still protected from the invasion of oil companies and the perverse influence of colonization. The complex was built with the greatest respect toward nature and the native peoples who live in this distant region: the Achuars. Twenty-eight structures of elliptical shape, in accordance with Achuar architecture, communicate with each other and manage to withstand the winds that relentlessly whip against them and the torrential rains that fall upon them all year long. Aside from the door hinges, not a nail, not a single nail, it is stressed, has been hammered to assemble these structures. Electricity is generated by solar panels, washroom and kitchen soaps are biodegradable, trash is reduced to compost and all plastic containers are returned by plane to their manufacturers for recycling. Come night-time, there is not a single artificial light between the *cabañas*, so as not to disrupt the life of nocturnal animals. When night falls and deepens the shadows of the trees and as the sun's rays cast a last glimmer of light before disappearing behind the trees raising their long silhouettes charged with mystery toward the starry sky, we suddenly enter a timeless world where space is no longer a dimension and fall asleep looking forward to the following day.

All the rooms are immaculate and pleasantly decorated with curios made by the Achuar Amerindians, and they have private bathrooms, where modern meets picturesque. Every bathroom has a hot-water tank that is heated by solar energy during the day. Moreover, each *cabaña* opens out on to a little balcony

with a few comfortable chairs where, after a day in the forest, guests can relax peacefully and contemplate the calmness and beauty of the lake spread out at their feet. Families will be happy to know that *cabañas* able to accommodate up to four people are also available.

All hikes are lead by excellent nature guides as well as an Achuar guide. The latter perfectly complements the explanations provided by the nature guide and also sees about opening narrow paths with the help of a dexterously-handled machete. The possibilities of observing fauna in its natural habitat are excellent. During our visit, we had the good fortune to see freshwater dolphins, giant sea-otters, caymans, turtles and an astonishing number of birds as exotic as they were spectacular. To give travellers a brief idea of what awaits them, approximately 300 kinds of trees and over 400 species of birds exist over an area measuring a mere hectare!

The food here is delicious and, even though most of it is brought in from the Sierra and the Costa, there is a little garden where the hosts grow manioc and pineapples. A common room with a bar and a small library allows travellers to have a quiet drink while learning more on the subject of the Amazon.

In other respects, a countless number of trees and plants have no precise names, as is the case in many remote places. Biological stocktaking is therefore necessary in order to determine the names and characteristics of this abundant biomass. This is a long and exacting task that requires a specialized work force as well as money. The proprietors foresee erecting a biological research station that would contribute on the realization of this task and hope to find investors. Moreover, in 15 years, this magnificent complex will belong exclusively to the Achuar people.

The staff is obliging and does its utmost to respond to their guests' every need.

Travellers should keep in mind that due to sudden changes in temperature, it is preferable for visitors to organize their itinerary with a certain amount of scheduling flexibility. In fact, the small plane that travels back and forth between Macas for Kapawi cannot take off if the weather is stormy. Travellers should therefore avoid mapping the course of their itinerary too rigidly, so as not to miss their next flight to another destination.

Zamora

Though Zamora is a simple little village with a little under 10,000 inhabitants, it is the capital of the province of the same name.

Nambija

Nambija is a small western Andean village, perched at an altitude of about 2,600 metres, that is currently experiencing gold rush. In fact, the mountain is furrowed with numerous galleries and caves where a few thousand modern prospectors employ traditional and rudimentary methods of extraction. They thus expose themselves to serious mining accidents like the one that buried about one hundred workers a few years ago. In addition to the dangers posed by

natural accidents, risks attributed to criminal human behaviour make it so that workers live in fear and anxiety, and it is not uncommon to encounter some of them openly carrying guns on their belts like in the old days of the gold rush...

 PARKS

Parque Nacional Yasuní ★★

Established in 1979, Yasuní park, situated in the province of Napo, constitutes the country's vastest national park with its colossal surface area of 679,700 hectares. Despite its impressive fauna, comprising monkeys, falcons, royal herons and giant armadillos, getting a chance to observe them is unlikely. Nevertheless, visitors will certainly have the opportunity to appreciate its flora, rife with a multitude of species. The park's forest vegetation is riverside and lakeside. Various types of forests shelter a multitude of trees and tropical plants such as the *dacanranda*, a tree that supplies a kind of wood sought after by cabinet makers. On account of its great biological wealth, this region is a "biosphere reserve" as defined by UNESCO's program on humans and the biosphere. Ironically, access to the region that contains the park's most interesting fauna is forbidden and is the private domain of the oil companies.

The small native community of the Huaoranis lives in the park. The Huaoranis were formerly known under the pejorative name of "Aucas", which means "savage" in Quichua. Little is known about these Amerindians who inhabit Parque Nacional Yasuní except that they do not speak Spanish and were among the last natives to come in contact with the Western world. In the last few decades, the intrusion on the part of missionaries and, more recently still, oil companies in search of black gold have given rise to frictions between the Huaoranis and these unwelcome plunderers who are attempting to set up shop on their territory.

Reserva Faunísta Cuyabeno ★★★

Established in 1979, the Reserva Faunísta Cuyabeno is a park considered by some to be Ecuador's most beautiful natural territory next to the Galápagos Islands. Located in the province of Sucumbíos, to the east of Lago Agrío and to the north of Parque Nacional Yasuní, this reserve covers 655,504 hectares of territory and boasts spectacular fauna and flora. The tropical forest shelters numerous species of animals who roam around the innumerable watercourses and under the dense foliage of huge trees. This is where you have the highest probability of observing animals in their natural habitat outside the Galápagos. Among those that visitors might encounter are caymans, monkeys, snakes, countless species of birds (eagles, toucans, parrots...) and even dolphins, who frolic in the freshwater rivers of Amazonia. Unfortunately, despite the exceptional lushness of this verdant expanse, and only a few short years after its creation, the government decided to grant oil companies the right to drill into the subsoil of the State's new El Dorado. As a result, the inevitable happened: oil spills of varying sizes occurred in this jewel of greenery, and Amerindian communities were forced to find refuge elsewhere. As a solution to this problem, the communities were compensated and the reserve's borders were retraced and expanded, making access more difficult but, also, better protecting the area. Today, the government is being forced to deal with many pressures exercised by oil companies that wish to exploit the park's subsoil. Cofans, Quichuas, Secoyas and Sionas are some of the tribes who inhabit the reserve. The park is only accessible through specialized guides or a tour company (see p 247).

Reserva Biológica de Limoncocha ★

Created in 1985, this biological reserve covers an area of 13,000 hectares and extends out from the shores of Limoncocha's magnificent lake, the natural habitat of over 400 species of birds such as the toucan, the parrot and many other representatives of tropical winged fauna. Monkeys and caymans can also be spotted in this lovely spot.

 ACCOMMODATIONS

The Northern Oriente

Papallacta

The **Las Termas de Papallacta** hotel *($30; pb, hw, ℜ, ≈; reservations in Quito: Calle Nuñez de Vela 913 at Naciones Unidas, Edificio Doral II, 1 piso, 15, ☎ 02-537-398, ⤶ 02-435-292)* is nestled in a relaxing setting. The establishment offers small, clean and well-tended bungalows, which can accommodate two to four people, around a few swimming pools.

Baeza

The city of Baeza has few tourist facilities. Those who wish to spend the night there will have to make do with rudimentary establishments such as the **Hostal San Rafael** *($8)* or the **Mesón de Baeza** *($8)*.

San Rafael

Those who wish to visit the Cascada de San Rafael can stay close by, at the **San Rafael Lodge** *($65; pb, hw, ℜ; reservations in Quito, Avenida Gonzáles Suárez, ☎ 02-469-846 or 02-544-600, ⇆ 02-469-847)*. Clean and well-equipped cabins are offered. The outfit belongs to the Quito hotel.

Tena

Located right near the bridge, the **Hostal Traveller's Lodging** *($10; pb, ℜ)* is a popular spot with budget travellers. The rooms are very plain, but the staff is friendly.

Lago Agrío

The majority of Lago Agrío's hotels are much like the city itself: noisy, dirty and devoid of charm.

Those who have checked out the El Cofán hotel's rooms and concluded that they simply do not have the means to offer themselves this luxury can resort to the **Hotel Cabaña** *($10 to $12)* or the **Hotel Guacamayo**. Rooms are spartan and noisy but inexpensive.

The **Hotel El Cofán** *($35; pb, ℜ, tv; Avenida Quito at 12 de Febrero, ☎ 830-009)* is definitely the cleanest, the safest and, of course, the most expensive in Lago Agrío. Indeed, the price of these rooms can seem much too steep for what they are truly worth, but visitors should remember that, despite everything, there are none better in the city, nor in the surrounding area...

Lodges in the vicinity of Lago Agrío

Travellers who wish to visit the Reserva Faunística Cuyabeno at a leisurely pace, in a completely original way, while benefiting from comfort and enjoying excellent food as well as the presence of unequalled nature guides, can choose to travel the waterways of Amazonia on board the **Flotel Orellana** *(for information, contact Metropolitan Touring, see p 53)*. Despite its odd resemblance to the old river boats that, not so long ago, used to navigate the Mississippi, this boat, fitted out as a floating hotel, was built in 1975, right near the small oil-producing village of Coca. This peculiar boat cheerfully navigated along the Río Napo until 1991, but was then forced to change its home port because of the presence of too many visitors, colonists and oil companies in this region who were causing the animals to flee. Measuring 45 metres in length by eight metres in width, the *Flotel* is propelled by a 3,100 horse-power engine and travels at a speed of five to 10 knots. It can accommodate up to 48 passengers in 22 cabins. Each cabin has a storage space, a private bathroom and a shower with hot water. All cabins open out on the bridge and have fans. The bar is ready to welcome guests and serves unlimited amounts of coffee from as early as 6:30am. In the same room, a small library offers a wide range of books on the Amazon.

Moreover, a doctor resides in one of the cabins and is available 24 hours a day.

Visits are made in the following manner: the *Flotel* navigates along the Reserva Faunística Cuyabeno's waterways and drops anchor at strategic points along the banks of the river. Travellers are then divided into groups and invited to take their place in small motor-propelled crafts. These crafts make their way to the different paths, which visitors are free to explore. There is an excursion with an overnight on terra firma, under a thatch roof covered by a mosquito net, for the complete exotic experience. On another day, the pleasures of discovery will lead visitors to a huge six-storey observation tower, culminating at 120 metres in height and erected around a tree even taller than the tower itself.

During the stay, a day is dedicated to meeting one of the indigenous peoples who live inside the Parque Cuyabeno on the shores of the Río Aguarico: the Cofans. It is important to remember, however, that these Amerindians are not circus animals parading for the pleasure of outside visitors. Firstly, visitors do not go to their village but, rather, to a neutral territory designated as the "Visitors Center". Secondly, it is expressly forbidden to take their picture. Despite the fact that they may be dressed in jeans and T-shirts and sporting digital watches, Cofans try to maintain their dignity. Thanks to Metropolitan Touring, it will nevertheless be possible for visitors to exchange a few words with these Amerindians and to purchase artifacts from them.

Those who wish to venture even deeper into the heart of the tropical forest can go to the **IMUYA** and **IRIPARI** campgrounds. These two camps are located beyond the territory serviced by the *Flotel*, right near the Peruvian border.

The IMUYA campground can accommodate approximately 20 people. "IMUYA" means "river of the howling monkeys" in *Pairocá*, the language of the Siona Amerindians. This is not by sheer coincidence, as the howler monkeys often manifest their presence with screeches. Moreover, everything here runs on solar energy and all trash is reduced to compost.

The IRIPARI campground was built in 1991 around the lake of the same name, Ecuador's biggest; it consists of a group of wooden structures covered in straw. Showers and bathrooms are shared. In this camp, everything runs on solar energy. Moreover, chances of observing freshwater dolphins nearby are fairly high at about 90%.

The **Cuyabeno Lodge** *($531 per person for a stay of four days and three nights; reservations in Quito, Avenida Coruña 1349 and Orellana, ☎ 02-552-617, 02-553-826 or 02-553-818, ✉ 02-565-261, P.O. Box 1703-402-A, nmundo@uio.telconet.net)* resembles a small indigenous village buried in the greenery of the Reserva Faunística Cuyabeno and erected along a murmuring river. It consists of a group of inconspicuous *cabañas*, covered with thatch roofs, built on piles and scattered here and there around a main building that houses the kitchen and dining-room. There is no electricity, but the *cabañas* are equipped with comfortable beds covered by mosquito nets and have private bathrooms with cold water showers. All the structures are linked to each other thanks to a footbridge that plunges into the forest, whence a path starts, allowing visitors to explore the wonders of nature. Made-to-measure excursions are organized. Guests can thus quietly navigate along the waters of the park and observe the countless winged species or even see friendly freshwater dolphins. Kayaks are also at the disposal of visitors. Come night-time, the canopy of heaven as well as myriads of phosphorescent insects will offer guests a starlit scene of infinite beauty; and meandering along Amazonian rivers on board a boat, visitors can also make out caymans lazily stretched out on the banks of the river. Accredited guides are more than competent and will do their utmost to satisfy your every desire. The outfit is managed by the Nuevo Mundo tour company, one its proprietors being the president of the Ecotourism Association of Ecuador.

Misahuallí

Travellers who are easy to please and whose budgets are limited can stay at the little **Hotel El Paisano** *($10; a block away from la Plaza)*.

The price/quality ratio offered by **El Albergue Español** *($20; pb, ℜ; reservations in Quito:* ☎ *02-584-912)* is unquestionably one of the best in town. The rooms are clean and offer a view of the Río Napo; the staff is friendly and obliging.

Sometimes referred to as the "Butterfly Lodge", the **Cabañas Aliñahui** *($30; pb, ℜ; reservations in Quito: Calle Río Coca and Isla Fernandina,* ☎ *02-253-267,* ⌨ *02-253-266)* are scattered along the sides of a hill, amidst close to two hectares of greenery bordering the Río

Napo. The rooms are spartan but comfortable. The staff sees to the organization of excursions into the tropical forest according to travellers' wishes. Those just passing through can play games of table tennis and have access to a volleyball court. A parking lot is available to the brave souls who have made the trip by car from Quito.

The **Misahuallí Jungle Hotel** *($30; sb, ℜ; reservations in Quito:* ☎ *02-520-043)* houses visitors in relatively clean and plainly decorated *cabañas*. It is, nevertheless, one of the city's good hotels. The staff is friendly.

Lodges in the vicinity of Misahuallí

Clinging to the side of a hill overhanging the Río Napo, the **Casa del Suizo** *($80 for two people for one night; ℜ, ≈, pb; reservations in Quito, Calle Reina Victoria 1235 at Lizardo García,* ☎ *02-509-115 or 02-508-871,* ⌨ *02-508-872)* belongs to the same proprietors as the Sacha Lodge. Its first stone was laid in 1986. At the time, a few rather rustic-looking rooms lodged visitors just passing through. Today, the main building encompasses the reception desk, a willowy observation tower allowing visitors to take in the scenery, a bar and a huge restaurant able to accommodate up to 150 people. Visitors can lounge on the terrace surrounded by a garden of flowers and take full advantage of the two swimming pools. One hundred and forty-five beds are distributed among approximately 50 *cabañas* that can accommodate the same number of people. Each *cabaña* is stylishly decorated, immaculate and lit by electricity, and has a private bathroom with a hot water shower. This establishment will perfectly suit those who wish to visit the rainforest without depriving themselves of modern comforts. Moreover, the food is delicious and the reception and service are impeccable, but a profound sadness may wring the hearts of travellers whose gaze is captured by the presence of many animals caged for the sole purpose of attracting onlookers...

The **Cabañas Anaconda** *(reservations in Quito:* ☎ *02-545-426)* are also on the Río Napo, a little farther along the Casa del Suizo. A dozen rustic *cabañas* with thatched roofs doze under the dense foliage of trees and receive groups of travellers. No electricity or hot water.

Coca

The **Hotel Oasis** *($10; pb; near the bridge)* offers rooms that will suit travellers who are not too demanding and whose budgets are limited.

For those who wish to spend a few more dollars, the **Auca** hotel *($15; pb, ℜ; very close to the* terminal terrestre*)* offers clean, unevenly decorated *cabañas* of various sizes.

The best hotel in town is **La Misión** *($30; pb; ℜ; reservations in Quito:* ☎ *02-553-674,* ≈ *02-880-260)*. Clean and comfortable rooms, but devoid of charm.

Lodges in the vicinity of Coca

The **Sacha Lodge** *($525 per person for a 4-day stay; reservations in Quito: Calle Reina Victoria 1235 at Lizardo García,* ☎ *02-509-115 or 02-508-871,* ≈ *04-508-872 or 04-222-531)* is located around two hours and 30 minutes from Coca along the Río Napo.

In 1991, Beni Ammeter, a Swiss who had been living in Ecuador for 25 years, decided to buy a piece of land in the rainforest in order to build facilities meant to accommodate visitors. The following year, the Sacha Lodge was inaugurated and the adventure began. Today, over an expanse of 1,200 hectares, there are seven cabins, each containing two large beds and barred windows that open out on a small balcony where hammocks are slung.

Two hours away from Coca by boat along the Río Napo is the **Hacienda Primavera** *(for reservations, contact the Ecotours tour company, Calle Robles 610 at Juan León Mera,* ☎ *02-226-890)*, which comprises a dozen rustic *cabañas*.

Off the beaten path, deep in the rainforest, three hours away by boat along the Río Napo, the **Selva Lodge** *($700 per person for a 4-day stay; reservations in Quito: Avenida 6 de Diciembre 2816 at James Orton,* ☎ *02-550-995,* ≈ *02-567-297)* receives much praise from visitors who stop there. The rooms are kept by an American couple, Eric and Maggie Schartz, and distributed among approximately 15 solidly-built *cabañas*, modestly decorated but with private bathrooms. The beds are covered by mosquito nets, but there is no hot water. One of its features is a 40-metre-high observation tower allowing visitors to take in the dazzling panorama at a single glance. Right near the complex, a butterfly farm is another interesting sight that will undoubtedly please travellers attracted to the colourful world of lepidopterans. Contrary to what people may believe, the staff does not amuse itself by catching these butterflies in the forest in order to bring them back here. The farm was built for the purpose of breeding butterflies. As a result, over 30,000 butterflies are sold every year throughout the world to botanical gardens or other organizations with the aim of promoting the wealth and beauty of tropical forests.

The **Hostería Yuturi** *($340 per person for a 4-day stay; Avenida Amazonas 1022 at Joaquín Pinto,* ☎ *(02) 522-133)* is situated five hours away by boat from Coca and offers rustic accommodations and typical hikes in the rainforest.

Puyo

Make no mistake, despite its name, the **Hotel Europa Internacional** *($10; ℜ, pb; Avenida 9 de Octubre at Orellana)* bears absolutely no resemblance to charming and comfortable European hotels, but will be perfectly suitable for travellers just passing through and with limited budgets who only plan on staying for one night.

For a few dollars more, the **Hotel El Araucano** *($16; hw, ℜ, pb; Calle Marín)* definitely has the best rooms in town. Though short on charm and elegance, they are adequate and well-equipped.

Approximately five kilometres from Puyo, in the direction of Tena, the **Hostería Safari** *($20; pb, ℜ, ≈;* ☎ *885-465)* offers small, clean and equipped *cabañas* in a quiet and relaxing setting. This is a good alternative to staying in Puyo, especially since guests get to enjoy the calm of the Amazonian forest.

The Southern Oriente

Macas

The rooms at the **Hostal Esmeralda** *($10; tv, hw, pb; Calle Cuenca and Soasti)* are spartan but prove to be relatively clean. Service is friendly.

Those who wish to afford themselves a little more comfort can opt for the **Hotel Peñon del Oriente** *($20; tv, hw, ℜ; Amazonas and Comín;* ☎ *700-124,* ↩ *700-450)*. The rooms are modern, clean and bright.

 RESTAURANTS

The Northern Oriente

Lago Agrío

Like its hotels, the city's restaurants are hardly inviting. If eating here is absolutely necessary, head for the restaurant in the El Cofán hotel.

Coca

For a quick and simple meal, try the **Escondido** *($)*, an unpretentious little restaurant near the river.

The Hotel **La Misión** *($$)*'s restaurant is, without a doubt, one of the best places to eat at in town. The menu offers a good choice of dishes featuring chicken, beef and pork.

Misahuallí

The **Hotel El Paisano's** *($)* little restaurant offers a vegetarian menu that changes daily. Those who have a little more money to spend can go to the **El Abergue Español** *($$)* hotel's restaurant. The menu offers a variety of meat and fish dishes.

Puyo

The **Chifa Famosa** *($; Calle Eslad Marin and 27 de Febrero)* offers simple cuisine featuring Chinese food.

The **Mesón Europeo** *($$; Avenida Zambrano)*, a house converted into a restaurant, offers a large choice of grilled meats such as very appetizing filets mignons and porterhouse steaks.

The Southern Oriente

Macas

Although the **Chifa Pagoda China** *($$; Amazonas 1505)* restaurant's decor is somewhat flashy, portions are as generous as they are delicious. The menu offers many chicken, shrimp, pork and beef dishes prepared in the Oriental style.

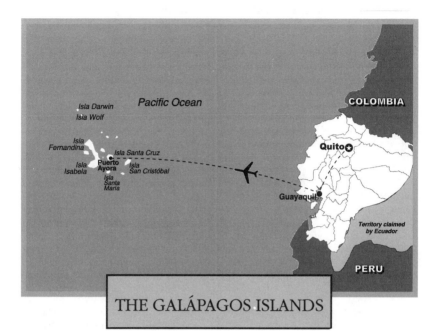

THE GALÁPAGOS ISLANDS

It is difficult, if not impossible, not to be amazed and charmed by the Galápagos Islands. To come here is to step out of time and into a fantastic, spectacular, insular world, where there is little to disrupt the tranquillity of the extraordinary flora and fauna that reign more or less supreme over this strange, isolated territory.

Where else could you find such a motley collection of animals—Californian sea lions, flightless cormorants, prehistoric-looking land and marine iguanas, flamingoes, gigantic tortoises that bear witness to bygone days, the smallest penguins in the world, and all sorts of other curious, mysterious creatures—all sharing the same territory? Indeed, there is no other place on the planet quite like the Galápagos.

The history of the Galápagos Islands might date back to the dawn of time, but it has only been recorded since March 10, 1535. On that day, a boat that had set out for Perú from Panamá, led by the bishop Fray Tomás de Berlanga, was forced off course by the strong ocean currents. The boat drifted westward into theretofore unexplored territory in the Pacific. Some time after running out of potable water, the crew spotted land on the horizon and hastened to drop anchor and explore the islands, thus becoming the first visitors to the archipelago. Unfortunately for them, all they found were giant tortoises, sea lions, iguanas and countless species of birds.

An official report describing the men's brief stay on these volcanic islands was sent to King Charles V. Too busy colonizing Inca territory and amassing South American gold, the Spanish showed no interest in the islands.

Eleven years later, in 1546, a few Spanish soldiers wishing to escape Francisco Pizarro's tyrranical regime decided to desert his army and head out to sea. The ocean currents forced their boat right through the Galápagos. The men, who were no match for the currents and had very little sailing experience, were unable to land on any of the islands that loomed up before them then disappeared in the dense fog that was gathering. Convinced that the islands were enchanted, they named them Las Islas Encantadas.

Thanks to Fray Tomás de Berlanga's report, however, the Galápagos Islands appeared in an atlas under the name Insulae de los Galopegos (Islands of the Tortoises) in 1574.

Over the next three centuries, pirates and corsairs used the Galápagos as a hideout and supply base before attacking the Ecuadoran and Peruvian coasts, causing serious problems for the native species. They used the trees to make fires to warm themselves, while the giant tortoises provided an excellent source of fresh meat that could easily feed an entire crew.

The whaling industry also caused tremendous damage to the islands and its marine inhabitants. The holds of ships were filled with giant tortoises for the sailors to eat, a practice that continued until the end of the 19th century.

On February 12, 1832, Ecuador officially took possession of the Galápagos by establishing a colony of exiled soldiers and prisoners on Isla Floreana and naming the group of islands the Archipiélago del Ecuador. Three years later, on September 15, 1835, Charles Darwin arrived at the Galápagos during a scientific expedition. In the course of his five-week stay, the young English naturalist, who was 26 at the time, visited just four or five of the islands and recorded a series of fascinating observations on the flora and fauna. These notes would support his famous theory of evolution, expounded in *The Origin of Species by Means of Natural Selection* (1859). His theory of evolution is based on the fact that species can adapt over generations in order to survive. For many years, this book was a source of controversy in conservative and religious circles, whose members fiercely disputed its content.

In 1892, the Galápagos Islands were officially named the Archipiélago de Colón in honour of the 400th anniversary of Christopher Columbus's first voyage.

The Ecuadoran government declared the islands a national park in 1959. That same year, the Charles Darwin Foundation was established in order to help preserve this unique ecosystem. UNESCO designated the archipelago a World Heritage Site in 1978.

The Galápagos are named after the shape of the shell of the giant tortoises that abounded here in the era of the Spanish pirates. These shells, which curve up at the edges, bear a strange resemblance to the *galápagos* saddles used in Spain in those days.

Chances are you will only visit this magnificent place once in your life. Rather than embarking on such an adventure uninformed, it is important to understand clearly what it entails. Don't forget that a trip to the Galápagos is expensive—very

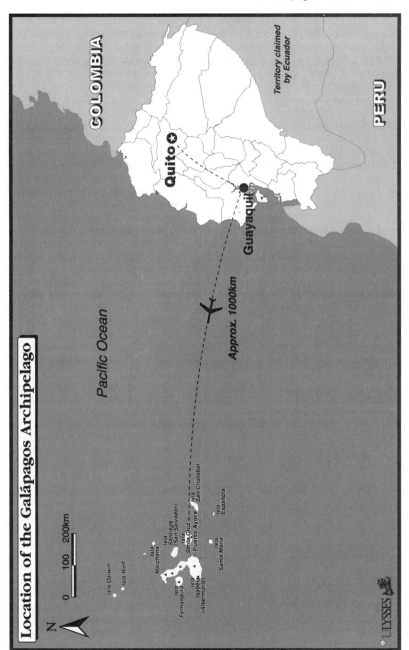

Location of the Galápagos Archipelago

expensive. The plane ticket costs over $300, the entrance fee for the park $80, and a week-long cruise nearly $1000. Factor in your personal expenses, and the trip adds up to about $2000! Furthermore, the Galápagos are not a big seaside resort like Cancún or Acapulco, much less a Disney World-style amusement park. Only four of the islands (Santa Cruz, Floreana, San Cristóbal and Isabela) are partially inhabited, and their total population is just over 10,000. Their total land area is 8,000 square kilometres, 97% of which is protected; the remaining 3% is set aside for human habitation. To protect and preserve the plant and animal life, park authorities and the Charles Darwin Station have decided to limit access to the islands to about 51 sites. Only a few islands may be visited without an authorized guide. For the past few years, tourism has been prohibited on a number of islands so the scientists can carry out research there. None of the hotels on the Galápagos has more than two stories, and aside from two or three places with very pretty rooms, the accommodations are rudimentary. Finally, even the most luxurious boats don't offer the same level of comfort as the big cruise ships that crisscross the Caribbean Sea.

The "Lost Paradise": Threats and Conservation

Because of its isolation from the rest of the world and its rare and highly distinctive flora and fauna, the Galápagos are often seen as a lost paradise. Today, the threats facing the archipelago outnumber the measures taken to protect it—so much so that it is to wonder if this paradise is not on its way to being lost and gone forever.

At the dawn of time, when these islands emerged from the sea, they were nothing but an ordinary cluster of volcanic rocks. Today, they are home to a wide variety of plants and animals with unique characteristics. The Galápagos were never connected to the mainland. Up until four centuries ago, nothing lived on the islands but endemic plants and animals that had gradually managed to make their home here through natural processes and led a completely self-sufficient existence.

These plants and animals came to the Galápagos by air and by water. Some seeds floated to the islands, while others were carried over by birds or simply by the wind. The vast majority of these species came from South America, the others from Central America. All the plants and animals found here have adapted to the environment over the centuries.

In order to eat and reproduce, the animals had to become acclimatized to the environment. Certain land iguanas thus became marine species, and some sea turtles moved permanently onto the islands, becoming land tortoises. Those tortoises from the islands of Española and Isabela have an unusually long neck that enables them to reach food formerly inaccessible to them. Darwin's (or Galápagos) finches (see p 272), which originally came from the mainland, have also evolved by adaptation. The shape of their beak gradually changed so that they could survive here. The finches thus differ from one island to the next, having adapted to the food available to them.

Over the centuries, these changes brought about an ecological equilibrium among the various plant and animal species. This equilibrium was disrupted

The Galápagos Islands

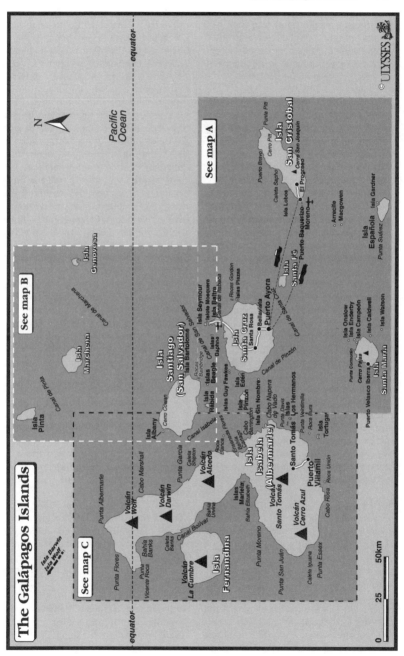

See map B

See map A

See map C

N

Pacific Ocean

equator

equator

© ULYSSES

Isla Darwin
Isla Wolf

Punta Flores
Volcán La Cumbre
Isla Fernandina
Punta Vicente Roca
Bahía Banks
Caleta Banks
Punta Espinosa
Canal Bolívar
Bahía Elizabeth
Punta Moreno
Punta San Juán
Caleta Iguana
Punta Essex

Punta Albermarle
Cabo Marshall
Volcán Wolf
Volcán Darwin
Punta García
Caleta Shipton
Volcán Alcedo
Bahía Urvina
Isla Isabela
(Albermarle)
Volcán Santo Tomás
Santo Tomás
Volcán Cerro Azul
Puerto Villamil
Cabo Rosa
Roca Unión

Islas Marielas

Islas Flores
Roca Blanca
Bahía Cartago

Cerro Cowan
Isla Albany
Canal Isabela
Isla Pinta
Canal de Pinta
Isla Marchena
Canal de Marchena
Isla Genovesa

Isla Santiago
(San Salvador)
Isla Bartolomé
Islas Bainbridge
Rocas Beagle
Islas Beagle
Canal de San Salvador
Isla Seymour
Islote Mosquera
Canal de Itabaca
Isla Baltra
Isla Rábida
Isla Guy Fawkes
Isla Pinzón
Isla Sin Nombre
Cabo Douglas
Cabo Nepera
Isla Eden
Rocas Gordon
Islas Plazas
Bellavista
Isla Santa Cruz
Santa Rosa
Puerto Ayora
Canal de Pinzón
Canal de Santa Cruz
Isla Santa Fé
Islas Los Hermanos
Cabo Barrington
Isla Tortuga
Roca Vendimilla
Punta Cormorant
Punta Cevallos
Cerro Pajas
Isla Santa María
Puerto Velasco Ibarra
Isla Onslow
Isla Enderby
Isla Campeón
Isla Caldwell
Isla Watson
Arrecife
Macgowen
Puerto Bravo
Cerro Pitt
Punta Pitt
Cerro San Joaquín
El Progreso
Isla San Cristóbal
Caleta Sapho
Caleta Lobos
Puerto Baquerizo Moreno
Isla Lobos
Isla Española
Punta Suárez
Isla Gardner

0   25   50km

when man arrived here, less than 400 years ago. For various reasons, rats, cats, horses, dogs, pigs, cows and goats were gradually introduced by pirates, whalers and colonists.

Pirates used the archipelago as a place to hide out from their enemies and stash their booty. As they had long distances to cover, they would stock up on tortoises to feed their crews. The tortoises weighed between 175 and 225 kilograms each, so donkeys and horses were brought to the islands to help the pirates carry them to their ship. The men also left cows and pigs here in the hope of eating them on their next visit. Whalers also filled up their ships' holds with giant tortoises. Like the pirates and the whalers, the first colonies on the islands were highly detrimental to the flora and fauna, as the settlers cleared land for farming and killed tortoises and other animals for food. The animals introduced onto the Galápagos by human beings now constitute the greatest threat facing the endemic species. For over 300 years, these animals have been reproducing at an incredible speed, causing great harm to the islands' fragile ecosystem. Pigs, like cats, rats and dogs, feed on tortoise eggs. In addition to competing for the tortoises' food, donkeys and horses trample on their eggs and on the endemic flora.

In the late 1970s, wild dogs ravaged large colonies of land iguanas on the islands of Isabela and Santa Cruz. Today, only two of the islands in the archipelago, Fernandina and Genovesa, are inhabited exclusively by endemic species.

There are three ways to eliminate the animals introduced by man. The first is to poison their food; this practice proved successful with the wild dogs on Isla Isabela. The second is to introduce bacteria that kill off a specific species. This method is very tricky, and no one wants to take on the responsibility of issuing an order to unleash bacteria without knowing the side effects. For example, if the buzzards eat the goats infected with the bacteria and are affected by it in turn, the already fragile ecosystem could suffer even greater damage. The third method, hunting, is still the most common. Unfortunately, it is not very effective, as the islands are large and often have luxuriant vegetation where the animals can take shelter. Furthermore, the animals reproduce faster than they are eliminated.

In 1954, the Galápagos were declared a province of Ecuador. Today, anyone can come here to live. As a result, the population is growing at the alarming rate of 10% annually—faster than anywhere else in the country. Many Ecuadorans move to the islands thinking that everyone here benefits from the influx of dollars. Unfortunately for them, this is not the case. Though over 50,000 tourists visited the Galápagos in 1996, the job prospects remain poor. Moreover, the new arrivals did not grow up in an environment as fragile as the archipelago's and are not used to complying with so many restrictions.

What's more, to satisfy an increasing foreign demand, many Ecuadorans are taking up fishing and killing off sharks, whose fins are considered a delicacy in certain countries. Over the past decade or so, the number of sharks has dropped nearly 50%! In the early 1990s, about 20 tons of hammerheads, some whole, but mostly their fins, were found on an illegal fishing boat. The smugglers were immediately fined. Still, for obscure reasons, Ecuadoran laws have not been modified since the middle of the century; as the fines have not increased for decades, they are now too nominal to deter fishermen from breaking the law. The Galápagos are probably the only place in the world where you can swim alongside a three-metre-long hammerhead shark without any danger of being attacked. However, if these creatures continue to be hunted, they might start attacking swimmers — or simply disappear altogether.

Fishing for sea cucumbers, better known in Spanish as *pepinos del mar*, is another alarming problem threatening the ecology of the islands. Sea cucumbers have the ability to reprocess certain kinds of organic waste and thus help purify the water. Asians are crazy about sea cucumber, which they consider a delicacy. Consequently, many Ecuadorans and other pirate fishermen cast their nets here, dangerously disrupting the archipelago's fragile ecosystem. Although fishing for sea cucumbers has been formally banned, people continue do so illegally, blinded by the lure of the profit they can make on this rare merchandise.

The archipelago is barely patrolled. A single boat, the *Guadalupe River*, provided by the Americans, is responsible for monitoring all fishing being carried out on the immense territory of the Galápagos. To make matters even worse, this boat often just sits at the dock, as there is not enough money to pay for its fuel.

The problems facing the Galápagos are thus serious, and it is urgent that solutions be found.

The Flora of the Galápagos

Vegetation exists on the Galápagos Islands because seeds were carried here by air and by sea. About 10% of the seeds were brought here from the mainland by ocean currents, 60% by birds and 30% simply by the wind. About 99% of the flora comes from South America, the remaining 1% from Central America. The plants on the archipelago have all adapted to the environment over the centuries. Still, due to variations in climate, altitude and degree of exposure to the wind, the distribution of the flora is very uneven; there are no fewer than seven distinct zones of vegetation on the islands.

1. The coastal zone: This narrow strip between the land and the water is home primarily to mangrove trees and brush, as well as colourful succulents.

2. The arid zone: This zone extends from the coastal zone to an average elevation of 100 metres. It features unusual plant life that has adapted to the dry climate (mainly cactuses), as well as the *palo santo*, a bush with greyish branches that are completely bare of leaves except during the rainy season.

3. The transition zone: This zone stretches to an average altitude of 250 metres and is characterized by the presence of three trees, the *palo santo*, the *pegapega* and the *guayabillo*.

4. The *scalesia* zone: This moist zone extends to an elevation of 200 to 400 metres and is blanketed with mosses and ferns, including the *scalesia pedunculata* or *lechoso*, a tree-sized fern with milky sap. The *lechoso*

has no branches, but rather a stem covered with flowers.

5. The brown zone: This zone owes its name to the colour of the mosses that hang from the ends of the *lechosos* in the upper part of the *scalesia* zone, on the leeward (rather than windward) side of the islands.

6. The *miconia* zone: This zone extends to an altitude of up to 600 metres and is distinguished by the presence *miconias*. This endemic species of bush has dense foliage and is only found on the islands of Santa Cruz and San Cristóbal.

7. The pampas zone: The tree fern is the only large plant that has managed to survive among the ferns, lichen and aquatic plants in this wet, misty and perpetually windswept area at the top of the islands (higher than 600 metres).

The Fauna of the Galápagos

The following pages contain a brief list of a few of the species you might encounter during your stay on the Galápagos Islands.

Waved albatross (*albatros ondulado* or *de Galápagos*): This magnificent seabird has a yellow beak and a wavelike colouring on its breast, hence its name. It can fly and coast in the wind for weeks without touching the ground. Isla Española is one of the only places in the world where the waved albatross nests. The albatrosses' display ceremony is a fascinating spectacle that lasts nearly half an hour and involves all sorts of graceful greetings, swinging movements, whistles and cries. There are about 12,000 albatrosses in the archipelago, but they only nest on Española, starting in mid-April, before heading back out to sea in mid-December. In order to take flight, these birds need fairly strong winds and high cliffs, which explains why they have chosen to live on Española. Albatrosses generally live farther south, in the South Seas.

Whales: Several species of whales share the waters around the Galápagos (rorquals, lesser rorquals, sei whales, sperm whales, killer whales, blue whales and humpback whales, to name but a few). These cetaceans rarely swim near boats, however, and can generally be observed only from a great distance.

Galápagos hawk (*gavilán de Galápagos*): This diurnal bird, an endemic species with dark brown plumage and yellow feet, is one of the chief predators of baby tortoises. It is nearly 60 centimetres long and is found mainly on the islands of Bartolomé, Española, Fernandina, Isabela, Santiago and Santa Fé.

Flightless cormorant (*cormorán no volador*): A seabird that has gradually lost the use of its wings over the centuries, this endemic species is the largest cormorant in the world. The wingless cormorant moves about easily in the water and feeds on fish. Because of its size and the fact that it is isolated on Isla Fernandina, it is safe from predators. In fact, Fernandina is one of the few islands on Earth where no animal has ever been introduced by man. It is easy, if distressing, to imagine what terrible things could happen to this bird if wild animals were inadvertently brought to Fernandina.

Dolphin (*delfín*): Recognizable to all by its shrill laugh, which never fails to

Bird Life on the Galápagos Islands

Seabirds

Albatros ondulado or *de Galápagos*	Waved albatross
Cormorán no volador	Flightless cormorant
Piquero enmascarado	Masked booby
Fragata común	Frigate-bird
Fregata reál	Magnificent frigate-bird
Pelícano café or *pardo*	Brown pelican
Piquero patas azules	Blue-footed booby
Piquero patas rosas	Red-footed booby
Pájaro tropical	Red-billed tropicbird
Gaviota de cola bifurcada	Swallow-tailed gull
Gaviota de lava	Lava gull
Gaviota de Franklin	Franklin gull
Golondrina de mer	Storm petrel
Petrel Hawaiano	Hawaiian or dark-rumped petrel
Pufino	Audubon's shearwater
Gaviotín	Tern
Pinguino de Galápagos	Galápagos penguin

Land Birds

Canario (María)	Yellow warbler
Pájaro Brujo	Vermillion flycatcher
Papamoscas de Galápagos	Lage-billed (Galápagos) flycatcher
Cucuve de Galápagos	Galápagos mockingbird
Cucuve de San Cristóbal	San Cristóbal or Chatham Mockingbird
Cucuve de Española	Hood mockingbird
Cucuve de Floreana	Floreana or Charles mockinbird
Paloma de Galápagos	Galápagos dove
Aguatero	Dark-billed cuckoo
Martín de Galápagos	Galápagos martin
Pachay	Galápagos rail
Gavilán de Galápagos	Galápagos hawk
Lechuza de campanario	Barn owl
Lechuza de campo	Short-eared owl

Darwin's (Galápagos) Finches

Pinzón terrestre de pico pequeño	Small ground finch
Pinzón terrestre de pico mediano	Medium ground finch
Pinzón terrestre de pico grande	Large ground finch
Pinzón terrestre de pico agudo	Sharp-beaked ground finch
Pinzón de cactus	Cactus finch
Gran pinzón de cactus	Large cactus finch
Pinzón arbóro mediano	Medium tree finch
Pinzón arbóreo grande	Large tree finch
Pinzón artesano (Carpintero)	Wood pecker finch
Pinzón de manglar	Mangrove finch
Pinzón vegetariano	Vegetarian finch
Pinzón cantor	Warbler finch

Lake and Lagoon Birds

Flamenco	Flamingo
Patillo de Bahamas	White-cheeked pintail
Tero real	Black-necked stilt
Garza blanca	Common egret
Garza vaquera	Cattle egret
Falaropo	Northern or red-necked phalarope

Shore Birds

Garza morena (azul)	Great blue heron
Garza de lava	Lava heron
Garza nocturna (Huaque)	Yellow-crowned night heron
Zarapito	Curlew or whimbrel
Ostrero Americano	American oystercatcher
Vuelvepiedras	Turnstone
Chorlitejo	Plover
Playero	Sandpiper
Aguila pescadora	Osprey

Marine Iguana

make both children and adults smile, this friendly sea mammal can be spotted early in the morning—usually swimming behind a ship.

Marine iguana (*iguana marina*): This jagged-backed saurian, the only reptile in the world to feed on seaweed, is a perfect example of Darwin's theory. In order to find food, this herbivore can dive to a depth of up to 10 metres, but rarely goes deeper than three metres because of the threat of predators. Its flat tail and sharp claws helped it to adapt to the sea. The marine iguana can even drink salt water and eliminate the salt through its nasal glands by sneezing. Its life span is about 30 years.

Land iguana (*iguana terrestre*): Threatened with extinction because of repeated attacks by wild dogs, this creature is found mainly on the islands of Plaza Sur, Isabela, Santa Cruz, Fernandina and Seymour. An herbivorous reptile, it is particularly fond of cactus. Its breeding season is from November to March.

Flamingo (*flamenco*): This bird is easily recognizable by its pink colour; supple, sinuous neck; long, thin legs and webbed feet. It frequents the salty lagoons on the islands of Floreana, Rábida and Santiago, and feeds almost exclusively on shrimp, which explains the colour of its skin.

Masked booby (*piquero enmascarado*): This bird owes its name to the black feathers around its eyes and yellow beak. Its wings and tail are tipped with black, while the rest of its plumage is white. It is the sturdiest of the boobies. Because of its strong constitution, it can take on bigger fish out in the deeper waters farther offshore. It is found mainly on the islands of Española and Genovesa.

Red-footed booby

Blue-footed booby (*piquero patas azules*): This seabird is distinguished by its blue feet and its mating ritual, an altogether charming spectacle. To seduce its mate, it stiffens its legs and walks around her, proudly displaying its blue feet, then points its beak and wings skyward and issues sharp, piercing cries. It is the smallest of the boobies and the one most often spotted. The female is slightly larger than the male and the black rings around her eyes are a darker shade of black. She usually lays two eggs. Most of the time, only one chick survives, as the two have to compete with each other for food. A relatively lightweight bird, the blue-footed booby dives near the coast to feed, then nests peacefully on the ground. However, scientists based on Isla de la Plata (west of Puerto López), whose animal life is similar to that of the Galápagos, observed that some blue-footed boobies built their nests on tree branches in 1996. They have yet to determine if these birds are a particular subspecies of booby or common boobies simply protecting themselves from predators.

Red-footed booby (*piquero patas rojas*): Unlike the vast majority of blue-footed boobies, at least those found in the archipelago, the red-footed booby nests peacefully in the trees. Its blue beak and red feet contrast with its light brown plumage, making it one of the most elegant birds in the Galápagos. It is found mainly on the remote islands of the archipelago, most notably on Genovesa, home to the largest colony of red-footed boobies in the world (about 250,000 birds). The island is one of the few nesting places for red-footed boobies on the planet.

Frigate-bird (*fragata común*): This webfooted seabird has a long, hooked beak and black plumage, and is most

Frigate-bird

conspicuous during the mating season. During this period, the male puffs up the huge red pouch at the base of his throat in order to attract the attention of females. His black silhouette can often be seen gliding over the islands of Darwin, Floreana, Genovesa, Española and Wolf.

Magnificent frigate-bird (*fregata real*): Unlike the common frigate, the magnificent frigate-bird hunts for food right near the islands. Another difference between the two is that the female of the latter is easier to identify: she has white feathers under her beak and a delicate red ring around her eyes. The magnificent frigate-bird can be found on the islands of Genovesa, Seymour, Wolf, Darwin, San Cristóbal and Isabela.

Galápagos penguin (*pingüino de Galápagos*): This little palmiped is 40 centimetres long and has black and white plumage. It is found mainly in the cold currents around the islands of Isabela and Fernandina. In addition to being flightless, this endemic species is also clumsy on land, but moves about quickly and gracefully beneath the waves of the Pacific. It is able to exist on the Galápagos because of the strong, cold Humboldt Current, which originates in Antarctica, runs along the shores of Chile and Peru then veers westward out to the Galápagos at Ecuador.

Mockingbirds(*cucuves*): There are four kinds of mockingbirds on the archipelago: the San Cristóbal, Hood, Floreana and Galápagos mockingbirds. This is the second greatest number of subspecies, right after the famous Darwin's (Galápagos) finches, of which there are 13. The mockingbirds are no longer than 30 centimetres and are distinguished by their curious, squawking, nervous, even insolent behaviour.

Lava gull (*gaviota de lava*): This endemic species has dark grey plumage and white rings around its eyes, while its beak and legs are black.

Swallow-tailed gull (*gaviota de cola bifurcada*): This other Galápagos gull is the only nocturnal gull in the world. An endemic species, it has large black eyes with red rings around them. Its black beak is speckled with grey, and its legs are red. Once stalked by predators during daylight, it now hunts for food at night.

Sea lion (*lobo marino*): The sea lion has a longer neck than the seal and is found on the shores of many islands in the archipelago. Each male, commonly known as *el macho*, takes over a

Brown pelican

territory and mates with the numerous females living there. Weighing in at 175 to 255 kilograms, the male protects his females and offspring from shark attacks and other males wishing to move in on his territory. The male rules over his territory until he is expelled by a stronger *macho*. There are no seals in the Galápagos. The sea lion has well-developed pectoral flippers, while the seal uses its caudal flippers to swim. The biggest difference between the two creatures is their ears: the sea lion's are tiny, the seal's invisible.

Galápagos fur seal (*foca peletera* or *lobo de dos pelos*): Pushed to the brink of extinction by the incessant attacks of hunters in the first part of the 20th century, the fur seal is smaller than its cousin, the sea lion. It has two coats, one short and one long; a large head and big eyes, and is also nocturnal. There are about 35,000 fur seals scattered about the islands of Fernandina, Santiago, Isabela, Marchena, Darwin and Wolf. The male's weight hovers around

80 kilograms, while the female generally weighs two times less.

Brown pelican (*pelicano café*): This large, webfooted bird has brown plumage and a white head. It is found mainly on Española, but also on the islands in the centre of the archipelago. It is easy to recognize, with its long beak and big, expandable pouch, in which it stores fish for its offspring.

Darwin's (Galápagos) finches (*pinzón de Darwin*): These birds made the Galápagos world-famous after Darwin observed them attentively during his visit in 1835 and used his notes as the basis for his famous theory of evolution, published in 1859. There are 13 different species distributed on almost all the islands in the archipelago, and another on Isla de los Cocos, west of Costa Rica. The main difference among the various finches is the shape and size of their beak. Darwin observed that as the finches evolved, their beaks changed shape to enable them to survive and feed in the environment in

Sea Turtle

which they were living. Among the 13 species of finches found on the Galápagos are the vegetarian finch, the small, medium and large tree finches, the small, medium, large and sharp-beaked ground finches, the cactus finch, the large cactus finch, the mangrove finch, the woodpecker finch and the warbler finch.

Manta ray (*manta*): This flat, cartilaginous fish has powerful, triangular fins and swims about near the ocean floor. It can reach gigantic proportions.

Hammerhead shark (*tiburón*): This creature has unfortunately become famous for the purportedly aphrodisiac qualities of its fins. Since the early 1990s, countless numbers of hammerheads have been caught, mutilated, and sold to wealthy Asian buyers. Although they do not ordinarily attack scuba divers, they could develop into hunters if this unfortunate practice continues.

Giant (Galápagos) Tortoise (*tortuga gigante* or *galápagos*): The most

popular reptile in the Galápagos deserves its name; it can grow up to two metres long and weigh more than 230 kilograms. An herbivore, it has no teeth and placidly digests its food over a period of 10 days. Untold numbers of giant tortoises were killed by pirates and whalers, who used them to feed the crews of ships sailing the Pacific. Today, there are only two types of tortoises in the archipelago, distinguished by the shape of their shell. Those with a shell that curves up in the front, like a saddle, can lift their head to reach food, while those with a dome-shaped shell find their food on the ground. The male tortoise can be distinguished from the female by its large tail. In 1979, three months before a volcano erupted on Isla Isabela, the tortoises on the southern part of the island started moving quickly to the north, leading scientists to conclude that the animals' feet are so sensitive that they can feel the movement of the magma reaching boiling point before an eruption. The females lay their eggs between June and December. The giant tortoise generally lives at the top of the islands and differs greatly from the sea turtle (described below).

Pacific green sea turtle (*tortuga marina*): There are eight known species of sea turtles in the world, and four of them live in the archipelago. One of these is the black turtle, supposedly found nowhere else on earth. It lives near the shore and feeds on seaweed, as well as the roots and leaves of mangroves on land. The other sea turtles live and feed exclusively in the water, and only come up onto the beach to reproduce. The mating season for these species is mainly in December and January, but they lay their eggs year round, albeit generally between January and June. Each year, the tortoises leave several hundred eggs on the beaches of the archipelago. Shortly after the eggs hatch, the baby tortoises' instincts drive them to the sea. Their main predators are sharks and certain marine mammals, such as killer whales. Newly hatched tortoises can be devoured by crabs and stray dogs.

 # FINDING YOUR WAY AROUND

By Plane

The airline **TAME** offers flights from Quito and Guayaquil from Monday to Saturday. A return ticket costs $300 from Guayaquil and $370 from Quito. The flight lasts an hour and a half. There is only one departure and one arrival per day in Baltra. When you arrive at the Baltra airport, you will have to pay $80, plus about $5 of municipal taxes. You will then be given a list of park regulations. These are important and should be carefully heeded.

If you are going on a pre-planned cruise, someone will be waiting for you at the airport to take you to your boat. However, if you intend to organize your tour of the islands on the spot, go straight to Puerto Ayora, on the island of Santa Cruz. From the Baltra airport, you'll have to take a bus and a boat, and then another bus to reach Puerto Ayora. The trip takes about an hour and a half and costs around $4.

For several years now, the airlines **SAN** and **SAETA** have been offering daily service (except on Thursdays and Sundays) between Quito-Guayaquil and the island of San Cristóbal. The ticket prices are on a par with **TAME**'s. However, make sure that your cruise starts at San Cristóbal; if it sets out from Santa Cruz, you are likely to have trouble getting there. There is no air service between the two airports.

Island Hopping

The Galápagos are scattered across an area of 8,000 square kilometres; 97% of this territory is protected, while the remaining 3% is set aside for human habitation. In order to protect and preserve the flora and fauna, park authorities and the Charles Darwin Station have decided to limit access to the islands to about 51 sites, which are linked by hiking trails so that visitors can admire the natural wonders. Only a few islands may be visited without a certified guide. There is no regular service between the islands. In fact, there are only two ways to reach the sites. The first is to sign up for an organized cruise with an itinerary that has been planned far in advance, the second to stay in Puerto Ayora or Puerto Baquerizo Moreno and organize a short excursion or a cruise through one of the agencies located there. These agencies charge an average of $50 per person per day, but offer many different kinds of guided excursions to suit visitors' needs.

By Boat

The **Ingala** company offers boat service from Puerto Ayora to Puerto Baquerino Morena twice a week, on Tuesday and Saturday morning, with return trips on Wednesday and Monday morning. The trip will cost you about $40 one way.

Landing on the Islands (Wet and Dry)

To prevent any destruction to the archipelago's fragile ecosystem, the boats drop anchor at a certain distance from the islands. Visitors are then transported to the island in question in small boats called *pangas*, which can only carry about 10 people at a time. From the *panga*, visitors either have to walk or wade to the island. In the latter case, visitors have to take off their shoes and roll up their pants, then slowly get out of the *panga* and walk to the beach. If the soles of your feet are sensitive, you can wear sandals. In the former case, visitors climb out of the *panga* right onto the volcanic rocks. Be careful: these rocks can be damp and slippery.

PRACTICAL INFORMATION

When to Go

The high season is from June to August and from early December to late January. During these periods, there is limited space on the boats and in the hotels, and the prices climb.

The Climate

The Galápagos Islands have a dry, temperate climate year round. There are two seasons, however: the rainy season, from January to June, and the dry season, from July to December. During the rainy season, the temperature is pleasant and the showers are short and infrequent. This is the best time for water sports, as the sea is warmer than it is during the dry season. During the dry season, the wind rises a bit and the sky is occasionally overcast.

Local Time

An hour behind the mainland.

Electricity

As there is no emergency generator in the archipelago and the existing generators are very old, the electricity is cut off every day at midnight and turned back on at 5am for the sake of economy.

How to Visit the Galápagos

Many travel agencies in Quito, Guayaquil and even your home country can easily arrange for you to take a cruise through the Galápagos. Of course, this option is more expensive, as there are several intermediaries involved. These agencies offer all sorts of itineraries, as well as various different kinds of boats. Some excursions cost over $1,000 per person for a week; in these cases, the boats are more comfortable, the food is excellent and the naturalist guides are highly qualified. It is possible, however, to tour the islands in one week for about $800. If you wish to reserve a cabin on a ship, it is imperative that you deal with an agency in Quito, Guayaquil or in your country, as it is very difficult to make telephone calls to the islands.

It is also possible to arrange a tour of the archipelago once you get to Isla Santa Cruz. This option can be more economical, but also has certain drawbacks. If you're on a tight schedule, you'll have to take the first cruise offered to you, and some of the islands that most interest you might not be on the itinerary. Furthermore, the best boats are often full. During the high season, even small boats are hard to find. Still, if you do chose this option, in order to avoid any misunderstanding, ask to see the boat before signing the contract, which should clearly indicate the itinerary, the length of each visit and whether or not meals are included.

About a hundred boats of all different sizes sail the waters of the archipelago. The quality of the guides, food and rooms varies from one to the other. Of course, the biggest and most expensive boats offer more amenities, and also have more powerful motors, enabling them to cover long distances faster. The smaller boats generally offer more personalized service, but move more slowly and sometimes get tossed about when the sea gets rough.

Those who can't stand sleeping on the water can climb aboard for a cruise that stops at certain islands, where they can stay overnight in a hotel. A few agencies offer this type of trip. The most noteworthy is **Metropolitan Touring** (see p 53), whose boat, the *Delfín*, has a powerful motor that enables it to travel to some of the more remote islands. This agency is a veritable institution in Ecuador. It was the first to organize trips to the Galápagos in the 1960s. It has several luxury cruise ships and a sailboat with room for 11 passengers. Its cruise ship, the *Santa Cruz*, is considered one of the best in the archipelago and can accommodate up to 90 passengers. The boats have spacious cabins with private bathrooms equipped with hot water, and each crew includes outstanding naturalist guides and a doctor. Moreover, the meals served on board are remarkably good.

The **Nuevo Mundo** tour company *(Avenida Curuña 1349 at Orellana, P.O. Box 402-A,　☎ 02-552-617, ≈ 02-565-261, nmundo@uio.telconet. net)* has two smaller boats offering much cozier quarters. The staff are extremely professional. Many a traveller has sung the praises of this company.

Angermeyer's Enchanted Excursions *(Calle Fosh 769 at Avenida Amazonas, Quito,　☎ 02-569-960, ≈ 02-569-956)* and **Quasar Naútica** *(Avenida Shyris 2447, Quito,　☎ 02-446-996,*

↔ *02-436-625)* offer yacht tours of the islands.

The **Canodros SA** agency *(Guayaquil, Calle Luis Urdaneta 1418 at Avenida del Ejército,* ☎ *04-285-711,* ↔ *04-287-651, eco-tourism1@canodros.com.ec, http://mia.lac.net/canodros)* is reputed for the quality of its services.

Unlike most other agencies, **Ecoventura** *(Quito, Avenida Colón 535 at Avenida 6 de Diciembre,* ☎ *02-507-409,* ↔ *02-507-409, Guayaquil,* ☎ *04-201-206,* ↔ *04-202-990, ecosales@ecoventura.com.ec)*starts its island tours in Puerto Baquerizo Moreno, on Isla San Cristóbal.

The **Galasam** agency *(Avenida 9 de Octubre at Avenida Gran Pasaje Building, 11th floor, office # 1106, Guayaquil,* ☎ *04-306-289,* ↔ *04-313-351, galapagos@galasam.com.ec, http://mia.lac.net/galasam/galasam. htm; or Calle Pinto 523 and Avenida Amazonas, Quito,* ☎ *02-507-079 or 02-507-080)* is known for its inexpensive excursions to the islands.

Some agencies include scuba-diving in their excursions. **Galamazonas** *(Tomás Martinez 102, Guayaquil,* ☎ *04-563-333 or 04-563-060,* ↔ *04-563-771; or Avenida 10 de Agosto 6116, Quito, P.O. Box 09-01-5600,* ☎ *02-241-555,* ↔ *02-546-994)* is definitely one of the best of these. Its boats are well-equipped and its staff highly competent. This agency also offers standard tours.

The owner of the **GALÁPAGOS sub-aqua** agency *(Avenida Charles Darwin, Puerto Ayora, Santa Cruz, in Guayaquil*↔ *04-304-132)*, Fernando Zambrano, has about 15 years of scuba-diving experience, as well as solid knowledge of oceanography, and organizes interesting tours of the underwater world. This is one of the few places in the archipelago where you can take a scuba-diving course.

Tipping

A delicate subject, tipping is often the source of endless debates among the people concerned. Whether it be in a restaurant or at a hotel, the clients and the service staff don't always agree on how much money should be left. In restaurants, some customers are convinced that they should only leave 15% (before tax), while the waiters assert that this minimum amount should be calculated after tax. In short, the situation in the Galápagos is the same as everywhere else. For example, most of the best cruise ships have better guides and thus generally offer better service; to the guides and the waiters, better service means a good tip. Like waiters, the guides usually earn a nominal base salary and often depend on gratuities to survive. In principle, if you are able to afford a trip to the Galápagos or an excellent meal in a good restaurant, you can afford to tip accordingly.

Isla Santa Cruz

Tourist office (CETUR): Avenida Charles Darwin, open Mon to Fri 8am to noon and 2pm to 4pm.

Telephone centre (EMETEL): On the way out of Puerto Ayora, in the direction of Baltra. It is extremely difficult to make a phone call to the mainland. Be patient.

Post office: In Puerto Ayora, beside the church. Letters take a long time to reach their destination, and sometimes get lost. If you have important mail to send, it is best to wait until you are back on the mainland.

Bank: Banco del Pacifico in Puerto Ayora, Avenida Charles Darwin (beside the Solymar hotel), Mon to Fri 8am to noon. The exchange rates are not as good here as in Quito or Guayaquil. It is not possible to use your credit card to withdraw money, but the souvenir shop across from the bank will advance you some cash on your credit card.

Terminal terrestre (bus station): In Puerto Ayora, opposite the volleyball court. There is bus service to the airport every morning at 8am; the office opens at 7am. The trip costs about $5 and takes about an hour and a half.

 EXPLORING

The names of the islands vary; some have one name, others several. In addition to a geographical designation, they also bear the names of pirates, captains, admirals, kings and important visitors who sailed the waters of the archipelago.

Isla Baltra

Most tourists who visit the Galápagos arrive by plane at the Baltra airport. The landing strip was built by the Americans during World War II; at the time, it was the longest in South America. The Americans also built a military base to protect the Panama canal. In those days, the region was swarming with land iguanas, but according to the residents of the archipelago, when the soldiers had nothing to do, they would amuse themselves by using the creatures as targets for shooting practice. As a result, there are no more iguanas today. It should be noted, however, that the wild animals introduced onto the island were also partially responsible.

Shortly before the war broke out, in 1933, a rich, eccentric American named Allan Hanrock had the idea of capturing about 70 land iguanas on Baltra and bringing them to the island of Seymour. The iguana population there is now at about 200.

It takes 15 minutes to reach the little dock where passengers board the ferry to Isla Santa Cruz. Once there, a bus will take you to Puerto Ayora. The trip takes nearly two hours in all and costs about $5.

Isla Santa Cruz (Indefatigable) ★★

Isla Santa Cruz is the most populous island in the archipelago. The main town is **Puerto Ayora**, the commercial hub of local tourism. Most of the hotels, restaurants and souvenir shops are located on Avenida Darwin, which runs through the town.

In 1959, 100 years after Charles Darwin published his famous theory of evolution, the foundation that bears his name was founded in Brussels, after a team of scientists carried out feasibility studies on the unusual plant and animal life flourishing on Isla Santa Cruz. It was thus that the **Charles Darwin**

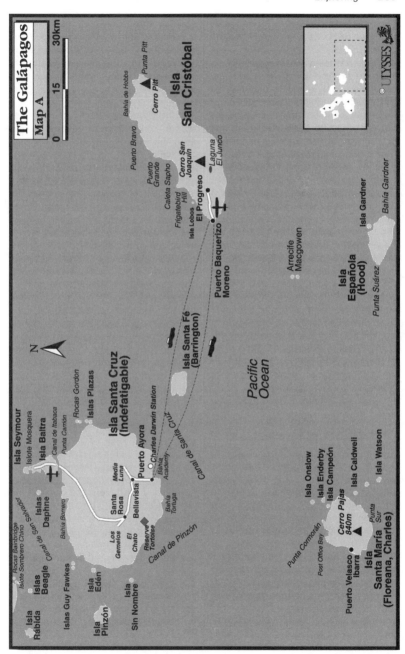

Station *(Mon to Fri 8am to 6pm; beside the Hotel Galápagos, a 15-minute walk east of the centre of town)* was inaugurated five years later, in 1964, in order to find solutions for the many problems afflicting the flora and fauna on the islands. The station endeavours to protect the animal and vegetable species, eliminate non-endemic animals that threaten the survival of native species and educate the public about environmental issues. It works in collaboration with UNESCO, UICN/IUNC (International Union for Nature Conservation) and the national park. It has trails leading through an arid area abounding in cactuses and houses the **giant tortoise breeding and incubation centre**, among other facilities. During the laying season, researchers gather up the eggs and take them to the Centre. Once they have hatched, the tortoises are kept under observation until the age of five, at which time they are set free on their island of origin. This process was started in 1970 in an effort to preserve the existence of these endangered tortoises. It has already proved successful: two endangered subspecies have been saved.

Right near the Centre, you can see a giant tortoise known as Solitary George, the last survivor of his species. He was found in 1971 on Isla Pinta by a group of scientists who had come to the island to conduct research on seabirds. A week later, an expedition was organized to bring the tortoise to Santa Cruz. He has been kept in captivity in the hope that one day a female mate might be found for him. An enormous reward has been offered to anyone who finds a partner for him anywhere in the world.

Located in the Charles Darwin Station, a **scientific library** *(Mon to Fri 9:30am to noon and 1pm to 4:30pm)*, open to the public, contains a wealth of information about the Galápagos Islands.

The little **Van Straelen Museum** is also part of the scientific station. It deals with the evolution of the islands over the years.

The shops at the station sell souvenir t-shirts. All proceeds go directly to finance the scientists' research.

Visitors are not yet required by law to enlist the services of a guide to visit the **Tortoise Reserve** *(5 km from the village of Santa Rosa)*. Nevertheless, you are strongly advised to hire one, as the territory is vast and signs are rare, making it is easy to get lost. Over the past few years, a number of accidents, some fatal, have occurred as a result of people losing their way and being unfamiliar with the environment. In the reserve, you can observe the famous giant tortoises in the wild, and even have the pleasure of renting horses and riding about where you will. Don't forget to bring along some water. You can also hop over to nearby **Rancho Mariposa**, a private piece of land owned by Steve Divine, which is abounding in giant tortoises, particularly between the months of October and June. The ranch also has a small, unpretentious restaurant that serves simple but decent food. For more details, contact one of the numerous agencies on Santa Cruz.

The magnificent "white" sand beach of **Turtle Bay** lies a half-hour walk from the centre of Puerto Ayarta. Free of hotels and restaurants, it is a pleasant place to relax and go for a swim.

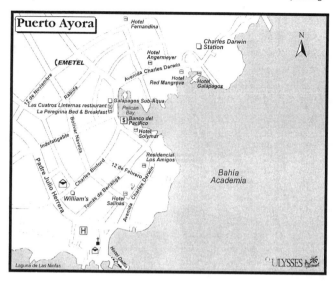

Los Gemelos (the twins) *(on the Baltra highway)* are the lava formations of two craters about 30 metres deep, located right near the road.

The **Media Luna** (half moon) is a semicircular crater located less than two hours' walk from Bellavista. You can admire some magnificent orchids along the way.

The shards of pottery in **Whale Bay** *(on the western part of Isla Santa Cruz)*, which is accessible by boat, indicate that pirates and whalers came here in the past.

Accessible only by boat, **Cerro Dragon** *(on the northwest part of Isla Santa Cruz)*, a new tourist site, owes its name to the prehistoric-looking land iguanas that roam peacefully about here. There is no guarantee that you will see any of these creatures, as they were hunted for many years and have only recently reappeared on the island. The trail that winds its way amidst the cactuses starts out by running alongside a brackish lagoon where you might get to see a few flamingoes.

Isla Plaza Sur y Norte ★★★

These twin islands were named after General Leonidas Plaza, the former president of Ecuador. Located east of Santa Cruz, they sit face to face, but visitors are only permitted on Plaza Sur. This island has an area of just one square kilometre, but is home to an impressive number of sea lions and land iguanas. A trail leads to the southern part of the island along a cliff that offers a magnificent view of the sea and the winged fauna. Due to its proximity to Puerto Ayora (about two hours by boat), Isla Plaza Sur is one of the most heavily visited islands in the archipelago.

If you have a chance, take a swim with the sea lions, but don't venture too far onto their territory as they can bite if they feel threatened.

Isla Seymour ★★

Located north of Baltra, Seymour has an area of two square kilometres but is home to one of the largest colonies of magnificent frigate-birds in the archipelago, as well as a large number of blue-footed boobies. Other avian species that have taken up residence here include the famous Darwin's, or Galápagos, finches and the swallow-tailed gull. Sea lions and a few land iguanas also inhabit the island. The iguanas were introduced onto the island from Baltra by the eccentric American millionaire Allan Hanrock in 1933.

Here, you can take a stroll along the beach and watch the pelicans and marine iguanas. Because of its proximity to Santa Cruz, Seymour, like Plaza Sur, attracts a large number of tourists each year. Consequently, the trails here are beginning to be dangerously beaten. Out of respect for the inhabitants of the archipelago, be careful where you step and for heaven's sake stay on the trails.

Isla Moquera ★★

Set between Seymour and Baltra, this little island stretches barely 120 metres and offers less spectacular attractions than Seymour. Still, it is home to an impressive colony of sea lions, probably one of the largest in the archipelago. Aside from the sea lions, there is not much to see, as there is little vegetation. However, visitors can go swimming or snorkelling in the limpid waters around this little sand bank.

Isla Santa Fé (Barrington) ★★

This little island (24 km^2), located 20 kilometres southeast of Santa Cruz, emerged nearly four million years ago, making it one of the oldest islands in the archipelago. It is crisscrossed by two marked trails. The first runs through a large forest of giant cactuses with trunks up to a metre around. The second invites you on a short walk across some rocky terrain. It is easy at the beginning, then soon becomes steeper and ends at the only place in the world where you can find land iguanas (conolophus pallidus) remarkable for their more robust shape, larger crest, bright red eyes and drab colours.

Isla Daphne ★★★

Access to this island, located west of Seymour, is relatively limited. Due to the various scientific studies being conducted here, Isla Daphne can only be visited once a month by a single boat with room for no more than 12 people. A couple of English biologists have been studying the famous Darwin's finches here since 1973.

Isla Daphne's geology is distinguished by the emergence of two craters made up of a light, porous rock called tuff, which is composed of compacted volcanic ash. There is a trail leading to the top of the two craters, in which a number of blue-footed boobies have set up residence. Visitors might see a confrontation between the boobies and the frigate-birds. The latter are notorious air bandits, and often attempt to steal the boobies' food in flight.

When they have a chance, they also try to spirit away the boobies' eggs.

Isla Santa Maria
(Floreana or Charles) ★★★

Isla Santa Maria covers 173 square kilometres and lies in the southern part of the insular world of the Galápagos; it is one of the five inhabited islands in the archipelago. It takes its Spanish name from one of Columbus's caravels, while the name Floreana refers to the first president of the republic, Juan José Flores, who annexed the Galápagos during his time in office. Finally, the Charles in question is Charles II of England.

In 1807, an Irishman by the name of Patrick Watkins became the first person to settle on Isla Santa Maria. He had the reputation of being a heavy drinker who spent his days in a perpetual state of intoxication. A few years later, he stole a boat and set sail for Guayaquil with a few slaves. Watkins reached his destination, but the slaves were no longer on board; no one ever found out what happened to them.

The island was officially annexed by Ecuador on February 12, 1832, when General Villamil established a colony of exiled soldiers and prisoners here.

A little less than a century later, in 1924, a Norwegian ambassador in Ecuador returned to his native country and illegally sold plots of land on Isla Floreana to about 200 families, assuring them that they would be able to raise crops and animals on their new property. What the future inhabitants did not know was that the island is almost all lava and rock, and that the Ecuadoran government, in an effort to populate the archipelago and develop the farming industry there, was giving a free piece of land to anyone who would settle on one of the islands—a practice that continued until the 1950s. The Norwegians brought tractors, donkeys, goats and seeds, but soon realized that they had been swindled. Disappointed but determined, they tried to settle the island anyway. Two years later, they had to give up, leaving their domestic animals behind. Today, these animals constitute one of the greatest threats to the archipelago's ecosystem.

In the beginning of the 20th century, the island was the scene of some very strange events. In 1929, a German dentist named Friedrich Ritter and his assistant, Dore Strauch, decided to leave Berlin and settle permanently on Floreana. Ritter was a vegetarian who had had all his teeth removed in order to avoid cavities. Furthermore, he wanted to prove to the world that human beings could survive way past the age of 100 if they lived in harmony with nature. Three years later, another German couple, the Wittmers, left their home in Cologne with their son in order to build a house on Floreana and lead a quiet life there. At the time, these "Robinson Crusoes" attracted the attention of the entire world and became so famous that even the luxurious yachts of American millionaire Allan Hanrock stopped here to pay them a visit.

All this interest in Floreana also attracted the attention of an eccentric Austrian baroness and her three lovers, two Germans and an Ecuadoran. Baroness Wagner-Bousquet, who had an arrogant air about her and walked around wearing an aviator's cap and a revolver on her hip, was determined to build a luxurious hotel for millionaires called the Hacienda Paradiso on

Floreana. Needless to say, they didn't all get along. Then, curiously, one by one, all these individuals started to disappear. In 1934, the Ecuadoran simply left the island; the baroness and one of her lovers went missing and the body of the other lover lost washed ashore. The dentist died after eating a poisoned chicken, and Dore Strauch went back to Germany. In 1963, Heinz Wittmer died of a heart attack. Today, Margaret Wittmer, her son and her grandson still live on Floreana. Many books have since been written about these strange events, including *Floreana*, by Margaret Wittmer and *Isle of the Black Cats*, by Gustavo Vascónez Hurtado, but no one really knows what happened. The Wittmer family lives in the little community of **Puerto Velasco Ibarra**.

Post Office Bay is a reminder of the inauguration of the postal system on the island of Floreana. In 1793, Englishman James Colnett came here to study the area's whaling possibilities. In order to facilitate communication between the islands and the mainland, he set up a wooden barrel in which people could put their letters. The mail was then forwarded to its destination by ships that stopped at the island. Today, the island residents encourage travellers who stop at Floreana to continue this tradition. In 1812, to step briefly back in history, the Americans sent David Porter to attack the British fleet, but he did not succeed in capturing a single English whaler. He did, however, hear about the famous barrel on Floreana and decided to take a closer look at it. He then proceeded to read all the letters inside it. The whalers were in the habit of writing to their families to tell them where they were heading. This made it possible for Porter to know where to

find the English and capture them. Furthermore, he easily convinced the crew members to work for him—a more appealing option that being trapped in the ship's hold and fed on dry bread and water.

Less than 500 metres behind the wooden barrel, there is a small cave that you can lower yourself into using a rope.

The magnificent "green" sand beach of **Punta Cormorant** attracts sea lions. Behind the beach, there is a small trail leading to a lagoon where scores of flamingoes and other species of birds can be admired.

Right near Punta Cormorant, you'll find the *corona del diablo* (devil's crown), the remains of a volcano cone, which has been sculpted by the sea. Its slopes are home to several avian species. The waters around the cone are one of the best places on the island for snorkelling. Be careful, though: the underwater scenery is beautiful, but the strong currents can carry off inexperienced or imprudent snorkellers.

Isla Española (Hood) ★★★

Isla Española is the southernmost island in the archipelago. It takes at least 10 hours to get here from Santa Cruz. The best time to visit the island is between the end of March and the end of December. During this period, the famous waved albatrosses can be observed here. The first site is called **Punta Suárez**. Upon your arrival, you will no doubt be greeted by mockingbirds, who will come inspect your shoes and maybe even alight on your head or your hands. Don't worry: these birds are simply very bold and

Isla Isabela, island of calm and relaxation.

The stunning masked booby, safe from predators.

A sea lion, one of the Galápagos' charmers.

curious. From there, a trail leads through several colonies of blue-footed boobies, marine iguanas and perhaps waved albatrosses. The colony of blue-footed boobies is one of the largest in the Galápagos. You'll also have a chance to see a geological formation showing a crack in the lava. When the water accumulated in the crack is compressed by the force of the waves, a stream of water shoots into the air. When the sea is fairly rough, the stream can go as high as 20 metres. The second site, the pretty beach of **Garner Bay**, frequented by sea lions and land iguanas, is located in the eastern part of Española. Snorkelling fans won't want to miss exploring the fascinating, silent world at the bottom of the bay.

Isla San Cristóbal (Chatham) ★★

Since the construction of the airport in 1986, **Puerto Baquierizo Moreno**, the capital of the archipelago, has been attracting more and more tourists. Although it is easier to get a group of people together for a cruise from Puerto Ayarta, it is now possible to organize island tours from San Cristóbal as well. In addition, the mail (*correo*) boats and the Ingala vessels provide service between Puerto Baquerizo and Puerto Ayora, on Isla Santa Cruz.

The **Laguna El Junco** is one of the few sources of potable water on the island. It is located at an altitude of over 700 metres, offering an altogether spectacular view. To get there, you'll have to rent a car in Puerto Baquerizo Moreno.

A two-kilometre walk east of Puerto Baquerizo will take you to **Frigate-bird Hill**, which commands a magnificent view of the village.

Located on the northeast tip of San Cristóbal, **Punta Pitt** is surrounded by tuff formations. Several species of seabirds may be observed here, notably boobies and frigate-birds. This site was laid out in 1989.

The little bay of **Puerto Grande (Stephens)** was frequented by fishing boats and various other vessels for centuries. It pretty white sand beach is a pleasant place to go swimming.

Isla Santiago (San Salvador or James) ★★★

The fourth largest island in the archipelago, Isla Santiago lies northeast of Santa Cruz and has four interesting sites. **Puerto Egas** is definitely the most popular of the group, thanks to its colony of marine iguanas and other fascinating aquatic animal life. Puerto Egas was also a salt mine in the 1950s.

North of Puerto Egas, **Buccaneers Cove** was frequently visited in the 18th and 19th centuries by pirates and whalers hoping to stock up on fresh water. The landscape is embellished by the presence of countless seabirds perched on the cliffs.

Located on the eastern part of the island, **Sullivan Bay** is remarkable for its enormous stretches of cooled lava.

The brown sand beach of **Espumilla** is a good place for swimming. Flamingoes

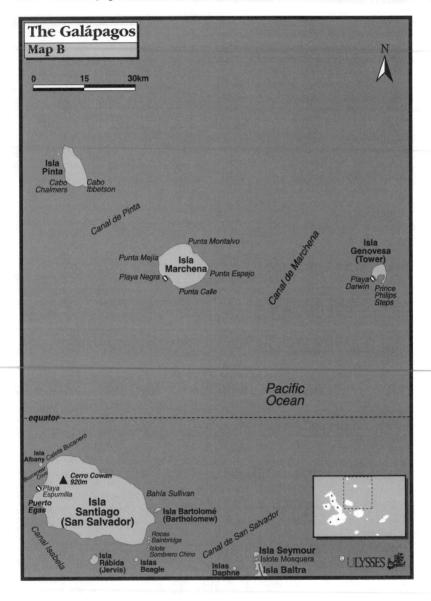

The Galápagos
Map B

0   15   30km

N

Isla
Pinta
Cabo
Chalmers
Cabo
Ibbetson

Canal de Pinta

Punta Montalvo

Punta Mejía
Isla
Marchena
Playa Negra
Punta Espejo
Punta Calle

Canal de Marchena

Isla
Genovesa
(Tower)
Playa
Darwin
Prince
Philips
Steps

Pacific
Ocean

equator

Isla
Albany
Caleta Bucanero
Buccaneer
Cove
Playa
Espumilla
Cerro Cowan
920m
Bahía Sullivan
Puerto
Egas
Isla
Santiago
(San Salvador)
Isla Bartolomé
(Bartholomew)
Canal de San Salvador
Rocas
Bainbridge
Islote
Sombrero Chino
Isla Seymour
Islote Mosquera
Canal Isabela
Isla
Rábida
(Jervis)
Islas
Beagle
Islas
Daphne
Isla Baltra
ULYSSES

sometimes frolic about in the small lagoon behind it.

Isla Bartolomé (Bartholomew) ★★★

Located east of Isla Santiago, Isla Bartolomé is one of the smallest islands (1.1 km2) in the archipelago, but also one of the most interesting. The landscape is truly remarkable, due to a recent volcanic eruption; 352 steps have been built in order to prevent erosion and offer access to the top, where you can contemplate one of the most sought-after panoramas in the Galápagos. After climbing all these steps, go relax on the beach or take a swim with the sea lions. Penguins, hammerheads and sea turtles can sometimes be spotted here.

Isla Rábida (Jervis) ★★

Isla Rábida, which lies south of Santiago, was named after a monastery that Christopher Columbus used to go to in his youth. It is known as the red island, for the simple reason that it has a pretty "red" sand beach (the lava here is rich in iron). A group of sea lions awaits visitors. One trail leads to a brackish lagoon where friendly flamingoes sometimes take up residence, while another runs through vegetation primarily composed of *palos santos* and cactuses, passing several volcanic formations.

If you take a boat ride along the steep, rocky shore, you might have a chance to see some fur seals.

Isla Sombrero Chino ★★

Located southeast of Santiago, Isla Sombrero Chino owes its name to its shape, which resembles a Chinese hat. The volcanic relief is particularly interesting here. Sea lions, penguins and marine iguanas are scattered all over the island.

Isla Genovesa (Tower) ★★★

Isla Genovesa was named after Christopher Columbus's birthplace. The northeasternmost island in the archipelago, located just north of the equator, it is definitely worth the trip if you're an avid birder. It truly deserves its nickname, Isla de los Aves. Picture nearly two million birds within an area of 14 square kilometres. Species found here include the red-footed booby, the petrel, the frigate-bird and the occasional blue-footed booby. The first site is the beach in **Darwin Bay**. The second, **Prince Philip's Steps**, thus named after the Prince's visit, is located in the east part of Darwin Bay. Genovesa, like Fernandina, is one of the few islands in the world where no animal has ever been introduced by man.

Isla Isabela (Albemarle) ★★★

Covering an area of 4,588 square kilometres and studded with active volcanoes and countless cones, Isla Isabela is the largest island in the archipelago and the home of its highest peak, Wolfe volcano (1,707 m). Statistics buffs might be interested to know that the greater part of the volcano is located underwater. If you could see its base, you'd discover that the volcano is actually 4,600 metres high.

Founded in 1887, **Puerto Villamil**, a charming little fishing village trimmed with long beaches, is located on the southern part of the island near several salt-water lagoons inhabited by flamingoes and frequented by various species of migratory birds.

There is a road leading from Puerto Villamil to the little town of **Santo Tomas**. Once there, you can either spend the night in the village or walk three hours to the top of the **Sierra Negra volcano** (1,390 m). The view is spectacular. The volcano's crater is 11 kilometres in diametre, making it the second largest in the world. Renting horses to get to the top is an appealing option.

It takes about five long hours to climb to the top of the **Alcedo volcano** (1,120 m). Once you get there, your patience will be rewarded by a spectacular view, as well as the company of some giant tortoises. It is possible, and even recommended, to camp right near the volcano. Inquire at the national park about getting a permit; the survival of the giant tortoises of Alcedo is seriously threatened, and an ecological disaster might well hit the site. The countless goats introduced onto the island are in the process of destroying everything in their path. A campaign to eradicate them is presently underway, but the scientists do not have adequate funding to finish their work. It is not too late, but they have to find a million dollars for the year 1997.

In the northernmost part of Isla Isabela, **Punta Albemarle** was the site of an American military radar station during World War II. Today, cormorants and marine iguanas can be observed here.

Tagus Cove might interest history buffs. The site was named after a British warship that came to this very spot to stock up on fresh water in the early 19th century. Since then, a number of people have decided to leave a record of their own presence here, as indicated by the scores of unsightly signatures. A 126-step wooden staircase enables visitors to take in a pretty view of magnificent Darwin Lake, which is nestled in an immense crater. The trail ends at a fairly high altitude, where, if the sky is clear, you can admire the numerous volcanoes rising up proudly on the horizon.

After enjoying some hiking, visitors can turn to another pleasant activity: sailing merrily over the waves of the Pacific, right near the site, for a look at the scores of crabs that embellish the steep, rocky shores and the sea lions lounging lazily in the sun. Penguins sometimes let themselves be carried along by the cold currents that encircle the island.

Punta Moreno, a lava formation, is studded with lagoons occasionally inhabited by flamingoes.

Isla Fernandina (Narborough) ★★★

Located west of Isabela, Isla Fernandina has an area of 642 square kilometres and is one of the youngest islands in the archipelago. It is also one of the few islands on Earth—and the largest of those—where no animal has ever been introduced by man. This island is home to an active volcano, La Cumbre, which last erupted in 1988.

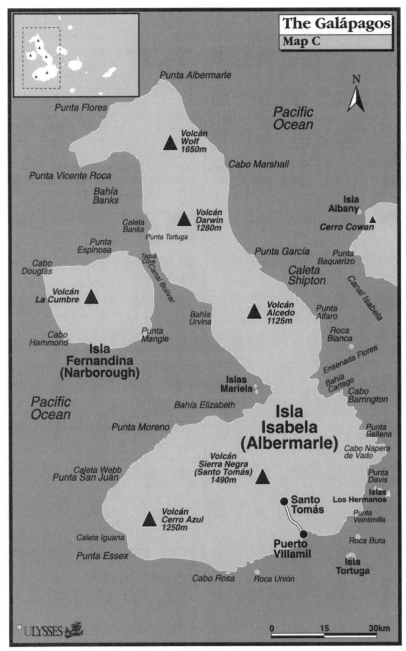

The Galápagos
Map C

N

Punta Albermarle

Pacific
Ocean

Punta Flores

Volcán
Wolf
1650m

Cabo Marshall

Punta Vicente Roca

Bahía
Banks

Isla
Albany

Caleta
Banks

Volcán
Darwin
1280m

Cerro Cowan

Punta Tortuga

Punta
Espinosa

Punta García

Punta
Baquerizo

Cabo
Douglas

Tagus
Cove

Caleta
Shipton

Volcán
La Cumbre

Bahía
Urvina

Volcán
Alcedo
1125m

Punta
Alfaro

Canal Bolívar

Canal Isabela

Roca
Blanca

Cabo
Hammond

Punta
Mangle

Isla
Fernandina
(Narborough)

Ensenada Flores

Islas
Mariela

Bahía
Cartago

Cabo
Barrington

Pacific
Ocean

Bahía Elizabeth

Isla
Isabela
(Albermarle)

Punta
Ballena

Punta Moreno

Cabo Napera
de Vado

Volcán
Sierra Negra
(Santo Tomás)
1490m

Punta
Davis

Caleta Webb
Punta San Juán

Islas
Los Hermanos

Santo
Tomás

Punta
Veintimilla

Volcán
Cerro Azul
1250m

Caleta Iguana

Roca Bura

Puerto
Villamil

Punta Essex

Isla
Tortuga

Cabo Rosa

Roca Unión

©ULYSSES

0   15   30km

An impressive number of marine iguanas, penguins, sea lions, cormorants and some penguins can be found at **Punta Espinosa**.

Some islands are off-limits to the public because their ecosystems are too fragile. These include **Pinta**, **Marchena**, **Wolfe**, **Darwin** and **Pinsón**.

 OUTDOOR ACTIVITIES

  Swimming and Snorkelling

Traversed by the Humboldt Current, the waters off the archipelago are relatively cool (around 20°C) for this altitude. The waters are at their warmest from January to the end of May. Nevertheless, the cool waters aren't enough to keep swimmers away from the beautiful marine plants and wildlife. Snorkellers are advised to gear up with the basics (a mask, snorkel and fins).

The waters off the "white"-sand beach at **Turtle Bay** on **Isla Santa Cruz** are lovely for swimming.

In **Plaza Sur**, you can swim with sea otters, but don't encroach too much on their territory as they've been known to bite when they feel threatened.

Swimming and snorkelling are both popular in the waters around **Isla Mosquera**.

The waters surrounding the "devil's crown" (*corona del diablo*) on **Isla Santa Maria (Floreana or Charles)** are one of the best snorkelling sites in the archipelago.

Swimmers should test the waters off the pretty white-sand beach in the **Puerto Grande (Stephens)** bay on **Isla San Cristóbal**.

On **Isla Santiago (San Salvador or James)**, snorkellers explore the sea bottom off **Puerto Egas**, while swimmers are attracted to the brown-sand beach of **Espumilla**.

The long white-sand beach on **Isla Bartolomé (Bartholomew)** is enjoyed by snorkellers and swimmers alike.

 Bird-watching

Sea birds congregate on the cliffs of **Isla Plaza Sur**.

The largest colony of frigate-birds of all the islands is located on **Isla Seymour**. Blue-footed gannets are also present in large numbers.

Isla Daphné is another good place to spot frigate-birds and gannets.

Between March and the end of December, **Isla Española (Hood)** is a good place to admire the famous albatrosses of the Galápagos as well as colonies of blue-footed gannets.

Gannets and frigate-birds can be seen at **Punta Pitt** on **Isla De San Cristóbal (Chatham)**.

All sorts of sea birds can be observed on **Isla Santiago (San Salvador or James)** north of **Puerto Egas** in **Buccaneers Cove**.

Isla Genovesa (Tower) is almost made for birders. There are numerous red-footed gannet colonies, as well as countless other winged species including petrels, frigate-birds, and occasionally blue-footed gannets.

Pink flamingoes and numerous other seabirds congregate at **Puerto Villamil** on **Isla Isabella (Albemarle)**.

Bike rentals: Beside the Chinese restaurant Asia on Avenida Charles Darwin in Puerto Ayora.

 ## ACCOMMODATIONS

Puerto Ayora

For several years, budget-wise travellers in search of simple, modestly decorated rooms have been welcomed at the **Residencial Los Amigos** *($8; Avenida Charles Darwin, facing the TAME offices,* ☎ *05-526-265)*. The owner, Rosa Rosero, is friendly and will help you figure out the Galápagos Islands.

Though the rooms at the **Hotel Darwin** *($8; Avenida Charles Darwin;* ☎ *05-526-221)* leave a bit to be desired and completely lack any decoration, the price is admittedly hard to beat.

The **Sir Francis Drake** *($10;* ≡*, pb,* ℜ*; Calle Padre Julio Herrera at Charles Winford,* ☎ *05-526-221)* hotel rents out relatively clean rooms that are dismally austere and gloomy. The bathrooms are private, but are located in the hotel's inner court, a few steps from the rooms.

Run by Jehovah's Witnesses, **La Peregrina** *($10; sb; Avenida Charles Darwin)* bed & breakfast has a few modestly decorated and inexpensive

rooms. The staff is friendly and offers laundry service.

For a few more dollars, and just a few steps along Avenida Darwin, the **Hotel Las Palmeras** *($12; pb,* ≡*; Calle Tomas de Berlanga at Bolívar,* ☎ *526-373, in Quito* ☎ *02-237-098)* rents out clean, well-equipped rooms.

Like its neighbour the Hotel Las Palmeras, the **Hotel Salinas** *($12; pb; Calle Tomas de Berlanga at Bolívar,* ☎ *05-526-107)* offers economical accommodations. Spread on two floors, the 24 rooms each have a ceiling fan and are relatively clean.

The 26 rooms of the **Hotel Lirio del Mar** *($12;* ≡*, pb,* ℜ*; next to the Hotel Palmeras,* ☎ *05-526-212; in Guayaquil* ☎ *04-460-865,* ⊷ *04-460-607)* are spread over three floors. They are clean, modern and spacious, but lack charm.

Close to the Hotel Angermeyer, about a 10-minute walk from the bus stop, the **Fernandina** *($18;* ≡*, pb, hw,* ℜ*; Quito* ☎ *02-538-686 or* ☎ *02-441-678)* guesthouse rents out some 15 clean rooms with hardwood floors and showers with electrically heated water.

The **Hotel Fiesta** *($20;* ℜ*, pb,* ≡*; towards Tortuga Bay,* ☎ *05-526-440)* will appeal to those looking to escape the bustle of Puerto Ayora. The establishment has six clean, spacious and functional *cabañas* along with a few rooms adjoining the main building. Guests can lounge about in the hammocks slung in front of the hotel after a fay of hiking. The staff is friendly and courteous.

Right next to the bank, the **Hotel Solymar** *($25, $30, $35 or $45; pb,* ℜ*;*

Avenida Charles Darwin) has a pleasant waterfront location and is known above all for its terrace, where guests can have breakfast while quietly observing the marine iguanas. The best rooms have ceiling fans, waterfront access and a balcony. The rates are a little lower for rooms on the first floor, though they do open onto the sea. Plain, poorly ventilated rooms, located at the back, are also available.

You might miss the **Red Mangrove Hotel** *($40; pb, hw, ℜ; towards the Charles Darwin Scientific Station; for reservations in Guayaquil ☎ 04-880-618, ↯ 04-880-617)* if you aren't careful, and you certainly wouldn't want that. Right before the Galápagos Hotel, this charming little spot built amidst the mangroves is ideal for a stay by the water. Three quaint rooms open onto the sea magnificently, and a fourth gives onto the back, though all are extremely well kept. The dining room is adorned with a hammock and comfortable chairs and boasts a terrace with a view of the Pacific. The romantic setting and the friendly personnel, who organize all kinds of excursions, give this place one of the best quality-price ratios in Puerto Ayora.

A few steps from the jetty, **Ninfa's** *($54 bkfst incl.; ≡, ≈, pb, ℜ)* rents out 25 spacious, clean and well-equipped rooms spread over two floors. Those on the second floor are decidedly brighter. Pool and ping-pong tables keep the guests busy throughout the day. The owners have their own boat and organize tours of the islands.

The **Hotel Angermeyer** *($95; ℜ, ≈, pb, ⊛, hw; Avenida Charles Darwin at Piqueros, a few minutes from the Station, in ☎ and ↯ 05-526-277; for reservations in Quito, ☎ 02-222-198, ↯ 02-230-981)* is an old backpacker meeting place that was transformed into a luxury hotel. A lovely pool traversed by a small bridge lies in the interior court surrounded by palms and flowers and chirping birds. Patrons can enjoy a cool drink while gazing at the horizon from the terrace above the second floor. Everything besides the stove works on solar energy. The 21 spacious, clean, pastel-toned rooms and the friendly, English-, German- and Spanish-speaking staff make this one of the best hotels in Puerto Ayora.

Chirping birds and lazy iguanas hidden amongst five hectares of luxuriant vegetation are the backdrop of the **Hotel Galápagos** *($95; ℜ, pb, hw; right before the Charles Darwin research station, ☎ and ↯ 05 526-330, from Guayaquil ↯ 04 564-636)* and its 14 clean and airy rooms with a view of the sea. After a day of walking and admiring the natural riches of the archipelago, you can stretch out in one of the hammocks hanging under the thatch-roofed hut, while sipping a *piña colada* and taking in the vibrant sunset...

For a peaceful, romantic and altogether memorable stay, the **Hotel Delfín** *($95; ℜ, ≈, ⊛, pb, hw; for reservations see p 53)*, only accessible by boat, welcomes you into an enchanting setting. Guests can stretch out on a charming and peaceful private beach after a day of exploring the islands. Those who prefer fresh water can opt for the lovely in-ground pool right just up from the beach; with its large patio and chaises longues, this is the perfect spot to dry off in the sun. The rooms are steps from the beach and pool and spread over two floors. They are all clean, bright, spacious and decorated in pastel tones. The staff are very willing and speak English, German and, of course, Spanish. Most of the guests here are passengers of the *Delfín II* cruise ship owned by Metropolitan Touring.

Isla Isabela

Camping near the Alcedo volcano is a possibility here. Permits are available at the national park office.

Isla San Cristóbal

The **Hotel Galápagos** *($15; east of the village)* is one to keep in mind if you're on a tight budget.

One of the best hotels on the island is also one of the most expensive. Besides offering clean, well-equipped rooms, the **Gran Hotel San Cristóbal** *($30; pb, hw, ℜ)* has its own private beach for travellers in search of a little tranquillity.

 RESTAURANTS

Puerto Ayora

The small **El Booby** *($; next to the bus stop)* restaurant is modestly decorated, but prepares excellent fish and seafood.

A few canteens open up for business around 7pm near the post office. One

name to look for is **Williams** *($)*. The place is small, only three or four tables (not a lot of elbow room), and the decor nonexistent, but the food is beyond reproach. You are the guests of the Esmeraldas family, who have settled in the Galápagos and prepare delicious dishes from the Costa. Be sure to try one of the many fish dishes prepares with coconut milk.

The small **Hotel Red Mangrove restaurant** *($; Avenida Charles Darwin)* doesn't have a menu per se, but the owner will prepare excellent dishes if given enough warning. The stunning view of the sea is an added bonus.

Next to the La Panga nightclub, **La Garrapata** *($$; Avenida Charles Darwin, next to the church)* is a popular meeting place for tourists. The cuisine is simple and varied and consists mainly of meat, pasta, fish and seafood. You can pay with a credit card but it will cost you about 10% more.

Tired of fish and seafood? Try the excellent **Las 4 Lanternas** *($$; facing Pelican Bay)* Italian restaurant. They have a pretty terrace, and serve excellent homemade pizzas and lasagna. Pleasant ambiance and friendly staff.

The **Hotel Angermeyer restaurant** *($$; next to the hotel)* has an excellent daily special of the catch-of-the-day variety. Poultry and meat also figure on the menu. A small covered terrace giving on to Avenida Charles Darwin has been set up for outdoor dining; there is also a cosy interior dining room.

ENTERTAINMENT

Puerto Ayora

Despite the fact that the electricity is usually turned off around midnight every night, a few places have their own generators and sometimes stay open until 2am. Depending on the season, a few bars and nightclubs cater to the tourists. The **Disco-Bar La Panga** *(Avenida Charles Darwin, next to La Garrapata restaurant)* is frequented by tourists and locals alike, come nightfall. Pool tables.

The **Bar de Frank** *(Avenida Charles Darwin)* is a simple little bar with a good DJ. There are a few tables outside on a terrace facing the sea.

 SHOPPING

Puerto Ayora

Avenida Charles Darwin is lined with shops selling t-shirts, books, film and suntan lotion. Remember that everything you buy in the Galápagos is more expensive than on the mainland. Before heading to the archipelago, therefore, stock up on essentials like film and suntan lotion. Profits from the sale of t-shirts at the Charles Darwin research station go towards research.

Incidentally, for an unknown reason, most stores do not accept Visa; MasterCard is by far the most popular credit card.

Bookstore: The Libreria Galapaguito, in Puerto Ayora, next to the Hotel Angermayer, sells new and used books.

GLOSSARY

GREETINGS

Goodbye	*adiós, hasta luego*
Good afternoon and good evening	*buenas tardes*
Hi (casual)	*hola*
Good morning	*buenos días*
Good night	*buenas noches*
Thank-you	*gracias*
Please	*por favor*
You are welcome	*de nada*
Excuse me	*perdone/a*
My name is...	*mi nombre es...*
What is your name?	*¿cómo se llama usted?*
yes	*no*
no	*sí*
Do you speak English?	*¿habla usted inglés?*
Slower, please	*más despacio, por favor*
I am sorry, I don't speak Spanish	*Lo siento, no hablo español*
How are you?	*¿qué tal?*
I am fine	*estoy bien*

I am American (male/female)	*Soy estadounidense*
I am Australian	*Soy autraliano/a*
I am Belgian	*Soy belga*
I am British (male/female)	*Soy británico/a*
I am Canadian	*Soy canadiense*
I am German (male/female)	*Soy alemán/a*
I am Italian (male/female)	*Soy italiano/a*
I am Swiss	*Soy suizo*
I am a tourist	*Soy turista*

single (m/f)	*soltero/a*
divorced (m/f)	*divorciado/a*
married (m/f)	*casado/a*
friend (m/f)	*amigo/a*
child (m/f)	*niño/a*
husband, wife	*esposo/a*
mother	*madre*
father	*padre*
brother, sister	*hermano/a*
widower widow	*viudo/a*

I am hungry	*tengo hambre*
I am ill	*estoy enfermo/a*
I am thirsty	*tengo sed*

DIRECTIONS

beside	*al lado de*
to the right	*a la derecha*
to the left	*a la izquierda*
here	*aquí*
there	*allí*
into, inside	*dentro*
outside	*fuera*
behind	*detrás*
in front of	*delante*
between	*entre*
far from	*lejos de*
Where is ... ?	*¿dónde está ... ?*
To get to ...?	*¿para ir a...?*
near	*cerca de*
straight ahead	*todo recto*

MONEY

money	*dinero / plata*
credit card	*tarjeta de crédito*
exchange	*cambio*
traveller's cheque	*cheque de viaje*
I don't have any money	*no tengo dinero*
The bill, please	*la cuenta, por favor*
receipt	*recibo*

SHOPPING

store	*tienda*
market	*mercado*
open	*abierto/a*
closed	*cerrado/a*
How much is this?	*¿cuánto es?*
to buy	*comprar*
to sell	*vender*
the customer	*el / la cliente*
salesman	*vendedor*
saleswoman	*vendedora*
I need...	*necesito...*
I would like...	*yo quisiera...*
batteries	*pilas*
blouse	*blusa*
cameras	*cámaras*
cosmetics and perfumes	*cosméticos y perfumes*
cotton	*algodón*
dress jacket	*saco*
eyeglasses	*lentes, gafas*
fabric	*tela*
film	*película*

gifts	*regalos*
gold	*oro*
handbag	*bolsa*
hat	*sombrero*
jewellery	*joyería*
leather	*cuero, piel*
local crafts	*artesanía*
magazines	*revistas*
newpapers	*periódicos*
pants	*pantalones*
records, cassettes	*discos, casetas*
sandals	*sandalias*
shirt	*camisa*
shoes	*zapatos*
silver	*plata*
skirt	*falda*
sunscreen products	*productos solares*
T-shirt	*camiseta*
watch	*reloj*
wool	*lana*

MISCELLANEOUS

a little	*poco*
a lot	*mucho*
good (m/f)	*bueno/a*
bad (m/f)	*malo/a*
beautiful (m/f)	*hermoso/a*
pretty (m/f)	*bonito/a*
ugly	*feo*
big	*grande*
tall (m/f)	*alto/a*
small (m/f)	*pequeño/a*
short (length) (m/f)	*corto/a*
short (person) (m/f)	*bajo/a*
cold (m/f)	*frío/a*
hot	*caliente*
dark (m/f)	*oscuro/a*
light (colour)	*claro*
do not touch	*no tocar*
expensive (m/f)	*caro/a*
cheap (m/f)	*barato/a*
fat (m/f)	*gordo/a*
slim, skinny (m/f)	*delgado/a*
heavy (m/f)	*pesado/a*
light (weight) (m/f)	*ligero/a*
less	*menos*
more	*más*
narrow (m/f)	*estrecho/a*
wide (m/f)	*ancho/a*

new (m/f)	*nuevo/a*
old (m/f)	*viejo/a*
nothing	*nada*
something (m/f)	*algo/a*
quickly	*rápidamente*
slowly (m/f)	*despacio/a*
What is this?	*¿qué es esto?*
when?	*¿cuando?*
where?	*¿dónde?*

TIME

in the afternoon, early evening	*por la tarde*
at night	*por la noche*
in the daytime	*por el día*
in the morning	*por la mañana*
minute	*minuto*
month	*mes*
ever	*jamás*
never	*nunca*
now	*ahora*
today	*hoy*
yesterday	*ayer*
tomorrow	*mañana*
What time is it?	*¿qué hora es?*
hour	*hora*
week	*semana*
year	*año*

Sunday	*domingo*
Monday	*lunes*
Tuesday	*martes*
Wednesday	*miércoles*
Thursday	*jueves*
Friday	*viernes*
Saturday	*sábado*
January	*enero*
February	*febrero*
March	*marzo*
April	*abril*
May	*mayo*
June	*junio*
July	*julio*
August	*agosto*
September	*septiembre*
October	*octubre*
November	*noviembre*
December	*diciembre*

WEATHER

It is cold	*hace frío*
It is warm	*hace calor*
It is very hot	hace mucho calor
sun	*sol*
It is sunny	hace sol
It is cloudy	está nublado
rain	*lluvia*
It is raining	está lloviendo
wind	viento
It is windy	hay viento
snow	nieve
damp	húmedo
dry	seco
storm	tormenta
hurricane	huracán

COMMUNICATION

air mail	*correos aéreo*
collect call	*llamada por cobrar*
dial the number	*marcar el número*
area code, country code	*código*
envelope	*sobre*
long distance	*larga distancia*
post office	*correo*
rate	*tarifa*
stamps	*estampillas*
telegram	*telegrama*
telephone book	*un guia telefónica*
wait for the tone	*esperar la señal*

ACTIVITIES

beach	*playa*
museum or gallery	*museo*
scuba diving	*buceo*
to swim	*bañarse*
to walk around	*pasear*
hiking	*caminata*
trail	*pista, sendero*
cycling	*ciclismo*
fishing	*pesca*

TRANSPORTATION

arrival	*llegada*
departure	*salida*
on time	*a tiempo*
cancelled (m/f)	*anulado/a*
oneway ticket	*ida*

return	*regreso*
round trip	*ida y vuelta*
schedule	*horario*
baggage	*equipajes*
north	*norte*
south	*sur*
east	*este*
west	*oeste*
avenue	*avenida*
street	*calle*
highway	*carretera*
expressway	*autopista*
airplane	*avión*
airport	*aeropuerto*
bicycle	*bicicleta*
boat	*barco*
bus	*bus*
bus stop	*parada*
bus terminal	*terminal*
train	*tren*
train crossing	*crucero ferrocarril*
station	*estación*
neighbourhood	*barrio*
collective taxi	*colectivo*
corner	*esquina*
express	*rápido*
safe	*seguro/a*
be careful	*cuidado*
car	*coche, carro*
To rent a car	*alquilar un auto*
gas	*gasolina*
gas station	*gasolinera*
no parking	*no estacionar*
no passing	*no adelantar*
parking	*parqueo*
pedestrian	*peaton*
road closed, no through traffic	*no hay paso*
slow down	*reduzca velocidad*
speed limit	*velocidad permitida*
stop	*alto*
stop! (an order)	*pare*
traffic light	*semáforo*

ACCOMMODATION

cabin, bungalow	*cabaña*
accommodation	*alojamiento*
double, for two people	*doble*
single, for one person	*sencillo*
high season	*temporada alta*

low season	*temporada baja*
bed	*cama*
floor (first, second...)	*piso*
main floor	*planta baja*
manager	*gerente, jefe*
double bed	*cama matrimonial*
cot	*camita*
bathroom	*baños*
with private bathroom	*con baño privado*
hot water	*agua caliente*
breakfast	*desayuno*
elevator	*ascensor*
air conditioning	*aire acondicionado*
fan	*ventilador, abanico*
pool	*piscina, alberca*
room	*habitación*

NUMBERS

1	*uno*	30	*treinta*
2	*dos*	31	*treinta y uno*
3	*tres*	32	*treinta y dos*
4	*cuatro*	40	*cuarenta*
5	*cinco*	50	*cincuenta*
6	*seis*	60	*sesenta*
7	*siete*	70	*setenta*
8	*ocho*	80	*ochenta*
9	*nueve*	90	*noventa*
10	*diez*	100	*cien*
11	*once*	101	*ciento uno*
12	*doce*	102	*ciento dos*
13	*trece*	200	*doscientos*
14	*catorce*	300	*trescientos*
15	*quince*	400	*quatrocientoa*
16	*dieciséis*	500	*quinientos*
17	*diecisiete*	600	*seiscientos*
18	*dieciocho*	700	*setecientos*
19	*diecinueve*	800	*ochocientos*
20	*veinte*	900	*novecientos*
21	*veintiuno*	1,000	*mil*
22	*veintidós*	1,100	*mil cien*
23	*veintitrés*	1,200	*mil doscientos*
24	*veinticuatro*	2000	*dos mil*
25	*veinticinco*	3000	*tres mil*
26	*veintiséis*	10,000	*diez mil*
27	*veintisiete*	100,000	*cien mil*
28	*veintiocho*	1,000,000	*un millón*
29	*veintinueve*		

INDEX

■ ULYSSES TRAVEL GUIDES

☐ Affordable Bed & Breakfasts in
   Québec . . . . $12.95 CAN
                      $9.95 US
☐ Beaches of Maine . . . . $12.95 CAN
                      $9.95 US
☐ Canada's Maritime Provinces . . $24.95 CAN
                    $14.95 US
☐ Chicago . . . . $19.95 CAN
                    $14.95 US
☐ Cuba . . . . $24.95 CAN
                    $16.95 US
☐ Dominican Republic . . . . $24.95 CAN
                    $17.95 US
☐ Ecuador Galapagos Islands . . . . $24.95 CAN
                    $17.95 US
☐ El Salvador . . . . $22.95 CAN
                    $14.95 US
☐ Guadeloupe . . . . $24.95 CAN
                    $16.95 US
☐ Honduras . . . . $24.95 CAN
                    $16.95 US
☐ Martinique . . . . $24.95 CAN
                    $16.95 US
☐ Montréal . . . . $19.95 CAN
                    $14.95 US
☐ Nicaragua . . . . $24.95 CAN
                    $16.95 US
☐ Ontario . . . . $24.95 CAN
                    $14.95 US
☐ Panamá . . . . $24.95 CAN
                    $16.95 US
☐ Portugal . . . . $24.95 CAN
                    $16.95 US
☐ Provence - Côte d'Azur . . . . . . $24.95 CAN
                    $14.95 US

☐ Québec . . . . $24.95 CAN
                    $14.95 US
☐ Toronto . . . . $18.95 CAN
                    $13.95 US
☐ Vancouver . . . . $14.95 CAN
                    $10.95 US
☐ Western Canada . . . . $24.95 CAN
                    $16.95 US

■ ULYSSES GREEN ESCAPES

☐ Cycling in France . . . . $22.95 CAN
                    $16.95 US
☐ Hiking in the Northeastern
   United States . . . . $19.95 CAN
                    $13.95 US
☐ Hiking in Québec . . . . $19.95 CAN
                    $13.95 US

■ ULYSSES DUE SOUTH

☐ Acapulco . . . . $14.95 CAN
                    $9.95 US
☐ Cartagena (Colombia) . . . . $9.95 CAN
                    $5.95 US
☐ Cancun Cozumel . . . . $17.95 CAN
                    $12.95 US
☐ Puerto Vallarta . . . . $14.95 CAN
                    $9.95 US
☐ St. Martin and St. Barts . . . . . . $16.95 CAN
                    $12.95 US

■ ULYSSES TRAVEL JOURNAL

☐ Ulysses Travel Journal . . . . . . $9.95 CAN
                    $7.95 US

QUANTITY	TITLES	PRICE	TOTAL
		Sub-total	
NAME:		Postage & Handling	$8.00*
ADDRESS:		Sub-total	
		G.S.T.in Canada 7%	
		TOTAL	

Payment: ☐ Money Order ☐ Visa ☐ MasterCard

Card Number:_____Exp.:_____

Signature:_____

ULYSSES TRAVEL PUBLICATIONS
4176 Saint-Denis, Montréal, Québec, H2W 2M5
(514) 843-9447 fax (514) 843-9448
* $15 for overseas orders